Princeton Theological Monograph Series

Dikran Y. Hadidian
General Editor

6

THEOLOGY BEYOND CHRISTENDOM

Essays on the Centenary of the Birth of Karl Barth,
May 10, 1886

By permision, EVZ—Verlag Zürich

THEOLOGY BEYOND CHRISTENDOM

*Essays on the Centenary of the Birth of Karl Barth
May 10, 1886*

Edited By

John Thompson

PICKWICK PUBLICATIONS

Allison Park, Pennsylvania

Copyright© 1986 by **Pickwick Publications**
4137 Timberlane Drive, Allison Park, PA 15101

Library of Congress Cataloging-in-Publication Data
Theology beyond Christendom.

   (Princeton theological monograph series; 6)
   1. Barth, Karl, 1886-1968—Addresses, essays,
lectures. I. Thompson, John, 1922-   . II. Series.
BX4827.B3T44   1986   230'.044   86-2377
ISBN 0-915138-5-9

Printed and Bound by Publishers Choice Book Mfg. Co.
Mars, Pennsylvania 16046

Contents

Preface

The contribution of Karl Barth (1886-1986) to christian thought and life has been so massive that it is difficult to grasp it as a whole and in detail much less assess its contemporary relevance in this year of the centenary of his birth. Certain features, however, stand out as particularly characteristic of his theology. Herbert Hartwell's phrase gives a neat summation when he states that for Barth "Jesus Christ is the key to God, the universe and man." This 'christological concentration' means beginning where God himself begins, with his own being, act and will in his Son Jesus Christ by the Holy Spirit. It implies in consequence, trinity, election, reconciliation, creation - both an exclusive concentration on the God-man in his act and an inclusive comprehension of man and the cosmos. The gospel of grace, of God's yes to man and choice of him is wholly good news and encompasses the whole of life. It envisages too a community of faith, of those who in life and witness correspond to what God has done for all and whose life is formed and sustained by the word of God in holy scripture. It enables a theology seeking to follow the biblical thought form - from God to man. It entails also a very specific hermeneutic bound to the object of faith and wholly determined by it. Not only the nature of holy scripture and the church but ethics and social and political life are embraced by this comprehensive vision and stem from it.

The theology of Karl Barth has thus a remarkable realism but also an openness not only to the whole christian tradition but to secular thought as well. Respectful freedom in relation to tradition is the watchword of his writings. His life and work manifest an impressive unity, an obvious simplicity combined with a rare and subtle complexity. The issues of the present day, while in many ways different from those in his time, are nonetheless to be faced and tackled from the centre which he has made the pivot of his theology. A right understanding and grasp of what he has written will yield in large measure the answers he might have given to the issues of our time. For him the last and central word was a name - that of Jesus Christ - the truth of God and man. Barth did not live long enough to complete his life work and the Church Dogmatics remained both his great memorial and an *opus imperfectum*. However he did live to see it accepted by many and challenged by others. As he himself would have said he did not want to create a school or even to be called a Barthian but to set before men and women the centre of faith, life and theology, namely, God in Christ by the Holy Spirit and the significance of that for man and the universe.

Barth was a legend in his lifetime for he, more than any other man, was responsible for setting the Church and its thinking (especially in Europe) on a different basis from previous decades, namely, God in his relation to man rather than the reverse. His literary output and his church and other involvement combined with his rich human qualities all ensure that his influence will long out last him. He has been compared in stature to great figures of the past like Thomas Aquinas and John Calvin and as one of the great church fathers of the twentieth century if not the greatest theological genius of our time. Even those who most disagree with him will not dispute the power of his writings, their influential nature and the place that he will have in history.

The present series of essays is an attempt to express something of the main themes of his theology as expounded particularly in the *Church Dogmatics* and to show their relevance to various areas of life. They are offered as a grateful tribute to one whose life and work have been and are a constant guide and inspiration to many and the consequences of whose thought in many areas have not yet been worked out. In presenting them to the public one can only reiterate Barth's own concern that the Church and its theology should not follow him but, helped by him remain true to its object-God's revelation and reconciliation in Jesus Christ our Lord and all that this means for the Church and the world.

J. Thompson

Contributors

Ray S. Anderson	Professor of Ministry, Fuller Theological Seminary, Pasadena, California, U S A.
Christina Baxter	Lecturer in Theology, St. Johns College, Nottingham, England
Geoffrey W. Bromiley	Senior Professor of Church History and Historical Theology, Fuller Theological Seminary, Pasadena, California, U S A.
Thomas W. Currie III	Minister of Brenham Presbyterian Church, Brenham, Texas, U S A.
Colin E. Gunton	Professor of Christian Doctrine, University of London, England
Alasdair I.C. Heron	Professor of Systematic Theology, Institut Für Systematische Theologie, Erlangen University, West Germany.
Stuart D. McLean	Professor of Christian Ethics, The Graduate Seminary, Phillips University, Enid, Oklahoma, U S A.
Harold P. Nebelsick	Professor of Doctrinal Theology, Louisville Presbyterian Theological Seminary, Kentucky, U S A.
J K.S. Reid	Emeritus Professor of Systematic Theology, University of Aberdeen, Scotland.
H. Martin Rumscheidt	Professor of Historical Theology, Atlantic School of Theology, Halifax, Nova Scotia, Canada.
Thomas A. Smail	Rector of Sanderstead, South Croydon, London, England
John Thompson	Professor of Systematic Theology, Union Theological College, Belfast and External Lecturer in Historical Theology, Queen's University, Belfast, N. Ireland.
Thomas F. Torrance	Emeritus Professor of Dogmatics, New College, Edinburgh, Scotland
W.A. Whitehouse	Emeritus Professor of Theology, University of Kent at Canterbury, England.

The Being and Act of God
By Thomas W. Currie III

Eberhard Busch, in his meditation at the memorial service for Karl Barth, took as his text, Psalm 103:1, "Bless the Lord, O my soul, and all that is within me, bless his holy name."[1] Busch's words, uttered in thanksgiving and praise, are not only profoundly moving when read today but also provide a student of Barth with an excellent starting-point from which to view his life's work. The Psalm invites us first to "bless the Lord" and then and only then summons "all that is within me" to "bless his holy name." Busch writes:

> Christians tend to forget again and again that we are to begin with this beginning ... We would like to begin elsewhere, with ourselves, with our faith or lack of faith, or with our dialectic. We would only too gladly praise a label, a cipher, an interpretation, a point of departure. But by beginning at such a place, we cannot move forward; only too clearly does such a beginning end in "myself." What we would praise then, is "all that is within me," not the Lord. However, with 'his holy name" we can, we must begin. And we must begin here not because by choosing a "non-label" we escape the power of labels; not because our souls have granted to the Lord this name, but rather because he has this holy name, because his name **is** holy. Indeed, we begin with the blessing of his holy name because he himself has made a name for us ... "a name which is above every name" (Phil. 2:9). That is the beginning **God** makes, which God makes with **us**: our true beginning, behind which we cannot retreat, from which we can only advance.

Busch continues:

> It is a special legacy of Karl Barth to us that he has drawn our attention to this beginning ... God is −for Karl Barth refused to participate in those explanations and clarifications in which theologians so eagerly begin "somewhat" with God, but rather (more strongly than this one cannot speak of our true beginning; i e, the beginning God makes with us): God is God. To be sure, it is not simply a matter of having made this discovery once. Indeed it can very well happen that one remains standing under this now discovered beginning and desires to exchange it for one's own point of departure, or

even to leave this beginning behind in the opinion that hav-
ing dealt with it once, one has finished with it. Karl Barth has
shown instead that one must remain there, that with this
beginning one must again and again begin. That is why . . .
even in old age . . . he was, precisely in the view of the begin-
ning of faith, still decisively, a beginner, a "stud. theol."
[2]

I have quoted this passage at such length because it seems to me, more so now on the centenary of his birth than even twenty years ago, that the distinctive contribution of Karl Barth to Christian theology consists precisely in the attentive concentration and cheerful consistency with which he begins with this beginning. For Barth, theology has to do with God. True, other theologians have said the same thing in other, or even the same words. True, Barth means something quite specific in his understanding of this beginning. Yet more so than any other, and in a way both more receptive and more skeptical of competing claims, Barth has no hidden agenda in appropriating this beginning for theology. For what isolates him from his peers ancient and modern, and at the same time enables him to take them seriously, and even generously, is finally not a matter of style, method or humor (though these matters are not to be overlooked) but rather the imense clarification he has brought about in his understanding of God and the beginning of his ways and works with us. The caricatures of Barth, that he does not take humanity seriously, that he has stormed the gate of heaven, that he ignores the difficulty of faith for his twentieth century contemporaries, all are rooted in the dissatisfaction with his beginning and the consistency with which he celebrates and reflects on this beginning. At least this much must be granted to the caricatures then, that they have sniffed out what was for Barth impossible, namely to think humanity, or creation, or even our experience apart from God. Why this is so I will try to indicate in this essay, but that it is so and that the answer has something to do with Barth's understanding of God's being and his act follow directly from his decision "to begin" where he begins.

This means, and here too the significance of Barth for theology is apparent, that in reaching the powerful clarification he does in his understanding of God, something new happens also for theology, namely, that as a discipline it too is transformed. If Barth's contribution is to be fully assessed, if his starting-point has enabled us to think of

God in a new way, then our very notion of what it means to be a theologian will also be read in a new light. That this might prove to be a continuing gift of Barth to us today is of no little significance in view of the contemporary confusion and cheerless tedium of so much present-day theological reflection. So deep has this confusion become that some have questioned whether theology is any more a field of rational discourse, its own grammar, language and methods being idiosyncratic to the theologian.[3] If our own theologies (called "Legion" for they are many) are more private and less coherent today, it is testimony, I think, not to a more complex or difficult world but rather to a conscious and widespread decision to begin theological reflection somewhere else than where God begins his pilgrimage with us. In any case, the result has been a loss of clarity in theology, a deep uncertainty as to its purpose, and a withdrawal from the vulnerable yet happy position of "following after" God's beginning in making himself known.

On the other hand, when one reads Barth today, one is struck not only by the conceptual clarity of his thought, not only by the skepticism with which he views new and not so new affirmations concerning man's needs and possibilities, but also by the sheer joy he brings to the enterprise of describing the being and activity of the God who presents himself as the subject-matter of theology. For Barth, theology is, in view of its subject-matter

> *a peculiarly beautiful science. Indeed, we can confidently say it is the most beautiful of all the sciences. To find the sciences distasteful is the mark of the Philistine. It is an extreme form of Philistinism to find, or to be able to find, theology distasteful. The theologian who has no joy in his work is not a theologian at all. Sulky faces, morose thoughts and boring ways of speaking are intolerable in this science. [4]*

Of course, as Barth points out, only God can keep us from this sin of *taedium* but that is just the point: theology's language and concepts find their sustenance and strength in their service to the God whose Word has made a beginning for these words also. Here too, "our help is in the name of the Lord." (Ps. 124)

The question of theology's starting point, of its beginning, is inseparable then from the question concerning the being and act of God whose beginning with us raises this question authentically for the first

time. The question of theology is the question of God. Eberhard
Jüngel points out what this means for Barth when he notes that Barth
thinks consistently and exclusively as a theologian.[5]. "What this
signifies is shown by his question concerning the being of God. This
question does not arise out of questioning; neither does it invent a
problem which sooner or later faces the more or less radical questioning that calls something or eveything into question. The theological
question concerning the being of God *reflects* on the being of God.
This means, however, that the being of God which is the subject of
theological inquiry *precedes* the question."[6]

Whereas, as we shall see, other theologians might very well say that
theology has to do with God, or even that theology begins with God,
the incontrovertible strength (and difference!) of Barth's theology is
that, for him, the very question is rooted not only logically but actually
in God's self-enacted being.[7] The consequences of this starting-
point for theology are not just the negative ones that have so fas-
cinated Barth's critics, viz., the denial of any kind of natural theology,
or even the observation that Barth is not *primarily* interested in a perceived congruence between the being and act of God and our experience of him, but also are to be found, positively, in his view that the
subject-matter of theology is the God who fulfills what he does, or to
put it another way, whose being is not added to or subtracted from by
his act but who *is* his act in his determining to be himself in this way
and no other. Hans Frei has noted the specific consequence for the
doctrine of Jesus Christ. "He is not the incarnate Lord who, as a separ-
able or added action, performs and undergoes the reconciliation of
God and man. He *is* the reconciliation he enacts."[8]

Note well: to think as a theologian, according to Barth, is not to
begin with God as a presupposition, hypothesis or project of thought.
"All really radical questioning sets aside human presuppositions."[9]
Rather, what is at stake here for Barth is his understanding of God's
being as active within himself, whose unity and integrity, whose life
and activity are seen here too in that *he* opens the way, on the basis of
his good pleasure, for questioning, drawing these questions on to the
particular circle of knowledge which is knowledge of God. Here is
both the logical and actual ground of such knowledge in the unity and
diversity, the coinherence and particularity of God's being in act.
Along this path God's being *moves,* and moves ahead of us, preceding
our questions and not dependent upon them or the predicates we

may wish to assign to him. Not only in his act but in his being himself the ground and fulfillment of that act does this God assign his own predicates. Yet, precisely in so doing, he makes possible a genuine encounter between himself and us. He is free; yet his freedom does not consist in his isolation from us but in his decision to be who he is with us. Here, as the free God binds Creation to himself, and does so in such a way that Creation, or humanity, or "the world" cannot be thought of except in terms of the unity of this binding decision, and in such a way that God himself cannot be thought except in the light of this same unity, knowledge of God arises. The locus of this decision, the place where God and humanity coinhere, is Jesus Christ. He not only is the beginning of all the ways and works of God but he is also, in the original sacrament of his humanity, the beginning of all the ways and works of our knowledge of God, the actual and logical ground, the ontic and epistemic basis for theology. "In the beginning was the Word." (John 1:1) And on the basis of this Word responsible language concerning the being of God is possible.

To speak of Jesus Christ as the place where God begins with us is to raise the question of God's being and act in its most compressed and critical form. Even to speak of Jesus Christ as the "place" of God's beginning with us raises problems, in that it implies a "place" of God's being apart from his decision in Jesus Christ. But for Barth God's beginning in Jesus Christ tells us not just something of his *act* of revelation but also something of his *being,* such that this act is not fully apprehended as God's act until it is seen as rooted in his being who he is as Father, Son, and Holy Spirit. His act of revealing is grounded in his being.[10] That is why Barth is compelled, at the *beginning* of his *Church Dogmatics* to explicate the doctrine of the Trinity precisely in the context of his discussion of the doctrine of revelation. The revelation of God in Jesus Christ is the act in which God interprets his being. As such, this act of self-interpretation not only provides the hermeneutical basis for our understanding of God but also indicates that because God does so interpret himself, he *can* interpret himself. His act then is not estranged from his being but is fully appropriate to it. God's being in his act of self-interpretation is grounded in his act of being Father, Son and Holy Spirit. "God," as Jüngel remarks, "corresponds to himself."[11] His act of revealing in its threefold form (Revealer, Revelation, and Being-revealed) is itself the root of the doctrine of the Trinity. Thus, this particular doctrine is truly understood as speaking of God insofar as it refers us to the ontic ground in God himself of the event of revelation. Here, Barth's basically realist axiom, "God is toward us what he is antecedently in himself" indicates the unity of God's being and act, and closes the door to any dualistic attempts to separate one from the other, either by means of an intrinsic theological ontology or some pre-determined decision as to what is possible for us to know. Barth's decision to *begin* with the God who is attested in Scripture and revealed in Jesus Christ is consistently carried through to the end.

The result is that for Barth it is the triune God who is known under the doctrine of God, not an experience of our limitations, much less an apophatically purified notion of being itself. And yet, just here, in the absence of any presupposed capacities within ourselves, Barth finds that the being of God in his act of self-interpretation creates not only knowledge of *God* but also true knowledge, i.e. conceptual understanding appropriate to God's being in his act. Barth believes we can know God in such a way, that our knowing, while remaining ours and not his (i.e. indirect and *per analogiam fidei*) is nevertheless real and true knowledge. This is the source of his confidence, his *"hilaritas"* as Bonhoeffer noted,[12] which allows him to undertake the theological task with such zest and diligence.

Yet precisely here many theologians, ancient and modern, part company with Barth. At stake is not their belief in the possibility of knowing God. Of that they are only too sure. The question concerns the ground of that possibility. Barth, almost alone of theologians since Anselm, sees his possibility arising exclusively from the event of revelation itself. The possibility of knowing God is, for Barth, rooted in the reality of God's self-interpreting act. Because God has made himself known, it is possible to know him. For that reason alone, and because he sees in this act God's great positive gift of himself, Barth refuses to do anything else but celebrate and witness to God's beginning with us. This is also the true source of his ironical skepticism toward natural theologies of left or right and his good-humored rejection of them as finally futile. That is to say, his skepticism is not part of some Calvinist baggage (e.g. *finitum non capax infiniti*) or Swiss rationalism, but instead is rooted in the most basic affirmation of the faith, namely, that "the Word became flesh and dwelt among us full of grace and truth; we have beheld his glory . . . ."(John 1:14)

To appreciate Barth's achievement in insisting that knowledge of

God arises solely on the ground of his self-giving, or to put it more strictly, that God's declaration of himself in his act corresponds and is rooted in his being Father, Son and Holy Spirit, it might be helpful to examine some alternatives. What would happen if the act of God was viewed as separate from his being? Traditionally, Protestant theology has concentrated on God's act. Indeed, one of the great achievements of the Reformation was the liberation of the doctrine of God from speculative notions of "being itself." The rediscovery of Scripture in both Lutheran and Calvinist circles led to the development of dynamic new categories in which to speak of God. John Calvin, for example, begins his *Institutes* with the *knowledge* of God the Creator,[13] not with an essay concerning the being of God. So also he goes on to speak of the *knowledge* of God the Redeemer and the way in which we receive the grace of Christ.[14] Though the *Institutes* are structured around the Apostles' Creed, nowhere does Calvin provide us with an explicit doctrine of the Trinity. Still, implicitly the doctrine emerges at every point, and Calvin, as is well-known, was not above defending it vigorously. With Melanchthon though, the Protestant tendency to dismiss questions of being received its formalization in the axiomatic epistemological claim: *hoc est Christum cognoscere, ejus beneficia cognoscere.* As the 17th century hardened the Protestant lines theology's concentration on the act of God to the exclusion of his being (i.e. rehearsing the "benefits" of Christ) opened a serious gap between God as he is known in his act toward us and the ground of these acts in God's triune being. To take one example, the act of God in reconciling the world in Jesus Christ was cut off from its ground in the freedom and love of God's triune being, such that to explain this act required that it be refracted back through the believer's faith, becoming then less and less a statement about God and more and more a statement concerning the believer's appropriation of that act. Hence, the possibility of knowing God was severed from the reality of the event of Jesus Christ and lodged itself in the disposition of the believer and in the assessment, quite independently made, of his limitations and possibilities. The result of this split for such doctrines as election and predestination was tragic. And worse, what had once been seen as a possibility for God now became more and more the subject-matter of theology, knowledge of God became increasingly vague and oblique, not to say utterly ineffable. That is why in Barth's view, Schleiermacher is not the enemy of orthodox Protestant

Scholasticism so much as its true child. By the beginning of the 19th century theology could no longer talk of God's being at all, only of the effect of his act upon us, and of our capacities, aesthetic, religious, and moral. Part of Barth's appreciation for the work of Feuerbach consists precisely in the latter's recognition that the emperor's new clothes were decidedly scanty and that theology's language referred not to God at all but to man. The charge levelled by Barth at the whole of Protestant theology from the 17th century onward, including his debates with Harnack, Brunner, and Bultmann was a protest against this split between the being and act of God, and specifically against what he perceived as the effort to widen it further by grounding the knowledge of God in some hitherto hidden epistemological key. More was at stake here than the niceties of theological method. For if, as Barth thought, God himself was not the basis for our knowing him, then the problem would not be the positing of human capacities -- of that he was sure there would be no end -- but rather the problem would be whether for all our knowing and speaking we would be knowing and speaking of *God.* The knowledge of God himself, of his saving activity, of his blessing, his giving and forgiving was at stake.

Barth's protest in part was a protest against theology's digging its own grave, but here again his protest was not rooted in a gloomy predetermination concerning what is possible for humans to know, but rather in the great positive of God's own act of establishing knowledge of himself in Jesus Christ. From the perspective of grace (i.e. the reality of God's being in his act toward us and the grounding of that act within himself) it is not only possible to speak truly of God, it is permitted. It is a gift; here too God gives. Theology, as it attends to the reality of God's self-interpretation can but receive, can but be grateful. What may be of epistemological concern elsewhere (How can I know God?) as what may be of ethical concern elsewhere (What is the good?) is not primary here. Theology proceeds with these questions behind it. What is primary is the reality of God's being in his act and the ground of that act in the activity and eternity of God's triune life. From this reality proceeds every possibility, noetic and ontic. And in light of it, language concerning God's being is as warranted as the restriction to strictly noetic categories is not.

If language about God's being has been a problem for Protestant theology, Roman Catholic theology, at least in its Thomistic aspect, finds it difficult to speak of God's act. It is true that Thomas understands God to be the subject-matter of theology.[15] Moreover, he believes that the theological task achieves its clarity, direction and coherence from its relation to God. Problems arise, however, when Thomas seeks to ground his knowledge of God in a notion of "being" apprehended apart from God's act. This ontological *datum*, independently derived, provides for Thomas a place where Creator and creature may approach one another and knowledge of God can be established. Moreover, Thomas presupposes in his concept of the "active intellect" an activity on the part of the creature which brings the being of God to speech. The question to be raised here is whether, if Thomas' doctrine of God is in fact the subject-matter of theology, such a being is in *need* of man to make sense of the theological task. E. L. Mascall, a faithful interpreter of Thomas, has argued that the latter's idea of God functions primarily to explain man's existence to himself.[16] In which case, one might be forgiven for wondering whether Barth, who in many other ways was willing to follow Thomas, (e.g. in his endorsement of Thomas' dictum: *Deus non est in genere.*) cannot do so here for much the same reason that he could not follow Schleiermacher, namely, not because of Thomas' use of ontological language but because the presupposition on which the use of such language was based rested not on the act of God in graciously revealing himself (where in fact it is warranted) but rather on an abstraction from an anthropological determination concerning human needs and capacities. In Barth's view, Thomas' doctrine of God can finally only confirm and explain man to himself. It cannot contradict or call into question precisely the place of man. And it cannot do this because finally it rests not on the self-enacted movement of God but rather on a predetermination of human capabilities. However one assesses Barth's understanding of Thomas – and about this there has been a good deal of debate – the basic question concerning the possibility of contradiction, and the separation of God's act from his being, will not go away.

Of course, a third alternative is to create some kind of synthesis between being and act. Dietrich Bonhoeffer, in his book *Act and Being* [17] attempts just this sort of synthesis, in part to escape a post-Kantian preoccupation with the "knowing" or "believing I." However, this attempt to balance the concepts of act and being, recovering ontological language to set beside affirmations of faith, may put us closer to a synthesis, but no closer to an understanding of God's being in his act.

One is left then, with Barth's approach, with his beginning. Twenty years after his death, a hundred years after his birth, Barth's contribution to the theological task seems as distinctive as ever. There have been in the interim, many theologians, some students of Barth, who have begun elsewhere and who have sought new points of departure in speaking of God on a basis other than the possibility God himself provides. Indeed, in some ways, Barth seems just as towering and lonely a figure now as at any time during his rather event-filled life. He has not been much followed in his skepticism of religious possibilities, in his lack of interest in the question of unbelief, in his refusal to baptize a particular ideology as a preamble to the faith. Those efforts, which seek to split the possibility of knowing God away from the ground in God himself, go on apace. Somehow though, I do not think Barth would be surprised, much less discouraged. For his skepticism was always rooted in his profound sense of gratitude, of good cheer in the face of the miracle God has wrought in becoming flesh. Barth's unique strength and his gift to those of us who labor today are not seen just here in that his work is profoundly un-tragic, but happy. He did not take *everything* seriously, and often what was of great concern to ancient and modern theologians he treated with an almost blithe, though not irresponsible freedom. The question he continues to pose to us, especially in his insistence on the unity of God's being and act in the event of revelation, is simply whether we can proceed in any other way than he did, and if so what it means if we do. A return to an analysis of sinful man and his needs and possibilities? A new natural theology based on an ideological anthropology which forces human beings into the Procrustean shape of a "new man"? A return to the old dialectic of law and Gospel, religious capacity and sense of the infinite? What amazes in reading Barth today is not how out-dated he is but how far ahead of us he still appears. And so, even to those who have not followed and cannot follow him he seems a haunting figure, serenely and infuriatingly confident that Jesus is Lord, even over the Babel of our theologizing. Hans Frei has asked whether Barth's achievement marks the end of an era or rather the "narrow gate" through which all future theology must pass. His answer is a fitting conclusion to our own investigation into Barth's "beginning." He writes:

> *On the other hand, it may be that at least in the form which*
> *Barth gave it, this way of theologizing won't come crashing*

down, but that it will remain to haunt and comfort the rest of
us with its iron and yet gay consistency, when we are less
daring in our ways of doing theology. For what he was about
was neither some anthropology in the guise of Christology,
nor yet a deductive Christological system. He was about the
conceptual unfolding of a rich variety of beings and relations,
all of them good and right, and all of them real in their own
right, and all of them refer figurally to the incarnate, raised
and ascended Lord who has promised to be with us to the
end, and at the end. Has Christian theology succeeded in setting us another task instead of this?*[18]*

Notes

1. Eberhard-Busch, *Karl Barth 1886-1968, Gedenkfeier im Basler Munster;* Zurich; EVZ-Verlag, p. 13
2. *Ibid.,* p. 13f; my translation.
3. Paul Holmer, *The Grammar of Faith,* San Francisco; Harper and Row, 1978. cf. especially Holmer's first chapter for an acute analysis of the contemporary theological quagmire.
4. Karl Barth, *Church Dogmatics,* II/1, The Doctrine of God, Edinburgh; T. & T. Clark, 1957; p. 656.
5. Eberhard Jüngel, *The Doctrine of the Trinity,* a translation of *Gottes Sein ist im Werden,* Grand Rapids, Michigan; William B. Eerdmans, 1976; p. xix.
6. *Ibid.,* p. xix
7. Hans Frei, "Karl Barth Theologian" in *Reflection,* Yale Alumni Bulletin, 1969, p. 8
8. *Ibid.,* p. 6
9. E. Jüngel, *op. cit.,* p. xix.
10. Cf. *C.D.* II/1, p. 259, where Barth maintains: "If the Word of God forbids the question of God's being as a particular question, or leaves us in doubt about this particular ques-tion, it means that it gives us no real revelation of God."
11. E. Jüngel, *op. cit.,* p. 106.
12. Dietrich Bonhoeffer, *Letters and Papers from Prison,* London; SCM Press, p. 77.
13. John Calvin, *Institutes of the Christian Religion,* Edited by J.T. McNeill and translated by Ford Lewis Battles, Philadelphia; The Westminster Press, Book One.
14. *Ibid.,* Book Two and Book Three.
15. Thomas Aquinas, *Summa Theologica,* new Blackfriars edition, Thomas Gilby, O.P., Vol. Ia, 1-11.
16. E.L. Mascall, *He Who Is,* London: Libra Books, 1943, p. 96. Mascall writes: "The very essence of our argument has been that the only hope of explaining the existence of finite being at all is to postulate the existence of a being who is self-existent."
17. Dietrich Bonhoeffer, *Act and Being,* trs. B. Noble, London; Collins, 1962
18. H. Frei, *op. cit.,* p. 9.

On The Trinity
John Thompson

I. Introduction

"The doctrine of the Trinity is what basically distinguishes the christian doctrine of God as christian, and therefore what already distinguishes the christian concept of revelation as christian, in contrast to all other possible doctrines of God or concepts of revelation."[1] In making these affirmations Karl Barth is countering the view that one begins thinking about God by asking: do you know him or does he exist? On the contrary the reality and nature of the knowledge of God spring from his self-revelation in Jesus Christ attested in Holy Scripture. When faith reflects on this and seeks understanding of it, it leads inevitably to the Christian view of God as triune. In other words the affirmations one makes about Jesus Christ and the triune God are two sides of the one reality. They are intimately related and mutually condition each other. While Barth's theology is characterised by a 'christological concentration' this does not and cannot mean that all theology can be reduced to christology, but rather that Jesus Christ is - to use Hartwell's perceptive phrase -"the key to the understanding of God, the universe and man."[2] "Even Christ's centrality is meant to point to (and not away from) - the centrality of the triune God."[3] The Scripture's testimony to God's revelation in Christ is "at one and the same time testimony to him who is the author of revelation and to what is achieved in those who receive the revelation."[4] It has a threefold form, in each aspect of which we meet with the one God. Thus the biblical testimony to revelation as the sole basis of our knowledge of God requires us to speak of God as triune. The doctrine of the Trinity is, in Barth's view, not explicitly biblical but implicitly so; it is "an immediate implicate of revelation."[5] The fact, however, that revelation is identified with Jesus Christ indicates that he is the key to our understanding of God the Father and the Holy Spirit and is further proof that Christology and Trinity are distinguishable but inseparable.

II. The Place of Trinity in Dogmatics

For Karl Barth revelation is the self interpretation of God and he is

13

known as the triune God. For this reason the doctrine of the Trinity is both the foundation and the goal of dogmatics, just as the triune God himself is the basis, centre and goal of all christian faith, life and worship. Barth, therefore, places this doctrine at the forefront of dogmatics since it is the fountainhead of all true knowledge of God. He writes: "In giving this doctrine a place of prominence our concern cannot be merely that it have this place externally but rather that its content be decisive and controlling for the whole of dogmatics. The problem of the Trinity has met us as the question put to the Bible about revelation."[7] Since this is so two consequences follow. Formally, it means beginning theology with the doctrine of the triune God, and, materially, that the content of the doctrine must find its place in and inform every area of christian life and thought. This in fact has happened in both ways since the doctrine stands at the forefront of the *Church Dogmatics* and at the same time gives both structure and content to the whole. In other words it is in this way that Barth has determined the nature of the *Church Dogmatics* and given to the whole its principle of interpretation. "The placing of the doctrine of the Trinity at the beginning of the *Church Dogmatics* is therefore a hermeneutical decision of the greatest relevance because on the one hand the whole *Church Dogmatics* finds its hermeneutical foundation here; on the other hand with just this decision the hermeneutics itself finds its own starting point."[8] This is seen in Barth's thinking in two ways: first, the prolegomena to the *Church Dogmatics* begins with the doctrine of revelation, with the Trinity as the primary truth derived from it and continues with the incarnation of the Word and the outpouring of the Holy Spirit; secondly, the rest of the *Church Dogmatics* is trinitarian form and has this doctrine for its main content and goal. In summing up and illustrating Barth's use of the trinitarian basis and structure of the five volumes of the *Church Dogmatics* John Godsey writes: "Thus the 'revelation', which is 'christocentric', is simply the revelation of the triune God: the Father, the Son, the Holy Spirit. From this perspective we can appreciate the division of the *Church Dogmatics* into five main parts: (1) the doctrine of the Word of God, which investigates the basis for the revelation of the triune God; (2) the doctrine of God which deals with the knowledge and reality of the one God who reveals himself in threeness; (3) the doctrine of creation, which concerns the activity appropriated to the Father; (4) the doctrine of reconciliation, the activity appropriated to God the Son; (5) the doctrine of redemption, the activity appropriated to God the Holy Spirit."[9]   This 'christocentric' revelation of the triune God is not only the basis of each doctrine but also its crown. Creation, election and reconciliation are all led from this basis to a peak in the doctrine of the Trinity. Moreover, while the essence of the doctrine is contained in volume I it reaches greater depths and enrichment in the doctrines of God, election and reconciliation. Claude Welch to some extent questions this conclusion when he writes: "The use of the trinitarian concept in later portions of the *Dogmatik*, while important as pointing to Barth's notion of the centrality of the doctrine and as providing an illustration of an attempt to make the Trinity truly an informing first principal of the doctrine of God and dogmatics generally, does not, however, add anything essentially new to the understanding of either the content or the place of the doctrine as Barth has elaborated these in the basic statements in the *Doctrine of the Word.*"[10] In one sense this is true since the basic issues of the doctrine are dealt with there. In another it is not entirely correct, since in the doctrine of reconciliation Barth integrates it much more fully into the material centre of the faith in the atonement, and thereby gives new insights into the being and action of God as triune. The already profound treatment in the Prolegomena is related more fully to the economy of salvation and particularly to the humanity of Jesus Christ and to his cross and resurrection. It is this aspect we now take up in this essay with belief that Barth in fact does add something decisive here for our understanding of the Trinity.

III. The Trinity and Reconcilation

In his definitive treatment of the Trinity in the *Church Dogmatics* (Vol. I/1) [11] Barth's interpretation is analytic and not synthetic; it has its basis in the fact of God's revelation in Christ and proceeds to analyse this content rather than make a synthesis on the basis of other doctrines. That there were inherent dangers and even weakness in Barth's earlier treatment has been pointed out and also acknowledged by him. [12] Revelation as God's self-interpretation must mean, in the condition of our sinful humanity, reconciliation or atonement, and this links it much more specifically than in his earlier writing to the cross.

In his doctrine of reconciliation Barth undertakes a far-reaching revision of former dogmatic theology in relation to the person and work of Christ.[13] They are seen in inter-relationship and unity. The person of Jesus Christ as the God-man is interpreted in the light of the two states of humiliation and exaltation and related to the three offices of Christ as prophet, priest and king. Jesus Christ is the Lord (divine) who humbles himself (humiliation) to become the servant (priest). In the same act he is the servant (man) who is exalted (exaltation) to Lordship (King). In this way he effects our reconciliation and as the God-man (unity) is its guarantor and witness (prophet). This significant reshaping of traditional christology and soteriology, while maintaining the essential truths of the older formulations and continuing necessary distinctions, seeks to avoid the dangers of divisions and abstractions which the former loci contained.

Barth continued to affirm strongly the truth of the incarnation but its focus and the point from which it is understood is that of reconciliation centred in the cross and resurrection as the integrating factor in the being and work of Christ. It is from this point that the whole life of Christ is to be retrospectively viewed and evaluated.

A. THE LORD AS SERVANT [14]

1. The Humiliation of the Son

The Son of God humbled himself in becoming man, condescending to our low estate as sinners, accepting the wrath and curse of God due to us for sin and the sentence and condemnation of death pronounced on man. In this way he bore the judgment of God on all human unrighteousness. This is his humiliation to the depths of the cross - the outer aspect of reconciliation. In this way he conceals but does not deny his deity; on the contrary it is his supreme affirmation of it *sub contrario in cruce*. Jesus Christ reveals in this deepest humiliation the nature of God and what is possible for him. The actuality of reconciliation on the cross reveals a possibility in God to be both high and lowly, to be God not merely in exaltation but in humiliation. It is at the same time a critique of all conceptions of God which regard him as only other - worldly, exalted, static and immobile. What God can do - the possibility of his humiliation to the depths of the cross - is shown by what he has done in his freedom, love and grace.

Barth is attempting here to answer the question - given the humiliation of the Son in reconciliation, how is this possible for God? His answer leads to a trinitarian basis. It is possible because it reflects a relationship in God himself between Father and Son - a direction downwards in God making possible the Son's condescension to us. Barth points out that this has its prototype in God's dealings with Israel where he stooped to this small nation even though it was often disobedient and merited exclusion and judgement. In other words the incarnation, reconciliation and the nature of the triune God are already adumbrated in God's actions in Israel and cannot be properly understood without them.[15]

2. *The Obedience of the Son*

Equally, if not more, important is the second, inner aspect revealed in God's reconciling action in Christ, namely its character as obedience. The human obedience of the man Jesus in union with the Son is made possible by and reflects the prior obedience of the Son to the Father. Barth points out that there is nothing arbitrary, capricious or accidental about what God does in Christ in his obedience unto death. On the contrary it reflects a necessity based in God's being and will, yet freely determined in grace. If Jesus Christ the crucified reveals the true being of God "we cannot refuse to accept . . . supremely the obedience of Christ as the dominating moment in our conception of God."[16] This has clearly profound implications for our whole way of thinking about the relation of Father and Son and the nature of the triune God.

From the perspective of the Son's condescension to the cross we see the true nature of God as both 'obedient in humility' and as 'majestic in mercy'. The point that Barth makes is the difficult one that in God himself there is an 'above' and a 'below', a 'prius' and a 'posterius', a superiority and a subordination. This in no way denies but rather confirms and expresses God's unity in differentiation. God does not need 'another' - the world outside himself - to be his partner or antithesis; he has all this originally and properly within himself. "God is both One and also Another, his own counterpart, co-existent with himself."[17] These distinctions and relationships within the one God indicate that unity is not to be defined or understood as singleness or solitariness in a unitarian way. The nature of God is open, free, an event, a history of one with another - a dynamic and living reality. The above and below imply no gradation, degradation or inferiority in God. By contrast they indicate an inner order, a high God but also a dimension downwards, a God who rules and commands in majesty and is obedient in humility. At the same time he can only be the One and the Other because "he is also a Third, the One who affirms the one and equal Godhead through and by and in the other two modes of being, the One who makes possible and maintains his fellowship with himself as the One and the Other."[18] He is the whole God in each mode of being; none exists for itself or apart from the others but each subsists in its relationship to the others. He is God in the totality, interplay and history of these relationships. What takes place between them is the history of these relationships which are the basis and possibility of human history and of salvation history at its centre. God's work *ad extra* is not alien to his being *ad intra* nor does it endanger it in any way, but rather it is "the strangely logical final continuation of the history in which he is God."[19] He is in humiliation on the cross and in obedience what he is before in himself - majestic and high in a relationship of obedient humility. In speaking in this way Barth is affirming an obedience and humility of the Son in relation to the majesty of the Father in the eternal life of God by the power of the Holy Spirit.

If the Son is obedient to the Father and the Father commands, is there not a danger of subordination or inferiority in God and can he be God as such? Barth recognises and refutes the twin dangers of subordinationism and modalism. The Son's obedience must be conceived as an obedience as Lord with no inequality or inferiority in the divine Being. Paradoxically, the Son is not only obedient but shares with the Father in his majesty, just as on his way to the depths of the cross the Father accompanies the Son on it. Barth writes: "In his humility and compliance as the Son he had a supreme part in the majesty and disposing of the Father."[20] One must not, therefore, see obedience (in the Son) as indicating an inferiority to the Father but rather as the expression - the central expression - of their relationship. These distinctions indicate that the Father is primarily majestic in commanding love and the Son primarily obedient to the Father, but each shares in the being and work of the other. It is in this way that God is God and is triune; in this differentiated relationship he is Father, Son and Holy Spirit, one God.

W. Kreck puts it in this way:

> *The God who reveals himself in Jesus Christ is not only in the heights but also in the depths, not only the Lord but also servant, rules not only in power but can, at the same time, meet us in weakness. It is right therefore, as the doctrine of the Trinity has always sought to do, to make distinctions in God without division in order to be able to state that God wholly identifies himself with us without giving up being God. These are, therefore, no trifling speculations or metaphysical phantoms when a distinction is made between God the Father and God the Son, between an above and a below, between one who commands and one who obeys, between one who is Lord and Creator of all life and one who goes to death, yet nevertheless to confess that he is one God.* [21]

3. The Awakening and Resurrection[22]

The cross as the climax of the life of Jesus and the consummation of his reconciliation manifests the height of God, the deity of Christ in utter humiliation. All this would, however, be known by us and closed off from us were it not for the raising of Jesus from the dead (Awakening) and his appearances (Resurrection). The cross was itself a history between Son and Father - an obedience in humility of the Son and Father, a giving up to death as a curse. That this is not the ultimate word the resurrection manifests. By contrast it is an action, as it were, in the reverse direction from Father to Son.

The awakening or raising of Jesus from the dead has, as the act of the Father (and not primarily the Son's own act), various aspects. It is a free act of divine grace of the Father to the Son. If the Son, who is at the same time the God-man, suffered and died on the cross it is the Father who raised him from the dead, not in any way to complete reconciliation but to manifest the true nature of the work on the cross. It is at the same time as much an act of grace of the Father in resurrection as it was in giving the Son to death on the cross. Barth can venture the bold thought that this was not merely an event in time and space but also an event between the Father and the Son in the divine life where the Son is the mere recipient of the grace of God. "Certainly in the resurrection of Jesus Christ we have to do with a movement and action which took place not merely in human history but first and foremost in God himself, a movement and action in which Jesus Christ as the Son of God had no less part than in his humiliation to the death on the cross, yet only as a pure object and recipient of the grace of God."[23] In this relationship the Son is basically passive and the Father active. This attitude corresponds to the obedience of the Son to the Father. If the Son submits to and carries out in obedience on the cross the will of God the Father, thus reflecting the very nature of the eternal relationship of Son to Father, this second step in Barth's thought is, however difficult, at least logical and comprehensible. But since the Son is divinely obedient and submissive, humbled to the depths of the cross, it is the Father's pleasure and gift to raise him from the dead. To think otherwise is to minimize the significance of the obedience and condescension to the cross as well as the free act of grace God the Father performs. "No, not simply as man, but even as the Son of God Jesus Christ is here simply the One who takes and receives, the recipient of a gift, just as in his death on the cross it is not only as man but as the Son of God that he is wholly and only the obedient servant.[24] This signifies that just as the Mediator, the God-man, dies on the cross in obedience, in raising him from the dead and giving him life, it is primarily the Father who acts.

In summing up the relationship of the cross and the resurrection to both the deity of Christ and the inner life of the triune God Klappert states: "The trinitarian statements of the *Church Dogmatics* make clear - even beyond what Barth states - that he understands the doctrine of the Trinity as an interpretation of the relationship of Son to Father articulated on the cross, of Father to Son manifest in the resurrection and of the creative confirmation of Father and Son in cross and resurrection. According to Barth the doctrine of the Trinity interprets the relationship between cross and resurrection; it is the taking up of the differentiated relationship of cross and resurrection into the conception of God."[25] In this way Barth relates his earlier doctrine of revelation more specifically to what happens in reconciliation.

4. The Confirmation of the Significance of the Cross as Atonement [26]

The cross is the completed event of reconciliation needing no fulfillment or completion by us. The resurrection is, however, God the Father's yes to this act carried out by the Son in obedience. It is God's ultimate verdict on his Son's work. It confirms this work as that of the Judge who was judged in our place. It was the Son's justification, "the divine approval and acknowledgement of the obedience given by Jesus Christ, the acceptance of his sacrifice, the proclamation and bringing into force of the consequences, the saving consequences, of his action and passion in our place."[27] It is a threefold justification - of the Father who willed it, of the Son "who willed to suffer this event" and of all sinful men. One must see the third aspect as the work of God by the Holy Spirit; again a trinitarian pattern emerges.

It was by the Spirit (Hebrews 9, 14) that Jesus offered himself without spot to God and by the same Spirit he was raised from the dead. The triune God is involved in the whole act of reconciliation and is known precisely here. His revelation is reconciliation. Barth sums up: "The fact that Jesus Christ was raised from the dead by the Holy Spirit and therefore justified confirms that it has pleased God to reveal and express himself to the crucified and dead and buried Jesus Christ in the unity of the Father with the Son and therefore in the glory of the free love which is his essence."[28] It is an affirmation of God's 'yes' hidden under the 'no' of the cross, of eternal life in death, of salvation in condemnation. There could be no more intimate relationship than this between what God is (as triune) and what he does in reconciliation. The noetic expression of salvation in Christ by the Holy Spirit has its ontic being and reality in the triune God.

B. THE SERVANT AS LORD[29]

In the second aspect of the one movement of God in reconciliation man (in union with the Son of God) is exalted to Lordship, to share in the divine life and love. The question remains, however, to be answered: how, having completed reconciliation objectively for us, is this subjectively ours? Barth gives a twofold answer to this question. First, the resurrection opens up and gives to man true knowledge of what God has done for him in Christ; secondly, the Holy Spirit makes the objective subjectively real in the community (the Church) and the lives of individuals. Indeed so intimate (almost identical) are the work of Christ and that of the Spirit that Barth can speak of "the Holy Spirit as the self-revelation of the man Jesus."[30] In this section Jesus is seen as the royal man exalted by his union with the Son and we are made one with him by the Holy Spirit.

But since the Holy Spirit leads from the *source* in the royal man Jesus to the *goal* of the community and faith, and is himself the *mediation* between them, we can discern a threefold pattern in this history.[31] The Spirit, however, is not only the Spirit of Christ; he is both himself divine and is also referred to as the Spirit of God or of the Lord or of the Father. It is the relationship between these two - the threefold pattern of the Spirit's work in salvation and the reality and basis of this in the divine background that Barth proceeds to explore in what Otto Weber calls one of the most controversial but at the same time one of the most rewarding sections of the *Church Dogmatics*.[32]

In the work of the Spirit in relation to Jesus and the community there is both a *formal* and a *material* relation to the Trinity. The formal relationship is the threefold structure; the material content of this is *God* at work in each and the link between them is analogy. What happens here corresponds, formally at least, to the triune nature of God. We cannot, however, say that the man Jesus as origin of the christian life is materially identical with God the Son. The one material identity in both is the Holy Spirit who, in the history of salvation and in God himself, is the transition from the one to the other, from Jesus to us and between Father and Son. It is this material coincidence, Barth argues, that is the supreme reason why one should view and interpret the doctrine of the Trinity from this standpoint. There is a double material coincidence and identity. The Holy Spirit is himself divine, is also a distinct mode of being of the triune God, while at the same time he is the transition between Jesus and ourselves.

What, however, does all this signify for the doctrine of the Trinity? It cannot be seen as a *vestigium trinitatis*. It means first, that in the work of the Holy Spirit in salvation history there is "repeated and represented and expressed what God is in himself." He reveals in his action among us "the fellowship, the unity, the peace, the love which there is in God ... the fellowship of the Father and the Son."[33] Secondly, since he is a divine mode of being and is active as God the Holy Spirit, the mediation between God and man is a *divine* mediation. It is in fact no less than that unity, mediation, fellowship and peace by which Father and Son themselves exist and co-exist. So great and so high is our reconciliation that it is based in the very being of God himself. Barth can therefore sum it up in this way: "In what takes place between the man

Jesus and us when we may become and be christians God himself
lives."[34] He lives as Holy Spirit but as the Spirit of the Father and the
Son and is never alone. It is the whole, divine, triune God alive and
active here in a dynamic and teleology reflecting and conveying his
own life to men. The dynamic of the movement is within God and
towards us; the teleology is the goal both of God's own life in the Spirit
and of our sharing in the knowledge of God in reconciliation. "The
Father lives with the Son, and the Son with the Father, in the Holy
Spirit who is himself God, the Spirit of the Father and the Son. It is as
this God that God is the living God."[35] At the heart of our experience of becoming and being christian we have to do with this living God who lives and loves in freedom as triune. God lives as triune;
he is free, loving and gracious as such: otherwise we are describing
another God.

Barth can put the matter in a more difficult, even questionable way.
In this earthly sphere where the transition from Jesus to ourselves is
concerned we meet with both a problem and its solution, namely, the
problem of "distance and confrontation, of encounter and partnership." Since, however, we have here a spiritual problem we must see it
as not merely human but as reflecting "the problem of God's own
being"[36] the answer and solution to which is the Holy Spirit. Barth
ventures again the further bold thought that the Holy Spirit is the
divine solution to both our problem and to God's. "In the first instance
distance and confrontation, encounter and partnership are to be
found in (God) himself."[37] In other words since Father and Son are
distinct from and over against one another this poses the problem as
to how they are really one. At the same time the solution transcends
the problem; indeed the problem is only known as such in the light of
the solution. This means that "what is primarily in God is the transition which takes place in that distance, the mediation in that confrontation, the communication in that encounter, the history in that
partnership."[38] And this is the work of the Holy Spirit in the communion and union of Father and Son in love, in a "history in partnership."[39]

When this takes place something ultimate is happening; God is
God and is alive, a history is taking place, a unity in distinction in a
threefold relationship which is forever renewed, dynamic, active and
loving. It is in this act that we see the being of God - a being in becoming. The *being* of God is in the *active* relationship of Father and Son in

and by the Holy Spirit as one God. It is in and by the Holy Spirit that "the history, the transition, the mediation and the communication between the Father and the Son take place and are revealed as such."[40] An important emphasis of Barth's is that the Spirit is God not merely in and for the union of Father and Son but as such active *pro nobis* and *in nobis*. It is in his being in transition in God that he is at the same time his being in transition for us. So the triune life as the free life and love of God is the basis, the power and the possibility of all his actions *ad extra* and particularly in our reconciliation.

Finally Barth points out that Jesus in his relationship to us reflects the nature and action of God. This is seen in a twofold way. The distinction, confrontation, encounter and partnership between Jesus and us mirrors "the distinction with which he is in himself the Father and the Son." Likewise the transition, mediation, communication and history reflect and correspond to "the union of the Father and the Son in the Holy Spirit as his own eternal living act." In being our God he is thus true to himself and manifests himself as God. In exalting us in Christ by the Holy Spirit we, by his free grace, participate in the triune life of God "and in the problem of this life, and its answer and solution."[41]

IV. DISTINCTIVE FEATURES OF THIS DOCTRINE

In many places in his exposition Barth's statements imply and in fact forestall the modern thesis chiefly associated with Karl Rahner that "the 'economic' Trinity is the 'immanent' Trinity"[42] and vice versa. God is as he reveals himself, as he acts in reconciliation. Barth sums it up as follows: "We have consistently followed the rule, which we regard as basic, that statements about the divine modes of being antecedently in themselves cannot be different in content from those that are to be made about their reality in revelation. All our statements concerning what is called the immanent Trinity have been reached simply as confirmations or underlinings or, materially, as the indispensable premises of the economic Trinity ... the reality of God which encounters us in his revelation is his reality in all the depths of eternity."[43] The identity and continuity of the divine being and act in himself and in reconciliation are constantly and clearly affirmed. "In the work of the reconciliation of the world with God the inward divine relationship between the One who rules and commands in majesty and the One who obeys in humility is *identical* with the very different relationship between God and one of his creatures, a man."[44] Again, Barth writes: "He is in and for the world what he is in and for himself ... He is in our lowliness what he is in his majesty ... He is as Man, as the man who is obedient in humility, Jesus of Nazareth, what he is as God."[45]

(a) The Trinity and Salvation

This particular emphasis on the reality of reconciliation as the key to the understanding of the nature of the triune God has certain important consequences in Barth's theology.

It excludes any basis for natural theology or philosophical ideas about God. If the cross is the centre and meaning of God's reconciling act, it reveals his true being in particular acts and relationships. It involves, as both Torrance [46] and Jüngel [47] point out, the grounding of our doctrine of the triune God in the fact of the truth of our salvation and thus in faith, worship and doxology. The act of God's reconciliation of us, his identification with us in his Son on the cross is the sole basis for the ontological affirmation of the reality of the triune God. Since the being of the one true God is in Jesus Christ the crucified, this involves thinking of and re-defining God from this centre.

It is the *being* of God which is revealed in his *act* and it is he who comes to us. God does not hold himself back or come to us as an intermediary but comes as true God in the fullness of his deity and the reality of his triune life as God in the person of the Mediator. Nor can this be the result of any necessity in God save that which he has freely chosen. That he has chosen one possibility for ever excludes all others; as manifesting his will it has this sure ground and its necessity here alone. The economic and immanent Trinity, while in one sense identical, must not be interpreted either as tautological or in a way that fails to see the economic as the result of the free grace of God. The economic Trinity is both an expression of how God is in himself (immanent) and how he acts in the freedom of his grace towards us.

Barth's view is also a critique of the older Protestant and Roman Catholic procedure of beginning with a section in dogmatics on the *de Deo Uno* and proceeding from this to interpret the *de Deo Trino*. The danger ensues of trying to fit the Trinity into an already preconceived idea of unity, whereas the Christian conception of God is from beginning to end trinitarian in character - the unity of God is a unity in Trinity. One cannot, however, simply imply that all who followed this path failed to reach a proper view of God nor does Barth make such a judgement. But he does, nonetheless, point out the hidden dangers of it as a source of error. In fact, in the formulation of doctrine a bare unity was actually transcended (except by Unitarians) by the trinitarian view of God.

(b) Deus pro nobis in Cross and Resurrection

The centering of God's act of reconciliation in the humiliation of the Son and the exaltation of man as God's primary will for man indicates a dimension in God which can only be described in trinitarian terms. That God reveals himself in reconciliation in this differentiated relationship of humiliation and exaltation, of above and below, and that in this way he is God for us, *Deus pro nobis,* indicates that this is how he is in himself-majestic and yet humble, One who is both high and lowly without any inequality. In himself, to put it in Barth's expressive terms, "as Father, Son and Holy Spirit, God is, so to speak, 'ours in advance'."[48] There is already in the divine life a direction downwards, a majesty and lowliness indicating a distinction in God as Father and Son which is the basis and possibility of incarnation and atonement, of his being and action for us.

The perspective from which Barth works is the cross as the climax of Jesus' earthly life revealed in its meaning in the resurrection. But if the cross is central it is in the history of suffering that the triune God is revealed. Barth is more careful than many modern theologians in relating the significance of the cross to the triune God. With almost all contemporary theology he rejects the Greek idea that God is *apathetic,* an unmoved, unfeeling being. How could he be when in his Son he enters into the passion of the man Jesus? Patripassianism is excluded but its grain of truth is accepted. The cross of Christ cost God. God shows his very nature there. The humiliation of the Son shows the mercy of the Father. The Father is intimately involved with the Son and the Spirit in the act of redemption. "He does not count it too high a cost to give and send his Son, to elect him to take our place as the Rejected, and therefore to abase him. It is not at all the case that God has no part in the suffering of Jesus Christ even in his mode of being as the Father. No, there is a *particula veri* in the teachings of the early Patripassians. This is that primarily it is God the Father who suffers in the offering and sending of his Son, in his abasement . . . This fatherly fellow-suffering of God is the mystery, the basis, of the humiliation of his Son; the truth of that which takes place historically in his crucifixion."[49]

While Barth can say this he can also state that this does not endanger God's 'self-sufficiency' or perfect 'beatitude'.[50] He holds together both God's involvement with us in the suffering of the man Jesus and his perfection of being as triune. He can in fact go so far as to say that it is only in and through the humiliation and suffering of the Son that we can know who God is, God in his exalted and perfect life. In this respect he makes the affirmation that the almighty God "exists and speaks in the form of one who is weak and impotent."[51] This in no way means that God contradicts himself - even the God-forsakenness of Jesus on the cross cannot be so interpreted. The Son of God in union with the man Jesus did indeed die as Redeemer but in this self-surrender and acceptance of death he did not give up being God, give away the deity, his oneness with the Father. He "does not give himself away. He does not give up being God in becoming a creature, in becoming man." In accepting and entering into the contradiction of man against himself and suffering under it he yet acts as Lord over it. "He is not untrue but true to himself in this condescension." Rather in the most intimate union with the Father his deity is affirmed, the life of God is manifest and triumphant in the midst of death, its curse and judgement. Death, while accepted and experienced, is not Lord. God is in Jesus. "He overcomes the flesh in becoming flesh."[52]

The constancy or immutable nature of God does not mean, therefore, an impassible Lord but one who has within himself the infinite flexibility and resources which make it possible for him to be both high and lowly and so to be God. He is sovereign Lord in the suffering and death of his Son which is in a measure that of the Father too. One must resist the idea that there is any lack in God filled out by his becoming man or suffering as such or that the cross reacts on God and changes his nature.[53] Much less must one accept the idea of the cross as a tragic entanglement from which God himself has in some way to be rescued. God's being, as Jüngel points out, is indeed a being in act, a being in becoming - in the act of 'suffering'.[54] The suffering of God is not something new in God resulting from the incarnation and cross; the reverse is rather the truth: the nature of the self-humiliation and the cross point back to what is the eternal nature of God. So God's suffering, his going to death in his Son is a real passion in which he participates but not something which alters him. It is one way in which what he always is is revealed; it is in fact the only way we know him. He lives as God in the death of his Son and in this way is victorious over sin and death.

Let us try more precisely to see what this means. The depth and alienation of the Son on the cross is clearly not alien to God, however opposed to him are the actions and persons that led to the cross. On the contrary, God is known as God, as the perfectly holy, constant, loving, living God precisely in this action. He is neither limited to it, confined by it nor known apart from it. God is as he has been made known and acts in the cross and its suffering.

If this is so and he is revealed as majestic in mercy and obedient in humility, for all the strong language about the suffering of God, Barth never specifically spells out what exactly is meant by this. Jüngel draws some conclusions from Barth's premises by saying that there is in God not only an aspect which is positive and active but one which is passive and obedient, not only a giving but a receiving. This is what corresponds in God to the suffering and obedience of the Son in his death. Jüngel guardedly states that the suffering of God, consists in this that as Son he "is able to suffer and die as a man."[55] He is able, furthermore, as Father, to share in some measure in this. The passion of God is therefore that attitude of God as Father to Son and Son to Father by the Spirit whereby he possesses the potentiality to enter savingly into the wholly different and contrary actuality of our God-forsakenness and sin and in fact does so. In doing so he takes it to himself, destroys it and frees us from it. For Barth therefore there is movement but not change in God. God must remain and be wholly God else man cannot be reconciled to him.

(c) Triune God as Event and Analogy

A further consequence of Barth's basic premise is that reconciliation as an event in the history of salvation, a movement in a particular time and place, reflects the very being of God himself. It is a being in act. It is a movement first within God himself as Father to Son by the

Holy Spirit which Barth describes in terms of dynamic and teleology. The movement from God to God, from Father to Son is in this irreversible order and the telos or goal is the union of both in the Holy Spirit. In the same way there is a telos and a dynamic - indeed the same dynamic - in God's action for us. He moves in sovereign freedom in humiliation in the Son to us and into our situation and lifts us up into union with himself. There is, therefore, not only a dynamic within God but one which reaches out, embraces us and returns us God. In this movement God is the living, loving God. It is a movement within God which opens out and includes us within the divine life and love.

To say, as we have seen, that the economic Trinity is the immanent Trinity and vice versa is true. But it requires an important sharpening and qualification. God is both God in himself as Father, Son and Holy Spirit and for us; there is, therefore, both an identity and a distinction between the two. In the first instance God's being *ad intra* as Father, Son and Holy Spirit is one with his being *ad extra.* In the second God's being and action *for us* corresponds to his being as triune. One must stress fully both sides to do justice to Barth's thought and to the relationship between the immanent and the economic Trinity.

We look now briefly at how this is seen in Barth's doctrine of reconciliation. The humiliation of the Son is analogous to the nature of God who is obedient in humility as Son to Father. At the same time the exaltation of Jesus as true and royal man corresponds to his divine Sonship. This is "the twofold but single will of God"[56] in exaltation and abasement reflecting the height of the Father and the depth and subordination of the Son. Barth expresses it in this way: "what is represented and reflected in the humiliation of God is the mercy of the Father" and "what is represented and reflected in the exaltation of the man Jesus is the majesty of the Son."[57] This denotes, represents and reflects the riddle of "the existence of Jesus Christ."[58]

In full accord with this close relationship between economic and immanent Trinity Barth supports the Western acceptance of the *Filioque;* his doctrine of reconciliation confirms this where the Spirit is the Spirit of Christ. Just as he (the Spirit) unites God and man in Jesus Christ and unites us with Christ so this reflects what he is and does in the divine life. Barth remains from beginning to end Western and Augustinian in his conception of the Spirit as the bond of love between Father and Son. At the same time his view of the nature of God based exclusively on revelation and his dynamic conception of the relations of the 'persons' within the Trinity strike a note closer to Eastern trinitarian thought. The emphasis, too, on the knowledge of the triune God as intimately related to worship and doxology points in the same direction. In this sense Barth's is truly a 'catholic' conception of the Trinity.

Where one has queries about Barth's exposition is in one part of his section on the Holy Spirit. As we have seen the use of analogy permeates the *Church Dogmatics* but is somewhat overdone and strained in Volume IV/2. The problem of the transition from Jesus to ourselves is seen by analogy as pointing to a problem in God, namely, that of the relationship between Father and Son which is solved by the person, work and union of the Holy Spirit. It is true that Barth poses the problem from the solution, sees the negative, as always, in the light of the positive, but it is a dubious way to state that God has a problem with himself which he has to deal with and solve. This could only be true if one temporarily omitted the work and place of the Holy Spirit and Barth clearly has no intention of doing this. The point that he is making is quite clear and could be put otherwise. It is, namely, that Father and Son can only be seen in proper relationship by and with the Holy Spirit. But is it not an abstraction (which Barth otherwise opposes) to think of them in any kind of isolation from him? To do so would indeed lead to a problem in God himself - in fact would lead to a different conception of God than the trinitarian which Barth so rightly and vigorously espouses. This kind of approach and bold language were better avoided. Having said this, however, Barth otherwise gives a profound, convincing exposition and powerfully relates reconciliation to the being of the triune God.

NOTES

1. *C.D.,* I/I, p. 301. cf *C.D.,* IV/I, p. 338. "The christian thought of God is trinitarian."
2. H. Hartwell, *The Theology of Karl Barth: An Introduction.* London: Duckworth, 1964, p. 96.
3. G.W. Bromiley, *Introduction to the Theology of Karl Barth.* Edinburgh: T & T Clark, 1979, p. ix.
4. Claude Welch, *The Trinity in Contemporary Theology.* London: S.C.M., 1953, p. 164.
5. Ibid., pp. 161 ff.
6. E. Jüngel, *The Doctrine of the Trinity, God's Being is in Becoming.* trs. Horton Harris, Edinburgh & London: Scottish Academic Press, 1976, pp. 15 ff.
7. *C.D.,* I/I, p. 303

8. Jüngel, op.cit., p. 5 Colm O'Grady writes: "The internal and formal as well as material significance of the doctrine of the Trinity in Barth's theology has been very seldom brought into sufficient relief by his commentators." *The Church in the Theology of Karl Barth*, London: Chapman, 1970, p. 84. O'Grady himself has shown how Barth's doctrine of the church has a trinitarian structure.

    It should, however, be pointed out that, while Barth regarded the Trinity as central to and determinative of all theology, he did not necessarily see it as always having to be treated first. When asked about this Barth commented: "You could move from any point in the dogmatic realm to the Trinity." *Karl Barth's Table Talk (T.T.)*, recorded and edited by John D. Godsey, Scottish Journal of Theology Occasional Papers, No. 10, Edinburgh: Oliver and Boyd, 1963, p. 50.

9. Godsey, op.cit., pp. 3-4. See also O'Grady, op.cit., pp. 85-86.
10. Welch, op.cit., p. 163.
11. *C.D.*, I/I, where the editors state that "studied in connexion with volume two on the doctrine of God, the claim may well be made that it is the greatest treatise of its kind since the *De Trinitate* of St. Augustine." p. ix.
12. E. Jüngel points out that Barth's treatment of the Trinity in volume one of the *Church Dogmatics* suffered from a certain formalism which is corrected in volume four when it is related more to the humanity of Jesus Christ in reconciliation rather than the earlier more formal concept of revelation. *God As The Mystery Of The World*, trs. Darrell L. Guder, Edinburgh: T & T Clark, 1983, p. 351.n.22.

    Barth himself grants later that in speaking of the relation of Father and Son in revelation and reconciliation he should "have begun with the humanity of Jesus Christ." *T.T.*, p. 52.
13. *C.D.*, IV/I, pp. 128 ff.
14. Ibid., pp. 157 ff.
15. Ibid., p. 199.
16. Ibid.
17. Ibid., p. 201.
18. Ibid., pp. 202-203.
19. Ibid., p. 203.
20. Ibid., p. 209.
21. W. Kreck, *Grundfragen der Dogmatik*, Munich: Chr. Kaiser, 1970, p. 84. This is a change in Kreck's view of Barth at this point. Cf his review in 'Die Lehre von der Versöhnung, Zu Karl Barths Kirchliche Dogmatik, IV/I and IV/2', *Theologische Literaturzeitung* 1960/2, p. 89, where he queried Barth's view of an 'above' and a 'below' in God and hence of a divine obedience of the Son. Cf however, P.T. Forsyth, for an anticipation of Barth's view that there is an obedience of Son to Father in the triune life of God. *Marriage: Its Ethic and Religion*, London: 1912, p. 70.
22. *C.D.*, IV/I, pp. 297 ff.
23. Ibid., p. 304.
24. Ibid.
25. Berthold Klappert, *Die Auferwecking des Gekreuzigten. Der Ansatz der Christologie Karl Barths im Zasammenhang der Christologie der Gegenwart*, Neukirchen: 1971, p. 306
26. *C.D.*, IV/I, pp. 304-309.
27. Ibid., p. 305.
28. Ibid., p. 309.
29. *C.D.*, IV/2, passim, especially pp. 264 ff.
30. Ibid., p. 333.
31. Ibid., pp. 330 ff.
32. Otto Weber, *Karl Barths Kirchliche Dogmatik*, Neukirchen: 1983, p. 254.
33. *C.D.*, IV/2, p. 341.

34. Ibid., p. 342.
35. Ibid.
36. Ibid., pp. 342-343.
37. Ibid., p. 343.
38. Ibid., p. 344.
39. Ibid.
40. Ibid., p. 345.
41. Ibid., p. 346.
42. Karl Rahner, *The Trinity*, trs. Joseph Donceel, London: Burns and Oates, 1970, pp. 22 ff.
43. C.D., I/I, p. 479.
44. C.D., IV/I, p. 203. Italics mine.
45. Ibid., p. 204.
46. Thomas F. Torrance, "Towards an Ecumenical Consensus on the Trinity," *Theologische Zeitschrift*, 31/6, 1975, pp. 337 ff.
47. E. Jüngel, states that "The mystery of the Trinity is the mystery of salvation." "Das Verhaltnis von 'ökonomischer' und 'immanenter' Trinität," *Entsprechungen: Gott-Wahrheit-Mensch*, Munich: Ch. Kaiser, 1980, p. 270.
48. C.D., I/I, p. 383.
49. C.D., IV/2, p. 357.
50. Ibid., p. 346. Cf C.D., II/I, pp. 57-58, 306, 659.
51. C.D., IV/I, p. 176.
52. Ibid., p. 185.
53. Jürgen Moltmann writes: "the cross has a retroactive effect on the Father" with a mutual relationship between economic and immanent Trinity so that "the cross determines the inner life of the triune God from eternity to eternity." *The Trinity and the Kingdom of God*, trs. Margaret Kohl, London: S.C.M., 1981, pp. 160-161.
54. Jüngel, *The Doctrine of the Trinity*, p. 85.
55. Ibid., p. 86.
56. C.D., IV/2, p. 351.
57. Ibid., p. 357.
58. Ibid., p. 358.

The Nature and Place of Scripture in the Church Dogmatics

Christina A. Baxter

Karl Barth presents an immense number of theoretical observations and practical examples of the nature and place of Scripture in his *Church Dogmatics*. A brief theoretical introduction will therefore be followed by a selective study to highlight distinctive features of his method.

The nature of Scripture is summarized thus by Barth:

> *The Word of God is God Himself in Holy Scripture. For God once spoke as Lord to Moses and the prophets, to the evangelists and apostles. And now through their written word He speaks as the same Lord to His church. Scripture is holy and the Word of God, because by the Holy Spirit it became and will become to the Church a witness to divine revelation.* [1]

Consequently it is wrong in Barth's view to equate Scripture to revelation; rather "revelation engenders the Scripture which attests it."[2] This attestation or witness is epitomised visually for Barth by Grünewald's crucifixion, where John the Baptist points from himself to the Lamb of God.[3] But it is not religious art alone which has given rise to Barth's basic understanding of Scripture, for he is convinced that this is the way in which the biblical documents understand themselves.[4] "We have not sought or found this answer at random. We have taken it from the Bible" he claims.[5] If both the Old and New Testament are witnesses, it is because "Jesus Christ has called the Old and New Testaments into existence:" his Incarnation "... is what the Old Testament as a word of prophecy and the New Testament as a word of fulfilment both proclaim as having happened . . . ."[6]

Thus all is witnessing to Scripture's central content: Jesus Christ. "The Bible says all sorts of things, certainly; but in all this multiplicity and variety, it says in truth only one thing - just this: the name of Jesus Christ, concealed under the name Israel in the Old Testament, revealed under his own name in the New Testament . . . ."[7] For Barth this recognition issues in a hermeneutical principle which he articulates thus: "the object of the biblical texts is quite simply the name

Jesus Christ, and these texts can be understood only when understood as determined by this object."[8]

Such a deeply theological understanding of Scripture has not lost
touch with the reality of the human author's frailty and sinfulness
however. Barth is most explicit: "As truly as Jesus died on the cross ...
so too the prophets and apostles ... even in their function as witnesses,
even in the act of writing down their witness, were real historical men
as we are, and therefore sinful in their action and capable and actually
guilty of error in their spoken and written word."[9] This Barth
regards as "... miracle, that here fallible men speak the Word of God in
fallible human words."[10] Such an assertion might lead the unwary
to suppose that it becomes necessary to weed out the errant human
words from the infallible Divine words, but Barth prohibits any such
attempt. The miracle of the grace of God is that these scriptural witnesses have been justified and sanctified. Thus:

> *If God was not ashamed of the fallibility of all the human
> words of the Bible, of their historical and scientific inac-
> curacies, their theological contradictions, the uncertainty of
> their tradition, and, above all, their Judaism, but adopted and
> made use of these expressions in all their fallibility, we do not
> need to be ashamed when He wills to renew it to us in all its
> fallibility as witness, and it is mere self-will and disobedience
> to try to find some infallible elements in the Bible.[11]*

The Divine Word is pleased to be joined with the human word, so
". . . Holy Scripture is like the unity of God and man in Jesus
Christ."[12]

For this reason, despite the biblical "capacity for errors"[13] Barth is
not prepared to stand in judgement over any part of Scripture to try to
ascertain its veracity. Rather the opposite is required: "... we have to
subordinate ourselves to the word of the prophets and apostles; not as
one subordinates oneself to God, but rather as one subordinates oneself for the sake of God and in his love and fear to the witnesses and
messengers which He Himself has constituted and empowered."[14]
Barth is convinced that God has graciously chosen to make Scripture
theologically reliable, and consequently "... the message which Scripture has to give us, even in its most debatable and less assimilable
parts, is in all circumstances truer and more important than the best
and most necessary things that we ourselves have said or can
say."[15]

The manner of God's making Scripture theologically reliable is in a double act of revelation. The first is in giving Himself to be known, objectively, for example in the person of Jesus, and subjectively in the giving to the apostles the capacity to know Him. The first "act" of revelation thus straddles objectivity and subjectivity and engenders the record known as Scripture. The second act of revelation is God giving Himself to be known, objectively in the Scriptural record, which is wholly about Jesus, and subjectively in the giving to the readers the capacity to know Him. This second "act" of revelation equally straddles objectivity and subjectivity, and is never completed or finished for the relationship between God who is giving Himself to be known, and the reader who is receiving the capacity to know God is a continuing relationship: it has to be "new every morning" or it is not knowledge of God at all.[16] Although the apostles witness to this, neither they nor the written words of Scripture, still less the readers of Scripture "possess" this revelation: - it is the free gift of a sovereign God.

I. The Role of Scripture in the Church Dogmatics

With this theoretical introduction in mind, we turn to an examination of the role that Scripture plays in the *Church Dogmatics*. A full study is impossible within the scope of this essay, so Barth's attitude will be elucidated from those sections where he outlines the relationship of men to women. Since one cannot find examples of all Barth's characteristics in any single section, the picture is bound to be partial. Nevertheless this choice shows Barth's mature style at work, displaying characteristic features.

Barth's exposition of "Man and Woman" may be found in his ethical volume of "The Doctrine of Creation" developed in conscious dependence on his earlier sections "Man in his determination as the Covenant Partner of God" and "Creation and Covenant."[17] They are not unrelated to his earlier affirmation of the Trinitarian God, and his later elaboration of "The Doctrine of Reconciliation."[18] However, it is possible to trace a development in his thought through the three chosen chapters.

In developing his understanding of humanity, Barth engages with the traditions of the past, with theologians, poets and others, and with Scripture itself. We are offered in the large print the conclusion which he has drawn from this process, generally without detailed reference either to other scholars or to the Bible. In the excursus however, he includes for the readers' benefit, "... the voices which were in my own ears as I prepared my own text, which guided, taught or stimulated me, and by which I wish to be measured by my readers."[19] Amongst these voices he identifies the Bible as "... the basic text upon which all the rest and everything of our own can only wait and comment."[20] Thus we literally see, *in print*, how Barth regards dogmatics as passing beyond Scripture, whilst nevertheless remaining dependent on it. He drew a clear distinction between exegetical theology which "... investigates biblical teaching as the basis of our talk about God". and dogmatics which "... does not ask what the prophets and apostles said, but what we must say on the basis of the apostles and prophets."[21]   "Biblical   exegesis   is   the   decisive   presupposition and source of dogmatics"[22] but dogmatics is "... a relative movement away from exegesis"[23] the danger of which he readily acknowledges whilst asserting its inevitability.

It is important to recognise that Barth has to make a judgement about which parts of Scripture are relevant to the topic under consideration, and this judgement can considerably influence his conclusions. In the case of the creation of humanity it may not be controversial: Barth turns to the Genesis creation stories, which he regards as the *locus classicus* of the debate, then to other texts touching on his subject.[24] It is the aim of our author never to ignore any text which might be considered to be relevant to his discussion, [25] but within this inclusive aim he often selects one or two passages which are for him "central", "normative" or comprehend the others. Thus he refers to Ephesians 5:22-33 as "... the *locus classicus* for the point at issue".[26] This selection and personal perception of texts can be extremely influential in Barth's theology for it precedes his written exegesis and dogmatics.

One of the interesting features of the earliest chapter under discussion (§41) is that Barth develops his dogmatic theology in tandem with his exegesis of Genesis. This is one of the major ways in which Barth uses Scripture in the *Church Dogmatics*. Almost a quarter of his biblical citations and references fall in excursts which are giving extended consideration to a single passage of Scripture.[27] This fact alone encourages an examination of Barth's exegetical method; and extended consideration to a single passage of Scripture.[27] This fact alone encourages an examination of Barth's exegetical method; and this is reinforced by the recognition that Barth frequently offers incidental exegesis elsewhere. We begin where Barth began, with historical criticism.

Despite disagreement amongst scholars as to Barth's readiness to engage with the historical-critical method, there is plenty of evidence to show that he was prepared to employ it in the *Church Dogmatics* whenever he considered it relevant to his purposes.[28] He never accepts its conclusions unthinkingly, for his concern is always whether the methods of criticism are appropriate to the text under consideration. When he judges that this is the case, he is happy to employ the discoveries that it has made; where he judges otherwise he selects those parts of the conclusions which are consistent with his view of Scripture. The historical-critical method is always an aid to exegesis rather than a tool for analysis for Barth.

A few examples must suffice. Barth relies predominantly on source criticism in his discussion of the Genesis passages. Genesis 1 is attributed to a Priestly source, "P", perhaps from Mesopotamia,[29] and Genesis 2:4-3:24 is a "Yahwistic account", "J" from a more arid area.[30] Barth relies on H. Gunkel's work for background details to help his exegesis.[31] Barth assumes an editor or redactor who gave us the final form of Genesis, and whose comment, for example in Genesis 2:24 may be recognised, on dominical precedent, as the revealed Word of God.[32] The redactor's intention is a crucial clue to understanding the text for Barth.[33]

There is little if anything in our sections which might pass for textual or form criticism, although Barth employs them elsewhere.[34] Textual comments are confined to examination of the Septuagint translation and less frequently the Vulgate.[35] The only hint of form criticism is discussion of the precise nature of the Genesis stories, which Barth concludes are "sagas",[36] but this is an important decision because it enables appropriate interpretion.[37] Wherever historical-critical methods are employed by Barth, his chief concern is to discover the author's intended meaning: "My aim is to convey the subject-matter or reference of what the author says in this particular text".[38] Hence grammatical points, the gender of a noun,[39] a plural,[40] or a preposition[41] may be deeply significant. The common use in the relevant testament may establish the correct sense.[42]

Barth uses background details to determine the exact intention of the author or redactor, although he depends on secondary sources for this.[43] Thus he argues ". . . the author [of Genesis 1] undoubtedly knew this mythical conception . . ."[44] of Babylonian myth but ". . . he definitely could not and would not appropriately reproduce it."[45] Barth considers it significant that the myths of surrounding cultures have not simply been adopted, but rather "what emerges is not just one picture of a mythological world view, but several different and to some extent superimposed pictures."[46]

However important the cultural context of the original author or redactor, the immediate literary context, or the larger canonical context always give more reliable indications as to the intended meaning in Barth's view. Thus early church exegesis is criticised because it dealt with the opening chapters of Genesis yet "on the whole paid far too little attention to the rest of Genesis and the rest of the Old Testament."[47] This was a mistake because "the decisive commentary on the biblical histories of creation is the rest of the Old Testament."[48] Thus, Isaiah 45:18 may help elucidate whether Genesis 1 is really dealing with *creatio ex nihilo*.[49] At this point we begin to glimpse the decisive influence which Barth's notion of the unity of Scripture played in his exegesis.

> *It can and must be maintained that the Old Testament as a whole forms a single material context with the New, and that it is this context, and beyond the confines of the Old Testament, that Gen 2:18f. must be seen if it is to be rightly understood. It can and must be maintained that we are forced to affirm convergence rather than divergence, harmony rather than contradiction, once we see the focal point which is outside the Old Testament and identical with the central point of the message of the New.[50]*

This focal point is Jesus Christ himself; ". . . in Holy Scripture there are, of course, many human subjects . . . but it is more important to realise that in virtue of the unity of their theme, the many human subjects of scripture are visible and operative . . . as a single subject - of his fullness have we all received (Jn.1.16)."[51]

Barth recognises that affirmation of the unity of Scripture is a position of faith, and not universally demonstrable. This was the case even for the apostles: "Paul's daring equation of the man Jesus . . . directly with the divine image, is an unprecedented and radical innovation"; although it does not

> *represent any innovation in relation to the Old Testament, but pointed to its fulfilment. The decision whether this is the case is not an exegetical question.* **Then and always it is answered only in the form of faith and unbelief, by proclamation or denial.** [52]

Barth has espoused this position of faith for three reasons. First, he finds it to be consistent with the view which Scripture offers of itself. Second, it fits his theological position which is equally derived from Scripture. That is, "the unity of revelation guarantees the unity of the biblical witness in and in spite of all its multiplicity and even contradictoriness."[53] Third, he considers it to be justified by practice. However there is not a simple determination on Barth's part to maintain the biblical unity at any cost, and certainly not to reduce the texts to a "lowest common denominator".

Barth is not blind to contrasts. The law and prophets of the Old Testament, or the gospels and epistles of the New have recognisably different emphases.[54] In our sections, Barth recognises that although there may be ". . . unity about the theme", of the two creation accounts, nevertheless they ". . . can be brought into direct relationship, i.e., harmonised, only in an artificial way and by doing violence to the actual text."[55] But this is not Barth's way forward: each account must be read "as if it were the only one"[56], and only then may a higher harmony emerge. Barth reads these two stories characteristically, for his approach is frequently comparable to musical harmony. Each line of music may be read as a separate tune, although taken together a harmony is produced which in no way cancels the tune of any one part. Rather it requires them all, for when played as harmony a fresh but not totally new entity is performed. Barth treats Scripture in a parallel way. Each account is valuable. To reduce any one to the other is to lose part of the truth. The task of the dogmatic theologian is to perceive the higher harmony which may only be seen if each part is taken seriously.[57] Thus, in our case, there are two creation sagas.

> They not only describe the events with greatly varying
> interests but also in very different ways. Seen from the point
> of view of the other, each of these accounts reveals painful
> omissions and irreconcilable contradictions.[58]

A single history of creation is not possible, so Barth concludes that this is not what was intended.

Barth is occasionally prepared to concede substantial contrast. Concerning divorce, for example, he writes: "The gulf between the Old and New Testament view of the matter is unmistakable."[59] These cases may not yield a "higher harmony", so it becomes necessary to echo the biblical dialectic. Thus "the concession of divorce in the Old Testament is understandable, for the Old Testament witnesses were quite unable to think from the standpoint from which the New Testament witnesses were compelled to think."[60]

To summarise: we have seen that the historical-critical method is a tool that Barth uses to discover the author or redactor's intended meaning. But Barth is always keen to see this in the canonical context. This may best be elaborated by looking at his understanding of the image of God, showing first how that depends on his exegetical and interpretative method, before explaining how it gives rise to his dogmatic and ethical conclusions.

II. The Image of God

Barth begins his considerations with an observation about the text: Genesis 1 includes several creative acts of God, each commanded "Let there be" or "Let the earth bring forth".[61] There is a strange contrast in the creation of man, for this regards "God as capable of soliloquy expressly narrated in the plural."[62] The excursus shows that Barth has come to this conclusion after exegetical consideration. He finds unanimous agreement amongst the expositors that the plural is not just a matter of royal dignity, but is linked with the "image". Several things are noteworthy. First, Barth includes amongst his expositors not only H. Gunkel and G. von Rad but also J. Calvin. His knowledge of and reliance on many of the Reformers is notable, and most frequently this is found in reference to either M. Luther or J. Calvin.[63] Second, he characteristically rules out the possibility of understanding the plural merely as "a formal expression of dignity" of Persian origin, on the canonical ground that "it is foreign to the linguistic usage of the Old Testament."[64] Third, Barth recognises that this plural was probably original to the oral tradition from which this saga came, and concludes that the priestly redactor decided not to remove it. Its presence is therefore to be considered highly significant in the final form of the text.

Positively Barth then assembles a series of passages where the Divine plural may be found. This is also characteristic of his method. Often he traces themes or concepts in a testament or in the whole of Scripture, [65] so he is able to trace a "field" of biblical thinking into which he can then place this particular use. This is what happens here. Barth finds two kinds of use in the Old Testament: the one implies a plurality within the divinity; the other implies a consultative council of heavenly beings. Barth distinguishes between these very clearly on the basis of the wording of the two groups of texts. Genesis 1:26 pictures a concerted co-operative creature activity; an activity available to God alone, hence the plural must refer to the divinity. "How could non-divine beings even assist in an advisory capacity in an act of creation, let alone have an active part in the creation of man, as we are expressly told?" Barth asks.[66]

This is a fine example of Barth setting up theoretical possibilities for interpretation, which are then examined meticulously before a final decision is taken. It is important to note here that Barth has to rely not just on the text, but also on his understanding of God and the angelic host. He has already developed his doctrine of God, but the "ambassadors of God" have yet to be discussed.[67] Here a single reference from the Psalms makes clear Barth's developing angelology which will not allow the possibility of an angelic creation of man; but neither will the doctrine of God already established. Thus in a real sense, one of the deciding factors in this decision about exegesis is doctrine. Barth says as much: "If we think that what is here said about the Creator can finally and properly be understood only against the background of the Christian doctrine of the Trinity, we have at least the advantage of being able to accept everything that is said quite literally and without attenuation . . ."[68] Exegetically Barth frankly admits that Genesis 1:26 "speaks of a genuine plurality in the divine being, but it does not actually say that it is a trinity."[69] This is one of the classic places where Barth recognises exegesis cannot go as far as dogmatics. Exegesis must ask what does the text say and mean? Dogmatics must go beyond that to ask what does it signify and imply? In this case the text clearly says that God addresses himself in soliloquy as plural. The text means that plural to be taken literally and not metaphorically. But the text does not spell out the implications or significance of the plural. Barth highlights how exegesis at this point raises a question which neither the text nor the Old Testament can answer: Who is this "us"? That question remains unanswerable in terms of the Old Testament understanding of God; it has to be answered by the New Testament. It is only in the light of Christ that the significance of the implied plurality in God may be ascertained. Jesus Christ is "...the answer to the enigma of Genesis 1:26f."[70] In this respect, Barth considers early church exegesis which saw this as a reference to the Trinity to be more correct than the contemporary scholars, for he considers that the latter do not keep close enough to the wording or the context.

It was important for Barth to settle the significance of the divine plural, because on that decision depended the answer to his next question: how is man in the image of God? He begins by outlining two groups of answers offered by theologians and exegetes. The first group are not important to this discussion: Barth concludes this survey:

> We might easily discuss which of these and the many other similar explanations is the finest or deepest or most serious. What we cannot discuss is which of them is the true explanation of Genesis 1:26f. For it is obvious that their authors merely found the concept in the text and then proceeded to pure invention in accordance with the requirements of contemporary anthropology.[71]

This is anathema to Barth for it is subjecting the text to contemporary philosophy rather than vice versa: it is eisegesis not exegesis. Moreover it has failed to grapple with the text in its literary and canonical context until biblical warrant is found for a possible or definitive enterpretation. Finally it is dishonest because if these exegetes could not find in this text or related texts any hints as to how to understand the "image" they should have been honest enough to admit defeat and confess that neither the text nor the context gives any clue as to what the phrase might mean.

Barth does not feel himself compelled to admit defeat. Indeed his notion of the perspicuity of Scripture drives him on to seek biblical interpretation.[72] He admits that a second group of answers to the question of the "image of God" are "closer to the text".[73] These he discusses in detail before rejecting them. H. Gunkel's notion that the image is primarily the physical form of man is based on Genesis 5:3 where Adam is said to beget a son after his image. Barth counters that God's creation of Adam and Adam's begetting of Seth are not genuinely parallel activities. For this and other reasons Barth cannot agree that the image is physical likeness. However he has to take H. Gunkel seriously because he is following Barth's principle of trying to elucidate Scripture by reference to another related biblical text. It is chiefly a matter of judgement: Barth does not consider that the other passage is related; Gunkel does. It is buttressed by Barth's decision that biblical talk of God's hands or heart is not meant to imply that God and man have physical attributes in common.

B. Jacob's suggestion that the image is to be identified with man's domination is commendable in Barth's view because image and dominion are allied in the text.[74] However, Barth observes that the text offers no "technical connections" between the two. Arguing from silence, he suggests that if man's dominion were the content of the image, the saga or the redactor would have expressed it. Once again he detects eisegesis, for he considers it to be based on modern ideas, and thus rejects it.

W. Vischer takes the phrase "image of God" in the widest literary context of the Old Testament, concluding that it means man is "the true counterpart of God" capable of covenant relationship with Him.[75] Barth recognises the veracity of the observation as a summary of the Old Testament, but does not find adequate reason for thinking that it is the meaning of the phrase in Genesis 1:26.

Barth commends D. Bonhoeffer's interpretation that man resembles God in freedom, which is especially seen in the relationships of male to female, [76] although Barth judges that Bonhoeffer has not examined the text vigorously enough and has consequently drawn the wrong conclusion. Barth wants to be more thoroughly tied to the text which does not mention freedom. So he asks "Is it not astonishing that again and again expositors have ignored the definitive explanation given by the text itself, and instead of reflecting on it pursued all kinds of arbitrarily invented interpretations of the *imago Dei* ?"[77] The text drives Barth to conclude that the image of God in which man is created is the Divine inter-relationship: the I and Thou expressed in 'let us". Man corresponds to this in bi-sexuality; in being male and female; in finding himself encountered by one who is both wholly other and wholly the same. Barth's reply to the objection that the animal kingdom also experience bi-sexuality is of the utmost interest. Both his reading of the text and his observations of the natural world lead him to conclude that for humanity the only genuine differentiation is that the individual is either male or female whereas for animals there are differentiations of species.[78] It is not that the sexuality of man is in the image of God, for that would be to postulate sexuality in God, and that quite clearly belongs to creatures. Rather it is the relationship of differentiated persons.

Having satisfied himself as to the true meaning of the text, Barth goes on to discuss at some length the exact meaning of the Hebrew construction from which he concludes that it is *not* the case that man *is* the image of God, but "he is created in correspondence with the image of God".[79] This is an extremely significant theological point, for Barth claims elsewhere that there is no *analogia entis* between God and man, but only an *analogia relationis* [80] or *analogia fidei*.[81] Whilst this may be consistent with the text it has to be asked whether the text requires Barth to draw this conclusion, or whether in fact decisions he has already taken concerning the nature of man's relationship with God lead him to this point.

Given Barth's interpretation of the *imago Dei*, he cannot hold that the fall of man damaged or effaced the image; indeed he argues that nothing in Genesis or the rest of the Old Testament even hints that this is the case.[82] Consequently he rejects this theology for which there is no biblical warrant. Barth suggests that Old Testament prohibition of images was precisely because in creating man, God had created sufficient indication of his nature already.[83] Barth often "tests" his ideas by looking to see if the theory he has expounded helps to elucidate other less closely related passages.

It might be thought that in identifying the image as relationship between male and female, Barth was constructing grave problems for himself, granted his concept of scriptural unity, when he turned to that New Testament passage which asserts that Christ is the image of the invisible God.[84] But this is not a problem for him because Barth notes that the Colossian hymn to Christ which begins by identifying Christ with the image of God concludes by confessing that "He is the head of the body, the Church"[85] so that Barth concludes that "it is with them [the Church] that Jesus Christ is God's image."[86] "It is from this standpoint that the realism of the Pauline doctrine of the image of God is to be understood...."[87] So Barth's exegesis of other New Testament passages relevant to the idea all lead up to this conclusion. He draws together 2 Corinthians 4:4, Colossians 1:15 and John 14:9 to elucidate the Old Testament for he holds that Adam and Eve both prefigure Christ and His Church and are copies of them: "... it is He, the Son of God, who is first of all the bearer of the image in and after which God created man according to Gen. 1:26f."[88] This becomes the interpretative key to explain why Christians are to "... put on the new nature, which is being renewed in knowledge after the image of its Creator",[89] for it is unthinkable that they should be anything else if the image of God is rightly understood primarily as Jesus *and* His Church. Fuller consideration of the New Testament material is to be found in the later sections; immediately Barth has to consider how the second creation saga in Genesis 2 relates to the first.

There is genuine independent discussion of this narrative,[90] but Barth sees the climax of the story as the creation of women: "God did not create man alone, as a single human being, but in the unequal duality of male and female."[91] Barth comments that "the peculiar light which is thus shed on the brief statement of Gen. 1:27 cannot be an accident but was surely intended by the redaction which combined the two sagas."[92] Barth suggests that the divine decision that "it is not good that man should be alone" must be understood to say that "... it would not be good because solitary man would not be man created in the image of God, who Himself is not solitary."[93] Further, because of the christological interpretation already given to Genesis 1:26, Barth argues that man's own existence "... must always be an anticipation or type - the term usage is unavoidable if we are to explain the matter - of what the form of God's relationship to it will be in the coming covenant between them."[94] Barth's contention is that in creating man as male and female, God creates a picture of the covenant relationship that he will have with Israel, and the relationship Christ will have with His Church.[95] "The whole inner basis of creation, God's whole covenant with man, which will later be established, realised and fulfilled historically, is prefigured in this event, in the completing of man's emergence by the coming of woman to man." [96]

Having discussed the widest significance of the story, Barth focuses next on the relationship between man and woman which is implied by the creation narrative. He observes that although woman is an autonomous being, she is really part of man. He had to suffer loss so God might bring her forth, since man could not create his help-meet.[97] She is his glory, because "without her, he could not be the glory of God."[98] The story's implication that "... the relationship is not one of reciprocity and equality [for] ... man was not taken out of woman, but woman out of man, ... primarily he does not belong to her but she to him ..."[99] finds its antithesis in the editorial comment, "therefore shall a man leave his father and mother."[100] Thus Barth concludes that man's belonging to woman is secondary, for primarily she belongs to him. But this primacy of man to woman is a question of order not supremacy, honour or glory not shame: it is woman's glory to be second. Elsewhere Barth concludes that:

> Man speaks against himself if he assesses and treats woman as an inferior being, for without her weakness and subsequence he could not be man. And woman speaks against herself if she envies that which is proper to man, for his strength and precedence are the reality without which she could not be woman. [101]

Barth concludes that Genesis 2

> ... tells us that only male and female together are man. The male alone is not yet man, for it is not good for him to be alone; nor can the female alone be man, for she is taken out of man: They twain shall be one flesh. Hence Genesis 2 speaks of the covenant made and irrevocably sealed.[102]

Barth then assesses that place which Genesis 2 plays in the Canon. He notices that both Genesis and the Old Testament as a whole are keenly aware of the problems prevalent between the sexes, and yet two passages, Genesis 2 and the Song of Songs are included which deal with the male/female relationship both explicitly and positively. Barth asks himself the question: Why?

> *... The only explanation is that the authors of the creation saga and these love songs had in mind another covenant, stained and spotted, almost unrecognisable in historical reality, yet concluded, sealed, persisting and valid ... ... It is of this covenant, this God and this Israel that the witnesses to Yahweh's revelation had to venture to think when they thought of the beginning and goal of this covenant. What lies at the back of the creation saga is the thought of its commencement, and what lies at the back of the Solomonic love songs is the thought of its goal. [103]*

Barth hazards a guess that to the redactors of Genesis and the Song of Songs "love and marriage between man and woman became to them in some sense irresistably a parable and sign of the link which Yahweh has established between Himself and His people, which in His eternal faithfulness He has determined to keep, and which He for His part has continually renewed."[104]

Precisely what has Barth been doing with Scripture in his handling of Genesis 2? First he has taken it on its own merit, and tried to understand the story. But he has found himself forced back into the other creation narrative, and into one sentence from it, that concerning man created in the image of God, for he construes this whole story as a large elaboration of that statement.

However Barth is not content to try to explain this passage in the light of Genesis alone. It is to be found in the context of the Old Testament, and there he observes there is but one parallel passage which deals exclusively with the marriage relationship. These two passages Barth pictures as the "book ends" which portray the whole purpose of God's creation. Humanity was created so God could have a covenant/ marriage relationship with them. At the end the perfect rapture of his purpose will be accomplished. But between the "book ends" is the factual history of the Old Testament covenant relationship in which Israel, Yahweh's wife is repeatedly unfaithful. Indeed, were it not for the New Testament it would be hard to see Genesis 2 and the Song of

Songs as "book ends": they might rather appear as idealism and irrelevance.

Once again Barth's exploration of the Old Testament has left him with a question which cannot be answered without reference to the New. A single passage about marriage answers all the problems which he has raised about Genesis 2. That passage is Ephesians 5:25f., where Paul explains the marriage relationship, adding: "This is a great mystery and I take it to mean Christ and the Church."[105] Barth moves beyond exegesis into dogmatic exposition: in order to answer the question of the significance of this passage he has to establish some vantage point outside of the passage itself. This he finds in Ephesians. His rationale for this procedure is the unity of revelation which lies behind the Scriptural unity. "Eph. 5:25 can and may and must be taken into account as a commentary on Gen. 2.18f."[106] He then develops a further interpretation in the light of Ephesians. [107]

That this excursus is almost allegorical and certainly typological cannot be denied although Barth refutes the former allegation.[108] Many scholars might condemn it simply because of that. But we must consider what Barth is in fact doing. He has exegeted Genesis 2 in its own terms and in terms of its literary context, but he finds it has left him many unanswered questions. These he proposes to resolve in the canonical context. Thus he answers these questions:-

1. Why could man not be alone?
   - because Jesus was not to be alone.
2. Why was man not content with the animals?
   - because Jesus could elect those who were like him.
3. Why did man sleep while God created woman?
   - because Jesus slept the sleep of death so God could create the Church.
4. Why was woman taken from man?
   - because the Church's life was taken from the life of Jesus.
5. Why does man acclaim woman?
   - because Jesus first recognises the Church before she responds in faith to him.
6. Why does man leave father and mother to cleave to his wife?
   - because Jesus left his Father's glory to unite himself genuinely to humanity.
7. Why were man and woman naked and not ashamed?

- because Jesus and his church were not ashamed of their respective conditions before one another.

These questions and answers might be regarded as fanciful eisegesis, but Barth does not offer them as the basic exegesis of the passage. He regards it as "... the final word of exegesis rather than the first, but there can be no doubt that both the context and the independent features of these verses force us to look in this direction from the outset."[109] Barth's conclusion springs from his conviction that the text's "main intention" is "... the presentation of the establishment of man's bi-sexuality as a mystery."[110] In proceeding in this way, Barth effectively espouses the method of *sensus plenior* more associated with Roman Catholicism than reformed protestant scholarship.

Barth's contention is that "... the advent of the Son of Man ... [gives] to Gen. 2.18-25 a meaning which it could never have had to its Old Testament readers."[111] This is put more sharply in an earlier discussion about another Old Testament passage:

> *it can hardly be disputed that their writing is in fact perplexing. That it is necessarily so is best explained if we concede that the fact of which they wrote was itself perplexing and if we are ready to learn from the New Testament what the riddle in these data was,* **and at the same time how profoundly they were filled with hidden and revealed divine truth.** [112]

Barth regards the true significance of the Genesis stories as discoverable only when they are read in the light of the New Testament which gives the key to the *sensus plenior*. The legitimation of this *sensus plenior* for Barth is his theological conviction that the Old Testament speaks prophetically of Christ for he is the content of the whole Bible. [113]

It is interesting to note that in developing his theology on the basis of Genesis 1 and 2 he characteristically uses story as the basis of dogmatics. However it is also important to note that here as elsewhere Barth's interpretation of story is governed by overt theological statements. This is true not only of the Genesis 1 story which is understood in the light of the overt theological statement that Jesus is "the image of the invisible God" who "is the head of the body, the Church",[114] but also of the Genesis 2 story which is understood in the light of the

Ephesians statement [115] which makes it clear that marriage is a great mystery pointing to Christ and his Church.[116] Behind both these interpretations is found Barth's conviction based equally on overt theological statement, that in Christ "all things were created ... through him and for him"[117] from which Barth concludes of man and woman "... in their creation God had in mind His only Son Jesus Christ, and this Son in his human form and reality, so that this one man was and is and always will be the meaning and motive of all creation."[118]

III. Christology and Anthropology

We now turn to the second major section of the *Church Dogmatics* concerned with man and woman, upon which Barth will build his ethics. §45.3 begins by summarizing the conclusions Barth has drawn in §41.[119] The groundwork may be outlined thus:

> *In the fact of the duality of male and female which cannot be resolved in a higher synthesis, we have this constant so clearly before us that we can only live it out, however well or badly. There can be no question of setting this fact aside, or overlooking it in practice. There is no being of man above the being of male and female.[120]*

Barth freely admits that his conclusion depends not only on those parts of Scripture which discuss the nature of humanity, but "we took this path because Christology left us no option."[121] This section §45:3 follows closely upon §45:1 "Jesus, Man for other Men" where he builds up a picture of Jesus as a being directed to God and to his fellows.[122] Barth is convinced that "we must continue to base our anthropology on christology."[123] The consequence of this dogmatic decision is that Barth's choice of biblical material, and his exposition of it is all done with conscious reference to the person of Jesus Christ. We have already seen how that has been the case for Genesis 1 and 2. We must now examine what that implies for the two major excursus in §45:3. The first of these deals with New Testament passages which seem to offer problems to Barth's position; the second discusses in detail the major texts which Barth thinks support his case.

The most difficult text for Barth is Galatians 3:26f. where Paul writes; "Ye are all the children of God by faith in Christ Jesus ... there is neither male nor female: for ye are all one in Christ Jesus."[124] This, coupled with Jesus' rebuke to the Sadducees "For when they rise from the dead, they neither marry, nor are given in marriage; but are as the angels in heaven",[125] seems to suggest that Barth's thesis that "man never exists as such, but always as the human male or human female" [126] is untenable. It is characteristic of Barth to face head-on the problems posed by passages which seem to contradict his theory that differentiation and relationship are basic to the definition of humanity. [127] He argues that Galatians can be taken to mean that there is no place for national, social or sexual pride in the Christian church since all are in receipt of the grace of God. This common faith "... is one which makes impossible any exaltation of the one over the other or hostility of the one to the other ..."[128] Barth considers that "Paul is not saying that the antitheses are simply set aside and done away by the being of Christians in Christ."[129] Thus male and female continue to be appropriate categories even for those in Christ.

The question remains whether such differentiation will be maintained at the resurrection. Barth outlines the case of those who consider that humanity will then be sexless, refuting it on the single word from Mark 12:25, ωϛ. He observes that Jesus did not say humans would be angels, but as angels. Consequently he argues that Jesus' point is that at the resurrection they will no longer be subject to death, so marriage and procreation will cease to concern them, although they will live on a new earth, seeing God face to face. Barth concludes:

> *There is no reference here, and cannot be to an abolition of the sexes or the cessation of the being of man as male and female ... Thus in this synoptic passage Jesus certainly tells us there will be no continuation of marriage but not that woman will not be woman in the resurrection.[130]*

This bi-sexuality Barth affirms "... is something which he [man] cannot lose. For by it there stands or fall his creatureliness."[131]

Having established that his view can be maintained in the face of apparently contradictory biblical evidence, Barth turns to a detailed consideration of those New Testament passages which he believes give him grounds for maintaining the case he began to develop on the basis of Genesis. He begins by examining these in their own context.[132]

Barth begins with 2 Corinthians 11:2-4. To encourage the Corinthians not to fall away from faith, Paul uses the image of betrothal. The implication of the passage is that the Corinthians were brought into a marriage relationship with Christ through Paul's preaching of the gospel. "Between the real Jesus and the Corinthians something has taken place, a decision has been made, which cannot be reversed."[133] Although they may be deceived into impurity, the "marriage" that has taken place cannot be ignored. From this passage Barth concludes: "We maintain that Paul regarded it as right in elucidation of this thesis to recall the encounter of the bridegroom and the bride and therefore the primitive form of humanity as being in encounter."[134]

The same idea is found by Barth in Romans 7:1-6. The argument hinges on the analogy Paul draws between a woman whose husband's death sets her free to marry again, and the Christian community who are set free from the law of death by Jesus' crucifixion, so they may belong to him. ". . . In the death of Jesus Christ . . . they have become genuinely free - free to be the wife of this other, their Liberator, Jesus Christ risen from the dead."[135]

Barth suggests that these two passages are the places where Paul declares the relationship of Jesus to his community to be that of man and wife. Elsewhere this relationship is referred to as an aside in passages which are dealing primarily with something else. In this category he includes 1 Corinthians 16:12-20, 1 Corinthians 11:1-16 and Ephesians 5:22-33. Barth's excursus builds up to a climax in Ephesians for "no other passage makes the connection so emphatically."[136]

In 1 Corinthians 6:16-20 Paul discusses what things are permissable for christians. Barth explains that Paul argues that union with a harlot is unthinkable on the basis which is understood that christians are already joined to Christ in marriage. If a christian is to belong to a woman ". . . he cannot contradict but must correspond to the fact that he belongs to Christ";[137] that is, he must marry a christian woman. It is the logical outworking of the christian's unique relationship to Christ which concerns Paul, not legalism.[138] So Barth concludes that here too "Paul brings the concrete form of the fellow-humanity of man and woman, and sexual intercourse at the most concrete form, into connection with the relationship between Jesus Christ and His community, and derives his normative concept of the human - not without express reference to Genesis 2 - from this basic norm." [139]

The second text, 1 Corinthians 11:1-6 is discussed by Barth primarily to focus on the nature of the male/female relationship in Christ, rather than to discern prescriptive patterns for liturgy, which was arguably Paul's main intention. It is frequently the case that Barth has to draw out implications from texts whose main concern is something other than the topic Barth is discussing. He is aware of the danger of this while continuing to be persuaded of its necessity. He negotiates his way through this very complicated Pauline argument by taking two verses as the light to illumine the rest:

> *Nevertheless neither is the man without the woman, neither the woman without the man in the Lord. For as the woman is of the man, even so is the man also by the woman, but all things of God. [141]*

Here, Barth comments, Paul ". . . does not retract anything he has said in Gal. 3.28."[142] However it is equally true that the distinctions between male and female remain for Paul: ". . . there is true super - and subordination",[143] for this is a divine order. When signs of its disruption appear, as in the unveiled heads of worshipping women, the angels are distressed by this flaunting of God's purposes.[144] Moreover, according to Barth, Paul argues in verses 14 and 15 that this is naturally recognised universally. These two supporting arguments bolster the notion of male headship, the foundations of which are located elsewhere if we take verse 3 seriously. Barth characteristically pays careful attention to the order in this verse. There is neither an upward nor downward progression: it is not God, Christ, man, woman or *vice versa*. Rather the arrangement precludes a hierarchical interpretation, Barth suggests, for it is plain that Christ is a model for both sexes: "both superordination and subordination are primarily and properly in Christ."[145] This sheds a completely new light on both roles, for man can only represent Christ's superordination, and woman can only represent Christ's subordination. "His is the place of man, and His the place of woman."[146] Man is the "... one who has precedence, initiative and authority" while woman is the one who has "... to be led by him, to accept his authority, to recognise the order which claims them both as it is represented by him."[147] Thus Barth argues that the order of male and female in Christ is consistent with that created originally, for "... God's creation is not accidental ... it is solidly and necessarily grounded in Christ, with a view to whom heaven and earth and finally man were created."[148] This ordering is not "occasion either for the exaltation of man or the oppression of woman"[149] because in Christ the contradiction and estrangement between lordship and humility has been overcome. Although Barth goes on to speak again of the male/female relationship as a model of Christ and his church, it is fascinating that in this exposition he has taken 1 Corinthians 11 in direct connexion to Christ alone. In doing this he has picked up the suggestion of verse 3 that Christ has to be seen as a model for both male and female roles before their roles can be seen as a type of Christ and his church.

This is a good example of the way that Barth works out the practical implications of his belief that Jesus Christ is the subject of all Scripture. It is like the spokes of a wheel where all point in towards the centre, Jesus Christ, but they do so from different perspectives, and some are to be located nearer to the rim of the wheel than the hub. The task of the dogmatic theologian and the exegete in Barth's view, is not completed until the connexion between the hub, Jesus Christ and the text has been perceived. Texts may relate in differing but complementary ways, held together by the person of Jesus Christ.

Barth's final exposition in §45:3 deals with Ephesians 5:22-33 which he concludes is sufficient basis for thinking that "man in his relationship to woman represents Christ in His relationship to the community, and that woman in her relationship to man represents the community in its relationship to Christ."[150] Indeed Barth asserts that the original creation of male and female was not "... a primary thing ... but a secondary, the copy."[151] Thus, in creating man and woman, God already had Christ and the church in mind. The arrangement of Paul's argument in Ephesians 5 is significant: first "mutual subordination in full reciprocity",[152] then female subordination at the beginning and end of the section because the woman models the subordination required of all in relation to Christ. But since male subordination has to be combined with headship, it is the male to whom the greater part of the paragraph is devoted. The male role is complicated by the fact that although he is a type or representation of Christ, he must ever avoid the error of supposing he can create or save. Much is said of this role also, Barth thinks, because much must be said of Christ.

Twice Barth affirms that it is on the basis of this exposition that he can survey "the whole field".[153] Ephesians 5 gives the pattern for Barth's approach to all the passages in both testaments which seem to be relevant to the doctrine of man. But it is not only on the basis of Ephesians 5 that Barth comes to his dogmatic conclusions. The whole network which he traces between Genesis and the Song of Songs; the prophetic condemnation of Israel's unfaithfulness to Yahweh, and the New Testament passages which discuss the marriage relationship can only be sustained on the basis of decisions already taken by Barth about the Trinitarian God whose eternal purpose in his Son for his people is known clearly from other texts about redemption and eschatology.

IV. Ethics and Anthropology

The final section of this essay must consider how Barth's preparatory work forms the foundation of his ethical developments in §54:1 "Man and Woman".[154] Barth observes that a married couple are genuinely one, (Ephesians 5:31) and that union with a nonchristian far from being insignificant is regarded in the same way (1 Corinthians 6:6). Thus the divine command for man and woman to encounter one another completely prohibits considering physical sexual relations separate from their whole being.[155] It rather sanctifies that aspect of human life within the context of the whole. [156]

Barth then weighs the question of whether marriage is obligatory as the Old Testament seems to suggest, or whether celibacy is the highest calling as parts of the New Testament have been understood. For Barth the resolution of the apparent tension between the testaments is to be found in the advent of Christ, whose coming is like the axis or pivot on which the diverse evidence may be weighed. Whereas under the old covenant marriage and procreation was highly regarded as the Jews looked forward to the birth of a Messiah; after Christ that motivation is removed. Another opposite motivation against marriage emerges; the desire to please the Lord. Barth examines in great detail the overtly ethical passages dealing with marriage in Paul's letters.[157] His conclusion is that "there is a genuine Christian obedience which does not lead a man into marriage but past it" and "there is a genuine Christian obedience in . . . acceptance of marriage as a matter of special gift and vocation."[158]

What therefore are the prescriptions which may be laid down on this basis? First, God requires a person to be fully man or woman, acknowledging their own sexuality.[159] However, since Scripture gives no evidence upon which to dictate what are distinctively male or female characteristics Barth suggests that everyone is faced in different cultures with the question: "What does it mean for me to live in a way that does not deny my sexuality?"[160] This is an important question in Barth's view because it prohibits any attempt to transcend sexuality and claim to be "human" or some third transcendent type of person.

Second it is mandatory for man and woman to live in genuine openness to the other sex whether or not they are married. Consequently any attempt to escape this whether within the cloisters or the world is disobedience. It is also the ground on which Barth prohibits homosexuality. Although he refers to Romans 1, were that not to be part of the canon, his theological position would give him ground enough to take this stance. Indeed, in Barth's argument Romans 1 becomes the "check point" of a position already established.[161] In the bi-sexual relationship men and women ". . . are to consider one another, to hear the question which each puts to the other and to make responsible answer to one another."[162]

Third it is important to recognise a genuine sequence within their equality and mutuality whereby men are in a position of superordination and women a position of subordination. This sequence is to occur both inside and outside of marriage. Barth emphasizes that sequence is not license for men to dominate, but is a genuine differentiation of order which men and women must maintain if they are to be truly human, free and obedient to God. Both live under the obligation to maintain the divine order. The exegetical excursus simply recapitulates material Barth has covered before, and once again we see our author basing his ethical prescriptions on well developed doctrinal bases rather than on single texts even when these are cast in prescripture form.[163]

Fourth there are specific guidelines for marriage. Those who embark on it are to regard it as vocation; they must regard it as a life-long task to which they bind themselves: everything must be shared for it is "full-life partnership".[164] It is an exclusive partnership, for the choice of this person precludes all others from their life time. If it is to be lived in this kind of way it requires free mutual love, and a recognition that marriage is a private and public activity which the world needs to recognise.

It is clear at this point that Barth's ethics emerge out of his doctrinal conclusions and are not lifted like simple prescriptions from the text of Scripture. He could not countenance any such practice for he recognises the different emphases in Scripture which could seem to be commanding vastly different courses of action. It is only possible to deal with these adequately if an overall doctrinal mapwork has been established on which these commands can be placed. Only then is it possible to discern what are the universally binding mores and what are the particular examples. There is an excellent instance of this when Barth discusses monogamy and polygamy. The Old Testament practice, law and history does not lead to any clear pattern. Barth even argues that in Genesis 2 "... it is over-subtle to try to find in the words 'shall be one flesh' a reference to the necessity of monogamy (Calvin). *The necessity of monogamy follows only from the fact that the one Christ and His one community are one flesh in the one fulfilled covenant."*[165] The ethical command springs clearly out of doctrinal formulation for Barth in this case.

Finally it must be made clear that Barth not only begins his dogmatics with Scripture, then passes beyond it, but always checks his conclusions with Scripture. The same practice is to be found in his ethics. For example, having asserted that marriage like celibacy is a divine vocation, he discusses Matthew 19:1-12 which is not the ground of his assertion but rather the sounding board against which he checks the appropriateness of his description.[166]

Barth has been shown to recognise the complexity and diversity of the biblical material. His genius is that he is able to recognise and deal creatively with its diversity, and handle its complexity. Barth reads Scripture expectantly, imaginatively, always pressing on to discover what at the deepest level the Divine Subject will reveal of himself to the human subject exegeting single passages in the context of the whole. This essay has attempted to offer a neutral analysis of Barth's biblical method which is as complex and diverse as Scripture itself, so that the reader may decide how far Barth's method is appropriate.

Notes

1. Karl Barth *The Church Dogmatics* (Eng. trans. of *Die Kirchliche Dogmatik*) Edinburgh 1936-74. I/2 p. 457 [Hereinafter abbreviated to C.D.]

2. C.D. I/1, p. 115

3. ibid. p. 112

4. ibid. p. 111f.

5. CD I/2 p. 457
    cf. ibid. p. 462 "... the right doctrine of Holy Scripture ... must always be sought and found ... in Holy Scripture itself."

6. CD I/1 p. 115.

7. CD I/2 p. 720

8. ibid. p. 727

9. ibid. p. 528f.

10. ibid. p. 529

11. ibid. p. 531

12. ibid. p. 501

13. ibid. p. 508

14. ibid. p. 717

15. ibid. p. 719

16. CD IV/2 pp. 120-127

17. These may be found respectively at:
    CD III/4 pp. 116-240
    CD III/2 pp. 203-324
    CD III/1 pp. 42-329

18. Barth's trinitarian discussion may be found in CD I/1 pp. 348-489. At the beginning of his section "Man and Woman" Barth reminds the reader that God is "Deus triunus" CD III/4 p. 117.
    Barth's "Doctrine of Reconciliation" forms Volume IV of the *Church Dogmatics*. An example of reference forward to this may be found at CD III/2 p. 299 "... the covenant between Jesus Christ and His community, which is the secret of creation, is of such a kind that its Lord, Jesus Christ, is the one who for His community - ... gives Himself up to death in order to win it as His possession."

19. CD I/1 p. xii

20. ibid.

21. ibid. p. 16

22. CD I/2 p. 821

23. ibid. p. 883f.

24. e.g. Ps. 8:5 CD III/1 p. 192
    Col. 1:5 CD III/1 p. 203

25. e.g. Although there are no direct N.T. references to the relationship between the Holy Spirit and creation, he discusses three allusions to it. CD III/1 p. 57f.

26. CD III/2 p. 312
    cf. ibid. p. 309 I Cor. 11:11f. "text for this whole section".

27. See C.A. Baxter "The Movement from Exegesis to Dogmatics in the Theology of Karl Barth, with special reference to *Romans, Philippians* and *The Church Dogmatics*" (Ph.D. dissertation, University of Durham 1981), Appendix 3 Table 1 p. 472f. for further details.
28. See C.A. Baxter, chapter 1, pp. 7-77
29. CD III/1 p. 105
30. ibid. p. 63
31. ibid.
    cf.ibid. p. 241 "Gunkel has a fine observation on this point."
32. ibid. p. 303f.
33. e.g. ibid. p. 289 "... Gen. 1:27 cannot be an accident but was surely intended by the redaction which combined the two sagas."
34. See C.A. Baxter pp. 8-40
35. e.g. CD III/1 p. 104; 220 Septuagint
    ibid. p. 197; 278 Vulgate.
36. ibid. pp. 79-81
37. e.g. ibid. p. 278 "... a contradiction is to be seen only if we demand from the saga a pragmatics which as saga it cannot and will not offer."
38. CD I/2 p. 723
39. e.g. CD III/1 p. 51 "an indisputable masculine"
40. e.g. ibid. p. 191 "the divine plural"
41. e.g. ibid. p. 197f. be Μυστηριον
42. e.g. CD III/4 p. 123 Eph. 5:32
    cf. ibid. p. 142 Jer. 16:2
43. e.g. CD III/1 pp. 87; 201 etc.
44. ibid. p. 104
45. ibid. p. 103
46. ibid. p. 105
    ibid. p. 243
47. ibid. p. 64
48. ibid. p. 65
    cf. ibid. p. 200 ". . . the whole of the Old Testament confirms the witness of the creation saga."
49. cf. ibid. p. 103f.
50. ibid. p. 320f.
    cf. CD II/2 p. 389 "The Kingship of Jesus is ...the subject which they [the O.T. historical narratives] attest."
51. CD I/2 p. 674
52. CD III/1 p. 202 (my emphasis)
    cf. CD II/2 p. 388
53. CD I/1 p. 117
    cf. CD IV/3 p. 93 ". . . there is not a single trace of the notion of a plurality of divine revelations ..."
54. See CD I/2 p. 208
55. CD III/1 p. 229
56. ibid.
57. For a fuller discussion see C.A. Baxter pp. 179-181
58. ibid. p. 80
59. CD III/4 p. 205
60. ibid. p. 206
61. CD III/1 p. 182 Genesis 1:3 and 1:24 respectively
62. ibid.

63. The *Index Volume* of the *Church Dogmatics* makes it very clear how far Barth's use of these two men outstrips their nearest rivals for his attention - who are not Reformers, but S. Augustine, F. Schleiermacher and S. Thomas Aquinas. *Index Volume* pp. 185-205.
64. CD III/1 p. 191
65. For a fuller discussion see C.A. Baxter pp. 127-154
    cf. CD III/1 p. 195 Hos. 1:2f. etc.
66. ibid. p. 192
67. Barth's doctrine of God may be found in CD I/1 pp. 295-489 and CD II/1 and 2. "The Ambassadors of God" is in CD III/3 pp. 369-531.
68. CD III/1 p. 192
69. ibid.
70. ibid. p. 202
71. ibid. p. 193
72. cf. CD I/2 p. 712 "Holy Scripture . . . as Word of God . . . needs no explanation . . . since as such it is clear in itself. The Holy Ghost knows very well what He has said to the prophets and apostles and what through them He wills also to say to us. This clarity which Scripture has in itself as God's word, this objective *perspicuitas* which it possesses, is subject to no human responsibility or care. On the contrary it is the presupposition of all human responsibility in this matter."
73. CD III/1 p. 193
74. ibid. p. 194
75. ibid.
76. ibid. p. 194f.
77. ibid. p. 195
78. ibid. p. 196
79. ibid. p. 197
80. CD III/2 p. 220
81. CD I/1 p. 243f.
82. CD III/1 p. 200
    cf. CD III/2 p. 324
83. CE III/1 p. 200
84. Col. 1:15
85. Col. 1:18
86. CD III/1 p. 205
87. ibid.
88. ibid. p. 204
89. Col. 3:10
90. CD III/1 pp. 229; 239-249; 276-288
91. ibid. p. 288
92. ibid. p. 289
93. ibid. p. 290 commenting on Gen. 2:18
94. ibid.
95. e.g. Hosea refers to Yahweh's relationship to Israel as like marriage: Eph. 6 refers to the marriage imagery in respect of Christ and His Church.
96. CD III/1 p. 295
97. ibid. p. 298
98. ibid. p. 303
99. ibid. p. 301
100. ibid. p. 304

101. CD III/2 p. 287
102. CD III/1 p. 313
103. ibid. p. 314
104. ibid. p. 315
105. Eph. 5:32
106. CD III/1 p. 321
107. ibid. p. 321f.
108. CD III/4 p. 143
109. CD III/1 p. 325
110. ibid. p. 326
111. CD III/4 p. 205
     cf. CD III/2 p. 393 "the final exegetical word provided by the New Testament..."
112. CD II/2 p. 393 writing of the elect kings of 1 and 2 Samuel. [my emphasis]
113. For a fuller discussion see C.A. Baxter pp. 235-240
114. Col. 1:15 and 18
115. Eph. 5:32
116. For a fuller discussion of the relationship of story to statement see C.A. Baxter pp. 171-177
117. Col. 1:16
118. CD III/2 p. 137
119. ibid. p. 285ff.
120. ibid. p. 289
121. ibid.
122. ibid. pp. 203-222
123. ibid. p. 207
124. ibid. p. 295
125. Mk. 12:25 CD III/2 p. 295
126. CD III/4 p. 117
127. The exception would be his refusal to discuss demonology. See CD III/3 p. 519f.
128. CD III/2 p. 295
129. ibid.
130. ibid. p. 296
131. ibid.
132. ibid. pp. 301-316
133. ibid. p. 303
134. ibid. p. 304
135. ibid. p. 304f.
136. ibid. p. 312
137. ibid. p. 307
138. ibid. p. 308
139. ibid.
140. Barth makes it clear elsewhere that he does not consider that such prescriptions are forthcoming for contemporary practice. See CD III/4 p. 155f.
141. I Cor. 11:11-12 CD III/2 p. 309
142. ibid.
143. ibid. p. 310
144. ibid. on 1 Cor. 11:10
145. ibid. p. 311
146. ibid
147. ibid.
148. ibid. p. 311

149. ibid. p. 312
150. ibid. p. 310
151. ibid. p. 315
152. ibid. p. 313
153. ibid. pp. 313 and 314
154. CD III/4 pp. 42-329
155. ibid. p. 130f.
156. ibid. p. 132
157. ibid. pp. 144-148
158. ibid. p. 148
159. ibid. p. 149
160. ibid. p. 155
161. ibid. p. 165f.
162. ibid. p. 167
163. ibid. pp. 172-176
164. ibid. p. 189
165. CD III/1 p. 328 (my emphasis)
166. CD III/4 p. 185f.

Election and Covenant
W.A. Whitehouse

It is presupposed, in biblical faith, that *active life* is properly ascribed to God. Karl Barth suggests that the character of this active life may be indicated by 'perfect forms of love in which God is free' and 'perfect forms of freedom in which God loves'. It is with human selfhood in mind that such language is used to direct thought towards the more eminent reality whom men may call 'God', and the language has to be qualified, by ways of negation and of analogy, in an effort to avoid crude idolatry. This applies equally to the further point that in God such active life is *self-derived*. In any human person there is some capacity to give shape to the self which he or she is by intentions of will; some capacity for self-determination by 'acts of choice'. This capacity is of limited scope; it does not suffice to determine, or re-determine, the whole of that person's intrinsic being in any fundamental way. With God, however, we may have reason to affirm that 'voluntary election', self-determined and wholly self-determining, is intrinsic. Christian tradition derived, then, the thesis that he is 'God' in the tri-personal unity of Father, Son and Spirit. Nothing by way of action beyond his own being is necessarily entailed in this fundamental self-determination. It is by an 'election of grace' that this self-established deity of God provides ground for a created reality, which includes humanity, and humanity destined for intimate partnership with himself on a basis of free bi-lateral commitment to terms of promise and obligation; terms which bind the divine partner and the human partners into a shared life of 'covenant' loyalty.

This imagery, of self-committal in 'federation' - 'the action of uniting in a league or covenant' with chosen partners - is also drawn initially from human experience. When it is used to direct human thought to the works and ways of God, it has to be disciplined by proper respect for the love in which God is free and the freedom in which he loves. Thought so disciplined recognises his election as an election of *grace*. Hebrew tradition draws attention to a moment, epoch-making for human awareness that things may be so, when Abraham had the dream recorded in Genesis 15, 17-21. The 'word' from God - 'I will be your God and you shall be my people' - was expressed in vivid imagery. That the pronouns 'your' and 'you' had more extensive application came to be acknowledged when 'history' was extended backwards, by saga or legend, from Abraham to Noah and his household, sole human survivors of primordial divine wrath, with the rainbow becoming, for human imagination, 'the sign of the covenant which I have established between me and all flesh that is upon the earth, (Genesis 9, 1-17). This tradition reaches its 'Christian' climax in the words of benediction used to round off the Letter to the Hebrews (13, 20-21):

> *Now may the God of peace who brought again from the dead our Lord Jesus, the great shepherd of the sheep, by the blood of the eternal covenant, equip you with everything good that you may do his will, working in you that which is pleasing in his sight.*

and in the greeting addressed to readers of I Peter (1, 1-2):

> *To the exiles of the dispersion... chosen and destined by God the Father and sanctified by the Spirit for obedience to Jesus Christ and for sprinkling with his blood: May grace and peace be multiplied to you.*

Though the imagery of 'federation' continues to have its place in some areas of political life, it does so at present without any strong emotional appeal. The symbolic significance of 'blood' for the bonding of any such covenant is largely rejected by modern sensitivity as a suspect archaism. As for any theological 'doctrine of election' as a major item in Christian doctrine, acrimonious debate in the centuries that separate Calvin from Wesley created what T.H. Huxley called 'widespread ethical revulsion from the Evangelical preaching of an immoral Old Testament God, away from Calvinistic substitutionary atonement, man's total depravity, arbitrary predestination, and eternal punishment'. Is there, one might ask, a touch of archaic extravagance in Barth's decision to devote one quarter of his 'Doctrine of God' to a revised exposition of God's 'election of grace'?

The substance of that exposition is available to English readers in lucid summaries.[1] It departs, notoriously, from previous tradition. 'Barth claims . . . that the thought of sinful man's reconciliation with God in Jesus Christ and of God's fellowship with sinful men, thereby made possible for him and for man, was in the mind of God before the world and man were created and thus even before sin became a reality. The unparalleled precedence thereby given to the idea of reconciliation over creation and sin has to be seen in the light of Barth's teaching on creation . . . , the Nihil . . . and reconciliation . . . before its true meaning can be grasped'.[2] The theme itself, rather than scholastic discussion of Barth's treatment of it,[3] provides the substance of this centenary tribute. But his own initial statement of it deserves to be reproduced as a guide to further exploration.

> *The doctrine of election is the sum of the Gospel because of all words that can be said or heard it is the best: that God elects man; that God is, for man too, the One who loves in freedom. It is grounded in the knowledge of Jesus Christ because he is both the electing God and elected man in one. It is part of the doctrine of God because originally God's election of man is a predestination not merely of man but of himself. Its function is to bear basic testimony to eternal, free and unchanging grace as the beginning of all the works and ways of God.* [4]

I.

Serious questions can always be raised about any 'foundation of religious affirmation', and about the intellectual integrity of any 'theology' which serves to clarify such affirmation. Are we entitled to profess that there is, from 'God', some 'Word' which authorises us to speak in these human terms - 'election', 'covenant' - under the continuing discipline of Hebrew-Christian tradition? Jude, 'servant of Jesus Christ', in the apostolic age, urged his colleagues to 'join the struggle in defence of the faith, the faith which God entrusted to his people once and for all'.[5] This entrusted deposit has for its content 'the whole living fact of Christ and his saving acts, in the indivisible unity of his person, word and life'; and he is 'the incarnate embodiment of the Word and Truth of God in his own personal being'. In the power of his resurrection, he continues 'to make his mighty acts of redemption effective in the life and faith of all who are baptised in his name and who draw near to the Father through his atoning sacrifice'.[6] These Christian believers, once (as Paul puts it in

Romans 6, 17) 'the slaves of sin', but now 'obedient from the heart to the standard of teaching to which you were committed', were ready to describe their new condition and its source in the words already quoted from I Peter, 1,2. Here are modes of thought, and imaginative language, which have served in their time to express religious affirmation and to clarify it in theology. But, as P.T. Forsyth remarked in 1907, 'Theology must be modernised. It is fruitless to offer to the public the precise modes of thought which were so fresh and powerful with the Reformers, or the schemes so ably propounded by the dogmatists of the seventeenth century, and so severely raked by the Socinians'. But what, he asks, does the 'modernising of theology' mean? 'If theology is to be modernised, it must be by its own Gospel', a Gospel which he goes on to spell out as a 'Gospel of the Grace of God', historically actualised through 'the Eternal Sonship, the Mediatorship and the Resurrection of Jesus Christ'.[7] This Gospel of the Grace of God is proposed to human minds in testimony, found in 'Scriptures of the Old and the New Covenants', by acts of God which avail to overcome existing estrangement between himself and the race of human creatures. Reconciliation, grounded in grace yet secured by righteousness, is the goal of God's works and ways, with redemption for his damaged and imperilled human creation as the final prospect. In events of worldly history God takes action; in deeds which entail *self*-revelation to mankind; in events where he 'distinguishes himself *in* the world *from* the world'.[8]

This biblical testimony comes to its climax when Christian theology dares to go beyond Jewish theology in its affirmation of God's *personal presence*, in the man Jesus and as that man. The testimony has a form substantially 'historic'. It is clothed in language fresh and powerful in the imagination of earlier generations but not sacrosanct for their modern successors. There could be more cogent reasons than possible cultural ineffectiveness for submitting the imaginative work of our predecessors to radical criticism. Any 'arbitrary' acceptance of it could, in a changed culture, enslave our minds to some image of 'God' which, in its idolatrous inadequacy, goes to produce a religiosity which corrupts the human self whilst purporting to save and to fulfil it.

There are voices which invite us to consider the possibility of abandoning even the age-old practice of using the word 'God' as though this name referred 'to any structure or reality that was *there and given* (as objects of experience are there and given)'. And, less drastically perhaps, it may be said that 'the idea of a God who *acts* has become so problematic today that it receives scant attention'.[9] Can we, perhaps, despite these warnings (but not altogether despising them), improve our understanding of life lived by Christian faith, and our practice of it, by fresh attention to acts of God conceived as his 'election of grace' and properly described as 'the sum of the Gospel'?

II.

In my own corner of the English-speaking world, any reference to 'election' - meaning 'the eternal and immutable decree of God, from which all our salvation springs and depends' - conjures up a spectre of that 'Calvinism' which John Wesley urged the 27th Annual Conference of Methodists in 1770 to purge from their doctrine, thereby ejecting from his Methodist Movement all who had learned their Evangelicalism from George Whitefield. What is this spectral 'Calvinism'? Wesley, good Anglican as he was, could well have replied by pointing to the third chapter of the Presbyterian Westminster Confession of 1647, a chapter taken over unaltered into the (Savoy) 'Declaration of the faith and order owned and practiced in the Congregational Churches of England', made in 1658. The first two paragraphs affirm God's absolute sovereignty. With no violence to the will of creatures and no derogation from the liberty or contingency of second causes, with no share in the authorship of sin and with no consulting of conditional contingencies, God, by omniscient foreknowledge does 'from all eternity ... by the most wise and holy counsel of his own will, freely and unchangeably ordain whatsoever comes to pass.' And (par. 3): 'By the decree of God for the manifestation of his glory, some men and angels are predestinated unto everlasting life, and others foreordained to everlasting death'. What is said about the sovereignty of God provides awesome backing for this Scripturally supported statement; and reverent minds which may lack the inspired agility needed to accommodate the paradoxes implicit in the previous paragraphs will not, for that reason, question the plain story of predestination. The chapter goes on to say that 'means of salvation' for the elect, 'being fallen in Adam', are available by divine appointment; and the fact that these means are not evidently efficacious for so many of our fellow men is explained by the divine decision to elect some but not all.

To this primary affirmation of God in his divine authority there is added a less controversial account of world-history, established by acts of God in creation and providence, distorted by the fall of man, his sin and the punishment thereof, and redeemed by 'God's covenant with man', a 'covenant of grace, differently administered in the time of the law and in the time of the gospel', with an eloquent account of the Lord Jesus, whom 'it pleased God in his eternal purpose to choose and ordain ... to be the Mediator between God and man'. The prospect of salvation thereby established for human beings (whose status as covenant partners requires genuine freedom of will) is articulated in nine chapters which clarify what is promised in the Gospel of Jesus Christ. The Christian is summoned to recognise that his life has been subjected to a fourfold act of God: an act of *'effectual* calling' (to 'faith'), an act of 'justification', an act of 'adoption', and an act of 'sanctification'. In consequence, he discovers within his experience the realities of 'saving faith', of 'repentance unto life', of 'good works', of 'perseverance'in the state of grace, and of an 'assurance of grace and salvation'.

> *By this faith, a Christian believeth to be true whatsoever is revealed in the Word, for the authority of God himself speaking therein; and acteth differently upon that which each particular passage thereof containeth; yielding obedience to the commands, trembling at the threatenings, and embracing the promises of God for this life and that which is to come. But the principal acts of saving faith are: accepting, receiving and resting upon Christ alone for justification, sanctification and eternal life, by virtue of the covenant of grace. (XIV,2)*

I have described this Christian perception of world-history and this account of Christian experience as 'less controversial' than the thesis of 'election'which underpins it in 'Calvinist'theology. In its fidelity to Christian Scriptures it has a strong claim to catholicity; and in theological debates among Protestants in the seventeenth and eighteenth centuries it was generally agreed that a distinctively Christian account of prospects for human salvation must do justice to these selected elements. But to many persons of deep Christian sensitivity it has come to rank as the ideology associated with 'evangelically conserva-

tive' groups or movements, confident in their 'elitism' and complacent
in their spiritual, moral, not to say commercial, prosperity. In the two
hundred years which separate Calvin from Wesley, debate spiralled
around the essentially pastoral question about the psychological
effect on believers and unbelievers of a Gospel presented in these
terms. There was proper concern to produce in the Church an educated lay membership with instructed awareness of 'the way in which
we receive the grace of Christ; what benefits come to us from it and
what effects follow'. This is the title Calvin gave to the third book of his
'Institutes of the Christian Religion', and, notoriously, he eventually
placed his exposition of 'election' in that context, thereby departing
from tradition as found in Aquinas, say, and Zwingli, for whom divine
predestination was a theme linked with divine providence. We may,
with Barth, agree that the theme really comes to its own in the context
of acknowledging salvation through the grace of the Lord Jesus
Christ; but we may also find reason to doubt whether Calvin's theological workmanship was as sound as his instinct in this matter. What
he brought to the exposition of the election of 'Israel', old and new,
was a version of divine authority conceived in relation to an account of
natural and universal history with its own antecedent logic and ontology, into which the history of Israel, of Jesus Christ, of the Church, has
to be fitted.

> We call predestination God's eternal decree, by which he
> determined with himself what he willed to become of each
> man. For all are not created in equal condition; rather, eternal
> life is foreordained for some, eternal damnation for others.
> Therefore, as any man has been created to one or the other of
> these ends, we speak of him as predestined to life or to
> death. [10]

'That eternal decree', irreprehensible yet incomprehensible, has the
appearance of a predestined fate, to the outworking of which the
activity of God in Jesus Christ is merely instrumental. To this appearance Barth was as radically opposed in the twentieth century as
were Wesley and his fellow Arminians in the eighteenth century,
though on more adequate grounds.

Before taking a closer look at Whitefield's debate with Wesley, it is
worth noting that the 39 Articles of Religion, to which, as Anglican

clergymen, they both subscribed, contain clear indications of post-biblical uneasiness about psychological effects. The prospect of salvation, envisaged in those Articles, begins with a recognition that:

> *the condition of man after the fall of Adam is such that he cannot turn and prepare himself, by his own natural strength and good works, to faith and calling upon God. (art. 10)*

> *We are accounted righteous before God, only for the merit of our Lord and Saviour Jesus Christ by faith, and not for our own works and deserving; . . . a most wholesome doctrine, and very full of comfort. (art. 11).*

> *Predestination to life is the everlasting purpose of God, whereby (before the foundations of the world were laid) he hath constantly decreed by his counsel secret to us, to deliver from curse and damnation those whom he hath chosen in Christ out of mankind, and to bring them by Christ to everlasting salvation, as vessels made to honour. Wherefore, they which he endued with so excellent a benefit of God he called according to God's purpose by his Spirit working in due season: they through grace, obey the calling: they be justified freely: they be made sons of God by adoption: they be made like the image of his only-begotten Son Jesus Christ: they walk religiously in good works, and at length by God's mercy they attain to everlasting felicity. (art. 17).*

This carefully positive statement is supplemented, at equal length, by a piece of pastoral caution:

> *As the godly consideration of predestination, and our election in Christ, is full of sweet, pleasant and unspeakable comfort to godly persons, and such as feel in themselves the working of the Spirit of Christ, mortifying the works of the flesh and their earthly members, and drawing up their mind to high and heavenly things, as well because it doth greatly establish and confirm their faith of eternal salvation to be enjoyed through Christ, as because it doth fervently kindle*

> *their love towards God: So, for curious and carnal persons,*
> *lacking the Spirit of Christ, to have continually before their*
> *eyes the sentence of God's predestination, is a most dan-*
> *gerous downfall, whereby the devil doth thrust them either*
> *into desperation or into wretchlessness of most unclean liv-*
> *ing, no less perilous than desperation. (art. 17).*

This note of caution might, perhaps, have been usefully extended, in other terms, to cover hazards endemic to the evangelised elite as well!

'Election', as a doctrinal ingredient in Christian belief, can be seen in a more congenial light when preserved among those Christians whose church life could no longer be regarded as an established part of a 'Christian' society. (This observation does not apply in the same way to regions where the *dominant* form of church life was confessionally Calvinist). A dissenting congregation in Durham City (England) adopted in 1783 its own Articles of Faith. Articles 1-3 say what must be said about Scripture as the charter of Christian faith, about the reality of God and about his trinitarian being. Before going on to spell out the main themes of creation, fall, salvation, sacramental church life and hope for life beyond death, two paragraphs are inserted with an evident intention of establishing this new congregation's claim to be 'the people of God':

> 4. *We do believe that God, before the foundation of the world*
> *was laid, did choose a people unto life everlasting, according*
> *to his eternal and immutable purpose and the secret counsel*
> *and good pleasure of his will in Christ, out of his mere free*
> *grace and love, without foresight of faith or good works or*
> *perseverance in any of them or any other thing in the crea-*
> *ture, as conditions or causes moving him thereunto. And all*
> *to the praise of his glorious grace. (I Peter 1,2: Eph. 1, 4-7;*
> *Eph. 2,10).*

> 5. *We do believe that God hath appointed ordinances as*
> *means through which he conveys grace, by the operation of*
> *the Holy Spirit, whereby they are effectually called, justified,*
> *adopted, sanctified, and kept by his power through faith unto*
> *eternal salvation. (Rom. 8,30; Eph. 1, 5; II Thess. 2, 13).*

Anglicans, and Methodist Evangelicals still within the Church of England and anxious to stay there, did not have the same existential interest in making election a principal matter for affirmation as did their dissenting fellow-Christians in the eighteenth century. The same is true in general about Catholics and Lutherans. A distaste for 'Calvinism' could more readily be developed within the prevailing climate of enlightened rationality in the more socially comfortable churches. What should be noted is that where the theme of election remains fresh and powerful, its first bearing is on the election of the corporate 'people of God', and on the *theology* of this, rather than on its anthropological consequences. Once stress comes to be laid, almost exclusively, on individual interest, the stage is set for acrimonious debate.

III.

In 1740 John Wesley preached a sermon in Bristol on 'Free Grace', with Romans 8, 32 as his text.[11] It was printed and published, after Wesley had decided, by 'drawing a lot', that he was divinely authorised to 'preach and print' against election. He received a letter from his 'affectionate though unworthy brother and servant in Christ', George Whitefield (then at work in Bethesda, Georgia), which is a model of disarming courtesy coupled with devastating rebuke.[12] Wesley remained fixed in his stereotyped objections to stereotyped 'Calvinism', and the rift between his preachers and those associated with Whitefield and the Countess of Huntingdon was irreparably sealed thirty years later by the affair of the 1770 Conference Minutes, despite efforts by the Countess to hold the Evangelical Movement together and keep it all within the established Church.[13]

The theses of 'Remonstrant' theology (inspired by Jacob Arminius), and the debates they provoked at the Synod of Dort (1618-19),[14] provided familiar terms of reference for the contending brethren; but neither was chiefly moved by scholastic concern to fit a doctrine of election into a suitably 'reasonable' systematic theology. What interests Wesley is the *effect*, upon 'godly persons' on the one hand and upon 'curious and carnal persons' on the other, of 'a godly consideration of predestination and our election in Christ'. But what is to count as a *godly* consideration of this? In a sermon more temperate and more positive than the 1740 diatribe,[15] Wesley expounds, from Romans 8, 29-30, the thesis that God decrees that 'all who believe in the Son of his love shall be conformed to his image'. 'This and no more' is supported by 'the whole law and the testimony'.[16] God knows all believers; wills that they be saved from sin; to that end justifies them; sanctifies them; and takes them to glory. 'This, and *no more*'. The 'more', against which Wesley preached in the 1740 sermon, is 'the blasphemy contained in *the horrible decree* of predestination'. In any (Calvinist) doctrine of election 'the sense is plainly this: by virtue of an unchangeable, irresistible decree of God, one part of mankind are infallibly saved, and the rest infallibly damned; it being impossible that any of the former should be damned, or that any of the latter should be saved'. The consequences of any such belief, for Christian piety, are spelled out in the sermon with polemical logic. Whitefield, in his reply, takes up the points one by one, with the scrupulous care that a modern tutor might display in demolishing a demonstration of undergraduate crudity. Brash vituperation will not serve to settle the question as to whether 'election' is or is not 'a gospel doctrine'; and Wesley's resort to 'drawing a lot '(his abhorrence of the doctrine being already settled) is suspiciously like 'tempting the Lord'. 'Down with your carnal reasoning', he says at the end, 'Study the covenant of grace'. Wesley, of course, was entitled to reply that this is precisely what he had done, with special attention to the subjectivities of Christian religious experience.

To Wesley's first point, that 'predestination' makes nonsense of all effort to *preach* salvation, there is the obvious reply that preaching and hearing are God's appointed means for implementing divine election. The second and third points relate to an undermining of that cultivated 'holiness' to which the believer is moved by hope of reward and fear of punishment; and of that 'full assurance of faith' which is 'the true ground of Christian happiness' - a happiness unduly assailed by doubt and fear if it is grounded, not in experienced holiness but in speculation about an arbitrary divine choice. The fourth point is that 'this uncomfortable doctrine already tends to destroy our zeal for good works'. These are commonplace charges, brought by those who associate belief in election with 'antinomian' arrogance, rooted in concealed insecurity. They are not to be trivially brushed aside, and Whitefield rises to the occasion in replies which testify to an understanding of life lived in Christian faith which is more sensitive and less simplistic than that of his colleague. The tensions in that life, between faith and infidelity, are not to be eradicated by 'building upon our own faithfulness'; and some taste even of the 'darkness of dereliction' does not alienate us from the Christ of Gethsemane. In bitter final salvos, Wesley contends that the doctrine 'makes the Gospel unnecessary to all sorts of men', that it 'makes the whole Christian revelation contradict itself', and that it is 'a doctrine full of blasphemy'. In his comment on these charges, Whitefield effectively rebuts the imputation that, in holding this doctrine 'we join with modern unbelievers, in making the Christian revelation unnecessary'. 'No, dear Sir, you mistake. Infidels of all kinds are on your side of the question. Deists, Arians, Socinians, arraign God's sovereignty, and stand up for universal redemption'. 'Dear Sir, for Jesus Christ's sake, consider how *you* dishonour God by denying election. You plainly make salvation depend not on God's *free grace* but on man's *free-will;* and if thus, it is more than probable, Jesus Christ would not have had the satisfaction of seeing the fruit of his death in the eternal salvation of one soul. Our preaching would then be vain, and all invitation for people to believe in him would also be in vain'.

Whitefield admits, at the outset, that he himself believes 'the doctrine of reprobation', against which so many are 'generally prejudiced' - the doctrine 'that God intends to give saving grace, through Jesus Christ, only to a certain number, and that the rest of mankind, after the fall of Adam, being justly left of God to continue in sin, will at last suffer that eternal death which is its proper wages'. There is, in his mind, no inconsistency here with the truth that 'God is loving to every man, and his mercy is over all his works' - his mercy, though 'not his *saving* mercy'. Nor is there any wanton arbitrariness in God's exercise of supreme right to show saving love where he will. The 'approbation', implicit in divine foreknowledge, upon which election is grounded, is said, in Romans 9, 10-13, to have as its reason 'that God's purpose of election might continue, not because of works but because of his call'. 'But if, by God's foreknowledge, you understand God's foreseeing of some good works done by his creatures as the foundation or reason of choosing them, and therefore electing them, then we say that in this sense, predestination does not in any way depend on God's foreknowledge'.

Within the settled framework of eighteenth century debate the honours go to Whitefield; but it is Wesley's 'discrediting' of the election theme which has generally prevailed in Christian minds during the two intervening centuries. Is God's supposed treatment of the non-elect really compatible with 'the glory of his sovereign power' or 'the praise of his glorious justice' or, above all, with 'the freedom of his love'? The doctrine of election will not be rehabilitated, much less valued as 'the sum of the Gospel', without a radical re-appraisal of its place in Christian dogmatics, and of its substance, which avails to dispel the uneasiness focussed in these questions.

IV.

Calvin chose to remove exposition of the doctrine from its context in immediate sequel to the doctrine of God, where its evangelical content of 'election for obedience to Jesus Christ' might suffer distortion. He deferred it to the penultimate chapters of his treatise on 'The way in which we receive the grace of Christ: what benefits come to us from it and what effects follow'. Its relevance for faith was thereby focussed on the hope of individual salvation. In the Westminster Confession, though the theme is dutifully articulated after the chapter on the being of God and before the chapters on his works and ways in creation and salvation, it acquires serious prominence chiefly in the chapter on 'Effectual Calling' (c.X):

> *All those whom God hath predestinated unto life, and those only, he is pleased, in his appointed and accepted time, effectually to call, by his word and Spirit, out of that state of sin and death which they are by nature, to grace and salvation by Jesus Christ.*

They are 'called', 'enabled', 'made willing'; and so 'come most freely'.

> *Others not elected, although they may be called by the ministry of the word, and may have some common operations of the Spirit, yet they never truly come to Christ and therefore cannot be saved; much less can men not professing the Christian religion be saved in any other way whatsoever, be*

they ever so diligent to frame their lives according to the light
of nature and the law of that religion they do profess.

They are justly forsaken; 'justly' because they have chosen their fate and are truly responsible for it. Justice, on the part of God, is safeguarded by an extra clause about 'elect infants dying in infancy' and about 'all other elect persons, who are incapable of being called outwardly by the ministry of the word'.

The debate provoked by so stern a piece of theology is warranted and comprehensible. It has been conducted before the bar of human reason and governed by abstract consideration of the essential terms: omnipotence, goodness, justice, in God; and, in man, the human dignity of freedom, in its basic sense of genuine capacity in man to act of his own accord.[17] When 'willingness' is ascribed, whether to man or to God, two senses should be, but were not always, distinguished: 'willing, though unable to will otherwise' and 'willing, yet able to will otherwise'. The object of the debate was to dispel the spectre of arbitrariness and to establish fairness all round. Whitefield's thought, like Wesley's, was coloured by this debate, and we, whose minds are deeply attuned to it, stand in need of some deliverance from the culs-de-sac of predestinarianism and universalism for which alone it seems to provide. Whitefield's reference to 'Deists, Arians, Socinians' provides a possible clue to the source of modern frustration and consequent apathy. And we may associate with it Pascal's *cri de coeur*: 'God of Abraham, God of Isaac, God of Jacob: not of the philosophers and scholars!'. How shall we speak of the living reality, divine reality and human reality, which transcends the abstractions and is yet radiant with rationality?

When Heinrich Heppe's extracts from *'Reformed Dogmatics'* was republished in 1935, Barth observed in his Foreword that the dogmatics of those 'orthodox' centuries were 'too closely bound up with a form *not taken from the thing itself* but from contemporary philosophies for the substance itself not to have suffered as a whole as well as in detail'. The thrust of his own work in dogmatics has been to prise our minds out of traps created by schematisms of supposedly 'enlightened' understanding, biased as these are by presuppositions which jeopardise authentic knowledge of God and of our salvation by his free election of grace.[18] He does, of course, provide schematisms of his own, better conformed to the 'thing itself' as it comes to us through the Scriptural documents of the covenant of grace. Schematisms provided in the first half-volume on the doctrine of God provide a more apt preparation in that fundamental area for a satisfying account of 'election' than that available to earlier dogmaticians. From the constellation of divine attributes, spelled out as perfections of freedom and perfections of love to be acknowledged in God whose life is 'to love with freedom', Barth takes what is needed in order to put any debate about divine power and divine goodness on to a better foundation than that hitherto found for it. In a crucial opening section on 'Orientation', he identifies, in all serious doctrinal conceptions of 'election', three points of emphasis: God's *freedom* in the election of grace; the *mystery* of God in his free decision; God's *righteousness* in the mystery of his freedom.

Does the inclusion of 'mystery' have some more positive role than the one generally assigned to it in previous expositions, where, for the mentally honest observer, it serves all too often as an 'Emergency Exit' sign from the rigours of debate? The three pages just cited provide a moving, and indeed beautiful, account of the believer's response to this element of mystery. But if that response is to go beyond the silence of grateful wonder, there is more that should be said, in conformity with the Pauline reference to 'mystery' in Ephesians 1, 9. There the unquestionable authority 'hidden' in God's will is presented as being now an 'open secret'. Barth's only allusion of this text is in the note on p. 102f. where he acknowledges a debt to Cocceius for a suggestion that the concept of predestination should be traced back to the biblical concept of God's self-commital in 'covenant'. Ten pages later his proposal for a newly distinctive foundation for the doctrine of election is distinguished from earlier effort. It was envisaged in the seventh Gifford Lecture delivered in 1937 at Aberdeen, with the Scots Confession of 1560 as his guiding text. The authors of that Confession, so Barth claimed, declare that 'they wish the whole body of material which is called the doctrine of Predestination to be explained through Christology, and conversely Christology to be explained through the doctrine of Predestination'.[20] From the small print of an extended historical excursus in the *Church Dogmatics* I extract one passage which sets that foundation in place. In the debates of the late sixteenth and seventeenth centuries:

> The Reformed party were right to safeguard against the Remonstrants and Lutherans the tenet that the **causa efficiens impulsiva electionis,** that which motivates the will of God, is not to be sought outside God himself, but solely in his free good-pleasure. Thus it is not to be sought in a created reality forseen by God. Nor is it to be sought in the good will of man, or the use which he makes of divine grace, or the meritorious work of faith, or even faith itself, or prayer, or perseverance, or the dignity and worth of the race. Nor is it to be sought even in the **meritum Christi;** the obedience as such which was rendered by the man Jesus. All that is effect and result of divine election, but not its basis. The election itself is grace, free grace, having its origin and basis in God and not elsewhere... What was not seen, however, was that the correctness of this necessary thesis, and the power of the proclamation of free grace, are bound up with the fact that grace **in its origin** is **concretely determined and fulfilled in God.** Thus when we think of the origin of grace and the beginning of all things, we cannot and must not think either of divine caprice or of divine loving-kindness, for these are both general and therefore without real content. What we must think of is Jesus Christ.[21]

Abstract thinking leaves this *causa efficiens* shrouded in the mystery of God's hidden will; and then no human reasoning avails to dispel the taint of arbitrariness. Barth's rehabilitation of the doctrine rests on a basis of 'concrete' knowledge, mediated, however, by information which, to 'enlightened' minds, can at best have only the 'inferior' status accorded to 'accidental truths of history'. The propriety of Barth's epistemology is a topic beyond the scope of this particular essay. What results flow from it in this area of Christian doctrine?

V.

In his Gifford Lecture on 'God's Decision and Man's Election', Barth chose to present, in straightforward traditional language, 'what has taken place in Jesus Christ'. God has established lasting fellowship with man, who, seen against the background of human self-assertion, is 'not worthy of the least of all his mercies'. He has done so in depths of goodness which 'we can describe only haltingly by the word "grace". But grace is not arbitrariness; 'the divine freedom is not the whim of a tyrant'. God does not become unfaithful to himself when he shows towards us his incomparable faithfulness'. In thus being merciful, he is *just*. 'While it would be monstrous for us to make our human capacities and merits the ground for saying that God must have fellowship with man, it is perfectly normal that he should have fellowship with man at that point where he himself as man has taken man's place . . . thus finding in a human life and death, real, proper and active obedience'. 'If God looks at man in *Jesus Christ*, then his good-pleasure in man is the strictest justice, as is his decision to have fellowship with him'. That he will so look at man, in this and no other way, is the proclaimed content for that 'eternal and immutable decree of God' which in older dogmatics had a more abstract representation.

There is racial significance for all mankind in this divine decision. The rest of us *are* 'those whose place has been taken by Jesus Christ'. and, 'by the power of God's action', we become what we cannot be by claims based on strength or achievement. We are 'permitted to have fellowship with God, to be called, and to be, his child'. Seen from our side, this is an act of supreme mercy; but it is secured in proper justice. For it is in the *suffering* obedience of that elected life and death of Jesus that God finds satisfaction in man. And in that suffering Jesus 'makes all our incapacity his own, incapacity for which we are to blame, because it is founded on our unwillingness', 'He himself becomes the one who cannot choose salvation', who can choose only the curse of reprobation. 'He bears the whole boundless affliction of the curse which lies upon us' (see Gal. 3, 10-14). When God looks in judgement upon man exposed at Calvary, and sees there himself, in the form of man yet divinely self-expressed in the perfections of his love and freedom, and having there become the one on whom the curse is focally imposed, what becomes of our self-incurred rejection, the guilt of our unwillingness, the curse of our reprobation? They are 'covered', absorbed, annihilated, in the passion of divine love actualised with divine freedom; and justly so. 'Because that has happened . . . it is not merely the opportunity for our election which has been given. . . . We *are* already ...the elect of God. No-one and nothing can ever again tear us from his hand after he has laid it so completely and powerfully upon us'.

This is the evangelical truth to be declared in any Christian doctrine of election. But that doctrine has to deal with what Whitefield eloquently described as 'sovereign *distinguishing* love', electing with everlasting efficacy, yet discriminating between Isaac and Ishmael, Jacob and Esau, David and Saul, Paul and Judas, my gratefully responsive and my unresponsive neighbour who, to all appearances, cannot respond. In the works and ways of God there is *particularity*, to be understood, however, always in relation to this basic evangelical truth. Active election by God thus to be God in this covenant partnership with another, is the fundamental thesis, and bound up with it is the passive election of this other as a fit partner. But it can be misleading to construe this in terms of 'predestination', taken as the prerogative of sovereign Deity, with 'election' as one form of it and 'reprobation' as the other corresponding form. Reprobation is, of course, a standing *possibility*, unless and until all occasion for it in a sought-for partner is removed. This is consistent with the *love* which God is, as well as with the freedom in which he loves. But the majesty of divine freedom, and, in particular, the righteousness in which the freedom of his love finds expression, do not call for instances of individual final reprobation as proof of sovereignty and of the justice inherent in it. When our minds attend to the historical particularities in which truth about the covenant of grace is mediated to us, we must not construe them with reference to timeless abstractions of 'principle'. There *is* integrating principle, a 'beginning in God', whereby humanity comes to exist as object of his choice. The substance of that beginning has assumed its own historical particularity in Jesus of Nazareth, electing God and elected man already united in one person, and 'Word of God' through whom this election is mediated to historically created humanity.

Any modern critic, philosophically educated, who is inclined to accuse Barth of naive Biblical positivism, in his departure at this point from tradition, should reconsider, more particularly, the second part of his discussion of 'The Election of Jesus Christ' and its identity with 'The eternal Will of God'.[22] 'In the resolve of God, which precedes the existence, the possibility and the reality of all his creatures, the very first thing is the decree whose realisation means and is Jesus Christ ... It *is* the electing God and also the elected man Jesus Christ, and both together in the unity the one with the other.'This covenant of grace is 'the sum and substance of all the wisdom and power with which God has willed this reality (distinct from himself) and called it into being. It is the standard and source of all order and all authority within God's relationship to his reality'. 'And this decree of God is not obscure but clear'. In it, 'we do not have to assert a God of omnipotence and to cower down before him. . . . God's glory overflows in this the supreme act of his freedom: illuminating, and convincing, and glorifying itself; not therefore demanding a *sacrificium intellectus* but awakening faith'. By this will of God we must abide, because God himself abides by it, and because God himself allows us and commands us to abide by it.[23]

'We' must abide by it. Who are 'we'? We are individual human beings, each with his or her historical particularity. But, as such, we are also human beings in community with others. Between the basic reality of Jesus Christ, electing and elect, and individual experience of election, there is, in Christian testimony, a mediating concept of the 'elected community' - 'the people of God', 'Israel', historically actualised to *serve* as 'testimony and summons to the whole world' as locus for 'the presentation (the self-presentation) of Jesus Christ and the act of God which has taken place in him'.[24] This community, *called* on the ground of its election, but apt to resist its election, receives in history a 'passing' and then a 'coming' form. Resistance within it is drawn to a head, and overcome (mercifully and justly) in the person of its representative Servant-Lord; and in each of its forms its dual character is evident, but with a difference. In Israel of the 'old covenant' there are signs of pre-existent conformity to the coming Christ; and in the Church of the 'new covenant' there is still resistance to the Christ who has come. The difference in these two situations is elucidated by Barth with reference to the duality of 'hearing' the promise and command of election, and of 'believing'. All that happens throughout this history is eloquent of the mercy and the judgement of God; and, within the larger context of the promise of 'life', the threat of 'death' persists as the verdict on infidelity.

It is tempting to apply sociological analyses, in terms of 'elitism' and 'egalitarianism', to these corporate phenomena, with the same interest in abstract generality as that which produced debate about individual experience in terms of 'antinomianism' and 'pelagianism'. Barth, of course, does no such thing. What he has to say is directed and supported by running commentary on Romans 9-11. F.W. Camfield, in the earliest report given to English readers of this section of the *Church Dogmatics,* [25] distils from it the important thesis that Israel and the Church *together* mirror 'the divine rejection which became event in the crucifixion of the Son of God, and so of the world which passes away in him', and 'the divine election which was manifested in his resurrection, and so the new coming world of God'. They do this *together;* and though in the synagogue, Israel does not move from 'hearing' to 'believing', it still exists as the servant of God's electing purpose. 'The electing God and the elected community embrace even this Israel which steps into the void', choosing what God rejects. [26] (C.D. II, 2, 236. Cf. Romans 11, 1). In requiring us all to think again about the interrelations of Church and Synagogue within the elected community, Barth paves the way for less arrogant thought about 'rejection'. As Camfield puts it: 'We shall not say that the actual Israel was the direct object of divine rejection, and that the actual Church is the direct object of the divine election. That would attribute to each an independent election of its own and quite apart from the election in Christ. It would also presuppose a predetermination of God for rejection, existing quite independently of his election of grace'. 'Both Israel and the Church point to the divine promise which is fulfilled in Christ. They are, so to speak, the space round Christ', the sphere in which he, as electing God and elected man, operates in the world. [27]

So we come to the thesis that it is in *individuals* that God seeks and finds his partners in the Christ-created covenant. In the final section of his treatise, devoted directly to this topic, Barth looks for Biblical bearings in three long, and moving, pieces of exegesis which draw out the significance of the Scriptural instances of individual election, in choices made among intimately associated candidates for rejection, where others are passed over within the gracious counsel of God. These latter provide testimony to man's freedom to destroy himself, a perverse choice, not willed by God, and untimately 'void'. [28] Their godlessness, their ingratitude, whether stemming from ignorance or from willfulness, *seems* to give substance and actuality to *what God rules out.* Thus a shadow of rejection that all the individually elect know themselves to be elected, in and through one who, entering into the negative depth of this shadow, is able to dispel it. And the 'faithlessness' by which divine election is still opposed, though thus 'covered' by the all-powerful grace of God, is made to serve his purpose in

'strange', and truly 'tragic', ways. The choices recorded in the pat-
riarchal narratives; the use, for widely differing destinies, of identical
birds (in cleansing ceremony of Leviticus 14) and goats (in the Day of
Atonement ritual of Leviticus 16); the mutual involvement of Saul and
David in the establishing of monarchy within Israel; and the co-
existence of Israel and Judah, each with its 'prophet' locked in judicial
contest in I Kings 13: these are the selected instances - and one cannot
stifle doubts about possible extravagance in the exegesis.

The choice, by Jesus, of his apostles yields light on the 'direction'
and on the 'aim', bestowed upon the individual as elected, in continued intimate association with the world of candidates for rejection.
And in the third of these long exegeses, the theme is Judas, apotheosis
of 'rejected' and 'rejecting' Israel, taken into the company of the
disciples/apostles, but as one who must 'pass away' in his 'void' choice
and leave room for the apotheosis of the 'new man', elected by free
grace, the apostle Paul.

Barth's 'Christological' approach to what he acknowledges to be *the*
problem for classical doctrine - the individual election of 'the many',
and the paranesis in which Christian testimony should present it - differs from previous tradition in that he *equates* 'divine determination'
with 'salvation in Christ';[29] not with some twofold determination
anterior to this within the 'secret counsel of God'. The individual's
interest in this opportunity must be evoked by a paranesis which,
from the outset, transcends our 'natural' human proclivity towards
self-preoccupation and self-realization, with (to anticipate the anthropology of later volumes in the *Church Dogmatics*) 'pride', 'sloth', 'falsity'
as its sinful manifestations. Elected to witness and service, each among
the 'many' will begin to live 'that which he is in Jesus Christ', by 'faith'
and 'love' and 'hope'. It is important to remark, with Camfield, that 'we
shall radically misconceive election and predestination if we think of
it, as the old exponents of the doctrine so largely did, as a mere
stationary decree fixing in advance all that should follow after. . . .
What we have to do with is no dead decree, but the action of the living,
electing, God, upon the acts and decisions of men; an action in which
these acts and decisions are determined in one way or another, but
determined as *acts* and *decisions*, that is, as expressions of freedom'.
This does not create room for some abstract necessity of universal
acceptance to match the divine sovereignty of electing grace. But

neither does any 'eternal covenant of wrath correspond on the one side to the eternal covenant of grace on the other'.[30] Opinions differ as to whether Barth's treatment of possible eternal perdition for those whose existence bears the marks of 'rejected man' is adequate.[31]

We have from Barth an account of the living, electing, God, whose election of mankind for covenant partnership with himself is implemented neither by force, nor by bribery, nor by manipulation. There is no lapse into the language of despotism. Yet, the love in which he determines us for partnership with himself is free and sovereign, and its expression - indefeasibly divine - is secured by the constancy with which he remains true to himself in holiness. He so gives himself to his elected partner as to 'cover' the consequences for that partner of seeking to choose what God in his election has ruled out. When election is thus presented as 'the sum of the Gospel' - the spelling out of 'God was in Christ reconciling the world to himself' - it could plausibly be argued that it loses the special appeal to self-interest which it plainly had when it held a prominent place in theology, and in preaching focussed on the 'destiny' of individual believers and non-believers. To re-create that special force could well be disloyal as well as archaic. Can we, with Barth's help, restore the theme to the place it ought to have in Christian understanding, Christian preaching, Christian piety?

C.K. Barrett's response to Paul's words in Romans 8, 28-29 is to say that:

> The history and personal make-up of the Church are not due to chance or to arbitrary human choices, but represent the working out of God's plan. Only here can peace and security be found. Our own intentions, like our own virtues, are far too insecure to stand the tests of time and judgement. ... Predestination is the most comfortable of all Christian doctrines, if men will accept it in its biblical form, and not attempt to pry into it with questions which it does not set out to answer. It is not "a quantitative limitation of God's action, but its qualitative definition", the final statement of the truth that justification, and, in the end, salvation also, are by grace alone, and through faith alone'.[32]

Notes

1. F.W. Camfield (ed.) *Reformation Old and New,* Lutterworth Press, London, 1947, contains an excellent account by the editor in c.IV. More recently, G.W. Bromiley, *An Introduction to the Theology of Karl Barth,* Eerdmans, 1979, has a summary in c.VII.

2. Herbert Hartwell, *The Theology of Karl Barth: an Introduction,* Duckworth, London, 1964, 109. c.III, taken as a whole, provides a deeply perceptive *synoptic* view of the Christian theology in Barth's *Church Dogmatics* and demonstrates the pervasive structural bearing of the 'claim' spelled out by Barth in the first half of *C.D.,* II/2 on 'The Election of God'.

3. Important allusions to such ongoing discussion are available in articles recently published in *The Scottish Journal of Theology:* A.E. McGrat, 'Justification: Barth, Trent and Küng' (34, 6) C. Gunton, David Ford: 'Barth and God's Story' (37, 3) Bruce L. McCormack, 'Divine Revelation and Human Imagination: Must we choose between the two?' (37, 4). J.L. Walls, 'Can God save anyone he will?' (38, 2).

4. *C.D.,* II/2, p. 3.

5. N.E.B. version of The Letter of Jude, v. 3.

6. T.F. Torrance, 'The Deposit of Faith.' *Scottish Journal of Theology,* 36, 1.2.

7. P.T. Forsyth, *Positive Preaching and the Modern Mind,* London, 1907. Lecture 7, 'Preaching, positive and modern'. 168-171.

8. Karl Barth, *The Knowledge of God and the Service of God,* London, 1938, 21. For a full discussion of this epistemology of Christian faith, see *C.D.,* II/1, c.V. Whether Barth succeeds in the effort to clarify his contentions and to establish their cogency is a matter for continuing debate. That he has important insights, Anselmic and post-Anselmic, into the unique epistemological problems posed in relation to 'God', is beyond question.

9. See the article by Bruce L. McCormack already cited, where he examines the thought of Gordon Kaufman in *The Theological Imagination: Constructing the Concept of God,* Philadelphia, 1981, and related articles, where Barth is criticised for failure to dispense with 'arbitrary' (and in the last resort 'uncritical') acceptance of 'imaginative work' from earlier generations.

10. Calvin, *Institutes of the Christian Religion,* III, 21, 5. See the whole of 21, 1-5 for the background to this final formulation and note the associated ideas at the end of 21, 7: 'As Scripture, then, clearly shows, we say that God once established by his eternal and unchangeable plan those whom he long before determined once for all to receive into salvation, and those whom, on the other hand, he would devote to destruction. We assert that, with respect to the elect, this plan was founded upon his freely given mercy, without regard to human worth; but by his just and irreprehensible but incomprehensible judgement he has barred the door of life to those whom he has given over to damnation. Now among the elect we regard the call as a testimony of election. Then we hold justification another sign of its manifestation, until they come into the glory in which the fulfilment of that election lies. But as the Lord seals his elect by call and justification, so, by shutting off the reprobate from knowledge of his name or from sanctification of his Spirit, he, as it were, reveals by these marks what sort of judgement awaits them'.

11. Sermon CXXVIII in his *Collected Works.*

12. *Whitefield's Journals,* Banner of Truth Trust, London, 1960. 571-588.

13. The bitterness generated by this rift can have consequences, unintended no doubt, two hundred years later. In the book *My Dear Sister: The Story of John Wesley and the Women in his life.* completed by Maldwyn Edwards in 1974 and published posthumously by Penwork (Leeds) Ltd., the account of the 1770 Minutes episode and the Lady Huntingdon's attempts at reconciliation is selective to the point of misrepresentation.

14. See Barth, *C.D.,* II/2, 67ff. and 331, for his view of this *locus classicus* for post-Calvin debate.

15. Published in the three-volume edition of Wesley's *Sermons on Several Occasions,* London, Wesleyan Conference Office, 1876. Sermon LVIII.

16. Wesley's favourite rhetorical allusion to the norm for faith. R.A. Knox, in *Enthusiasm,* Oxford, 1950, 435f., concludes, fairly enough, that what Wesley meant was 'his own interpretation of the Bible'. Cc. XVIII-XXI of that book contain a most readable and balanced account of this eighteenth century episode, against the wider European background.

17. J.L. Walls, in the article 'Can God save anyone he will?', *Scottish Journal of Theology,* 38, 2, 155-172, makes a pertinent contribution to the analysis of that debate.

18. The 'presuppositions' arise within a prescription for 'reliable reasoning' which de-values the significance attaching to 'accidental truths' (notably those of 'history', as in Lessing's famous remark) by comparison with that of 'generality' reached by way of 'abstraction'. See Heppe, op.cit., VI.

19. *C.D.,* II/2, 30-32.

20. Karl Barth, *The Knowledge of God and the Service of God,* London, 1938, 69.
    Confessio Scotica. Art. VII: Why it behoved the Mediator to be very God and Very Man.
    We acknowledge and confess that this most wondrous conjunction between the Godhead and the manhood in *Jesus Christ,* did proceed from the eternal and immutable decree of God, from which all our salvation springs and depends.
    This is followed by Art. VIII: of Election, whose content, as Barth says, seems at first sight to be of a purely Christological character.

21. *C.D.,* II/2, 112. The non-Latin italics are not in the original text.

22. I have in mind more especially *C.D.,* II/2, 155-161.

23. *C.D.,* II/2, 157f.

24. Ibid., 205

25. Camfield, *Reformation Old and New,* 76-78.

26. *C.D.,* II/2, 236. Cf. Rom. 11, 1.

27. Ibid., 77.

28. The bearings of this symbol of negativity in Barth's thought are not so clear as one might wish. It has to be related to what he says about 'God and Nothingness' in *C.D.,* III,3, a task beyond the scope of this present essay.

29. In this respect his position has some affinity with that of so-called 'post-redemptionist' theologians, in older efforts to 'order' the divine decrees; though in that context his main affinity is with the 'supralapsarian' tradition. cf. *C.D.,* II/2, 324 and 325ff.

30. *C.D.,* II/2, 450ff. See Heppe, op.cit., 78.

31. The reader may judge for himself by studying the compact statement on pp. 449-458 of the treatise.

32. C.K. Barrnett, *The Epistle to the Romans,* London, 1957. 170f. The quotation in the last sentence is from Karl Barth, *The Epistle to the Romans* (English translation by E.C. Hoskyns, 1933) 346.

The Doctrine of the Holy Spirit
Thomas A. Smail

In a very real sense Barth's doctrine of the Holy Spirit was never written. In the uncompleted design of *Church Dogmatics* the person of the Holy Spirit and the eschatological context of his work were to have been the central content of the fifth volume. But, as is well known, his personal eschaton caught up with Barth before he caught up with eschatology and the projected Volume V never saw the light of day. One cannot but reflect that there was a certain appropriateness about that situation. In his last years "Barth ... told of his dream ... that some-one and perhaps a whole age, might be allowed to develop a 'theology of the Holy Spirit' a 'theology which now I can only envisage from afar, as Moses once looked on the promised land"[1] The image is perhaps significant. For Barth a theology of the Holy Spirit was an important ingredient of the land of promise. It was something towards which his whole theological journey had been leading, but like Moses he was excluded from it, not just because he was by then too old, but because his calling and distinctive preoccupations belonged to an earlier stage of the same journey. To change the metaphor, the architect who had built everything on such a strong Christological foundation could not easily move over to working from a pneumato-logical base.

Nevertheless, if Barth's characteristic base is in Christology, that certainly does not mean for him the exclusion of the Holy Spirit, but rather his inclusion. Barth's trinitarian theology insists that there can be no adequate speaking about the Son which does not involve a speaking of the Spirit in his relation to and distinction from the Son. If in Barth there is no treatment of the doctrine of the Holy Spirit in and for itself, his staunch adherence to the principle that *opera Trinitatis ad extra indivisa sunt* ensures that there is rich pneumatological material at almost every locus of the *Church Dogmatics.*

It is scattered over the many volumes of the work rather than gathered and treated systematically in and for itself, in a way that raises questions about both its internal consistency and its development as the work progressed. Barth could well have replied "to those who wondered how his doctrine of the Holy Spirit would have turned out, in the same terms in which he answered those who asked the same question about his eschatology. "Some of those who have questioned me I have put to confusion by raising the counter-question whether, to what degree, and with what attention they have read and studied the material already to hand. Others I have asked whether they have noted how much about the desired sphere of eschatology may be gathered indirectly, and sometimes directly, from the earlier volumes."[2]

That defines our task: to look at the material already to hand in *Church Dogmatics* and to see what may be gathered directly or indirectly from it about Barth's doctrine of the Holy Spirit. I am well aware that before CD there are earlier works of Barth that deal directly with pneumatology,[3] but restrictions of space demand concentration on CD on which what is presented here is almost exclusively based.

The Holy Spirit and Barth's Basic Approach to Theology

Despite his wariness of the word 'person' as one of the most slippery theological terms, Barth's whole approach to the God-man relationship was deeply personalistic. Like Martin Buber, Barth is in solidarity with the deepest insights of biblical religion in seeing the divine-human relationship as a personal encounter between a divine 'I' and a created human 'thou', a relationship that was brought into existence by the sole will and initiative of the divine 'I'. Barth is deeply concerned to affirm the integrity of that relationship, both as regards to the sovereign freedom of the divine Lord over against all his creatures, but also as regards the relative freedom of the human creature in his encounter with that Lord, on which the authenticity of his knowledge of God and of his response to him depends. Barth sees quite clearly that the biblical notion of the covenant between God and man would be nullified by an authoritarian and totalitarian domination of the Lord over his creatures that removed and excluded the need for and the reality of the personal human response to the sovereign grace that encounters us in Jesus Christ. The covenant requires the free human Amen for its completion just as it requires the free sovereign divine Yes for its inauguration. The gospel does not compel or overwhelm man from an objective standpoint outside himself; it sets him free to make an authentic response to the God of grace who comes to him in it.

It is precisely at this point that the fundamental activity of the Holy

Spirit in the covenant relationship comes into evidence. The Holy Spirit is the internal liberator of man who makes possible and guarantees his response to God, "The act of the Holy Ghost in revelation is the Yes to God's Word which is spoken by God Himself for us, yet not just to us, but also in us. This Yes spoken by God is the basis of the confidence with which a man may regard the revelation as applying to him. This Yes is the mystery of faith, the mystery of the knowledge of the Word of God, but also the mystery of the willing obedience that is well-pleasing to God. All these things, faith, knowledge and obedience, exist for man 'in the Holy Spirit!' "[4] The concern that the Spirit's response would not just be *for* us but also *in* us, that we should be able to provide the 'willing obedience' that the covenant requires, that man should be free to respond to God *for* himself, even if he cannot do so *by* himself - these are emphases that Barth shares with the liberal neo-Protestant theology of which he is otherwise so critical. Barth knows just as well as the liberal theologians that the man God is seeking is the man who shows that he is "a responsible grateful, hopeful person" whose understanding, will and imagination are involved in the response he makes.[5] As he puts it elsewhere, "It would be comfortless if everything remained objective. There is also a subjective element; and we may regard the modern exuberance of this subjective element, which had already been introduced in the middle of the seventeenth century, and was brought by Schleiermacher into systematic order, as a strained attempt to bring the truth of the third article into force."[6] In other words Barth desires to respect in his way the freedom and authenticity of man's response to God as much as the liberals do in their very different way. The basic 'I-thou' structure of his thought requires the relative freedom or responding man over against God as well as the sovereign freedom of God over against man. One aspect of this doctrine of the Holy Spirit is therefore designed to affirm that human freedom and to give a theological explanation of its actuality and possibility.

But Barth's consensus with Schleiermacher at this point is short lived. Schleiermacher's exposition of the third article of the creed is 'strained', because, in its concern for the liberty of the human subject, it neglects the Lordship of God over that subject even in the very act of making its subjective response to him. Barth rejects what he regards as the tendency of liberal protestantism on the one hand and of Roman Catholic theology on the other to see the freedom of man to respond to God as his own innate possession, his ability to know and relate to God as something that man has at his own disposal prior to and apart from God's act towards him in Jesus Christ. In their different ways the liberals reduce the Spirit of God to being the spirit of man and the Roman Catholics tend to make him the spirit of the Church. Barth's question to Schleiermacher is whether on the latter's anthropocentric view of the Spirit, "It can be avoided that the objective impulse must merge and disappear into the subjective one? Here (in Schleiermacher) the independence of the Word over against faith is not so assured as would have to be the case if this theology of faith were a genuine theology of the Holy Spirit. In a genuine theology of the Holy Spirit a dissolution of the Word cannot come into question. In Schleiermacher's theology of the Spirit such a dissolution comes in all earnestness into question."[7]

For Barth the Spirit is neither to be psychologised and seen as the inner core of man's own being, nor is he to be ecclesiasticised as the soul of the Church or the Christian tradition. Rather he is to be seen always as the Spirit of Christ. P.J. Rosato well describes the questions about the relationship between the freedom of God and the freedom of man that Barth's doctrine of the Spirit is designed to answer and the threats from right and left it is concerned to parry when he says, "Only the sovereign Spirit of the Word can bridge the immense gulf between Christ and the Christian which modern Protestantism since Schleiermacher and Roman Catholicism since Augustine have sought to abolish by either a metaphysical or an ecclesiological means of identifying the Spirit of the Creator and man. Barth has first to separate the Spirit radically from the experience both of the individual Christian and of the worshipping community. But then he must restore the essential connection between the Spirit and Jesus Christ. Other theologies have indistinctly associated the Spirit with human spirituality or with Church tradition to the detriment of His primary relationship to the historical revelation of God's Word in Jesus Christ."[8]

Thus Barth's pneumatology presupposes the freedom of the responding man against the initiating God and the covenant requirement of his authentic answer to God's speaking and acting, but it wants to emphasise above all that man's response does not come from himself, but has to be given to him by the Spirit. His capacity to know and belong to God is not his own possession and is not within his own power to realise. It has to be given him by God, and it is given to him not everywhere and anywhere but in the closest connexion with the incarnation of God's Word in Jesus Christ. Pneumatology is related basically and primarily neither to anthropology nor to ecclesiology but to Christology. Its anthropological and ecclesiological implications can be explicated only derivatively from its christological base. We shall therefore be advancing to the centre of Barth's concern when we consider these primary relationships.

Christology and Pneumatology in Barth.

God's goal in Christ is that he should fulfil his covenant with man and that man should fulfil his covenant with him. Jesus Christ is both God's gracious and saving self-giving to man and he is man's responsive self-giving to God so that in him the covenant is fulfilled from both sides. But the purpose of God's vicarious action on man's behalf in Christ is that men should come to participate in and make their own what Christ has done on their behalf. God's Word is not just to be spoken, it has to be heard; God's grace has not just to be given, it has to be received. That hearing and receiving are not human possibilities but are made possible only by the action of the Holy Spirit within man as he encounters the gospel. In CD I.1, in the context of his doctrine of revelation, Barth makes a very key statement about the role of the Holy Spirit in his theology, "the Spirit of God is God in his freedom to be present to the creature . . . And God's Spirit, the Holy Spirit, especially in revelation, is God Himself to the extent that He can not only come to man but also be in man, and thus open up man and make him capable and ready for Himself, and thus achieve His revelation in him. Man needs revelation for he is certainly lost without it. He thus needs to have revelation become manifest to him i.e. he himself needs to become open to revelation. But this is not a possibility of his own. It can only be God's own reality when it does happen, and therefore it can lie only in God's own possibility that it can happen. It is God's reality in that God Himself becomes present to man not just externally, not just from above, but also from within, from below, subjectively. It is thus reality in that He does not merely come to man, but encounters Himself from man. God's freedom to be present in this way to man, and therefore to bring about this encounter is the Spirit of God, the Holy Spirit in God's revelation."[9]

We may note several extremely important points from this highly significant passage:

1. It affirms man's incapacity to know God apart from God's coming *to* man in Christ and acting *in* man by the Spirit.

2. It establishes the closest concomitance between our knowledge of Christ and our knowledge of the Spirit. We have no knowledge of the Spirit except as the one who leads us to Christ. "As God, the Holy Spirit is a unique person. But He is not an independent divinity side by side with the unique Word of God. He is simply the Teacher of the Word: of that Word which is never without its Teacher."[10]

3. It affirms the deity of the Holy Spirit. If Jesus Christ is God and if only God can know God, then the Spirit who opens us up to God must be as truly God as the Word to whom he opens us. "... the child of God in the New Testament sense will never for a moment or in any regard cease to confess: 'I believe that I cannot of my own reason or power believe in Jesus Christ my Lord or come to Him.' God remains the Lord even and precisely when He Himself comes into our hearts as His own gift, even and precisely when He 'fills' us. No other intercedes with Him on our behalf except Himself. No one else speaks for us when He speaks through us except Himself ... The deity of the Holy Spirit is thus demanded."[11]

4. In this understanding of the action of God in revelation, there is the basis of a distinction between God the Son who comes to us "externally, from above" and God the Spirit who comes to us "from within, from below, subjectively". This distinction Barth uses to construct his doctrine of the immanent Trinity, which we shall examine later. But already here we have the delineation of a hypostatic distinction between God the Son who is the object of our knowledge, the one to whom we are related and God the Spirit, who is at work within us making that knowledge possible and enabling us to enter into that relationship. Implicit in this distinction is that subordination of the work of the Spirit to the work of Christ which, as we shall see, is characteristic of Barth's pneumatology as a whole.

When we look at what he says about the Spirit in the context of his Christology, this subordination becomes even more explicit to the point at which it becomes a real question whether the hypostatic distinctness of the Spirit is still being maintained. In IV.1 Barth can write, "We cannot say more of the Holy Spirit and His work than that He is the power in which Jesus Christ attests himself, attests Himself

effectively, creating in man response and obedience."[12] So in
IV.3 Pentecost is seen as one of the forms of the *parousia* of Christ. As
he comes in one way at Easter as he will come in yet another way at the
eschaton, so he himself comes at Pentecost in the form of the Holy
Spirit. This coming is "no less genuinely his own direct and personal
coming, His *parousia,* presence and revelation, than was his coming
then and there to his disciples in the Easter event, or than will be His
coming in its final and conclusive form as the Judge of the quick and
the dead."[13]

From all this it is clear that for Barth Pneumatology is totally determined by Christology: to speak of the Holy Spirit is simply to speak of
the extension of the power of Jesus Christ into the subjective sphere,
so that he may liberate men to believe in him, love him and hope in
him. In this subordination of the Spirit to Christ Barth shows himself
to be a faithful representative of the Western tradition. The identity of
the Spirit with Christ is sometimes so complete as to throw into doubt
the reality or the necessity of the hypostatic distinction between them
which in his doctrine of the Trinity Barth wishes formally to maintain.
It is no accident that Hendrikus Berkhof can quote passages from CD
IV in support of his own thesis that New Testament language about
the Spirit can be translated without remainder into language about the
action of the ascended Christ.[14]

In this connexion it is interesting that Barth, while making much of
the soteriological consequences of the doctrine of the virgin birth for
our understanding of how we receive Christ, has little to say about the
properly Christological implications of the same doctrine, so that
Rosato's attempt to find in Barth some sort of Spirit Christology foun-
ders for sheer lack of material.[15] Barth's own Christology is consistently pursued in terms of the incarnation of the Word and the role of
the Spirit in the constitution of the incarnate Word receives little attention. In this connexion, Barth has little to say about the baptism of Jesus
and of what it might mean that the Father gives the Spirit, not just to
the man Jesus, but to the incarnate Son, and that Son is therefore the
recipient as well as the dispenser of the Spirit. Such considerations
might suggest that there is a greater mutuality in the relations of Son
and Spirit than Barth allows. Son and Spirit are *homoousios* - of that
Barth is completely aware - but they are also hypostatically distinct
and sometimes Barth speaks as if the Spirit were only the mode of

presence and action of the ascended Christ.

At this point we are in a position to take a critical stance against the

thesis of P J Rosato that Barth has an independent interest in and concern for pneumatology over and against Christology. What we have
seen already shows that such a contrast is quite alien to Barth's
approach. For him, from the start, the work of the Spirit is seen
exclusively in terms of carrying over the work of Christ into the sphere
of human responsiveness, and as the *Dogmatics* proceed, the tendency
to make the Spirit simply a mode of Christ's present action becomes
more and more accentuated, although of course the trinitarian distinction between them is never formally abandoned. As he goes on,
Barth's pneumatology can be more and more completely expressed
by the Pauline statement, "Now the Lord is the Spirit" (II Corinthians 3.17)

The Spirit and the Birth of Christ

We are now in a position to understand the significance of the doctrine of the virgin birth of Jesus for Barth's theology in general and for
his pneumatology in particular. He is the last great theological friend,
at least on the Protestant side, that this much contested doctrine has
had, and he returned to expound its importance again and again. For
him, as I have already hinted, it is a soteriological father than a properly christological importance. He is interested in the *conceptus de
Spiritu sancto* less for what it tells us about the constitution of Christ's
person and the trinitarian relationships in which he stands, than for
what it tells us about how the human nature that he assumed became
capax Dei, and how by analogy our human nature also is capable of
coming into relationship with God.

In other words, the virgin birth is of prime importance to Barth
because he perceives in it the historical enactment of the central principles of his pneumatology. Human nature in the person of Mary is
capable of receiving into itself the Word of God only in virtue of God's
action upon it in the creative power of the Holy Spirit. The Word is
what is received and the Spirit is the power that makes that reception
possible. From this transaction Joseph as the symbol of human power
and initiative is totally excluded.

It is through the receptivity of Mary that the Spirit works, but
against all Roman Catholic mariological synergism, Barth insists that
the so-called *Fiat* of Mary is the result and not the condition of the
Spirit's action upon her. Her consent to the incarnation is not a factor

external to the Spirit's action which she contributes, but is itself the fruit of the action of the awakening Spirit who alone gives her the true ability and the will to say Yes to what God purposes to give her.

And what is true of the human nature of the mother is true *a fortiori* of the human nature of her Son in whom the Word is incarnate. As the Spirit acts on Mary to enable her to conceive and bear the word, so the same Spirit sanctifies the human nature of Jesus and makes it capable of entering into hypostatic union with the Word of God. The virgin birth is important for Barth because it exemplifies in a paradigmatic way the basic axioms of his pneumatology. "Through the Holy Spirit and only through the Holy Spirit can man be there for God, be free for God's work on him, believe, be a recipient of His revelation, the object of the divine reconciliation."[16] And again, "The very possibility of human nature's being adopted into unity with the Son of God is the Holy Ghost. Here, then, at this fontal point in revelation, the Word of God is not without the Spirit of God. And here already there is the togetherness of Spirit and Word. Through the Spirit it becomes really possible for the creature, for man, to be there and to be free for God. Through the Spirit, flesh, human nature, is assumed into unity with the Son of God. Through the Spirit this Man can be God's Son and at the same time the Second Adam ... the prototype of all who are set free for His sake and through faith in Him."[17]

One could have wished that Barth had explored further the properly christological insight that he formulates here, the Spirit as the constituting bond of unity of Christ's person, a point on which the Chalcedonian formula itself has nothing to say. Barth might have got further along this line if he had considered Christ's baptism as carefully as he considers his birth. His main interest here is in the humanity of Christ as the prototype of human responsiveness, and the virgin birth as the historical demonstration that the responsiveness is possible only through the activity of God himself in the power of the Holy Spirit.

On its negative side this asserts that apart from the action of the Spirit in relation to the incarnation of the Word, man has no natural capacity for God or for revelation. Barth's emphasis on the virgin birth goes hand in hand with his dismissal of all natural theology on the one hand and all forms of work-righteousness on the other. Knowledge of God and obedience to God are possible only where man is freed for them by the Spirit, and the Spirit acts revealingly and sanctifyingly only in relation to the incarnation of the Word. In his polemic against Emil Brunner in the thirties Barth always implied that there was an internal connexion between Brunner's denial of the virgin birth and his readiness to entertain what Barth regarded as a modified natural theology.[18]

Thus the doctrine of the virgin birth encapsulates the central insights, both positive and negative, of all Barth's pneumatology: hence his continual emphasis upon it. Human nature can come into relationship to God only by being conceived, opened, visited, born again by the Holy Spirit and through him enabled to receive the Word.

To sum up our results so far, we have seen that at the centre of Barth's thinking is the connexion between Christology and pneumatology, between Christ and the Spirit. Christology is the objective basis of pneumatology: pneumatology is the subjective application of Christology. Or, to put the same thing in terms that Barth himself likes to use, Christ is God's action in the objective realm of *being* (the ontic realm) and the Spirit is God's action in the subjective realm of *knowledge* (the noetic realm). We participate in what God has done for us in the ontic realm in Christ, by coming to know Christ through the action of the Spirit, with the kind of knowledge that brings with it a real participation in and conformity to that which it knows.

Christology is the objective basis of pneumatology which gives it its entire content: pneumatology is the subjective application of Christology by which that content comes to effective revelation and reception. God's saving work happens in the first place *pro nobis*, vicariously on our behalf but apart from us, in the Son made flesh, in whom alone God's covenant is fulfilled from both sides. But in the Spirit all that comes to fruition *in nobis*, when God opens us up to know and benefit from what he has done in Christ, so that we begin to believe and hope in it, and respond in love to God's love for us.

All the rest of Barth's pneumatology is an exposition and application of that basic position, and in what remains we shall trace some of these applications. From the relation of the Spirit to Christ we can see how he is related also, to the scriptures, to the church, to man as such, and finally how he is related to the Father and the Son in the eternal life of the Triune God. We shall say something about each of these in turn.

The Holy Spirit and the Inspiration of Scripture

As the incarnate Christ is, for Barth, the primary form of God's word and Holy Scripture is secondary form, we must, according to him, understand the relation of the Holy Spirit to scripture by analogy from his relationship to Christ. As the humanity of Christ in all the reality of its human limitations is nevertheless capable of expressing and conveying God's revelation through the action of the Spirit upon it, so the real and limited humanity of the authors of scripture is capable of being inspired by the same Spirit, so that they become authentic witnesses to the Word Incarnate through whom God can speak and reveal himself. As the Spirit acted upon the humanity of Mary and enabled her to conceive and bring forth the Word, so in an analogous way the same Spirit acted upon the prophets and apostles and made them what they could not make themselves the conceivers and speakers of God's written word that bore witness to his self-revelation in Christ. Thus not only the living Word, but the written word, like the word preached, is conceived by the Holy Spirit in and through the real humanity of those who are enabled to receive it and give it forth.

Barth, like Calvin before him, was aware that the Spirit who was active in the writing of scripture must also be active in the hearing of scripture. Inspiration is not a quality that inheres in scripture as such. Scripture is the word of God only insofar as the Spirit acts each time it is read amd makes it again the speaking of God that can be heard as such. "If the Church lives by the Bible because it is the Word of God, that means that it lives by the fact that Christ is revealed in the Bible by the work of the Holy Spirit."[19] The Church cannot take the inspiration of the scripture for granted. It must pray "that the Bible may be the Word of God here and now, that there may take place that work of the Holy Spirit, and therefore a free applying of the free grace of God". [20] This emphasis on the Bible as the sword which the Spirit must take and wield again and again, rather than as a document that possesses its inspiration inherently, is a chief differentiation of Barth's doctrine of scripture from that of evangelical orthodoxy. For him the Spirit is present dynamic power who needs to be at work every time the word is read or spoken if it is to be heard and obeyed.

It remains true that the long treatment of scripture as God's word in CD I.2 is dominated by christological rather than pneumatological terms of reference. Barth is more interested in the authority of scripture than he is in its inspiration. The word is often seen as self-authenticating rather than receiving its authentication through the action of the Spirit. The pneumatological interest is by no means absent, but it is always subordinate to the christological centre from which Barth is all the time working.

The Holy Spirit, The Church and The Christian

For Barth the Spirit is primarily the Spirit of Christ rather than the Spirit of the Church, but, in distinction from all Protestant individualism, he sees the corporate body of Christians rather than the pious heart as the central scene of his activity. In CD IV the corporate application of Christ's work is given deliberate priority over the personal application in order to correct the individualistic bias of so much Protestant thinking at this point.

As we would by this time expect, Barth's ecclesiology is christologically rather than pneumatologically ordered: the church is seen less as the fellowship of the Spirit and more as the Body of Christ. That Body, since the Ascension and Pentecost, has two forms, Christ's heavenly Body in which he remains eternally incarnate as Man at the right hand of the Father, and his earthly Body which consists of those who believe, love and hope in him. That body of believers he has related to himself not in a new incarnation but in a real incorporation and sharing of life. The Holy Spirit is the bond of unity between Christ's heavenly Body in which he is incarnate and his earthly Body into which we have been incorporated. "The Holy Spirit is the power, and His action the work, of the co-ordination of the being Jesus Christ and that of His community as distinct from yet enclosed within it. Just as the Holy Spirit, as Himself an eternal divine 'person' or mode of being, as the Spirit of the Father and the Son, . . . is the bond of peace between the two, so in the historical work of reconciliation He is the One who constitutes and guarantees the unity of the *totus Christus*, i.e., of Jesus Christ in the heights and in the depths, in His transcendence and in His immanence . . . He is the One who constitutes and guarantees the unity in which He is at one and the same time the Heavenly Head with God and the earthly body with His community."[21]

It is worth noting in passing that in the light of such passage, one needs to question whether Avery Dulles' [22] classification of Barth's ecclesiology as falling within his Herald model is entirely justified. For the later Barth at least the Church is seen primarily as the Body of Christ, in accordance with his basic christocentric stance.

It is clear from our last quotation how Barth's christological and trinitarian norms shape his understanding of the work of the Spirit in the Church. Within the trinity, as we shall see, the Spirit is the bond of love between Father and Son, their hypostatic self-giving the one to the other. In Christology the Spirit is the One who makes possible the unity of God with human nature in the Incarnation. So in ecclesiology it is the Spirit who bridges the distance between Christ exalted in the heavens and yet present and living among his people. "In the work of the Holy Spirit it takes place that Jesus Christ is present and received in the life of His community of this or that century, land or place; that He issues recognizable commands and with some degree of perfection or imperfection is also obeyed; that He Himself actively precedes this people." [23]

This presence and lifesharing encounter between Christ and his people takes place in a particular way in the Lord's Supper where the Spirit is also and most typically active. "In the work of the Holy Spirit there takes place in the Lord's Supper, in a way which typifies all that may happen in the life of this people, that which is indicated by the great *Touto estin,* namely, that entity with its heavenly Lord, and the imparting and receiving of His body and blood, are enacted in and with their human fellowship as realised in the common distribution and reception of bread and wine."[24] The presence of Christ and the reality of our fellowship with him are not within our control and can never be taken for granted. They are always to be given again and again in the faithful grace of the Holy Spirit who holds Head and members together in one Body and continually awakens faith, love and hope.

But it is in the ecclesiological context we are at present expounding that Barth's doctrine of the Spirit shows most clearly its eschatological face. According to Barth Christ's reconciling work is done for *all* men, whereas it becomes clear in the life of the Church that the Spirit has been given only to *some* men; not all hear the gospel and not all who hear believe. For Barth the distinction between believers and unbelievers is not an absolute one, like that between elect and reprobate in Calvinist theology, but a relative one between those who have so far and those who have not yet believed. Because Christ is for all, the Spirit is promised to all, is in principle poured out on all flesh from Pentecost on, so that the Church as we know it is only preliminary, the first fruits of the Spirit and the promise of all that is yet to come. What the Spirit does now in Christians gives us hope and confidence about what he will yet do in those who do not yet believe. "Nothing of what the Spirit does, effects and accomplishes among and with and in Christians is not ready like a harnessed stream to be effective among and with and in non-Christians. And when there comes the hour of the God who acts in Jesus Christ by the Holy Ghost, no aversion, rebellion or resistance on the part of non-Christians will be strong enough to resist the fulfilment of the promise of the Spirit ... which applies to them too."[25] This confidence in the Spirit's power to bring all men to acceptance of the gospel is the subjective obverse of Barth's conviction that the objectively completed work of Jesus Christ is valid universally for all. It leads to the optimistic affirmation of the Church's vocation to evangelism - an evangelism that depends much more on the promise of the Spirit than the decisions of men.

Thus for non-believers there is a not-yet attaching to the promise of the Spirit. That is true in a different way for believers also, as they long for the still not fully possessed inheritance that is theirs as God's children. But here and now the Spirit has already begun his work among them, and amidst the tensions of the 'not-yet' and the 'here and now' of the Spirit, the emphasis must finally be on affirmation of what he has already done rather than on bemoaning what he has not done. "If we can and should long for the new order of the future world - and the Spirit Himself makes this unavoidable in His great promise for the last days - then we can and should also rejoice with unstinted gratitude in the order which is present already, being established by the pre-sence and action of Jesus Christ in the promise of the Spirit. Not only was God glorious in the past, and not only will He be glorious in the final fulfilment of His promise, but He is glorious here and now in the promise of His Spirit, He Himself being present and active yesterday, today and tomorrow."[26]

What is to be said corporately of the Church is also to be said per-sonally of the Christians who comprise it. In the published fragment of CD IV.4 Barth says that people become Christians by being baptised with the Holy Spirit, a term used not in the current Pentecostal sense of a subsequent experience of empowering and endowment with gifts, but in the sense of regeneration and conversion. "Baptism with the Spirit is effective, causative, even creative action on man and in man ... It cleanses, renews and changes man truly and totally ... It is ... his being clothed upon with a new garment which is Jesus Christ

Himself, his endowment with a new heart controlled by Jesus Christ, his new generation and birth in brotherhood with Jesus Christ, his saving death in the presence of the death which Jesus Christ suffered for him."[27]

In the analogy with Christ who was conceived by the Holy Spirit, Christians are born of the same Spirit, and this is a sovereign act of God's grace which they themselves cannot originate but that has to be given to them. But this does not mean the elimination of the human factor in the case of Christians any more than it does in the case of Christ. "The change which God has made (in man) is in truth man's liberation. It comes upon him wholly from without, from God. The point is that here as everywhere, the omnicausality of God must not be construed as His sole causality. The divine change in whose accomplishment a man becomes a Christian is an event of true intercourse between God and man . . . He (man) is not run down and overpowered, but set on his own feet. He is not put under tutelage, but addressed and treated as an adult . . . The faithfulness to God to which he is summoned is not, then, an emanation of God's faithfulness. It is truly his own faithfulness, decision and act. He could not achieve it were he not liberated thereto. But being thus liberated, he does it as his own act, as his answer to the Word of God spoken to him in the history of Jesus Christ."[28]

Here Barth is struggling with a problem deep at the heart of his doctrine of the Spirit. He wants to affirm that the work of the Spirit is sheer gift which no man can originate, control or earn and yet he also wants to affirm at the same time that the Spirit does not treat man as a passive object on which he exerts the external causality of irresistible grace, but rather liberates him into the freedom in which he can make his own authentic response and say his own spontaneous yes to the gospel. The Spirit does not deprive man of freedom, he rather gives him a freedom he did not and could not possess before. Barth refuses in principle to discuss how sovereign grace and human freedom are related, just as he refuses in principle to discuss how Jesus can be both God and man. Both are miracles of the Holy Spirit which can be revealed and believed but not explained. Arminians and synergists of all kinds find Barth deeply unsatisfactory at this point because he will not grant them their basic presupposition that human freedom is freedom *from* God. Barth, on the contrary insists that true freedom is *in*

God and in his Spirit. One might however concede that Barth might have been understood better at this point if he had been more willing to explain rather than simply assert his position.

The Holy Spirit and Man

As well as being the Word and the Head of the Church Christ is also true man as in God's purpose man was meant to be. So if we want to look at man as he is now, we must look at him in the light of the perfect man Jesus Christ. Barth's anthropology like all the rest of his theology is read off from his christological centre. Jesus Christ the true man is in the closest possible relation to the Holy Spirit. In fact it is true to say of Christ that he *is* Spirit, just as he is body and soul. In other words he is as constitutively related to God as he is to the physical and psychical equipment that comprises his humanity. Because he is God incarnate, "He breathes lastingly and totally in the air of the 'life-giving Spirit'. He not only has the Spirit, but primarily and basically he is Spirit, as He is soul and body. For this reason and in this way He lives. This is His absolutely unique relationship to the Holy Spirit."[29] Christ alone *is* Spirit, whereas all other men *have* the Spirit. Christians have the Spirit in a distinctive way as the one who awakens them to new life in Christ and begins to conform them to his likeness. In the language of IV.4, they are "baptized with the Spirit". The Spirit is the Lord and Giver of that messianic life into which they have entered.

But when we look at creation in the light of Christ we see that the same Spirit who gives new life to Christians gives life itself to all living men. It is only in relation to God that man can live at all; man comes to life, as Genesis makes clear, only when God breathes his own breath upon him. That breath or Spirit of God in its immanence in human life is what lets man live and be man; it is the human spirit which is also the Spirit of God.

Barth is at his most difficult at this point but several elucidatory points can be made. Spirit in Barth's doctrine of man is a mediating concept. He accepts the ambiguity of the biblical documents as to whether 'spirit' means Spirit of God or spirit of man. For him it means both and neither. It is Spirit of God because it is God's action totally dependent on his will and grace, and yet it is also the human spirit, because without it man cannot be. Spirit in this context in fact describes the dynamic relationship to God in which alone man has life.

Man does not possess spirit as part of his constitution like his body and his soul. Barth is not promoting a tripartite description of man as body, soul and spirit. Man *is* body and soul, he keeps insisting, but he only *has* spirit. "We must perhaps be more precise and say that he is, as the spirit has him. Man has spirit as one who is possessed by it. Although it belongs to the constitution of man, it is not, like soul and body, and as a third thing alongside them, a moment of his constitution as such. It belongs to his constitution in so far as it is its superior, determining and limiting basis."[30]

All this remains pretty obscure, but Barth seems to be saying that man could not *be* without the Spirit, but that his own life and being are not his own possession. He cannot exist outside his relationship to God but that relationship has to keep on being given to him by God.

Man's relation to God in this general way as his creature is the basis and possibility of his being related to God in Jesus Christ as a Christian, but only the Spirit on whom man's life depends can realise in him that possibility of new life. "By Spirit we have primarily and originally to understand the movement of God towards man and therefore the principle of human relation to him and fellowship with Him."[31] It is sometimes foolishly charged against Barth that for him only Christians have a relationship with God, but we should note here that his clear teaching in this anthropological context is that all men have the Spirit in this basic sense, because apart from God's ceaseless breathing upon them, they could not be alive. Life itself implies relationship to God in the Spirit.

Thus there are *three* ways in which men are related to the Spirit (1) the unique way of the man Jesus who *is* Spirit (2) The Christian way of believers who are baptised in the Spirit and (3) the general relationship shared by all men to whom God imparts life. Thus for Barth there are two distinct functions of the Spirit in creation and in redemption." As the Spirit of Jesus Christ, who, proceeding from Him, unites men closely to Him *ut secum unum sint,* He distinguishes Himself from the Spirit of God who lives as *vita animalis* in creation, nature and history, and to that extent in the godless as well."[32]

Barth's teaching about the Spirit in the context of his doctrine of man raises again questions we have already encountered in the context of ecclesiology and the Christian life. We are left wondering about how Barth's insistence upon man's utter dependence upon the Spirit for his life and being leaves room for a proper human freedom to act (and indeed to sin) over against God. But, more immediately germane to our own present enquiry, questions are raised here in the most acute form about what we might call the hypostatic status of the Spirit, who in Barth's anthropology tends to be described as a breathing, a relationship, a movement, an event, an action of God, so that one is left wondering if there is any need to go on describing him as a distinct 'person' or, to use Barth's own language, a distinct 'mode of being' in interaction and interrelationship with the Father and the Son. The Spirit tends to be seen here as simply God's way of relating himself to his creation, a mode of the divine action rather than a mode of the divine being, and it could be argued that what Barth says about the Spirit in his doctrine of man is consistent with a binitarian rather than a properly trinitarian doctrine of God. All of which leads to our next major topic.

The Trinity and the Person of the Spirit

For this material, we have to turn largely to CD I.1, which reminds us that we are raising the question of the trinitarian relationships of the Spirit at the end of our essay whereas Barth raised it very near the beginning of the *Church Dogmatics*. Despite the change of order, we may still claim to be in line with Barth's basic method, which holds that what the Spirit shows himself to be in his historical work *ad extra* is the revelation of what he is himself *ad intra* in the external being of God. It is therefore not inappropriate that, having surveyed what Barth says about the Spirit's historical work, we should ask what he says on that basis about trinitarian person.

In faithfulness to this method of moving from historical revelation to eternal being, Barth begins by establishing the deity of the Spirit on scriptural grounds and then ventures about as near a definition as he comes in a passage we have already quoted at (9) above. The distinction there made between Christ who is God's coming to man as man, and the Spirit who is God's presence in man to open him up to the coming of the Son, is the basis of his insistence that to open him up to the coming of the Son, is the basis of his insistence that revelation requires a threefold and not simply a twofold distinction in the divine action and being. The Holy Spirit is not to be identified with Jesus

Christ, the Son, on biblical grounds - a point that may not be as immediately obvious as Barth suggests but also because the Son is the principle of objective completed revelation and the Spirit the principle of the ongoing subjective reception of and response to that revelation. Both are the action of the same God and are therefore in the closest possible connexion with each other. But if they are not to be separated, neither are they to be confused. "Those who believe in Him (Christ) and confess Him believe in Him and confess Him as the exalted Lord. Thus the Spirit in whom they believe and confess and He who is the object of this faith and confession stand as it were on two different levels."[33]

So, Christ as the one confessed is to be distinguished from the Spirit who enables the confession. We have more than once had reason to ask whether in the working out of Barth's pneumatology, this distinction between Christ and Spirit is always carefully maintained, but here in his formal treatment of the trinitarian relationships, it is insisted upon.

On this basis Barth proceeds to argue that if *ad extra* the Spirit is God's presence in the other, opening it up to himself, the Spirit *ad intra* is the same: in the life of God he is the presence of the Father in the Son and of the Son in the Father. "This togetherness or communion of the Father and the Son is the Holy Spirit. The specific element in the divine mode of being of the Holy Spirit thus consists, paradoxically enough, in the fact that He is the common factor in the mode of being of God the Father and that of God the Son. He is what is common to them, not in so far as they are the one God, but in so far as they are the Father and the Son."[34]

Barth comments that this statement shows how impossible it is to conceive of the Holy Spirit as a distinct person in the modern sense of the term. But of course it also raises the question in what sense the common factor between Father and Son is himself a distinct third mode of being of the one divine Thou, and in what sense he stands over against the other two in properly personal relationship with them. In answer to this Barth makes the distinctively Augustinian point that the Spirit is distinct from Father and Son because he is the love with which Father and Son give themselves to each other. Since that love cannot itself be less than God himself, it is therefore to be seen as a distinctive mode of the divine being, as much as the Lover and the Beloved.

This however provokes the question that the Augustinian love-analogy has always raised, that love is a relationship of persons rather than itself a distinct third person. On this analogy cannot the Spirit be seen simply as the relationship of Father and Son, rather than himself a third eternal expression of the personal divine being?

Barth resists that conclusion; the love with which the Father loves the Son is no mere relation; it is a *self*-giving, so that the *self*-giving of Father and Son to each other is the Holy Spirit. That would seem to be the point of the following passage, "What is between them (the Father and the Son), what unites them, is, then, no mere relation. It is not exhausted in the truth of their being alongside and with one another. As an independent divine mode of being over against them, it is the active mutual orientation and interpretation of love, because these two, the Father and the Son, are of one essence and indeed of divine essence, because God's fatherhood and sonship as such must be related to one another in their active mutual orientation and inter-penetration. That the Father and the Son are the one God is the reason why they are not just united but are united in the Spirit in love; it is the reason why God is love and love is God."[35]

In other words, in so far as one can understand that very dense statement, Father and Spirit, and Son and Spirit are distinct from each other as modes of being of the one God, as the Giver is distinct from the Gift, granted that what is given here is the very self of the Giver. Barth does not explain further and, while it is clear that he affirms the Spirit as a hypostatically distinct mode of the divine being, the way in which he understands that distinctness remains in a certain obscurity, as it has always done in the Augustinian tradition that Barth follows very closely here. The same lack of clarity and indeed ambiguity about the hypostatic distinctness of the Spirit that we have seen at different points in Barth's treatment of the work of the Spirit is not wholly absent from his treatment of the Spirit in the life of the Trinity. His typically Western interest in the oneness of God and his tendency to see the Spirit as functionally subordinate to the Son makes this almost inevitable.

The Spirit and the Filioque

What we have already discovered about Barth's pneumatology helps to explain why Barth was a staunch defender of the Western teaching about the double procession of the Spirit from the Father and the Son, encapsulated in the *Filioque* clause of the Western version of the so-called Nicene Creed. His Christological centre which predisposes him to see the work of the Spirit in one-way dependence on the work of the Son points him decisively in that direction.

Barth is rightly critical of the Eastern doctrine of the procession of the Spirit from the Father alone, because it introduces an illegitimate contradiction between what we say on the basis of historical revelation about the Spirit being sent by the Son and what we say about the eternal life of God where the Spirit proceeds solely from the Father. Our access to the eternal relationships in God is solely dependent on the revealed relationships in history, so that what we say about the former must conform to what we know about the latter. Barth even confesses himself more than a little suspicious that the exclusion of Christ from the eternal origination of the Spirit might open the door to an independence of the work of the Spirit from the work of Christ on the economic level and might serve as a basis for a Christless mysticism which would be yet another form of natural theology.

But Barth's own position in this matter is far from invulnerable. He takes the Western line that for Christ to be fully divine, he must be involved in the origination of another divine mode of being, namely the Spirit. He will not be content with saying that the Spirit is breathed forth *per Christum,* a formula often thought to provide a mediating possibility of reconciliation between East and West. For Barth however it does not emphasise strongly enough the co-ordinating activity of the Son along with the Father and could be construed in a merely instrumental sense. Indeed Barth's understanding of the Spirit as the hypostatic love of Father and Son requires that he should have his origin in both, although of course the Son in turn has his origin in the Father.

In his stress on the full and co-equal deity of the Son, Barth fails to give sufficient weight to the priority of the Father as *fons et origio totius divinitatis,* which has its scriptural base in the Fourth Gospel, where the subordination of *both* Son and Spirit to the Father is as strongly emphasised as their co-divinity with him. Also it can be argued that the *Filioque* does justice to only one side of the biblical material about the relation of Christ and Spirit. Christ in his baptism and ministry is not only the donor and sender of the Spirit, but also the recipient of the Spirit, receiving from him both his humanity and his charismatic sonship. Thus Son and Spirit are not in a relationship of one-sided subordination of Spirit to Son, but in something much more like a mutual co-ordination and interdependence. The Son receives from the Spirit as well as the Spirit receiving from the Son, and if we read this back into the life of God we would need to affirm an involvement of the Spirit in the begetting of the Son as well as an involvement of the Son in the procession of the Spirit. Barth considers this possibility, but rejects it on the ground that the action of the Spirit in the incarnation has to do with the humanity of Christ only, and has no implications for the origination of the eternal Son.[36] On this we may comment that if what happens to the human Christ has no reference to the eternal Son, Barth's whole doctrine of revelation is attacked at its heart. In IV.1 [37] Barth argues that in the human obedience of Jesus we see an analogue of the divine obedience of the Son to the Father. Why on the same principle should the conception of the human Jesus by the Holy Spirit not point by precisely the same analogy of faith to a participation of the Holy Spirit in the eternal generation of the Son of God?

If Barth had paid more attention at this point to the Christological and pneumatological implications of the baptism of Jesus, the reception of the Spirit by the incarnate Son might have rescued his teaching from an unbiblical onesidedness at precisely this point. The Son is from the Father through the Spirit just as the Spirit is from the Father through the Son. The Western *Filioque*, as Eastern theologians have not been slow to point out, leads almost inevitably to a depression of the role and person of the Spirit in relation to the role and person of the Son. If the Son is divine because he co-originates another divine person, is the Spirit less than divine because he does not co-originate any divine person? It is not without significance that those theologians who stand most closely in Barth's tradition have not followed him in his defence of the *Filioque*. [38]

This tendency to subordinate the Spirit to the Son in a one-sided way is, as we have seen, present right through Barth's theology. It is certainly true that we must not separate the Spirit from the Son, but Barth's danger is to fail to assert the distinction between them which formally he wishes to maintain, so that pneumatology is in danger of being merged into Christology and the subjective is not sufficiently distinct from the objective so that it can be a God-given but also free response to it. Barth's intention is certainly to recognise the freedom and creative spontaneity of God the Spirit in enabling the response to revelation over against what is objectively given in Christ, but his christological concentration sometimes prevents this intention from being fully honoured.

In Barth's historical situation and as a much needed reaction against liberal subjectivism, his christological protest was essential. In our different historical situation fifty years later the Holy Spirit is at the centre of our thinking and practice in a way that was not so when Barth's theological enterprise took shape. Then the need was indeed for a christological Moses to lead the way from the liberal house of bondage. But, as Barth himself saw, that Moses was not likely to be himself the man best qualified to explore the promised land of a theology centered on the Spirit.

Nevertheless, whatever theological Joshua may yet arise to fulfil that task, will do it well, only if he remains true to Barth's central insights and co-ordinates his doctrine of the Spirit with a Christology that emphasises as clearly as Barth has done Jesus Christ as God's descent to man and man's return to God and as such both the recipient and the donor of the Holy Spirit whom he receives from the Father and pours out upon the Church now, but ultimately upon all flesh.

Notes

1. E. Busch, *Karl Barth: his life from letters and autobiographical texts,* trs. John Bowden, London: SCM Press, 1976, p. 494.
2. Karl Barth, *Church Dogmatics* IV/4 (Fragment), trs. G.W. Bromiley, Edinburgh: T & T Clark, 1969, p. vii.
3. Notably the lectures given at Erlangen in 1929 and translated into English in 1938 under the title of *The Holy Ghost and the Christian life,* London: Frederick Muller.
4. *C.D.,* I/1, (Second Edition), p. 453.
5. *Dogmatics in Outline* trs. G.T. Thomson, London: SCM Press, 1949, pp. 130-40.
6. Ibid., pp. 137-8.
7. Barth, *Protestant Theology in the Nineteenth Century: Its Background and History,* London: SCM Press, 1972, pp. 471-2.
8. Philip J. Rosato, *The Spirit as Lord: The Pneumatology of Karl Barth* Edinburgh: T & T Clark, 1981, p. 32.
9. *C.D.,* I/1, (Second Edition), pp. 450-1
10. *C.D.,* I/2, pp. 243-4.
11. *C.D.,* I/1, (Second Edition), p. 465.
12. *C.D.,* IV/1, p. 648.
13. *C.D.,* IV/3,1, p. 356. cf also *C.D.,* IV/2, p. 128.
14. Hendrikus Berkhof, *The Doctrine of the Holy Spirit,* London: Epworth, 1965, pp. 22-29.
15. P.J. Rosato, op.cit., especially chapters V and VIII.
16. *C.D.,* I 2, p. 198.

17. Ibid, p. 199.
18. E. Brunner and Karl Barth, *Natural Theology*, trs. Peter Fraenkel, London: Geoffrey Bles, 1946, p. 123.
19. *C.D.*, I/2, p. 513.
20. Ibid., p. 514.
21. *C.D.*, IV/3,2, p. 760.
22. Avery Dulles, *Models of the Church*, London: Gill and Macmillan, 1976. Especially Chapter V, pp. 71ff.
23. *C.D.*, IV/3,2, p. 761.
24. Ibid., p. 761.
25. *C.D.*, IV/3,1, p. 355.
26. Ibid., p. 359.
27. *C.D.*, IV/4, (Fragment), p. 34.
28. Ibid., pp. 22-3.
29. *C.D.*, III/2, p. 334.
30. Ibid., p. 354.
31. Ibid., pp. 356-7.
32. *C.D.*, I/2, p. 241.
33. *C.D.*, I/1. (Second Edition), pp. 451-2.
34. Ibid., p. 469.
35. Ibid., p. 487.
36. *C.D.*, I/1. (Second Edition), pp. 485-6.
37. *C.D.*, IV/1, pp. 186ff.
38. cf Alasdair Heron 'The *Filioque* in recent Reformed theology' in *Spirit of God, Spirit of Christ*, ed Lukas Vischer, London; SPCK, 1981, World Council of Churches, Geneva, pp. 110ff.

Creation and Anthropology
Stuart D. McLean

Introduction

Barth's anthropology is buried in the doctrine of creation (C.D. III/
2), and is, therefore, often skipped over in the reader's eagerness to get
to the more central doctrine of reconciliation (C.D. IV). Thus is overlooked one of the richest discussions of anthropology in the western
theological and philosophical tradition and also, perhaps more im-
portantly, one of Barth's most detailed expositions of his content and
method in relation to a subject available to our common experience
and reflection. On the other hand, his dialogical-dialectical method is
spelled out so deliberately (III/2/45 pp. 222-285) that one can better
appreciate its operation in the more traditional discussions of God,
Jesus Christ, and the God-person relationship. On the other hand, one
sees how theological his anthropology itself is – that in Barth's thought
Christology is the criterion for anthropology. Consequently, his doctrine of creation in general, and his doctrine of anthropology in particular, demonstrate the dependence of his whole theology on the
covenantal relationship of God to persons, persons to God, and persons to persons, as enacted and revealed in Jesus Christ.

Carefully analyzed, Barth's doctrine of creation (and specifically his
anthropology, III/2) is an antidote to common errors in Barth interpretation. To begin with he discusses anthropology with three interrelated and interdependent terms (a) *real man* – the interrelationship
between God and persons (the "vertical"); (b) *humanity* – interrela-
tionships between persons (the "horizontal"); and (c) *whole persons* –
the interrelationship of soul and body. For Barth the relationship with
God and with others is not constituted by "add ons" to man's original
equipment of soul and body, but by constituent relationships which
exist from the beginning. This is a radical departure from traditional
anthropology, and has major implications for understanding Barth's
theology. An insufficient realization of these aspects of anthropology
prevents an adequate understanding of reconciliation, and leads the
reader to interpret Barth in traditional and, I believe, mistaken ways.

111

This departure from a more traditional approach not only signals a different anthropology but also reflects Barth's assumption that relationship is the key to understanding God and persons – that is,
persons are entities that not only *have* relationships with other entities,
but *are* in fact constituted by such relationship.

Second, Barth's major contribution is missed if his peculiar understanding of relationship is overlooked. While it is true that the
dynamic-form of his understanding of relationship emerges from a
familiar family of dialectical-dialogical thinkers –the way he appropriates that tradition is uniquely influenced by Martin Buber –more
particularly, by the form of interrelationship in which human beings
participate i.e., not only through visual and bodily exchange and
encounter but, most especially, through verbal exchange and encounter. An understanding of the complexity of this exchange is important
in helping us discern the richness of dialogical-dialectical relationships as human beings relate to one another and to God and also in the
logic and language used to describe and discuss this content. Relationship involves *being with* (unity) and, because of this *being with*,
interaction and differentiation (separation). A linear sequencing of
these moments misrepresents the dynamic. Unity and differentiation
of a certain kind do not exclude but augment each other. The greater
the unity (and community) of this particular kind, the greater the
possibility of personal identity (individuality). However, the preposition "for" augments the preposition "with," and contributes
another aspect to his understanding of relationality. *Being for* another,
or God's *being for* us (as well as with another, or God's being with us),
points to the actional, interactional, and event character of the dialectic. While this emphasis points to agency, event, deeds, and work, etc.,
it is dialectically complemented by the equally important receptivity
and openness to what is done *for* one. Again, a linear sequencing of
these movements obscures the richness of the dynamic. The
dynamic-form of giving and receiving, of agency and receptivity,
penetrates to Barth's special use of a dialogical-dialectical understanding of interrelationship and interaction. Detecting the significance
Barth assigns these two prepositions (with and for) is a crucial insight
into his theology.

Another aspect of the dialectic, indicated by the prepositions *over/
under*, the nouns *superordination, subordination*, the adverbs *high/low*,
can also reveal the internal workings of his vocabulary. However the

order is initially stated, in somewhat conventional and seemingly linear terms, i.e., God superordinate to man, man superordinate to woman – Barth intends (I believe) radically to redefine these terms: i.e., in Jesus Christ, the Lord is revealed also as servant (IV/1), omnipotence becomes participation *with* and *for* the most alienated of creatures as servant (IV/1), a wife leads her husband in the true meaning of servanthood.[1] Thus, in his discussion the conventional and traditional – top-down and controlling concepts of hierarchy and leadership and the demeaning nature of servanthood – are radically transformed. For Barth servanthood and lordship are functions of one another. While order, initiation, and sequence are maintained, their roles are radically transformed by his understanding of the free and dynamic interplay of God's love and freedom as it is demonstrated, enacted, incarnated and revealed in Jesus Christ.

Third, these distinctions contribute not only to the recovery of the concept of covenant as a unique metaphor for understanding the Biblical materials, but also to a particular understanding of that term. While it is popularly acknowledged that covenant is a central category in Barth's theology, it is not often understood as a distinctive metaphor for summing up the relationality of Barth's understanding. Sometimes covenant is misunderstood as contract (an agreement between entities the violation of which, on the part of either, ends the agreement). More often it is misunderstood through the interposition of an organic or body metaphor, which, while affirming certain aspects of relationality, nevertheless falls short of the full orbed covenantal concept.[2] The contributions of the organic metaphor are especially appreciated in contrast to the mechanistic (*lex talionis*, the legalistic, Newton's understanding of cause and effect) which is the dominant metaphor in most modern cultures.

However, while relational and interactional, the organic metaphor does not fully capture or comprehend the dialectical-dialogical dynamic of Biblical thought. As commonly understood, this metaphor so overemphasizes the functions of unity and harmony in relationality that it down-plays the equally important dimensions, pointed to by such words as "encounter," "struggle," (e.g., *Israel*, "he who strives or struggles with God"), and differentiation. The organic metaphor allows little room for the radical assumptions about relationality to which we are led by the language about God's freedom, forgiveness, new beginnings and resurrection. In organic thought the character of life and God is governed by the web of interconnected-ness exemplified by the internal operations and dependencies of *one* body. In contrast the covenantal metaphor derives from the idea of interaction and interrelationship *between* bodies e.g., marriage, with special but not exclusive emphasis on linguistic exchange as the model for its dynamics. Both metaphors are significant departures from the mechanistic, cause-and-effect analysis of human condition-ing; both expand our limited thought forms for speaking of God, His creation, and reconciliation; but the biblical and Barthian contribution to theology is primarily informed by the covenantal.

Finally, organic thought handicaps our thinking about time. A growing, interconnected network moves from the past into the future, dependent not only upon itself, but on an environment which is similarly organically understood. Covenantal thought acknowledges not only the richness of this contribution but also the crucial contribu-tion of the concept of the future to biblical thought about life in relationship with God. God is a promise-making and promise-keep-ing Reality who is with us not only at our beginning, but also at our end; and through whom the dynamic of hope and expectation for the Kingdom, the new Jerusalem, significantly breaks into the present web of our relationships and makes us new.

Other biblical interpreters have convincingly demonstrated that the richness of the Biblical narrative will not yield to mono-meta-phorical interpretations. The Bible abounds with a variety of meta-phors, each of which, I would argue, has a significant role in the economy of Biblical interpretation (the mechanistic, the contractual, the organic, and others). Nevertheless, I believe that Barth has inten-tionally recovered the covenant as a distinctive root metaphor which has often been overlooked or collapsed into organic or contractual metaphors in the history of academic and ecclesiological interpreta-tion. This recovery, its detailed elaboration and centrality in his inter-pretation, significantly accounts for the insight, power, and authority which makes his contribution so important to the history of Christian thought.

These uniquely Barthian contributions to theological interpretation surface more clearly in his discussion of anthropology than in any other place in his *Church Dogmatics*. Attention to this discussion pro-vides a window for viewing, somewhat less darkly, the dynamic con-figurations of his interpretation of the Bible as the Word of God.

Therefore, the thesis underlying the following interpretation is that a dynamic understanding of relationality is crucial to an assessment of Karl Barth's thought; that this understanding is best grasped through his interpretation of dialogical-dialectical thought; and that it is encapsulated in the metaphor of covenant.

The following sections will discuss 1) Barth's interpretation of creation and covenant; and 2) the three uses of the term man.

The Relationship of Creation and Covenant

Creation and covenant are reciprocally related. The covenant is the internal meaning of creation, and the creation the external basis of the covenant.[3] But Barth has few specific references to the creation in general, the cosmos and the other animals; rather he focuses attention almost entirely upon the creature, man. Barth implies that theology and anthropology should not be determined by the changing paradigms of physics, biology, and social science.[4] He limits his statements about creation. God created the cosmos. He is Lord over the creation, and the creation praises Him in return. He doesn't comment on *how* the cosmos was created nor how the non-human aspects of creation praise Him. He avoids the problem of other theologies which attach themselves to a specific cosmology and subsequently allow it to influence their theologies. The Christian faith does not contain a specific cosmology. At this point, it should be non-committal and seek to free itself from any particular paradigm of physics. Thus, he is secondarily concerned with the cosmos itself, affirming that it is fundamentally good, the creation of a good and loving God.

For Barth, theology should reflect on the Word of God. Its primary focus is the relationship of God and man, and man and man. Jesus Christ reveals these relationships and thus becomes normative for understanding both man and God. Consequently, anthropology, the center of III/2, is based on Christology. Each section of III/2 will treat its special emphasis in terms of the God/man Jesus Christ.

After distinguishing man from the cosmos and other creatures (animals), Barth distinguishes his understanding of man from non-theological anthropologies. Scientific approaches to man (through physics, biology, psychology, and sociology) are faulted because their concern is not with the being of man but with appearances. Theological anthropology, on the other hand, does not deal merely with man as a phenomenon but with man himself. This means that if God is and is essentially related to man (and for Barth both are true), this relationship undergirds and conditions *all* other dimensions in understanding man. Thus, taking his holistic principle of interpretation seriously, any interpretation which excludes this basic relationship is flawed. The same rationale applies to man's relationship to man, and the soul's relationship to the body. If man is essentially related to man, to view man atomistically, and community as an aggregate of individuals, distorts the perception of man. If man's body and soul are dialectically related, to interpret the body or soul without the other fundamentally distorts. These three sets of relationships – God-man, man-man, and body-soul – form an essential gestalt which, in the nature of our human ways of knowing cannot be empirically understood. At least the basic relationship, relationship with God, cannot be empirically demonstrated, and the other relationships are distorted if not seen within this context. In principle, then, "scientific understanding" screens out the most crucial aspect of the gestalt. Exact sciences cannot know man as "creature of God."

Philosophical theories of man are also faulted in that they proceed from certain speculative ideas. They are not grounded in a reality which includes the actual relationship between God and man. For Barth, this relationship is not secondary, nor accidental, but a primary and essential dimension of man, and thus conditions all other aspects of understanding him. He claims that understanding man in Christological terms is not speculative but based on the concrete manifestation of a man – who is normative for all and who starts from "the other side" with the presupposition that *God is,* and *God and man are related essentially.* "It [theological anthropology] has a responsibility to make the claim of truth. We repeat that this does not mean that it cannot err, that it does not need continually to correct and improve itself."[5] Having shown why both the sciences and speculative philosophy are incomplete and uncertain clues to our manhood (personhood),[6] Barth has to face the question of how Jesus Christ can be normative for man when he is distinguished from man by his godhood, and man is distinguished from Jesus by his sin.

Each of the three following sections will discuss one of the aspects of anthropology: real man, humanity and the whole man.

Real Man: Man as the Creature of God
Christology: Basis for Defining Real Man

Barth begins this discussion with a statement about the *real man*, Jesus Christ, who is man *for* God and God *for* man. He sets forth six criteria of the real man, Jesus.[7] Then he applies these six criteria to man *in general*. These criteria are the minimal requirements by which other definitions of man's nature are evaluated. Barth says:

> *No definition of human nature can meet our present need if it is merely an assertion and description of immediately access- ible and knowable characteristics of the nature which man thinks he can regard as that of his fellows and therefore of man in general . . . [Man's self-knowledge is to be regarded as a vicious circle. The point at issue as Barth states it, is] . . . How does he [man] reach the platform from which he thinks he can see himself? . . . Who is the man who to know himself first wishes to disregard the fact that he belongs to God? [8]*

If man attempts to understand himself from a perspective which is not based on Jesus Christ, he misses real man, for the immediately know- able phenomena are (1) neutral, (2) relative, and (3) ambiguous. Whether or not those "immediately knowable phenomena" are genuine symptoms depends on whether they correspond to the criteria of real man. In themselves, the phenomena are silent.[9]

Six criteria for the evaluation of Jesus Christ as real man, and subse- quently, man in general, are set forth. Real man is man as he is related to God, or God is related to him, the "vertical" dimension of manhood – the dimension that includes and presupposes the other dimensions – humanity, and whole man. The uniqueness of Barth's method is that all definitions relate to the "internal" meaning of creation, covenant, and its fulfilled, actual, incarnated, and revealed manifestation to Jesus Christ.

These criteria set forth three major aspects of the God and man, relationship in Jesus Christ, and man's participation with Him.

First, *relationship* with God (to, from, with), and the order of that relationship (over, under) (points one and four, III/2, pp. 73-74).

Second, *deliverance* (for, action, will, works), and man's participation
in that deliverance in reconciliation (points two and five).

Third, the end (purpose) of the history of deliverance is in the
freedom, sovereignty, and *glory* of God, and man's participation in what
God does as the *service* of God (completed action of God in redemption), (points three and six).

Unpacking these six points reveals the dialogical-dialectical complexity of what one often, simplistically, calls the relationship of God
to man. They entail not only relationship (God with us), but also the
order of the relationship (Lordship and standing under); not only
God's deliverance (reconciliation), but also the outcome or completion of the action (the glory and service of God). The fullness of this
discussion of the "vertical" relationship provides Barth with a rich and
integrated theological repertoire with which to critique a variety of
definitions of man's nature. Autonomous definitions, man without
God, from Polanus (man as a rational animal) to Fichte (man exists
properly and concretely in the act of self transcendence) are easily
felled by Barth's method. Theonomous definitions from Karl Jaspers
to Emil Brunner are critiqued for their generality, their lack of certainty, and their failure to consider the attitude and action of God in their
definition of man.

The question for Barth has been what norm or criteria should be
used to establish a definition of real man? The major criteria are that
man is essentially a God-connected (related) entity, and that the
character and action of God, and man's response to that action is critical. He finds these criteria fulfilled in Jesus Christ, and what man
knows of his own definition is through participation in Him.

Barth further clarifies what he means in a discussion of the formal
and material dimensions of real man. The formal dimension is the
relationship between God and man – the fact that man is *from, to* and
with God. But this formal dimension is ensconced within the material
dimension. Both are made known to us in Jesus Christ, the God-man.
The material dimension is analyzed in four stages.

The Call and the Hearing of the Word

On the first level,

> *the two material and therefore primary statements in our
> exposition are: (1) that the being of man as a being with*

*Jesus rests upon the election (the call) of God; and (2) that it
consists in the hearing of the Word of God.[10]*

It is *first* the man Jesus who is elected or called by God.[11]

Here the *formal* definition of real man is given its first *material* content. To be a man is to be *with* the One who is the true and primary
chosen (elect) of God. Thus man is *with* God because he is *with* Jesus.
And "To the extent that he [man in general] is with Jesus and therefore with God, man himself is a creature elected [chosen, called] in the
divine election of grace."[12]

The second *material* statement is that the being of man as being with
Jesus consists in *listening to the Word of God.* Who is the one who has
heard? We know only that the man Jesus has heard, and, therefore,
that it is the being and existence of all men to be addressed and summoned. Because Jesus has *received* the Word of God, He is the sum of
the divine address to the created cosmos. He is not merely the bearer
of the divine address, but is Himself the divine address and summons.
Man is the creature whose being is from the first addressed, called, and
summoned by God. Man isn't first a kind of nature, which then has a
relationship with God, and finally is addressed by God. Rather, he is
from the beginning in the Word of God. Thus, "Men are those who are
summoned by this Word."[13] But, "To be summoned means to have
heard, to have been awakened . . .".[14]

Since Jesus Christ is *real man,* since He is *in* our sphere, since it
appears that we have been, as men, already fundamentally determined by our relationship with God in creation, the material dimension of the covenantal relationship is "objectively" already the
determination and destiny of all men. However, "subjectively," the
fact that man is *real man,* and has been summoned by God, is *known*
only by some.

The Being of Man as a History

On the second level of explanation, Barth sums up all that he has
said with the statement, ". . . *the being of man is a history* [not *has* a history, but *is* a history.]"[15] The contrast between the concept "history"
and the concept "state" (or "condition") may clarify this distinction.

Even when a "state" is very much in flux, it is never open to more than certain particular movements. History occurs when something happens to a being in a certain state, i.e., when something *new* befalls it, when something takes place upon and to the being as it is, when its circular movement is broken from without. In this instance, that which breaks in is the decision of God (God's freedom). The being of the man Jesus lies in the fact that God is *for* Him in this way and that He is *for* God. God gives Himself to Jesus as the deliverance in order that He may Himself be the deliverance. Thus, apart from the eternal will and counsel of God (apart from the inner Godhead), Jesus exists only in this history, i.e., in the particular history of the covenant, salvation and revelation inaugurated by God. "Jesus *is,* as this history takes place."[16]

Again, let us consider man in general in the light of these statements about "history." Man is the being (1) whose kinsman or brother is the man Jesus and (2) in whose sphere, therefore, this "history" takes place. "He [man] is with God, confronted and prevented and elected and summoned by Him, in the fact that this history takes place in his own sphere."[17] "Man is what he is as a creature, as the man Jesus, and in Him God Himself, moves towards him, and as he moves towards the man Jesus and therefore towards God.", [18] i.e., he is real man in this history which is the new (God's freedom) breaking into man's sphere.

The Being of Man as a Being in Gratitude

On the third level, Barth says that a more precise *material* definition of man is "a being in gratitude."[19] For,

> *If the Word of God in which man is, and is therefore historical, is a Word of divine grace, if he is thus summoned to hear and obey his Word . . . then the being of man can and must be more precisely defined as a being in gratitude.[20]*

Gratitude is the precise creaturely counterpart to the grace of God. In daring to cast himself upon God, he corresponds to the Word without which he would not be this human creature. "To be grateful is to recognize a benefit,"[21] a benefit which is a good which one has received. A benefit presupposes the action of a benefactor, an action which one could not perform for oneself but which, nevertheless, happens to one. But the true benefactor is God, the Creator of all benefits. He transcends the limits of the human condition and makes the being of man a history so that the being of man is a being open to the benefits of God.

However, "As it [the being of man] cannot be gracious to itself, it cannot tell itself that God is gracious to it. This it can only hear,"[22] can only receive. But as it does this, as it is content to be what it is by this Word, as it exists by its openness toward God, the question is decided that it is a being in gratitude. "It has not taken the grace of God, but the latter [grace of God] has come to it; it has not opened itself but God has opened it and made it this open being."[23]

When we see man as a being in gratitude we see him for the first time *in his own act*. It is the act in which he *accepts* the validity of the act which not he but God has done. "To see this acceptance as such is to see real man in his *own* action, not merely as the object but as the subject of the history in which his being consists."[24] God is a subject, and man can be considered an object. On the other hand, man is subject, having been addressed by God, distinguished from Him, and given His grace, as he responds to God as object. True both God and man are subject in one sense and object in another. The intersubjectivity of the interaction of grace (charis) and thanksgiving (eucharistia) is the history of the God-man relationship and constitutes the content of the being of man. However, what we are speaking of here is the being of the man Jesus, real man, upon which the being of man in general depends by participation. He (Jesus Christ) participates in our life and, consequently, we participate in His life, and hence in the life of God.

Barth is not defining man in general or "natural man," but Jesus Christ and the saved man who *consciously* participates in Christ. Certainly Barth argues that all men in general are saved by God, yet many are not aware of it or even reject it.

The Being of Man as Responsibility

The fourth level of Barth's understanding of man's being is responsibility.

Human being consists in thanksgiving, or response to God, and, therefore, in responsibility. In its own place and way, man's response is itself a word, a human word which is different from the Word of God. It is the word of thanks rather than the Word of grace. The being of man is an answer, a response, a being lived in the *act* of answering the Word of God. Thus, Barth says:

> Man is, and is human, **as** he performs this act of respon-
> sibility, offering himself as the response to the Word of God,
> and conducting, shaping and expressing himself as an
> answer to it.[25]

What makes him *real* man is that he is engaged in active responsibility to God.

Barth further develops this theme, "man's being-in-responsibility before God," as "inner notes:" (1) man's knowledge of God, (2) his obedience to God, (3) his invocation of God (call), and (4) the freedom which God imparts to him.

Barth has asserted that God decides for man by creating and sustaining him as man; in love He delivers him from sin as he works through His Son and Spirit. There is no question of a special *state* in which man finds himself placed. It is always a question of his act, as he thanks the God who tells him that He is gracious to him, as he moves to the God from whom he comes.

These four *material* dimensions of real man – hearing the call, man as "history," as gratitude (thanksgiving), and responsibility emphasize and highlight the dynamic interrelationship and interaction peculiar to Barth's dialogical-dialectical understanding of this vertical relationship, first as present in Jesus Christ, and then as persons participate in Him. Real man cannot be understood except in this covenantal partnership between God and himself, between the Creator and the creature. These elements explicate the dynamic aspects of the covenant which is the internal "history" and meaning of the creation. We next look at Barth's discussion of humanity, the second aspect of his discussion of anthropology.

Humanity: Man With Man

Jesus as Man for Man, the Basis for Understanding Humanity

According to Barth our natural knowledge of humanity is uncertain and "arbitrary,"[26] thus we need the Word of God in Jesus Christ to know ourselves. Hence, Christology again is the key. In order properly to understand humanity in general, it is necessary to investigate the humanity of Jesus.

Jesus is true man and true God. The humanity of the man Jesus means that He is the true creaturely *form* of man, i.e., the form of I-Thou human relationship.

> *If the divinity of the man Jesus is to be described comprehensively in the statement that He is man for God, His humanity can and must be described no less succinctly in the proposition that He is man for man, for other men, His fellows.* [27]

The distinctions between His manhood and those of others are two. 1) He is referred to other men, not partially, incidentally, or subsequently, but originally, exclusively, and totally. "In the light of the man Jesus, man is the cosmic being which exists absolutely *for* its fellows." [28] 2) In addition, he is human in the specific sense that His *special activity* is to be *for* God, i.e., be *the deliverer* of man.

The relationship in which Jesus binds Himself to man is wholly real. He is affected by the existence of His fellows. This relationship is not a "stoic calm," untouched by the problems and the fate of men. He is not passive; rather, He *actively* makes the cause of other men His own. He suffers, His vitals are affected. He sacrifices Himself to the need of men. He gives Himself to them. He puts Himself in their place. He makes their state and fate his own cause. However, man also needs something more than this suffering with; he needs a new beginning. Jesus Christ delivers man. He gives him freedom through His activity. Thus, the humanity of Jesus means that He is *for* man in a radical way.

From this basic affirmation Barth develops the following implications:

1. *Jesus is from his fellows.* ". . . Jesus has to let His being, Himself, be prescribed and dictated and determined by an alien human being (that of His more near and distant fellows), and by the need and infinite peril of this being."[29] Here Barth points to the I-Thou relationship. The "I" of the selfhood of Jesus is not found in isolation from others but in relationship to the "Thous" who are rebels from

God. The self or "I" of Jesus is given its meaning by them; his "I" as determined by these alien beings means that he becomes "... the Representative and Bearer of all the alien guilt and punishment transferred from them to Him."[30]

2. *Jesus is to His fellows.* "He moves towards the Thou from which He comes [i.e., his fellow-man]."[31] He is active only in the fact that he makes the deliverance of this alien being His exclusive task. He gives Himself freely to His fellows for their salvation. He offers Himself up for them. He, therefore, serves them.

3. *Jesus is with His fellows.* ". . . His being is both *from* and *to* His fellows, so that He is *with* them."[32] Thus, if we see Jesus at all, we see Him *with* His disciples, the people, His enemies, and "... the countless millions who have not yet heard His name."[33] We see Him determined by them and for them. In this way, He is supremely Himself. In this way, He is human.

4. *There is no alienation, distance, or neutrality between this human definition and the divine.* Although there is no distance between this human definition and the divine definition, His humanity is not His divinity. His divinity is from and to God; His humanity is from and to human persons. But His humanity is in closest correspondence with His divinity; they are in harmony with one another. "There is here a *tertium comparationis* which includes His being for God as well as His being for man . . .".[34, 35]

5. *His saving work not His own choice.* "The saving work in which He serves His fellows is not a matter of His own choice or caprice, but the task which He is given by God."[36] The activity and work of Jesus is not first His own work, but the choice and will of God, because God first, and not the man Jesus, is *for* man. Since Jesus is *for* God, it is not an accident that He is *for* man because God is *for* man. Jesus exists and lives in God's saving work. He is only Jesus because and as He is doing God's work.

6. *There is freedom in God but no caprice.* "If 'God for man' is the eternal covenant revealed and effective in time in the humanity of Jesus, in this decision of the Creator for the creature there arises a relationship which is not alien to the Creator, to God as God, but we might almost say appropriate and natural to Him."[37] God repeats *ad extra* a relationship which is proper to Himself, His own inner essence. He makes a copy of Himself. He imparts to the relationship between Jesus and man, the freedom and eternal love which is the inner essence of

God. Thus, this freedom becomes the true, yet ultimately mysterious, basis of Jesus which makes legitimate the designation of the term "divine" to Him.

Barth establishes a theological basis for understanding man in *general* from these six criteria. He sees the connection in the "fact" that Jesus Christ is both man and God.

When he refers to the correspondence and similarity between God and man, Barth points to a set of actions and relationships central to his theology. If this correspondence and similarity *(analogia relationis)* is understood, a crucial door is opened into the mansion of Barth's theology.

First, let us focus on the "form" which is the I-Thou relationship before we focus on the "dynamics" or "material" content of the relationship. The correspondence and similarity is between three different relationships: the I-Thou relationship *within* God Himself; the I-Thou relationship *between* God and man in Real Man (variously referred to as God's eternal covenant, man's being for God, the Divinity of Jesus); and the I-Thou relationship *between* man and man (or person and person), the humanity of man. Barth says,

> *If "God for man" is the eternal covenant [God-man] revealed and effective in time in the humanity of Jesus [man-man] ... but we might almost say appropriate and natural to Him. God repeats Himself in this relationship* **ad extra** *[God-man], a relationship proper to Himself in His inner divine essence [God-God]. Entering into this relationship, He makes a copy of Himself.[38]*

But what is copied? It is the *relationship* between Father and Son. "There is in Him a co-existence, co-inherence and reciprocity ... [but further] in this triunity He is the original and source of every I and Thou, of the I which is eternally from and to the Thou and therefore supremely I."[39] It is this *relationship* in the inner divine being (Father-Son) which is reflected in God's eternal covenant with man (God-man). This eternal covenant (God-man) is revealed and operative in time together with and through the humanity of Jesus (man-man).[40]

We have seen above that there is a necessary correspondence and similarity between the being of the man Jesus for God (His Divinity;

God-man) and His being for his fellows (His humanity; man-man). However, "The humanity of Jesus is not merely the repetition and reflection of His divinity, or of God's controlling will; it is the repetition and reflection of God Himself . . ."[41] It is the *imago Dei.*[42]

He speaks of the image as the "plurality in man," or "being man means being in togetherness: [as] man and wife."[43] Thus the image for Barth is the togetherness, the plurality of the I-Thou relationship.

He says, "image has a double meaning." Thus Barth sees the I-Thou-ness of our humanity not only as a reflection of the inner Godhead, but also as a reflection of the I-Thou form of real man (God-man). Both I-Thou relationships are the *imago Dei* and because they are both images; they are signs of one another. Thus, humanity (man-man) reflects and points to man's destiny which is to realize that we are covenant-partners of God (man-God).

Up to this point we have focused on the *form* of the *analogia relationis;* now let us consider the same three relationships, but from the perspective of the correspondence and similarity between the "content" or "material" or "dynamic" dimensions. This has to do with the actional dimension of the relationship, here referred to as the freedom and love of God. Barth says:

> *This is not a correspondence and similarity of being, an* **analogia entis** *. . . it is not a question of this twofold being. It is a question of the relationship within the being of God on the one side and between the being of God and that of man on the other. Between these two relationships as such – and it is in this sense that the second is the image of the first . . . There is an* **analogia relationis** *. . . The correspondence and similarity of the two relationships* **consists in the fact that the eternal love in which God as the Father loves the Son, and as the Son loves the Father, and in which God as the Father is loved by the Son and as the Son by the father, is also the love which is addressed by God to man.** [44]

The analysis of *analogia relationis* shows how Barth establishes his understanding of the *imago Dei* and the humanity of Jesus. By it Barth sets forth both relational (formal) and actional (material) aspects of the basic metaphor of covenant, the I-Thou dyad, present between Father and Son in the Godhead, between God and man, and between man and man.

The Basic Form of Humanity

· In the attempt to understand our humanity, we turn from the humanity of Jesus, man *for* other men, to the humanity of man *in general.* But it is difficult to see man in his real humanity because we observe him as a sinner, hence in contradiction to himself. Thus, there are fundamental *differences* between Jesus and ourselves; first, He is *for* man from the beginning; and second, He acts on behalf of man as his deliverer.

On the other hand, there are *similarities* between the humanity of Jesus and our own which are given and revealed in the fact that the man Jesus *can be for man.* Barth says, "Where one being is for others, there is necessarily a common sphere or form of existence in which the 'for' can be possible and effective."[45] Also, God is the creator not just of the man Jesus, but of all men, so that in all men there is a *basic creaturely form,* a creaturely essence which is given them by God. Further, being able to enter into the covenant revealed in Jesus implies a basic form *in common* between the humanity of Jesus and the humanity of man in general.

What then is the common form basic to our humanity? Barth says that the criterion for determining this human form is Jesus Christ, the humanity of Jesus. Accordingly, many definitions of humanity are inadequate. For example, any definition of man in which man is abstracted from the co-existence with his fellowman is false. Any definition of man as a being in and for himself, as a being opposed to or neutral about his fellowman, or wherein his humanity is subsequently or secondarily determined rather than seen as an essential and primary aspect of being with fellowmen, is false or inhuman. Positively stated, ". . . the humanity of each and every man consists in the determination of man's being as a being with others, or rather with other man."[46] "It is not as he is for himself but with others, not in loneliness but in fellowship, that he is genuinely human, that he achieves true humanity, that he corresponds to his determination to be God's covenant-partner."[47] Thus, through the criterion of the humanity of Jesus, Barth establishes a boundary line beyond which man exists in contradiction to his nature, i.e., in inhumanity.[48]

The Humanity of Man as the Being-With-the-Other

The background has been laid for an analysis of the humanity of man as *the being-with-the-other*. From my perspective Barth sets forth the most careful development of the basic form of humanity, the I-Thou relationship, available in theology, philosophy, or the social sciences. It is to be noticed that this definition does not necessarily depend on theology, for much of it has been arrived at by non-theologians or non-Christians, e.g., Buber and Confucius. However, *the criterion of its adequacy and its validity*, Barth says, depends upon theology.[49]

Barth develops an analysis of the "I" proceeding to an analysis of the "I am," to "I am in encounter with the other," to "I am in encounter essentially," to "I am as Thou art." Then he discusses four elements of the history of being-in-encounter.

But, first, Barth discusses what he does *not* mean by humanity. Things which might be said about man as an "empty subject," as he is man *without* his fellowman, have no "categorical" significance in the description of humanity for Barth. For example:

> . . . the fact that I am born and die; that I eat and drink and sleep; that I develop and maintain myself; that beyond this I assert myself in face of others, and even physically propagate my species; that I enjoy and work and plan and fashion and possess; that I acquire and have and exercise powers; that I take part in all the works of the race either accomplished or in process of accomplishment; that in all this I satisfy religious needs and can realize religious possibilities; and that in it all I fulfill my aptitudes as an understanding and thinking, willing and feeling being – all this as such is **not** my humanity.[50]

This if the "field" in which human being either takes place or does not take place, but it is not humanity. Rather, to be human one must exist in this field according to the categories of humanity, as a being *with* his fellowman, and in the encounter of the I and Thou. If man denies himself as essentially with his fellowman, all man's "participation in scholarship and art, politics and economics, civilization and culture" [51] will not reveal his humanity. The crucial question for man's humanity is the *enactment* of this history, i.e., the realization of the encounter in which "I am as thou art."

The four elements of this "horizontal" dimension of man, being-in-encounter follow.

"Being in encounter is (1) a being in which one man looks the other in the eye. The human significance of the eye is that we see one another eye to eye."[52] (Man, not things or the cosmos, sees and is seen. We don't know about animals). A man who is visible to another man is distinct from the one who sees him. There is an over-against-ness of two men as they see one another. When one man looks another in the eye, he lets the other look him in the eye. "To see the other thus means directly to let oneself be seen by him."[53]

More generally, being in encounter is a being in *openness* of the one to the other with a view to and on behalf of the other. In other words, the "I" doesn't hide himself or refuse to be seen by the other but rather the I and the Thou are *open* to one another. As one man is open to another, we give each other something, ". . . an insight into our being."[54] Therefore, as I see you and you see me and we are no longer closed to one another, I am not *for* myself, but *for* thee and thou *for* me. Where openness obtains, humanity begins to occur. This two-sided openness is the first element of humanity.

"Being in encounter consists (2) in the fact that there is mutual speech and hearing."[55] In seeing the other we are limited in our knowing him because we interpret him through our own concepts and by our own standards. Something more than separately formed views and arbitrary conclusions is required on both sides if we are to be in real communication with the other. Unless there is something more than the mutual look, we can still enter into this intercommunication *without* the other.[56]

This step in the I-Thou interaction is speech and hearing, which consists in both the *self-expression* of the I to the thou and its *reception*, as well as the *address* of the I to the thou and its *reception*.

> *Humanity as encounter must* **become** *the event of speech.*
> *And speech means comprehensively reciprocal* **expression**

*and its reciprocal **reception,** reciprocal **address** and its
reciprocal **reception.** All . . . four elements are vital.[57]*

*Being in encounter consists (3) in the fact that we render mutual assistance in
the act of being."*[58] The third step is being *for* one another, however
limited. In the strictest sense Jesus is *for* us, living *for* us, accepting responsibility for us. But in this respect, acting as the Son of God, he differs from us. Therefore, our *for* one another, our assistance to each
other in the basic form of our humanity, is not this kind of *for.*
Nevertheless, our *forness* corresponds to His *forness* so that we can say
that humanity is constituted by rendering mutual assistance to each
other. Our humanity cannot be less than *giving* and *receiving* assistance. What is assistance? For one thing, it is actively standing by the
other, standing so close that one's own action means help and support
to him.

It also means that one does not leave him to his own being and
action, but rather takes part in his anxiety and burden, accepting concern for his life. It means to live with the other. "As we see one another
and speak and listen to one another, we call to one another for assistance."[59] We cannot be *for* him in the strictest sense, only God can
be that, but we can be at his disposal. We can assist in meeting his
needs. We can support but not carry him, give him encouragement
but not victory, alleviate but not liberate. Thus, ". . . humanity consists
in the fact that we need and are capable of mutual assistance."[60] By
his very being man calls for assistance that only fellowman can give, so
when he calls for assistance he calls for fellowman.

However, if I refuse to let myself be helped, others cannot help me,
however much they would like to do so. Thus,

> *My humanity depends on the fact that I am always aware,
> and my action is determined by the awareness, that I need the
> assistance of others as a fish needs water. It depends upon
> my not being content with what I can do for myself, but call-
> ing for the Thou to give me the benefit of his action as
> well.[61]*

This notion of humanity is not idealistic, but ultimately realistic.
Man is not alone, but *with* his fellowman. He needs his help and is
pledged to help him. "To be human, and therefore to act accordingly,

confessing both the need of assistance and the willingness to render it, is supremely natural and not unnatural."[62] It is an obvious thing to do. Not to do so, to be by oneself, not assisting the fellowman, or calling for his assistance, is artificial. All man has to do is to see himself in the situation in which he actually finds himself and not try to construct another alien situation for himself.

"Being in encounter consists (4) in the fact that all the occurrence which we have so far described as the basic form of humanity stands under the sign that it is done on both sides with gladness."[63] We *gladly* see and are seen. We *gladly* speak and listen. We *gladly* receive and offer assistance. This last and final step of humanity, the *gladly,* is the secret of the preceding three stages. Without it, humanity suffers an essential lack and is empty. If man is only human *externally* in the I-Thou interrelationship of seeing, speech, and assistance, but does not do them "gladly," then he is *internally,* and thus essentially, inhuman. The real substance and soul of humanity is in the secret of the gladly.

Is not Barth actually referring to the freedom and gladly of the God-man covenant partnership? Apparently not. Barth says, that man belongs to God is the *great secret* of man. However, in this section he is not speaking of that secret but of a lesser one, the secret of man's creatureliness, his humanity. Even for the person who has not become aware of the covenant-partnership with God, there can be some realization of this human "gladly;" a freedom which is based on man's creaturely form.[64]

However, this lesser secret, the secret of humanity, remains a mystery. It can be indicated, pointed to, but not solved. The "gladly" does not penetrate the secret before which it stands, but stands as the *conditio sine qua non* of humanity.

It cannot be grounded or deduced from elsewhere but can only be affirmed as the living center of the whole. One can say that a *discovery* takes place. But a discovery implies that something is posited and given, not created by man's activity and/or ability. What is it? The gift consists in the fact

> *. . . that the one has quite simply been given the other, and that what he, for his part, has to give is again himself. It is in this being given and giving that there consists the electing and election, the mutual acceptance, the common joy, and therefore the freedom of this encounter.*[65]

Barth disavows the implication that this elaborate description of humanity with its "gladly" is Christian love or *agape*. Too frequently it has been the custom of Christian theologians to depreciate the fullness of humanity in order to contrast it with Christian love. In the process, Christian love has been identified as nothing more than the good humanist would also set forth. As a result the humanist cannot understand the real content of Christian love, and consequently, does not take it seriously. Thus Barth says, "At this final level of the concept of humanity we have *not* been speaking about Christian love."[66,67]

> *On the contrary, we have been speaking of the nature of the human creature. The same man who in the course of his history with God, in the fulfillment of his fellowship with Jesus Christ,* **will also** *participate in and be capable of Christian love for God and his fellow-men as brothers, is as such this creature . . . we have come to know as humanity. Humanity, even as we finally spoke of it in the secret of that free co-existence of man and man, is* **not Christian love,** *but only the natural exercise and actualization of human nature – something which* **formally is on the same level as the corresponding vital functions and natural determinations of other beings which are not men.** [68]

The fact that a man is a man involves the co-existence of man and man ". . . in which the one may be, and will be, the companion, associate, comrade, fellow and helpmate of the other."[69] This is human nature, humanity. The man who is determined "from above" to be the covenant-partner of God, is determined "down below" to the creature – fellow-man. "For all the difference in detail, he always lives with varying degrees of consistency and perfection the life characterized by this nature."[70] Again, *"What we have called humanity can be present and known in varying degrees of perfection and imperfection even where there can be no question of a direct revelation and knowledge of Jesus Christ."*[71] Thus the reality of human nature (humanity) and its recognition are not restricted to the Christian community.

> *The totality which we have described as humanity is the determination of human being as such irrespective of what*

may become of man in the course of his history with God.
We cannot, therefore, expect to hear about Christian love
when the reference is to humanity in the Christian doctrine
of the creature. [72]

Humanity, as the image of God, is a "sign" pointing to man's fulfillment in the covenant relationship with God. Although it is known with clarity through the revelation of God in Christ, humanity does not depend upon that *revelation* for its reality. Since Jesus Christ is the ontological form of *all* humanity in creation whether or not it is *recognized* as such, he is the reality of our humanity and can be and has been described by non-Christian thinkers.

The form of our humanity is the dialogical structure of the I-Thou relationship, of being-in-relationship-to-the-other, of mutually seeing, speaking, and listening, assisting, and doing all this "gladly."

Whole Man: Soul and Body

Barth's understanding of the individual person, whole man, is also dependent on Christology. To see whole man properly one must see him in the context first of real man, the God-man relationship, and second of humanity, the man-man relationship, both set forth in Jesus Christ. The discussion of the person then proceeds from the "outer" relationship with God (Spirit) to the "inner" relationships of soul and body. Finally the particular operations of the soul and body (perceiving, thinking, desiring and willing) are described. As usual, the "parts" are dialectically-dialogically related, no part can be understood without the other, although distinctions are made and priorities given.

The function of the Spirit in redemption brings man into a salvatory relationship with God where whole man is in the process of fulfillment. This has to do with participation in Jesus Christ through the Christian community. But the function of the Spirit *in creation and providence* (preservation) has to do with the relationship between the Creator and the creature, as such, and applies to all persons. Whereas, for Barth, the Spirit *in creation and providence* is most clearly known through Jesus Christ, creation and providence are *not* redemption. They precede it, and are preparatory to it.

When Barth says that man *has* Spirit, it means that God is there *for* him. Every moment that he breathes and lives he has a witness that

God turns to him in His free grace as Creator and Preserver, that He has willed him again and again *as a living being,* and that He has allowed him to become whole soul of his body.[73]

> *Since man* **has** *Him, the Spirit is certainly* **in** *man – in his soul and through his soul in his body too* . . . *But [Spirit]* **is the principle which makes man into a subject.** *The human subject is man as soul, and it is this which is created and maintained by the Spirit. But* . . . *the Spirit lives His own superior* . . . *life over against the soul and the human subject. He is not bound to the life of the human subject.[76]*

Barth makes a clear distinction between Spirit and soul, so that God is not identified with man, but the Spirit is efficacious in maintaining the soul in creation, however indirectly.

Let us see what Barth says about the soul and body in their interconnection and particularity.

Soul and Body in Their Interconnexion

Man is constituted as a unity within which there is an anti-thesis. There is creaturely *life* and creaturely *being.*[75] The former refers to the soul and the latter to the body, each in its interconnexion. Creaturely *life* is a *living* being, an individual *life* of a body which emphasizes man's *temporal existence.* Creaturely being is a living *being,* an individual life of the body which emphasizes *spatial form.* Man is one, i.e., an inwardly united and self-enclosed subject; therefore with man we speak not only of interconnexion, but also of unity.[76] This understanding of the soul and body relationship eliminates false spiritualization and false materialization. It also eliminates the dualistic interpretations of body and soul that have plagued Christian thought and had such devastating consequences for ethics.

The soul, as movement *in time,* as inner, fulfills itself in specific perceptions, experiences, thoughts, feelings, and resolutions, but it needs the body as movement *in space,* as outer, as means to execute the functions of the soul. Therefore, every trivializing of the body, or removal of the body from the soul, jeopardizes the soul. Every denial of the body is a denial of the soul.

The soul is life, the independent life of a corporeal being. Life in general means *capacity* for action, self-movement, self-activity, self-determination.[77] Independent life, the life of a specific subject, does not emerge except where the capacity for action of a corporeal being is not bound to a specific point in space. The function of the soul is related to time, hence the soul and its functions are not spatially bound. This is one basis for Barth's affirmation of freedom as *self-determination* in "natural man."

However, the process whereby we become conscious of ourselves as independent and self-determining is not merely an act of the soul; it also involves the body. As I live, I find myself able to become conscious that I am a soul.

> *And as I make use of this ability, my life itself and therefore my soul, executes a return movement to itself. I come to myself, discover myself and become assured of myself. It belongs to my capacity for action that I continuously do this ...[78]*

This life I live is the independent life of my physical body. This act is performed by the material body as well as my soul. Without the material body, I cannot be aware of objects different from myself, "I cannot distinguish myself from others as the object identical with myself, and cannot therefore recognize myself as a subject."[79] Consequently, I have need of the corporeal senses to determine myself as an object of my knowledge, which is decisive for my self-consciousness and is presupposed in my self-knowledge as subject. If the act, in which we become conscious of ourselves, is not both a soulful and corporeal act, the one within the other, then it does not happen at all. The soul and body can be distinguished but not separated, for I cannot answer for myself without at the same time answering for my body. Thus there is an interconnexion and unity between soul and body of the human being. Barth says that all rejection of this interconnexion, or attempts to deny it, can only mean a distortion of the nature of man.

Soul and Body in Their Operations

As man is in *this* relationship with God, i.e., in providence or preservation, as he has Spirit, two presuppositions emerge in regard to his creaturely nature. First, man is a *percipient being,* and second, he is an *active being.* But these operations refer to the functions of the whole self (body and soul) rather than to the distinction between the soul and body.

Initially, perception (percipient being) is understood as a compound act of two functions: *awareness,* which is external and related to the body; and *thought,* which is internal and related to the soul. However, the situation is more complicated than this, for the act of perception is single and the act of the whole man.[80] Thus not only the body but also the soul has *awareness,* and not only the soul but also the body *thinks.* Therefore, awareness is not only with the body. The body is the body of man's soul, yet he does not execute this act as soul, but as body, i.e., by means of his organs. Again, *thinking* is not only with the soul but with the body, the brain, nerves, and the whole organism. As man thinks, he leads the life of his body and is disturbed by what disturbs it, and when he dies, thinking ceases. So both awareness and thinking are functions of the soul *and* the body. There is a distinction without separation.

However, Barth says, the acts of awareness and thought, though they involve both soul and body, are *primarily* of the soul and *secondarily* of the body. An order exists between the functions. There is a special relationship of the body ascribed to the act of awareness (the outside of perception), although the soul also has awareness. This awareness of the soul is only possible as the body in its outer form is open to the other. "Body is the openness of soul. Body is the capacity in man in virtue of which another *can come* to him and *be for* him. Man has awareness, therefore, in so far as he is the soul of his *body.*"[81]

On the other hand, there is a special relation of the soul to *thinking* (the inner side of perception). "When I think, the other which I perceive *comes into* me, after it has come to me."[82] But the soul is man's self-consciousness taking place in and essentially related to the body, for the soul does not think without the body.

The soul is the capacity in virtue of which he can make another his own, in virtue of which the other can be not only *for him* but in him. Man thinks, therefore, insofar as he is the *soul* of his body.

Now Barth proceeds to the discussion of man as *active being.* As there is an inner and outer aspect to perception, so too there is an inner and outer aspect to action. The outer side of action is *desire* and the inner side is *will.* But, as soon will be seen, these are only functional distinctions within an essential unity. Finally, it will be seen that the same kind of dialectical-dialogical relationship which characterizes most of Barth's thought, wherein he speaks of relationships in terms of unity, differentiation, and order, will relate perception to action.

These functions of desiring and willing are differentiated for the purpose of understanding them as separate, yet related, having the same kind of relationship between them as we saw when Barth spoke of awareness and thinking. Although there is no partition between desiring and willing – both are soulful and bodily, and both are primarily of the soul and secondarily of the body –there is a *special relationship* of *desiring* to the *bodily* nature and *willing* to the *soulful* nature.

In the operation of *desire* the nerves of the brain and body participate. (Awareness is also involved [external bodily action] because particular sensible experiences [awareness] release in man particular desires and urges.) Thus, there is a special relation between desiring and the body. However "...the urge as such ...does not constitute the desire or aversion. If I am to desire or shun, it is necessary that I not only be *aware* of the *urge* concerned but that I affirm it, making it my own and committing myself ...to it [as a particular desire]."[83] That a man can do this or not do this, that he can accept or shun the material (urge) is not merely the response of his nerves, although it is that, it is also his "own affair."[84] This is where his will, as a function of his soul, participates in his desiring. This is what constitutes the most decisive participation of man's soul in his desiring. This indicates how desiring is not strictly a function of the body, but also a function of the soul (the will).

It is a matter of willing (and thus primarily a matter of the soul)that man is not only the object of desire, but also an object of man's will. Barth says, "...that I have a certain intention and come to a resolution with respect to it or to my relation to it; that I set it before me and put myself into the corresponding movement in relation to it,"[85] is a matter of my will. Desiring is presupposed. By the operation of the will a choice is made among several desires, so the self does not will everything it desires. To will means *to make up one's mind* (involving thought and awareness as well as desire)in respect to a desire. To will means that the "I" chooses. The "I" determines itself and its activity for the execution or the non-execution of its desiring. (What Barth describes as "will" is the process of the soul, but it can be realized only because the soul is the *soul* of the *body*.) It is the "I" who decides and determines the relation to the desiring of the body. When it elevates itself above, it becomes aware of itself only when it realizes the distinction between its desires and makes use of the power of will over them. When the "I" wills, it abandons its neutrality to itself and its desiring and takes a position over against them both. This is the act of the soul, the man's act. Once again Barth affirms freedom as self-determination or choice.

In summary, man is the percipient and active soul of the body which puts into effect his perception and action. Soul and body, and perception and action cannot be seen without each other, although they are not interchangeable. They have different functions, and one precedes the other. On both sides of perception and action there is a primacy of the soul, but at no level is the soul found without the body. Although there is a primacy of the soul, at no level can it be said that the soul only thinks and wills; it also senses and desires. Barth says,

> ... [man] does not think without sensing [awareness], nor will without desiring. But when he thinks and wills, he stands at a distance from his sensing [awareness] and desiring ... He becomes an object to himself. In this freedom to stand at a distance, pass under review and become object, he conducts himself as soul of his body. The body lacks this freedom. It can only participate in it.[86]

Although Barth's method for arriving at his description of whole man differs significantly from the physical and social sciences, his conclusions overlap with some basic insights of humanistic psychology. He affirms, with humanistic psychology, the interdependence and unity of body and soul. He refuses both materialistic and spiritualistic reductionisms. At the same time he affirms the distinctive functions of the body-soul complex – thinking, awareness, willing, and desiring, but always dialectically related and with a concern for the priority of certain of the functions – thinking and willing.

One must remember that whereas whole man is presupposed in the discussion of real man and humanity, Barth's chosen method for unfolding the discussion is significant –from real man to humanity to whole man. Barth would be unhappy if we saw these three aspects of person in linear sequence. His dialogical-dialectical method compels us to see them simultaneously interrelated. One must also remember that the God-person covenant, fulfilled in Jesus Christ, contexts and frames the discussion of the above. Whether this method, sequence and order holds up under long term critical assault one cannot judge. What one can assert is that Barth's revolutionary theological moves radically recast a large number of theological issues, not the least of which are anthropological. Persons are to be understood as essentially determined by linkages with God and fellow humans. They are essentially interrelational and interactional, defined by the peculiar dynamics of the covenantal relationship demonstrated through the God-person Jesus Christ.

Notes:

1. *Church Dogmatics* III/2, pp. 311-316. An important issue, for many, has to do with the superordination of man to woman, as he develops the connection, differentiation and order of the primary example in man's and woman's creation (Genesis 2), as well as the husband made head over the wife and head coverings (I Cor. 11:1-16). While Barth does not fall into the traditional patriarchial and hierarchical pattern, primarily because Jesus Christ is understood as *both* superordinate and subordinate, Lord and servant, nevertheless, elevating this structural differentiation (the only one) of human existence to theological-ethical prominence raises questions of whether a "too serious" reading of biblical texts does violence to the more important insight of the particularity of human beings, as they are in interrelationship with one another. Even within his theological-biblical framework one has difficulties when one refers this interpretation to God in Himself (the Triunity) and to Jesus Christ. The quasi-biblical literalism at this point seems unnecessarily to blunt the profundity of his major point about humanity.

2. Stuart D. McLean, "A Functional-Relational Understanding of Covenant as a Distinctive Metaphor" (Unpublished, 1980).

3. *Church Dogmatics*, III/1, pp. 94ff, pp. 228ff.

4. Cf. Thomas S. Kuhn, *The Structure of Scientific Revolutions* (Chicago: The University of Chicago, 1962).

5. These arguments are too lengthy to be made here. See *Church Dogmatics*, III/2, pp. 25ff.

6. Barth uses the generic man and manhood, and fellowman throughout the *Church Dogmatics*, while, contrary to my usual practice and intention, I have followed him in this essay.

7. *Church Dogmatics*, III/2, pp. 68-71.

8. Ibid., p. 75.

9. Some characteristics of man defined by non-Christians are true symptoms, but we do not know which are true except as they are viewed from the perspective of real man. Barth discusses these other anthropologies (naturalistic, ethical, idealistic, existentialistic, and theistic) in the light of these six criteria. The discussion follows at this point in the text (pp. 76-132). It is a fascinating and important discussion. Unfortunately, it cannot be summarized in the space available.

10. *Church Dogmatics*, III/2, p. 142.

11. Election means a special *decision* (of God) with a special *intention* (the delivery of man) in relation to a special *object* (man). The decision is God's free choice as an expression of His love.

12. Ibid., p. 145.
13. Ibid., p. 150.
14. Ibid.
15. Ibid., p. 157. Italics mine.
16. Ibid., p. 160. Italics mine.
17. Ibid.
18. Ibid., pp. 161-62.
19. Ibid., p. 166.
20. Ibid.
21. Ibid., p. 167.
22. Ibid.
23. Ibid., p. 168.
24. Ibid. Italics mine.
25. Ibid., p. 175. Italics mine.
26. Ibid., p. 207.
27. Ibid., p. 208. Italics mine.
28. Ibid. Italics mine.
29. Ibid., pp. 214-215.
30. Ibid., p. 215.
31. Ibid.
32. Ibid., p. 216. Italics mine.
33. Ibid.
34. Ibid.
35. See following discussion on *analogia relationis*.
36. Ibid., p. 217.
37. Ibid., p. 218.
38. Ibid.
39. Ibid.
40. The crucial link between the inner Godhead (Father-Son) and the humanity of Jesus (man-man, hence our humanity) is the being of the man Jesus for God. Since action and being define each other, for Barth, God's act of action of deliverance in Jesus Christ means His being and reality *ad extra*. Ensconced within action is the form of the relationship. This link establishes the relationship between God in Himself and humanity.
41. Ibid., p. 219.
42. The *imago Dei* has both dynamic (material, as defined by Barth) and form (structural) elements. Although we are lifting up the aspect of *form* for consideration at this point, he is also speaking of the material, actional, or dynamic dimension of the relationship. Common definitions of the *imago Dei*, "reason," "personality," "responsibility," or "original righteousness," are not shared by Barth.
43. John D. Godsey, ed., *Karl Barth's Table Talk* (Richmond, Va., John Knox Press, 1962), p. 57.
44. *Church Dogmatics*, III/2, p. 220. Italics mine.
45. Ibid., p. 223.
46. Ibid., p. 243.
47. Ibid.

48.	Barth elucidates this statement: Humanity is described as a being of man *with the other*. But only the humanity of Jesus can be absolutely described as being *for* man. The extent to which the being of the one man with the other also includes a certain being of the one *for* the other will have to be shown.

	Barth describes ". . . humanity as a being of the *one* man with the other." (Ibid. Italics mine.)

	"Fundamentally, we speak on both sides in the singular and not in the plural. We are not thinking here in terms of individualism. But the basic form of humanity . . . is a being of the one man with the other, and where one is with many, or many with one, or many with many, the humanity consists in the fact that in truth, in the basic form of this occurrence, one is always with another, and this basic form persists. Humanity is not in isolation, and it is in pluralities only when these are constituted by genuine duality, by the singular on both sides.

	The singular, not alone but in this duality, is the presupposition without which there can never be humanity in the plural." Ibid., pp. 243 - 244.

49.	"We need not be surprised that there are approximations and similarities. Indeed, in this very fact we may even see a certain confirmation of our results – a confirmation which we do not need and which will not cause us any particular excitement, but of which, in view of its occurrence, we shall not be ashamed. Why should there not be confirmations of this kind? *In this context we are not speaking of the Christian in particular but of man in general,* and therefore of something which has been the object of all kinds of 'worldly,' i.e., non-Christian wisdom. And surely it need not be, and is not actually, the case, that this worldly wisdom with its very different criteria has always been mistaken, always seeking humanity in the direction of Idealism and finally of Nietzsche, and therefore establishing and describing it as humanity without the fellow-man, the humanity of man in isolation. It would be far more strange if not the slightest trace had ever been found of fellow-humanity, of the humanity of I and Thou." (Ibid., p. 277. Italics mine.)

50.	Ibid., p. 249 Italics mine.

51.	Ibid.

52.	Ibid., p. 250. Italics mine.

53.	Ibid.

54.	Ibid., p. 251.

55.	Ibid., p. 252. Italics mine.

56.	The complexity of Barth's thought is at most points difficult to summarize without doing it injustice: however, the problem is especially accute when dealing with his analysis on the very complex interactional phenomena of speech and hearing.

57.	Ibid., p. 253. Italics mine.

58.	Ibid., p. 260. Italics mine.

59.	Ibid., p. 262.

60.	Ibid.

61.	Ibid., p. 263.

62.	Ibid., p. 264.

63.	Ibid., p. 265. Italics mine.

64.	This is not redemption, but neither is it independent from God's constant action; rather, it is related to God's activity operating in creation and providence.

65.	Ibid. p. 272.

66.	Ibid., p. 274. Italics mine.

67.   Christian love or agape "... is the action and attitude of the man who only *becomes* real and can only be understood in the course of his history with God. Love is the new gratitude of those who *have come to know* God as the Creator as the merciful Deliverer. As such it is the gracious gift of the Holy Ghost shed abroad in the hearts of Christians convicted of sin against God and outrage against themselves. ... In love they respond to the revelation of the covenant fulfilled in Jesus Christ, in which God comes to them as their merciful Father, Lord and Judge, and they see their fellow-men as brothers and sisters, i.e., as those who have sinned with them and found grace with them." (Ibid., p. 275. Italics mine.)

68.   Ibid., p. 275. Italics mine.

69.   Ibid., p. 276.

70.   Ibid.

71.   Ibid. Italics mine.

72.   Ibid.

73.   Ibid., p. 363.

74.   Ibid., p. 364. Italics mine.

75.   Ibid., p. 367.

76.   Ibid., p. 371.

77.   Ibid., p. 374.

78.   Ibid., p. 375.

79.   Ibid.

80.   Ibid., p. 400.

81.   Ibid., p. 401. Italics mine.

82.   Ibid. Italics mine

83.   Ibid., p. 408. Italics mine.

84.   Ibid.

85.   Ibid.

86.   Ibid., p. 418.

The First Commandment As Axiom For Theology: A Model for the Unity of Dogmatics and Ethics.

Martin Rumscheidt

I

On March 10, 1933 Karl Barth delivered an address in Copenhagen entitled "Das erste Gebot als theologisches Axiom." Two days later he repeated it in Aarhus.[1] It was the time of Barth's first visit to Denmark. (Thirty years later he returned to accept the prestigious Sonning Prize, awarded for outstanding contribution to European culture.) It was also the time when Adolf Hitler, six weeks in the Reich-Chancellery, was promulgating the Law for the Reorganization of the Civil Service which was eventually to cost Barth his position at the University of Bonn, the prelude to his expulsion from Germany in 1935. The Reichstag-building had gone up in smoke on February 27. and, the next day, Hindenburg signed a far-reaching decree for "the protection of the people and the state". Hitler had laid the foundation for his strategy to deal with what he called "treason against the German people". The so-called "fire-decrees" were, in fact, the legal instruments of the Nazi's permanent terror.[2] The composition of Barth's address falls, therefore, directly into the period of these and similar events in the political scene of Germany.

Like other writings of his, it is remotely possible to read that address 'as if nothing had happened'. Barth had been busy for nearly two decades fashioning a way of theology that rigorously honoured the biblical assertion that God is God and that we humans may not speak of God by speaking of ourselves in a loud voice. There is, consequently, a need for establishing in the area of dogmatics as clear an injunction as in the area of ethics which declares: "I am the Lord, your God; you are to have no other gods beside me!" Barth's address may be seen, then, as his pressing on with the task of reforming theology, that essential discipline in and for the Church's witness to the God of Holy Scripture.

Such a view is not totally inadequate; it is, instead, inappropriate to the author of that address. It must unfortunately, remain unanswered whether Barth would have acceded to the characterization of certain aspects of his work in terms of categories like 'political' or 'critical' theology *as they are understood by us in the nineteen-eighties*. Yet, it is the former category which is to be applied in this essay to Barth's address, "The First Commandment as an Axiom of Theology", in order to demonstrate the unity of dogmatics and ethics so typical of the theology of Karl Barth.

II

To this day minds are divided as to whether, how or with what success Barth took part in politics. Some observers even suggest that in regard to this question Barth's interpreters are to be divided, like those of Hegel, into right and left wingers. - Some factual observations are in order here. One can still visit today the parsonage of Safenwil where Barth, ministering to the congregation from 1911 till 1921, met not only the people with whom he organized labour-unions for textile-workers but also the owners and managers of their factories, people opposed to those efforts and who, in anger, called him the "red pastor". And just down the road, near the railroad-station, there still stands the union-hall where Barth delivered numerous 'political' speeches. On January 26. 1915 he joined the Swiss Social Democratic Party.[3] For nearly a decade after his arrival in Germany to teach at the Universities of Göttingen and Münster, he engaged in no such overt political activities. Then, in March 1930, he moved to Bonn where he succeeded Otto Ritschl, son of the renowned Albrecht Ritschl, in the chair of Systematic Theology. A year later, on May 1., Barth joined the German Socialist Party. To him "the German political situation was 'like sitting in a car which was driven by a man who is either incompetent or drunk' " as he wrote to Thurneysen.[4] The general elections in the Evangelical Church of July 23. 1933, even though strictly an ecclesial matter, were of a highly political nature as the issue was support of or opposition to Hitler and his platform for

Germany. One of the factions seeking election was called 'For the Freedom of the Gospel'; Barth was one of its candidates and won his election.[5]

It was foreign for most Germans that a theological figure would join a political party and, to top it off, then write a cabinet-minister about it and explain why he had done so.[6] Barth met more with suspicion than with solidarity, even during the Church-Struggle, when he was clearly the best ally church-people could have asked for. One reason for that was the generally negative attitude of German pastors and theologians towards the Weimar Republic. For most of them it went against the grain to become republican. Emanuel Hirsch, Barth's colleague at Göttingen, repeatedly assailed Weimar as an extremely distressing form of existence for Germans since they had no real authority in that government. Another highly regarded Lutheran theologian, Paul Althaus of Erlangen, developed a similar critique on the basis of the notion of "peoplehood" (*Volkstum*). When the National Socialists took power and it became clear that they had behind them an equally illustrious array of academics as had Kaiser Wilhelm II, when ninety-three signed a public manifesto of identification with his war policies on August 1. 1914, Barth wrote to the newly appointed Minister of Science, Arts and Education, Bernhard Rust. He told him in that letter, dated April 4. 1933, that, as a citizen residing in Germany, he would offer the new state the same loyalty which he had observed his own colleagues offer during the last twelve years to the Weimar Republic, given their rightist political orientation. That was, in itself, not only a repudiation of the enthusiastic reception the new state was enjoying but also an announcement of a different outlook on the theological enterprise that had to be engaged in. Barth went on to write: "My academic activities will not become involved in opposing the old system nor in supporting the new one. They will be shaped entirely by the imperatives of theological objectivity. I cannot accept the demand to leave the Socialist Party of Germany as a condition for the continuation of my teaching-position simply because I cannot expect any good to come from the denial of my political convictions, from the neglect to declare them openly, which such a step would imply. No good can come from such a thing for my students, the Church, the German people."[7] This was no declaration of resistance; Barth did want to stay in Bonn. But it was an indication that, as a theologian, he could not remain aloof from the political dimensions of the day and his personal involvement in them which by then had clearly become a matter of going against the stream.

There are autobiographical comments about that period which reinforce this conclusion. They show that Barth saw an urgent need for resistance against the new regime because a false 'god' was being worshipped by the Germans. In his judgement the policy of the National Socialists on religion and Church was designed to achieve a complete *Gleichschaltung,* homogenization, of the racial and imperialistic programme of the state and the faith and action of the Christian churches. That meant bringing into congruence the gospel of Jesus Christ and what Hermann Rauschning called the nihilism of the Nazis. [8] (In 1940 Rauschning, a one-time member of the Prussian General Synod, published a book about his conversations with Hitler in which he quotes him as saying that he intended to eradicate utterly Christianity from German soil. "One is either Christian or German, not both."[9]) In the first of his articles for the *Christian Century,* (speaking about the decade from 1928 to 1938, Barth wrote the following:

> *Doubtless between that time and today a considerable change in my position and line of action has taken place, not with regard to the meaning and direction of my accumulated knowledge but rather with regard to its application. For this change I am indebted to the führer!*
>
> *What happened? First of all this happened - and this one must keep clearly in mind while seeing the whole - there was given me a gigantic revelation of human lying and brutality on the one hand, and of human stupidity and fear on the other. And then this happened: In the summer of 1933, the German church, to which I belonged as a member and a teacher, found itself in the greatest danger concerning its doctrine and order. It threatened to become involved in a new heresy strangely blended of Christianity and Germanism, and to come under the domination of the so-called "German Christians" - a danger prompted by the successes of National Socialism and the suggestive power of its ideas . . .*
>
> *All that was indeed what in America is called an 'experience' and is, as such, so highly regarded there. But just what was the situation with regard to this 'experience'? In*

that first series of pamphlets, **Theologische Existenz heute,** *published in June 1933, I still had nothing essentially new to say. At that time I said rather just what I had always tried to say, namely, that beside God we can have no other gods, that the Holy Spirit of the Scriptures is enough to guide the church in all truth, and that the grace of Jesus Christ is all-sufficient for the forgiveness of our sins and the ordering of our lives. But now, suddenly, I had to say the same thing in a situation where it could no longer have the slightest vestige of an academic theory. Without my wanting it, or doing anything to facilitate it, this had of necessity to take on the character of a summons, a challenge, a battle cry, a confession . . .*

Accordingly, the ensuing repetition of my doctrine and teaching became - of its own accord and paralleling its deepening because of this new situation - practice, decision, action. And so one day, to my own surprise most of all, I found myself standing in the very midst of church politics, engaged in collaboration in the deliberations and decisions of the Confessional Church which had been assembling since 1934. . .

What was and what is at stake? Simply this, to hold fast to and in a completely new way to understand and practice the truth that God stands above all gods, and that the church in **Volk** *and society has, under all circumstances, and over against the state, her own task, proclamation, and order, determined for her in the Holy Scriptures. . . . there could have been no other outcome than that this truth of the freedom of the church, despite the claims of National Socialism, should come to signify not only a 'religious' decision, not only a decision of church policy, but also and* **ipso facto** *a political decision. A political decision, namely,* **against** *a state which as a totalitarian state cannot recognize any task, proclamation, and order other than its own, nor acknowledge any other God than it itself, and which therefore in proportion to its development had of necessity to undertake the oppression of the Christian church and the suppression of all human right and freedom. Behind this heresy, which I saw penetrating into the church, there stood from the very beginning the one who soon stepped out as the far more dangerous*

> *adversary, the one hailed at the beginning - and not least by many*
> *Christians - as deliverer and saviour: Hitler, himself the per-*
> *sonification of National Socialism. The church-theological conflict*
> *contained within itself the political conflict, and it was no for-*
> *tuitous happening that it revealed itself more and more as a politi-*
> *cal conflict . . .*
>
> *The antichristian and therefore antihuman essence of National*
> *Socialism revealed itself more and more distinctly. At the same*
> *time its influence over the remainder of Europe alarmingly in-*
> *creased in proportion. The lies and brutality, as well as the stu-*
> *pidity and fear, grew and have long since grown far beyond the*
> *frontiers of Germany. And Europe does not understand the danger*
> *in which it stands. Why not? Because it does not understand the*
> *First Commandment. Because it does not see that National*
> *Socialism means a conscious, radical, and systematic transgres-*
> *sion of this First Commandment.[10]*

As a man experienced in party-politics and, consequently, in political activity and as a theologian sharply alert to the perduring urge of
theology and Church to fashion links with philosophical systems and
secular powers in order to secure relevance and authority for the gospel, Barth moved decisively in 1933 to isssue a *theological* battle-cry to
the *political* order of the day precisely because that order had brought
the Church - once again - to sin against God. The ethics for political life
had to be a faithful theology; the theology called for had to be a political ethics if there were to be no other gods beside the God of Sarah and
Abraham. - What led to such a perception?

III

In September 1930 the National Socialists (N.S.D.A.P.) became the
strongest opposition party in the German parliament. The public discussions about this party were regarded by many as political discussions, that is to say, church-folk took the issue to be one of politics
and not of doctrine or religion. But during the next two years certain
events occurred that created the awareness that the Nazi's victory
would lead to problems of a different kind. With hindsight the story is
clear but then what was actually happening was so novel and un-
predictable to most Germans (and not only Germans!) that theology
and Church could catch on only with difficulty.

During the twenties some people had begun to say that a genuine engagement of the current political situation was conditional for a right understanding of the Word of God for us. For example, Emanuel Hirsch had stated that evangelical preaching was made possible only through a final and conscious solidarity with the fate and destiny of the German people, since those to whom that preaching was addressed were the brothers and sisters of that people and destiny. For him this was an internal problem of theological hermeneutics to be discussed like any other theological matter. And as long as this sort of populism was nurtured in one among several political groups, a political theology was one among other available theological options. Once National Socialism came along this changed dramatically. The adherents of this political theology now claimed that the ascendancy of the Nazis was not a political matter, not the fortuitous rise of this rather than another party to power, but was a theological matter: God had willed it, God's triumph was seen here by those who had eyes to see. Here is the hand of God at work in history and they who refuse solidarity with this national, this people's movement refuse solidarity with none other than the living God. What was really happening was that this political theology had subsumed in principle the Church's confession under, had evaporated it in, a political notion. Between a decided political theologian (of this genre) and an opponent there could be no community in principle.

Statements by Althaus and Hirsch give a good impression of this. Responding to an international, ecumenical gathering in Hamburg, meeting in June 1931, they declared in a joint statement that in face of the "continuing terrible war against Germany, all ecclesial relations to other bodies outside Germany should be broken off. In our present situation there can be no more genuine care for community than the demolition of the kind of deceptive aura [as that reigning at that gathering]."[11] Separately Hirsch said that the schism in the German conscience was terribly deep, that there was in fact now a drastic alienation of Protestant Christianity from the German consciousness. Only a radical will for truth -which meant the truth about Germany's destiny - could overcome the utter bankruptcy of the ecumenical movement in this enslaved Germany.[12] (It is necessary to state here that neither he nor Althaus were members of the N.S.D.A.P. at that time; Althaus, in fact, never joined.) Some time after Hirsch had made that declaration, Althaus stated that he gave himself unreservedly to the National Socialist movement since it did not really coincide with its external form as a political party nor its internal form as an ideology. In its inmost core National Socialism consists of the determined will of freedom on the part of the German youth; in that movement the injured pride of our great people, but also the brutal threat to its existence, has reached its strongest and most passionate expression.[13] (One wonders whether Althaus was aware of the remarkable parallelism of that comment to Karl Marx' dictum about religion as the expression of and the protest against real distress.)

Althaus, Hirsch and others made solidarity with the fate and destiny of the German people the precondition for responsible theological discourse; they had to make a separation between "movement" and "ideology" and demand solidarity with the movement in order to discern criteria for a critique of ideology. The consequence of a political theology forced them to bind the possibility of Christian community to conditions which Christian theology had never recognized as conditions at all. In addition, these conditions were from the outset exclusive: destructive of the Church!

While this political theology stipulated the engagement of a given political situation as conditional for the right hearing and understanding of God's Word, Barth's theology stipulated the sovereign action of God's Word as conditional for the right understanding of that political situation. Barth refused to regard such political theology even as a *Bindestrichtheologie*, a theology linked by a hyphen to another entity such as a culture-theology. For him such theology was plain heresy.

An address of early 1931 expresses his unease; it is entitled "Die Not der evangelischen Kirche" and he delivered it in Berlin on January 31, in Bremen on February 14 and in Hamburg the next day.[14] He distinguishes between an essential, necessary and healthy distress which arises for the evangelical Church from the fact that it is a church under the cross and a non-essential, unnecessary and unhealthy distress which arises for the Church when it is ashamed of the gospel and does not accept or recognize this distress. The former must be affirmed while the latter must be resisted. As examples of the latter Barth cited the assimilation of the message of the Church to categories like the current ideas of destiny, authority, order, and the like. He cited particularly the hyphenating of Christianity and race. What the German people needed, he said, was an *evangelical* Church and not a *German* evangelical Church.

A Church which affirms the necessary distress need not be ashamed of being in *that* distress and try to conceal it. It is, indeed, to give witness to it and thereby give God glory. Whenever, wherever and to the extent to which the Church exists in *that* form of visibility there will be no need to be distressed. Existence in those syntheses which hyphenations create will inevitably lead to shame. And the shame is the futile striving to be a *pompa ecclesia*, a pompous "outfit" as Karl Kupisch used to render that term.[15] (In 1924 an ecclesiast commented that when one compares the Church's parliamentarianism with that of the state, one could not escape noticing abundant senility, unworthy squabbling and empty mills here and dignity, active energy and ample achievement there.) A *pompa ecclesia* seeks to stress its public commission in slogans such as that of Bishop Otto Dibelius: the century of the Church. Such phrases, Barth said, fail to distinguish between confession of faith and contemplation of history. "I am aware that my words are harsh ones but I must not suppress them. As far as I can tell what is being proclaimed as gospel in the average sermon of our churches is, in spite of all the appeals to Scripture and all the Luther-pathos of these days, mysticism spiced with a bit of morality or morality spiced with a bit of mysticism and not the word of the cross as the Reformers saw it. Put in biblical language, it is an ideology of an elevated middle class that comes to expression here."[16] Dibelius was among the listeners and, eight days later, he responded in the same hall with a counter-address. He presented himself as a pragmatist and declared that he was no theologian or Christian theorist. Rather, he said, he was a man of Christian love and practice. Arguing that Barth, a Swiss, could of course not sense in its depth what moved the German heart in these days, [17] Dibelius climaxed his address with Luther's word: "For my Germans was I born, them will I serve."[18] The combination of German and Evangelical had once again emerged unscathed. (Responding to Barth's pamphlet *Theologische Existenz heute,* Hirsch also stated that Barth could not possibly understand the Germans, after all he was a bourgeois and a democrat.) [19]

The crescendo, jubilating the German fatherland that was loved with a burning love, grew and grew. The "Faith-Movement German Christians" moved from victory to victory. At Pentecost 1933, Walter Künneth and Helmuth Schreiner published a book called *Die Nation vor Gott;* each contributed three articles and together they wrote the foreword. Among other things they said the following there:

> *The epoch-making events of the first months of the year have given a new face to the German nation. The indestructible will of the Germans for self-preservation, unbroken by Versailles, has pushed its way towards political embodiment in a monumental national movement under the leadership of Adolf Hitler and with the blessing of the aged President. In conjunction with the heralded tradition of Prusso-German history and borne by the best populist forces, a new Reich of the German Nation is arising. It is to grow struggling against inner disunity and outer threats and this task calls all who love Germany to the front of the nation.*
>
> *This book, begun at a time when the swastikas did not yet wave over our land, can have no other aim in this hour of national awakening than to assist in the new upbuilding of the Reich. Seeking to do so, we proceed from the basic conviction that the great work of national renewal can be accomplished with benediction only if it is done in concert with eternal forces, over which people and state have no disposal, if it is done in obedience to God's orders and measured against God's relentless truth. Thus, the German nation stands before God in this hour of its destiny's reversal. As so often in its history, it will be decisive for the future of the Reich whether this claim from God's revelation to our people is heard or not. Our deliberations are meant to assist in calling for this ultimate and deep self-reflection which irrevocably leads to an encounter with God and then to lead forward to the existential task of giving that reflection political embodiment. We seek to give greater depth to our national thinking and to root it in the biblical revelation. At issue is the Church's theological word about the inner questions concerning the rebirth of our nation. And this word knows itself to be unconditionally responsible before the truth of the revelation of Christ; it also knows itself to be responsible for the life of the nation to which this word is spoken in deep love and solidarity with its fate. A populist state and our becoming a nation in this Reich need today more than ever a church and an evangelical proclamation that speak out of a super-*

> *terrestrial power bound to the authority of God. It is one of*
> *the burning tasks of this day to clarify from a position above*
> *the political the pending questions of a national politics of*
> *state and people, a politics rooted in faith. ... Agreement in*
> *every point is not what we seek, but it is essential that every*
> *discussion be shaped by the joyous will to be this nation and*
> *by the understanding of the Church's unique task in the*
> *totality of the people. Service to truth is our decisive service:*
> *the nation expects it and Church and theology are called to*
> *it. ... The Nation before God! This appeal of fate constrains*
> *us all, in the midst of all the passionate movement of our days*
> *and the concomitant, necessary urge to act, to hold still before*
> *the call of the Lord of history. [20]*

A characteristic feature of the argumentation that Barth faced was the alarming *habitus* of the German Christians to downgrade foundational, theological reflection in favor of their programs and assertions. One sees that, for example, in the minutes of a meeting which two pastors from Lübeck had on April 20. 1933 with the national leader of the German Christians, Joachim Hossenfelder. They enquired from him what the ecclesial politics of the Movement was to be. Among other things, they report Hossenfelder to have said that "the 'Faith-Movement German Christians' has no particular theology or dogmatics. Theology is nonsense; it interposes itself between people and Church. The confessional basis will, of course, stand but ministers now will need to obey, not to think. Our goal is to revolutionize the churches from below and to create a church-folk. Engage people from the SA for your congregations, people who have no positions of responsibility yet, preferably with a 'clean vest'; they need know nothing of theology. Let such people run things for you."[21] There is a stated preference of an ecclesiastical sergeant-major type over a theologically trained pastor.

Althaus, Hirsch and the renowned Reformation historian, Heinrich Bornkamm, were members of that 'faith-movement'. That *they* would not share the denigration of theology may be safely assumed, yet they seemed to accept the goals of the movement. In their theologies they spoke of the 'orders of creation' which they expressed in connection with the conviction that there was a communality of kind, of folk-ness and of history which had for Germans an obligatory nature. They pleaded for a recovery of certain great orders of life; after the era of individualism and secularism, in which fundamental values of life had been ignored and the individual robbed of sustaining ties, it was imperative to resist any further atomizing of folk-unity and to create new space for reflection on the primal factors of human community. These orders of creation, to be seen in marriage, family, people and state, were called by this name because God gives our sinful world its life and order out of divine, creative will and power. What people had in mind one can readily assess from their attacks on Versailles, the League of Nations, the Faith and Order Movement or the Stockholm Practical Christianity Group. International organizations were suspect because they relativized the orders of creation.

How was one to respond criticality in face of such a curious anti-theological stance that went with a specific theological outlook that supported a pronounced mythology of German folk-community? It is surprising to some extent that the response was shaped by theology rather than by ecclesial politics. Karl Barth made such a response, but his was not the only one. Another began by asking whether the Church, having been put into the quandary by history itself, had the inner resources to interpret this great transition in the fate of Germany from the viewpoint of God and take part in its creativity. Some specific *theologoumena* made their appearance in this discussion: God and folk, history and redemptive history (*Heilsgeschichte*), historical experience of God and biblical revelation; the transition of the fate of Germany was said to be a transition towards the rebuilding of nation and church from the forces of a world view of the Volk. Wilhelm Stapel, a theologian, made it plain what this world view was. He stated that the German Volk was not an idea of humans but an idea of God. As Israel had its *nomos* in the Decalogue, so the German people would have its *nomos Germanicos.* [22] Karl Barth's one-time theological companion, Friedrich Gogarten, expressed views about the theological assertions of the German Christians which led to an irreparable breach in their relations. Just prior to his departure for Copenhagen and the delivery of the address on the First Commandment, Barth discussed with Albert Lempp, the publisher of Christian Kaiser Verlag in Munich, where the journal *Zwischen den Zeiten* appeared, the discontinuation of that journal as a public gesture of distancing himself from Gogarten, a fellow-editor. The theological responses of the German Christians and those who sympathized with their goals held in common the conviction which was expressed by the Roman Catholic historian of the church, Joseph Lortz, that: "either this movement [National Socialism] pushes through to salvation or we land in chaos. No one refutes any more this ineluctable conclusion. Chaos, however, would be the destruction of the nation and the ruin of the German Church. And that ends the discussion."[23]

Here, then, was the position of one of the political theologies of the time, one to which the political revolution had become a theological principle of knowledge and interpretation. National Socialism and Christianity, Third Reich and Church condition one another, explain one another and have to justify themselves to each other. Solidarity with the National-Socialist Movement from a theological basis - that was the demand of political theology which Barth faced.

But can one simply counterpose another political theology, such as a Marxist or Western-democratic theology? Meet ideology with ideology? If neither a basically political nor a basically non-political argumentation can be brought into the field against such a political theology, then the only option is the theological argument. That is to say, the only option is to enquire whether the political decisions of this political theology, founded as they were on essentially theological reflections, could in fact stand up to a solid theological critique. The question, therefore, was not: was the political decision of the German-Christian theology in favour of National Socialism right or wrong, or whether theology could or should make political judgements at all. The question, rather, was: was this political decision arrived at in a theologically adequate manner? And Barth raised it in that way.

In August 1932 Barth wrote the preface to volume I/1 of his *Church Dogmatics*. He again manifests his zeal for the primacy of theology. "I am firmly convinced that, especially in the broad field of politics, we cannot reach the clarifications which are necessary today, and on which theology might have a word to say, as indeed it ought to have, without first reaching the comprehensive clarifications in and about theology which are our present concern."[24] He was pleading for a theology, neither political nor unpolitical, which became clear about itself before making any political judgements. Instead of a theology that allowed political events to define its milieu and locale, he strove for a theology which could give milieu and locale to political events.

"The First Commandment as Axiom for Theology" repeats and

confirms this position. The unconditional primacy of theology over politics Barth called for, a theology which vis-a-vis politics will not become politics but remain theology, was not a quasi-formal decision to be made but was something entirely appropriate to the subject of theology, the God who tolerates no other deities. It meant concretely that theology and Church, in matters of foundational concerns, could not tolerate commitment to fascism or anti-fascism, to Communism or anti-Communism as a *theological* axiom.

IV

The lecture itself consists of three parts. - In the first Barth defines the notion of an axiom for theology. The general meaning of 'axiom', as used, for example, in mathematics of logic, has to be distinguished from the meaning it has in theology. "An *axiom* is a statement which is sufficiently comprehensive and substantial to form the ultimate and decisive presupposition to the proof of all other statements of a definite scientific discipline."[25] An axiom is self-authenticating, needing no other statements for its proof. Since the concept 'axiom' is borrowed from non-theological disciplines, its *theological* use needs definition. The general concept of an axiom "contains *nothing* analogous to what it designates in its theological use."[26] Barth cites four points of divergence between the theological and the general use of this concept.

First, the theological axiom *is written*. It is of the essence of the Church and all that it does that it exists between the Word and the world. "The Church exists in her reading and proclaiming this document [sc. the Bible] as the unique witness of God's unique revelation: in reading, proclaiming and reading again; proclaiming, reading and proclaiming again."[27] The theological axiom has its validity in that it is written in a document that has authority for theology. In the general concept an axiom owes its validity not to its place in an authoritative document but to its self-evidence. Such an axiom "should be directly, immediately and generally perceptible and be persuasive precisely without formal authority and regardless of whether and where it is written."[28] Second, an axiom in the general sense has the character of a timeless and universally valid truth. How the truth of an axiom should come to be known personally or historically is quite incidental to the general understanding of axiom. Once perceived, the manner of its perception is irrelevant. The theological axiom, on the other hand, is a concrete historical event. It is God's act of becoming the God of actual human beings, it is the event of real people being concretely addressed by God. Thus, this axiom is understood only insofar as one is addressed. "They and only they understand the axiom of theology who in *their* time have to make do with the same temporally determined address of God which the Israelites in *their* time had to make do with for better or for worse."[29] Third, the form of the theological axiom is that of a commandment. At stake in this axiom is not some fact about God, but the question of human obedience or disobedience. "The theological axiom is, in essence, God's establishing a position, which means that human perception of it is, too, the occupation of a specific position. For if people do not hear what is being said to them it means not only that they are mistaken but also that they are disobedient. If they hear what is being said to them it means not only that they have rightly understood but also that they are obedient."[30] In the general sense, axioms are subject to human disposition, they lie in the sphere of human freedom and authority. No question, then, of obedience. With the theological axiom the relationship is reversed: "there *I* am lord, here I *have* a lord."[31] Fourth, the theological axiom, the First Commandment, is located in an identifiable relationship of God to humanity. The one who addresses stands to those addressed in a relationship of liberator to the liberated, of saviour to the saved. For the God who commands is the one who brought Israel out of Egypt, who acts as the Lord of history, of the people who are saved, justified, sanctified by this God. This axiom, then, is inseparable from the character and behaviour of the speaker in relation to those to whom the command is addressed. General axioms, on the other hand, can be understood independently of the sphere of revelation and response. Barth argues, and here he refers explicitly to principles drawn by some of his theological contemporaries from the 'orders of creation', that an axiom exhibiting the characteristic of neutrality and universality is not an axiom of theology.

In the second part of the address Barth discusses the particular content of the First Commandment as a theological axiom. "You shall have no other gods before me!" The commandment does not declare a general metaphysical principle, it is not a statement of philosophical monotheism. It does not deny that there are other gods. Instead, it is a prohibition: the Israelite is forbidden to 'have' other gods than the one who gives this commandment. If one could not have other gods because there are no such gods, there would be no point to the commandment; in other words, those other deities are real in a sense. And to have other gods means, according to Luther, whom Barth cites at this point, to place one's trust in one in whom one has faith, from whom one expects to receive what one loves and who will protect one against that which is feared. "Wherever is the heart of people, in other words, wherever is the foundation of their real and ultimate confidence and hope, the *primum movens* of their movement of life and also the basis of their lives' security, there also in all truth is their god."[32] As a human, and particularly an ecclesial activity, theology stands under the First Commandment. The responsibility of theology to this commandment is so fundamental that Barth draws the analogy between the role of commandment in theology and that of axioms in other disciplines. "Where in other sciences axioms have their place, in theology, prior to any theological thought or speech, at its source or root, there stands as foundation and critique . . . the commandment: You shall have no other gods before me!"[33] At every point theology is answerable to the question posed by the First Commandment:

> *Theology is asked over and over again where its heart, its concern and interest really lie and whether its heart is perhaps not divided secretly between this god and those other gods. It is asked, for example, about the concept of the highest* **good** *or highest* **value** *presupposed in its work. It is asked about the* **source** *from which it deduces its statements. It is asked about the practical* **motive,** *the* **intention** *according to which it phrases those precise statements in that precise manner. It is asked where it really comes from and where it is really going. And on every side other gods, other grounds and objects of fear, love and trust beside the* **deus ecclesiae** *are seriously in the running - also and precisely for theology. [34]*

The concrete temptation which faces theology, according to Barth, is to become dissatisfied with the narrowness of its basis. Why confine God to a book, a church, a particular point in history? And why not deal with that temptation in the manner of free human beings?

Beginning with that resolution Barth sketches its development in Neo-Protestantism from the Enlightenment through Schleiermacher, Ritschl and Troeltsch to his own contemporaries, especially to those who had been closely identified with him during the previous decade: Brunner, Bultmann and Gogarten. From this temptation derives the theology of 'and'. Other sources of theology are placed beside revelation and there appear theologies of revelation *and* reason, of revelation *and* religious experience, revelation *and* creation, New Testament *and* human existence, the commandments *and* the orders of creation. Against such theologies Barth puts the question of the responsibility of theology to the First Commandment. That question comes in three forms.

1) If theology is responsible to the First Commandment but wants to relate something else to revelation by means of that little, so weighty word 'and'[35], then it will be clear that revelation, rather than the other, must take central place in the interest and concern of theology. And so Barth asks whether Brunner's and Gogarten's zeal has not become centered in the other place.

2) If theology is responsible to the First Commandment then it will interpret its other sources in the light of revelation and not the other way around. Thus, the theology of Schleiermacher must be questioned as to whether Christ is not subject to the realm of religion. Brunner, Bultmannn and Gogarten must be asked whether primordial revelation, human existence or the orders of creation do not shape the interpretation of revelation rather than being determined in the obedience of theology to the First Commandment. "Must one not ask whether something like 'other gods' beside the *deus ecclesiae* have not been allowed into the discussion?"[36]

3) If theology is responsible to the First Commandment then it must not allow the identification of revelation with any other authority such as reason, existence, creation, experience, etc. Barth sees this danger in Protestant theology since Kant, where revelation became swallowed up in reason, Schleiermacher, where revelation became swallowed in religious self-consciousness, and Ritschl, where it became lost in culture. "And so also vis-a-vis Brunner and Gogarten I have to ask: is 'God' really more than another word for the neighbour? Is 'commandment' more than another word for the orders of creation? And vis-a-vis Bultmann: are theology and anthropology really interchangeable concepts?"[37] Against the assurances of such theologians that this is

not what is meant, that the orders of creation are part and parcel of the revelation of the only god, Barth asks: "why does one always speak and write those weighty books as if one did mean it that way?"[38]

The third, concluding part is given over to two observations on the importance of the theme of the address. First, Barth observes, the path of a theology of 'and' has already been explored in a careful manner in Roman Catholicism. Must Protestant theology, in following the same path in a manner that cannot be called careful at all, not ultimately reach the same point, the point namely where that path has to be left in obedience to the First Commandment? "Many roads lead back to Rome!" Barth warns [39], a warning he was to repeat in much the same context in his vigorous NO! to Emil Brunner a year later.

Second, Barth adds, no theology is ever justified by its conscientious fulfillment of the First Commandment. "Every theology has 'other gods' and most of all where they are least expected and noticed."[40] *Every* theology is subject to the challenge of this Commandment. It is the obligation of every theologian, therefore, to remind everyone of the First Commandment and to call in question the divided heart of the respective theologies. It is the forgiveness of sin and not the perfection of its obedience which justifies a theology. The question of the possible idolatry of another theology is for that reason a penultimate question.

> *When we have said everything that has to be said, the 'bond of peace' (Eph. 4.3) must also become visible, the knowledge of the utterly superior wisdom of the **Lord** of the Church, the promise 'behold, I am with you always' which, if we apply it to ourselves, we can apply to others no less than to ourselves. Only in a common hope can the necessary fight of theology be fought properly. For that should be the final thing that we must let ourselves be told, precisely by the First Commandment.[41]*

V

Barth's address has the form of dogmatics and a political content, showing what in this article is claimed to be the unity of dogmatics and ethics in Karl Barth. The point of the address is that Barth is striving for a foundation on which it becomes possible to offer resistance to National Socialism. At first glance what was said at Copenhagen and Aarhus appears irrelevant to that endeavour. Yet if such a foundation was in fact provided then the theological argument itself is no longer 'merely' a theological but also a highly political one. However *formal* Barth's argument appears, the ethical or material consequences of the basic theological position he had adopted in the address were easily drawn from what he had said. Barth's long-standing occupation with and critique of Neo-Protestantism, the fruit of which he had identified in the theology of the German-Christians, had provided him with the means to enter *materially* into their politics, which claimed a basis in the faith of the historic Church, as well as into their theology, which claimed the present political situation as needful for the perception of God's revelation. From the very beginning Barth's theology was no theology 'per se'! It was always ethical, to be precise, his 'christological concentration' had political relevance. The autobiographical comments cited earlier included the statement that "the church-theological conflict contained within itself the political conflict, and it was no fortuitous happening that it revealed itself more and more as a political conflict." As one reads on, one comes to the following sentences:

> *People have been* **very** *much astonished about the 'change' in my stand. They were astonished . . . when I became out-and-out political. That I have not always succeeded, in former times and also today, in expressing myself in a manner comprehensible to all, is part of the guilt which I certainly impute to myself when I see myself surrounded by so much anger and confusion. I should like to be allowed to say that anyone who really knew me before should not now be so very much astonished. As I see it, the majesty of God, the eschatological character of the whole Christian message, and the preaching of the gospel in its purity as the sole task of the Christian church are the thoughts which have been and continue to be the centre of my theological thinking. The abstract, transcendent God, who does not care for real people, 'God is all, human beings are nothing', the abstract, eschatological expectation that has no significance for the present and the just as abstract church, occupied only with this transcen-*

> *dent God, and separated from state and society by an abyss -*
> *all that existed not in **my** head, but only in the heads of those*
> *who have written reviews and even whole books about me.*
> *… Contrary to the opinion of many, to whom it seemed that I*
> *was drawing an empty bow for the sheer sport of it, I have*
> *had quite apparently an arrow on the string and have taken a*
> *shot. It would be well if some, looking at what has happened,*
> *would now at last comprehend how the whole thing was*
> *meant all along. [42]*

And how was it meant all along? Karl Barth's dogmatics is in the form of an historical-concrete content, namely Jesus Christ, a very specific human being - a Jew! - and his history. For the sake of that subject Barth worked out his penetrating critique, and a Marxian one at that, of religion, including the religion of the German-Christian 'God and folk' religion and the theologies of the 'and' already referred to. It was the astute observer of Barth's work, Hans Urs von Balthasar, who commented that specific political convictions may well have been present at the generation of a particular line of dogmatic thinking just as such thinking may well have led to particular practical and political consequences. The more profound one's acquaintance with Barth's theology the more evident the connection between these two dimensions. One may well conclude with astonishment how faithful Barth remained to his earliest convictions, both spiritual and worldly, and that they have changed so little in the midst of all the other changes Barth underwent.[43] The rigorous form of argument conceals the exegetical and the ethical-political studies which preceded it and on which it rests. Yet it is precisely that form of argument Barth follows, namely, that dogmatics is the criterion to which his political, more specifically, his ethical thinking is subject. "Barth 'works' inductively, that is to say, from below to above, while in his presentation he argues deductively, that is to say, from above to below. He must have known why he did so and, obviously, he expects his critics to subject themselves as well to the labours of this 'form', of this dogmatic concept, before they express their conclusions about him."[44]

'The First Commandment as Axiom for Theology' serves as a good model for that Barthian dogmatics in which neither dogmatics nor ethics are present 'per se' but appear in that creative interaction which Barth's life itself modelled so impressively.

Notes

1. The German text, published originally in *Zwischen den Zeiten*, vol. 11, 1933, pp. 297-314, may also be found in Barth's anthology *Theologische Fragen und Antworten*, Zürich: Evangelischer Verlag AG, 1957, pp. 127-143. An English translation is to appear in *The Way of Theology in Karl Barth; Essays and Comments*, ed. by Martin Rumscheidt, AllisonPark: Pickwick Publications, 1986.
2. That expression comes from Karl Dietrich Bracher, one of the leading current analysts of the Third Reich.
3. Eberhard Busch, *Karl Barth - His Life from Letters and Autobiographical Texts*; Philadelphia and London: Fortress Press and SCM Press, 1976, p. 82. (Cited as Busch)
4. Busch, p. 217.
5. Busch, p. 228.
6. Busch, p. 225.
7. Hans Prolingheuer, *Der Fall Karl Barth*; Neukirchen: Neukirchener Verlag, 1977, p. 233
8. Cf. Rauschning's important study *Die Revelution des Nihilismus*, Zürich, New York: Europa Verlag, 1938.
9. Hermann Rauschning, *Gespräche mit Hitler*; Zürich, New York: Europa Verlag, 1940, p. 50.
10. Karl Barth, *How I Changed My Mind*; Richmond: John Knox Press, 1966, pp. 45-7. (Cited as Mind)
11. Klaus Scholder, *Die Kirche und das Dritte Reich*, Vol. 1; Frankfurt, Berlin, Vienna: Propyläen Verlag, 1977, p. 213. (Cited as Scholder)
12. Scholder, p. 214.
13. Scholder, p. 214.
14. *Zwischen den Zeiten*, 1931, pp. 89-122.
15. Karl Kupisch was for many years the Church-historian at the Kirchliche Hochschule in Berlin; he had had long association with Barth. The rendition of *pompa ecclesia* into the German equivalent of 'a pompous outfit' was reported to the author by a former student of Kupisch. From that source also came the citation in parentheses.
16. Scholder, p.p. 156-7.
17. See Peter Winzeler, *Widerstehende Theologie, Karl Barth 1920-35*; Stuttgart; Alektor Verlag, 1982, p. 148. (Cited as Winzeler)
18. Karl Barth, *Der Götze wackelt*; ed. by Karl Kupisch, Berlin: Käthe Vogt Verlag, 1961, p. 62.
19. Winzeler, p. 148.
20. Walter Künneth and Helmuth Schreiner, *Die Nation vor Gott*; Berlin: Wichern Verlag, 1933, pp. vii-ix.
21. Scholder, p. 526.
22. Scholder, p. 131.
23. Scholder, p. 545.
24. Karl Barth, *Church Dogmatics*, I/1; Edinburgh: T. & T. Clark, 1975, p. xvi.

25. Karl Barth, *Theologische Fragen und Antworten.* p. 127. (Cited as Fragen)
26. *Fragen,* p. 128.
27. *Fragen,* p. 129.
28. *Fragen,* p. 130.
29. *Fragen,* p. 130.
30. *Fragen,* p. 131.
31. *Fragen,* p. 132.
32. *Fragen,* p. 134.
33. *Fragen,* p. 135.
34. *Fragen,* p. 136.
35. *Fragen,* p. 138.
36. *Fragen,* p. 140.
37. *Fragen,* p. 141.
38. *Fragen,* p. 141.
39. *Fragen,* p. 142.
40. *Fragen,* p. 143.
41. *Fragen,* p. 143.
42. *Mind,* pp. 48-9. - The text is slightly reset in this citation to agree with the German text as cited in the work referred to in note 18.
43. Hans Urs von Balthasar, *Karl Barth. Darstellung und Deutung seiner Theologie;* Köln: Verlag Jakob Hegner, 1962, p. 54.
44. Winzeler, p. 152.

Karl Barth's Understanding of Science

Harold P. Nebelsick

For Karl Barth, "Evangelical theology is concerned with Immanuel, God with us! Having this God for its object, it can be nothing else but the most thankful and [therefore] *happy* science."[1] Late in life, therefore, in 1962 when he wrote that statement, Barth had no hesitation in calling theology a *science,* even a *happy* science. There were times, however, when Barth spoke of theology as a science only in muted tones. In the first volume of his *Church Dogmatics* (1932), for instance, he could justify describing theology as a science, a "special science," only as "a relative and factual necessity," as over against the *other sciences.* In the early thirties Barth's reluctance to refer to theology as a science reflects his apprehension that, were theology to identify itself with "the sciences" too hastily, *the other sciences* would likely intrude upon *theology (the science of God).* Such uncritical identification would likely subject theology to alien principles rather than to its own principle.[2]

In the early thirties, then, when Barth embarked upon his third rather distinct period of development, his *Theology of the Word,* he was ambivalent about whether or not theology should be considered a "science" at all. "There is no necessity of principle, nor are there any internal reasons, why it should claim to belong to this genus."[3] The history of the designation of theology as a science is itself ambivalent. Both Augustine in his *de trin.* (XIV 1,3) and Thomas Aquinas in his *Summa theo.* (I, qu. 1, art. 2 & 6) refer to theology with the term, *scientia.* Also, J. W. Baier (*Comp. Theol. posit., Prol. 1, 15*) and J.F. Buddeus (*Instit. dogmat., 1724, I, 1, 28*) emphatically call theology a *scientia.* The older Leyden school, somewhat by contrast, cautiously spoke of *scientia vel sapientia* (Walaeus, *Loci comm. 1640, p. 4; Leidener Synopsis pur. Theol., 1624, I, 9*). For the most part however, Reformed and Lutheran theologians preferred the term, *doctrina.* J. Gerhard and D. Hollaz, for instance rejected the description of theology as *scientia* and chose the term, *sapientia.*[4] In view of this history, Barth was convinced that G. Wobbermin's statement that "theology has the greatest possible . . . interest in ranking theology as a real science, as a science in the strict and indeed the very strictest sense of the word" *(Richtlinien evang.*

Theologie, 1929, p. 25), is exaggerated.[5]

Nevertheless, from the time of the first edition of the *Römerbrief* onward, Barth himself found it necessary to call theology "a science" because of the nature of theology itself. Theology, as Barth explained in the first volume of his *Church Dogmatics* (1932), like the other sciences, is a "human concern with a definite object of knowledge". Also, like the other sciences, it "treads a definite and self-consistent path of knowledge and lastly, like the others, it must give an account of this path to itself and to all others who are capable of concern for this object and therefore of treading this path." This does not mean, however, that theology, even if it is known as a "science," would allow itself to be disturbed or hampered in its own task by what other sciences might prescribe. "As regards method, it has nothing to learn from them." [6]

Barth's determination to designate theology as a science, along with the fervor with which he repudiated the possible subordination of theology to the other sciences, is explicable on the basis of his own theological development. Beginning with the second edition of the *Römerbrief* (1922), Barth vehemently rejected the compromising theology of the nineteenth century when theology subjected itself to science's prescription for the understanding of knowledge and truth. Consequently, it had forgotten its own peculiarity, especially the peculiarity of its proper *object.*

> "Since the days of Schleiermacher, many encyclopaedic attempts have been made to include theology in the sciences. But the common objection may be made against all of them that they overlook the abnormality of the special existence of theology and therefore essay that which is radically impossible. The actual result of all such attempts has always been the disturbing or destructive surrender of theology to a general concept of science and the mild unconcern with which non-theological science, perhaps with a better sense of realities than theologians with their desire for synthesis, can usually reply to this mode of justifying theology."[7]

In repudiating the nineteenth-century *neo-Protestant liberal* theology of his student days that is still reflected in the first edition of the *Römerbrief* (1918), Barth also rejected the extraneous influence of science upon theology. Liberal theology, formulated under the impact of the Kantian idealist philosophy, had not only imbibed the culture of the day, it had founded itself upon it. Eventually it amalgamated itself with it with such thoroughness that Christianity and culture became inseparable. In the process, theology that had succumbed to Kantian idealism had also acquiesced in the demands of nineteenth-century science.[8]

I. The Commentary on Romans

The *Römerbrief* (1922), that marks the beginning of his "dialectical period", shows Barth to be profoundly influenced by his adoption of Franz Overbeck's devastating critique of so-called "Christian culture" and the religion of culture, *Kulturchristentum*. This, along with Kierkegaard's understanding of *God-as-other* and Dostoevski's judgment that the world lay under the shadow of death, provided him with the categories and the language to reject the easy, romantic, anthropocentric, optimistic, neo-Protestant theology of the nineteenth century along with it's generally too uncritical relationship to and acceptance of science as the touchstone of truth.[9] Ivan Karamazov's understanding of the *totaliter aliter* (the totally other) illustrated the real and unknown God. God was the *absolute contradiction*. Dostoevski's "Idiot," his Christ-figure, makes it plain that in spite of humankind's so-called "riches, health and righteousness," humanity's only option, when confronted with the truth, is death. The Grand Inquisitor, who attempted to present Christ and the Christian faith in a harmless, palatable way portrays the subtle but consummate betrayal of Christ. [10]

Buoyed by ideas such as these, Barth then perceived the complete contradiction between God and any and all human concepts of him. God's truth is the negation of culture, even and especially of the highest achievements of culture, including those of science, by which people delude themselves into thinking they could take life, reality and even faith into their own hands. Thus, the sciences of *this world* have no right whatsoever to intrude upon the science of theology. Any attempt that theology would make to subordinate itself to the demands of science, or even to reconcile itself with science, would represent nothing less than a betrayal of itself and of its proper *object* – the God of the Bible to whom theology is supposed to bear witness.

The controversy with science that Barth continued through the various prefaces of the *Römerbrief* centers primarily on the science of biblical criticism, *(die historisch-kritische Methode der Bibelforschung)*. Not that Barth would reject theology as a science or that he would reject the science of biblical criticism. Indeed, in that monumental manifesto that stands over all of his theology and with which he prefaced the first edition of *Römerbrief,* he admits the necessity and the significance of the *historical-critical method of biblical research.* "The historical-critical method of biblical investigation has its rightful place; it is concerned with the preparation of the intelligence – and this can never be super-fluous."[11] The fact that Barth preferred "the venerable doctrine of Inspiration" *(den alten Inspirationslehre)* as having "a broader, deeper, and more important justification" because, it was "concerned with the labour of apprehending, without which no technical equipment, however complete, is of any use whatsoever," in no way diminishes his respect for the scientific method of biblical interpretation, or what we would call the "historical-critical method."

The preface to the notorious second edition, (dated September 1921), was written coincidentally with Barth's leaving his pastorate in Safenwil to take up his teaching post as Professor of Reformed Theology in Göttingen. It was this edition in which Barth so worked over the first edition that "hardly one stone remained in its old place,"[12] that "burst like a bomb on the playground of the theologians," as Karl Adam put it. [13] In the preface Barth notes in all honesty, "I have been accused of being a declared enemy of historical criticism *abgesagter Feind der historischen Kritik)."*[14] He frankly admitted that he had protested against some of the recent commentaries on Romans. The protestations, however, were not directed against the so-called "critical school" simply because, "I have nothing whatsoever to say against historical criticism. I recognize it, and once more state quite definitely that it is both necessary and justified."[15]

Showing himself to be a better scientist than the "so-called scientific theologians," Barth apologized for his method in true scientific fashion. "The matter contained in the text cannot be released save by a creative straining of the sinews, by a relentless, elastic application of the 'dialectical' movement *(dialektische Bewegung).* The critical historian needs to be more critical." True apprehension of the content of a document is possible only by wrestling with "the ideas written in the text". Then, like a proper scientist who attempts to allow his mind to be shaped by the object *he is attempting to understand,* Barth explained, "Criticism, *(krinein)* applied to historical documents means for me the measuring of words and phrases by *the standard of that about which the documents are speaking."*[16]

The scientific investigation of textual documents, therefore, necessarily moves beyond the text itself into the matter the text intends to reveal. It is nothing less than a struggle that attempts to penetrate to the very heart of the matter that, in the first place, was the impetus that brought the text into being, that same matter that, even now, desires to make itself known.

> "Intelligent comment means that I am driven on till I stand with nothing before me but the enigma of the matter; till the document seems hardly to exist as a document; till I have almost forgotten that I am not its author; till I know the author so well that I allow him to speak in my name and am even able to speak in his name myself."[17]

Again, like the true scientist he was, Barth realized that he, like any other scientist, has assumptions, even a "system" perhaps. However:

> "... if I have a system, it is limited to the recognition of what Kierkegaard called the 'Infinite qualitative distinction' between time and eternity. And to my regarding this as possessing negative as well as positive significance: 'God is in heaven, and thou art on earth.' The relation between such a God and such a man and the relation between such a man and such a God, is for me the theme of the Bible and the essence of philosophy."[18]

Like every scientist then, Barth knew that his method of interpretation is founded on assumptions. The basic assumption is that he and the Apostle Paul were related to the same God. It is this God and none other, this God who has related himself to the Apostle Paul that, in the science of theology, is the *object* of investigation.

> "I embark on its [The Epistle to the Romans] inter-
> pretation on the assumption that he [Paul] is confron-
> ted with the same unmistakable and unmeasurable
> significance of that relation as I myself am confronted
> with, and that it is this situation which moulds his
> thought and its expression."[19]

Barth thus reiterates in other words that which he had already said in
the preface to the first edition, "Our problems are the problems of
Paul; and if we be enlightened by the brightness of his answers, those
answers must be ours."[20]

Assumptions, of course, are assumptions and again, in line with
proper science, Barth realizes that assumptions prove themselves or
are disproved only in the process of exploration. "Whether these
assumptions are justified or not becomes clear in the course of the
investigation when each verse comes to be examined and interpreted."[21] Barth knows also that all theological statements are tentative. For Barth, therefore, "theological statements end in only relative
certainty." They cannot be proven.[22] Barth's attitude here is identical to that of the scientist-philosopher Michael Polanyi who compares
the Christian faith to an heuristic impulse that "is never without a
sense of its possible inadequacy." Like an "heuristic impulse" too,
theology, "can live only in the pursuit of its proper enquiry."[23] Thus
Barth states:

> "I assume that in the Epistle to the Romans Paul did
> speak of Jesus Christ and not of someone else. And
> this is as reputable an assumption as other assump-
> tions that historians are wont to make. The actual
> exegesis alone decides whether this assumption can
> be maintained."[24]

"Is it reasonable," Barth asks, to approach the Epistle "with any other
assumption than that God is God?"[25]

"Paul knows of God what most of us do not know: and his Epistles
enable us to know what he knew." Although his critics chose to name
this trust in the Apostle Paul, his "system" or his "dogmatic presup-

position" even his "Alexandrianism", for Barth such an attitude was "the best presupposition even from the point of view of historical criticism"[26] It was exactly because of this assumption or presupposition that Barth was compelled to wrestle with what were considered to be "scandals to modern thought" that Paul had put forward, simply because it was in these "scandals" that "the characteristic and veritable discernment of Paul" were to be found.[27]

The main feature of Barth's method, therefore, is his intention of reading the text in such a way that it reveals to him *what* was revealed to Paul. Accused of being a "biblicist" he turns the epithet against his critics by saying that to be a "biblicist" means no more than to take the Bible seriously. It means to consider the text as worthy of study. It means simply, "I am prejudiced in supposing the Bible to be a good book, and that I hold it to be profitable for men to take its conceptions at least as seriously as they take their own."[28]

Having been accused of being a Philistine with regard to the historical-critical method, Barth in the "Preface of the Third Edition" written February, 1924 in Göttingen, took note with particular pleasure that even such a staunch critic as Rudolf Bultmann had given the second edition a favorable reception. "I conclude to my very great satisfaction that the original cry against the book as being an incitement to a Diocletian persecution of historical, critical theology was not necessary [*nicht nötig*]."[29] Barth's reply to Bultmann, who despite his favorable reception of the book, had criticized him, as it were, for believing the Apostle Paul not wisely but too well, indicates once again the depth of Barth's critical approach to the understanding of the Scripture. According to Bultmann, were one to be properly critical of the Bible, one would have to realize that "other spirits make themselves heard, as well as the Spirit of Christ."[30]

Barth's reply is directly related to his dialectical method at this stage, at least, caused him to perceive revelation and the witness to revelation as standing over against one another. His answer shows that for all of Bultmann's reputation as being a *radical critic* of the New Testament, Barth, in fact, is more radical than he. God, as well as the real *message of the Bible,* were *totaliter aliter.* There are in the Epistle no words at all that are not of "the spirits [of this age]." The Bible and all of its texts are *of this world.* "The whole is *litera,* that is, voices of those other spirits." It is illegitimate, therefore, Barth insists, to attempt to pick and choose among the passages and to claim that in some of the veritable spirit of Christ had spoken. "The problem is whether [or not] the whole must not be understood in relation to the true subject – matter which is – the spirit of Christ."[31]

Thus, Barth takes seriously, more seriously than Bultmann, the fact that the Apostle Paul is not with God in heaven or at least was not when he wrote the Epistle. Rather, like the rest of humankind, he was on earth and was "of this world." His witness, therefore, was no more but no less than human witness. This in no way, however, causes Barth to reject what Paul had written. Rather he insists that to understand an author one must "stand or fall with him." Bultmann's demand that he write "*with* Paul" and follow him into the unfamiliarity of his Jewish, Popular-Christian, and Hellenistic conceptions and "when the whole becomes too hopelessly bizarre, I am to turn around and write 'critically' *about* him and against him – as though, when all is strange, this or that is to be regarded as especially outrageous," seems to Barth to be completely illegitimate with regard to understanding the biblical texts. For him, such a procedure relegates the texts of Scripture to the category of "relics of a by-gone age". That attitude not only represents a failure to understand what the Bible is about, it is even "an error in literary taste."[32]

As to the criticism that his interpretation had certain affinities with the old doctrine of inspiration, Barth explains that, as expounded by Calvin, the doctrine is "at least worthy of careful consideration." "Is there any way," he asks, "of penetrating to the heart of a document – of any document! – except on the assumption that its spirit will speak to our spirit through the actual written words?"[33] This does not mean, of course, that there is to be no criticism of the letter by the Spirit. That, indeed, is unavoidable. It is, in fact, exactly this kind of critical interpretation that at one and the same time ties Barth to the text and frees him from it. "It is precisely a strict faithfulness that compels us to expand or abbreviate the text, lest a too rigid attitude to the words should obscure that which is struggling to expression in them and which demands expression." This is "a critical freedom of exegesis," which as Barth notes, was used by Calvin "in masterly fashion, without the slightest disregard for the discipline by which alone liberty is justified."[34]

What is needed, Barth insists, is to stand side by side with the Apostle Paul, "to discern in spiritual fashion what is spiritually intended," while at the same time realizing that "the voice with which we proclaim what we have received is primarily nothing but the voice of those other spirits." For, "No human word, no word of Paul, is absolute truth." It is, of course, necessary "to see beyond Paul," but this can be done only if we first "endeavour to penetrate his meaning."[35] Thus, as Calvin in his interpretation of Hebrews, chapter 11, had explained, we are able to "plant our feet" on faith, but that which we are given in faith is "far distant under our feet." So, too, Barth knows that faith is but the *"evidence of things not seen"*. Then in a complicated but profound statement in which he revealed his *dialectical method* at its core, Barth states, *"Evidence* means that things emerge into appearance. It is applicable only to that which concerns our senses."[36] The things of faith, however, lie beyond the evidence. "In the realm of faith the two apparent opposites – *evidence* and *things not seen* – struggle with one another and are united. It is precisely the hidden things, inaccessible to sensible perception, that are displayed by the Spirit of God."[37]

Barth's explanations did not stem the criticism of his work. In the "Preface to the Fourth Edition", written February 1924, he notes that Adolf Jülicher, one of his former professors at Marburg, had reviewed the book for a second time and said, as his "final word", that it "proceeded from the 'arrogance of a spiritual enthusiast'."[38] The literary organ of the Dutch Reformed Church was outraged by its "negative" character and warned its readers to "exercise great care in using it" since it was "foreign to piety."[39] Roman Catholics, on the other hand, specifically Erich Przywara, S.J., pronounced the book to be a "genuine re-birth of Protestantism." It was, he said, "a reappearance of the 'passionate fervor of the old Reformers'."[40]

The continued and mounting sales of the book, that made yet another edition necessary in 1926, continued to astonish Barth as much as the fact that, because of its popularity, people began to consider him to be an *authority* on its subject matter and on other things as well. He admits that when he wrote the book in his "peaceful parsonage in the distant valley of the Aar," although he thought he was producing something worthwhile, "it never crossed my mind to think that the apostle Paul, as I seemed to hear him, would awaken such an echo." Now firmly ensconced as a regular professor at the University of Münster where he had moved from Göttingen in 1925, Barth realized again (and this reveals his whole scientific attitude) that in doing theology it was not only difficult "to plow the field of Christian doctrine," it was necessary to remember that "each furrow is – of necessity – a new furrow."[41]

In the "Preface to the Sixth Edition" that was written the first Sunday in Advent, 1928, just after the publication of his *Prolegomena to Christian Dogmatics (Christian Dogmatics,* Vol. I.1), Barth notes the necessity of this constant scientific *aggiornamento*. While he agreed to have the *Römerbrief* go to press yet again in its second edition form, he also realized that he had moved from the position he had expressed in it. "I do not wish the book to go forth once more without saying that, were I to set to work again on the exposition of the Epistle, and were I determined to repeat the same thing, I should certainly have to express it quite differently."[42]

Thus from the history of Barth's most famous single work his *Römerbrief,* it is possible to show him as a *scientist* in the proper sense of the word, a proper *Wissenschaftler,* one who is fully cognizant of his presuppositions, his method, the time-boundness or temporality of his thought, and hence the transient and provisional nature of his own theology. His conclusions were serious conclusions. They were, however, no more but also no less than the conclusions of one who took with utter earnestness the task of attempting to reveal the nature of the *object* with which he was dealing in accordance with the assumptions that he trusted were appropriate to the *object* itself. The assumptions in turn were always open to critique. They proved themselves to be valid or invalid in the scientific process, in the procedure of investigation.

Far from giving up on science or denigrating it, both Barth's method and his explanation of it show that he fully intended to be more scientific than the so-called "scientific theologians" (*wissenschaftliche Theologen)* who continued their adherence to nineteenth-century neo-Protestantism in spite of Barth's critique. For all their claim to be "critical theologians," they were, according to Barth, *not critical enough.* They were blind to the human-centeredness – the *anthropocentricity* of their own "scientific presuppositions." Because of their anthropologically-oriented presuppositions, although they claimed to be doing theology, i.e., attempting to understand God, the real object of their investigations was humankind. In speaking about "God," therefore, they were only saying "man" in a loud voice.

II. The Harnack Correspondence

This difference between Barth and his critics is nowhere more evident than in the correspondence *(ein Briefwechsel)* between himself
and Adolf von Harnack as published in the church newspaper, *Die
Christliche Welt,* between January and May, 1923. The confrontation
was especially painful to Barth because, during his theological studies
in Berlin in the winter of 1906-7, he had considered Harnack, *the
theologian of the day.* He had been an enthusiastic student of Harnack,
had visited in his home, and had thought himself privileged to have
become a member of Harnack's seminar. He was, in fact so devoted to
study, that he had no time for the German capitol's famed theaters,
concert halls, museums or even to hear the Kaiser's renowned speech
against the opposition Central Party and social democracy.[43]

It was, however, this same Harnack who in 1914, along with many
of Barth's other teachers, backed the Kaiser's war effort by signing the
manifesto issued by 93 intellectuals supporting the Kaiser's military
initiative. Even worse, if there were a *worse* for Barth, Harnack himself
composed the Kaiser's Declaration of War that united the German
people behind the war with the famous phrase, "I know no parties any
longer; I know only Germans." Barth admits having experienced a
"twilight of the gods *(eine Götterdämmerung)* when he read the
manifesto and discovered, to his utter disbelief, the names of many of
his famous teachers. Religion and science had been entirely transformed into 42 cm. cannon. Further, Barth realized that the ethical
failure of his former teachers implied that "their exegetical and
dogmatic presuppositions could not be in order" either.[44] Theology had become a study of the god of culture, rather than of the God
of the Bible.

Barth's rejection of the nineteenth century neo-Protestant theology
represented by his teachers turned him back to the Scripture to study
it with new eyes and to listen to the Apostle Paul with new ears. The
Römerbrief was the result. Much to his surprise, as said above, the voice
of the Apostle Paul, as he had been enabled to hear it, achieved an
echo that he had simply not expected. As the echo resounded through
the lecture halls of the theological world and penetrated to the pulpits
of the church, it became the impetus for a new theological direction.

In August 1922 Barth, along with his friends, Eduard Thurneysen
and Friedrich Gogarten (who a dozen years later, much to Barth's

consternation, was to join the Nazi-inspired German Christian Movement), decided to publish a new journal. The new journal was baptized *Zwischen den Zeiten* after an article that Gogarten had written for *Die Christliche Welt* two years previously. The periodical, in which the major part of Barth's lectures and articles from the 1920's were to appear, served both to give the so-called *dialectical theology* a voice and to form it into a distinctive theological movement.[45]

In January 1923, the same month the first issue of *Zwischen den Zeiten* was published, Adolf von Harnack, the scion of nineteenth century liberal theology, addressed a letter: "Fifteen Questions to the Despisers of Scientific Theology" to the church newspaper, *Die Christliche Welt*.[45] Barth was only one of the persons Harnack had in mind when he wrote the original letter. Nevertheless, upon reading it, Barth felt addressed and wrote a reply: "Sixteen Answers to Professor Adolf von Harnack."[47] Harnack then answered with an "open letter to Professor Karl Barth."[48] Barth again replied with, "An Answer To Professor Adolf von Harnack's Open Letter."[49] Harnack then wrote a fifth and final letter closing the series, "A Postscript to my Open Letter to Professor Karl Barth."[50]

Understanding himself as having been accused of being a "despiser of scientific theology *(Verächter der wissenschaftlichen Theologie)*, Barth stated, as indeed he had already said in the "Preface to the Second Edition" of the *Römerbrief*, that far from being a despiser of scientific theology, he only criticized the particular form it had taken in current times *(ihre moderne Gestalt)*. He faulted it because it had not been properly scientific. In direct opposition to Harnack's assertion, therefore, that the scientific theology *(wissenschaftliche Theologie)* that had gained clarity and maturity only since the eighteenth century,[51] Barth asserted that the proper theme of theology had last been stated clearly by the Reformation.[52] He went on to reiterate the primary precept of his "dialectical theology." Human truth is human truth no matter what its development. God's truth is God's truth. It is a matter of *either-or*. We can never grasp God's truth. *Our* faith is always unfaith.[53]

This God-awakened faith will never be able to avoid entirely the necessity of a more or less radical protest against *this* world. All hope rests in that which is *promised* but *invisible (das verheissende Unsichtbare)*. Any theology that loses the understanding of the basic *distance* of faith over against *this* world, therefore, would in the same measure be forgetful of the knowledge of God, the *creator*. It is because of this utter contrast *(schlechthinige Gegensatz)* between God and the world that the cross is the only way in which we, as human beings, can consider the original and right unity of creature and creator.[54]

Barth's answer to Harnack's question as to whether the determination of the content of the gospel depends on the individual's own discovery *(Erfahrung)*, and experience *(Erlebnis)*, only or is subject to historical knowledge and critical reflection,[55] gave Barth opportunity to reassert his critical stance on *religion* as such. The one revelation of God *(die eine Offenbarung)* should be considered the theme of theology beyond even the "religion" and the "revelations" of the Bible. It is only through an act of the content of the gospel itself that historical knowledge is enabled to discern that the communication of the "content of the gospel" is at all possible.[56]

Thus, too, the so-called "experience of God" *(Gotteserlebnis)* that Harnack asked about is as different from the *faith* that is awakened by God as is heaven from earth. In fact *(in der Tat)* such "experience of God," does not distinguish itself from "uncontrolled fanaticism." The real experience of God, Barth insisted, "comes through preaching." Preaching, however, no matter what the state of the preacher's historical knowledge and critical reflection, comes through the word of Christ. The task of theology, therefore, is identical to the task of preaching. It consists of receiving the Word of Christ and of passing it on.[57]

Further, Barth insisted, in reply to Harnack's fear that in negating culture Barth would encourage a fall back into barbarism, that all culture as well as all statements about God stand under the judgment (das Gericht). Thus, the Gospel has as much and as little to do with barbarism as it has to do with culture. In the same vein Christianity is not a development that can be furthered by historical knowledge and critical reflection as Harnack had insisted. The way from the Old to the New World is *"not* a stairway in any sense whatsoever." Rather, "it is being born anew" *(ein neues Geborenwerden)*.[58]

Barth, in fact, does not shy away from applying his critical attitude to the question of the so-called "historical Jesus". When Harnack asked how reliable and critical knowledge of Christ could be gained except through critical historical study "so that a dreamed-up Christ *(ein erträumten Christus)* is not exchanged for the real one,"[59] Barth answered that the knowledge of the person of Jesus Christ as the center of the Gospel can come about only by "way of a God-awakened faith" *(Gott erweckten Glaubens)*. He then added with some pointed-ness, "Whoever does not yet know (and none of us really know this) that we *no longer know* Christ according to the flesh, should let the criti-cal scientific study of the Bible *(kritische Bibelwissenschaft)* tell him so."[60]

To Harnack's question that even if one grants that there are limi-tations to scientific theology, "is there any other theology having strong ties and a blood-relationship *(Blutverwandschaft)* with science in general?",[61] Barth answered by implying again that the so-called "historical critics" were not critical enough. Were theology again to return to proper objectivity *(Sachlichkeit)* and regain the courage to become a witness to the word of revelation and judgment in the love of God, then perhaps science in general would necessarily search for a stronger tie and a blood-relationship with theology rather than the other way around. If such were the case, it would be better for the scientists in general if the theologians knew what they were supposed to know.[62]

Harnack's second letter, his, "Open Letter to Professor Karl Barth," is a mixture of understanding and misunderstanding. He is frank to admit that Barth's answers had clarified some of the issues. For that very reason, however, their differences were even clearer than before.[63] Harnack understood full well, however, the basis of Barth's dialectic, namely that between the truth of God and our truth there is only contrast, only the relationship of "either-or." That being the case, he then complained that he could not recognize the "simple gospel" in Barth's presentation. Instead he saw Barth as being caught in an esoteric psychology and metaphysics.[64] He then went on to re-iterate his contention that contemporary scientific theology was the only possible way of grasping the object of theology in an epis-temologically valid way. He accused Barth of having transformed his theological teaching ministry into a preaching ministry *(Lehrstuhl in einen Predigtstuhl)* and insisted that rather than being identified with preaching, the task of theology is to be identified with that of science generally. Further, Barth's statement that "we no longer know Christ according to the flesh" meant for Harnack, that we no longer know the historical Christ, the Jesus Christ of the gospels. He then asked acute-ly, "If we do not use the historical-critical method for understanding Jesus Christ, what then?" Do we use, perhaps "a theory of the exclusive inner word" or one of the many other "subjectivistic theories"?[65]

Barth, in his extended answer to Harnack's "Open Letter" pointed out that Harnack's method of theology being a post-Enlightenment development would have precluded Luther and Calvin from being "scientific theologians" *(wissenschaftliche Theologen)*. He then continued, "If indeed, the quality of being scientific means 'objectivity' *(Sachlichkeit)*, it is rather the theologians since the eighteenth century whose quality of being scientific *(Wissenschaftlichkeit)* is to be called into question." By contrast Barth pointed out that even the classical thought of the Middle Ages and the theology of the seventeenth-century Protestant scholasticism were, in all probability, more instructive than was the chaotic business of the theological faculties of his own day. Not that theology is to be a simple repristination of the ancient thought of the church, however, for, "we in our time have to think *in* and *for* our time".[66]

Basic to all of this for Barth is that preaching and theology alike have to do with a single truth, a truth that is present here and now, if indeed it is present at all. It is "the truth that comes through the Word of Christ *(durch das Wort Christus)*. Therefore, for faith, preaching, and theology, *content* and *the way of understanding that content* are identical. God himself is alone the goal; so also, he is alone the way.[67]

It is exactly for this reason that for him there is no possibility that human statements, including the statements of the creeds or those of the Bible, are to be considered a direct historical apprehension of the heavenly reality. By the same token, the center of the gospel is neither the "historical Jesus" nor "a dreamed up Christ." "It is, rather, the *risen one,* or should we say, in view of our little faith and with somewhat more restraint, it is "the Christ who is witnessed to as the risen one".[68]

Moving back to the question of the historical-critical method of biblical research, Barth showed again that he was convinced of its value by saying that in the Bible, "we have to do with testimonies and only *with testimonies."* The only possibility of faith, therefore, is that God, who through the witness of Scripture has spoken the Word of Christ and through the same witness, as empowered by the *testimonium spiritus sancti internum* (the internal testimony of the Holy Spirit), also speaks to me, so that I hear it and having heard it, I believe.[69]

This correlation of Scripture and spirit was Barth's only confidence in objectivity. He had no trust at all in the pontifications of a science *(Papat einer Wissenschaft)*. For him, there was no evidence that the historical-critical method had any superiority over the subjectivistic urgings of the revivalists. Even "the testimony of revelation" *must* be understood as human, as a part of the unpleasant and dark cultural history (insofar as God himself does not intervene!). In that everything human is a relative thing, a witness, a parable, religious experience is definitely not itself *the absolute*. In no way does it stand on the pinnacles or heights of development as Harnack would seem to imply. It is indeed, however, a *reference to the absolute*, whether it is so understood or not. Therefore, that which is historically and psychologically understandable, that which we know in reference to ourselves and others as "faith" is a witness and a symptom of that work and miracle of God upon us. This miracle of the faith was created through the Word and is deepened in the Word.[70]

That being the case, any continuity between what Barth calls *Geschichte* (history) and *Offenbarung* (revelation) is quite impossible. "I repudiate every continuity between here and yonder *(hier und druben)*. I assume a dialectical *relation* that points to an identity that cannot be either set out or presumed." It is precisely in the *No* of culture in its attempt to reflect God, the *No* which in the faith of revelation is to be stated as pointedly as possible, in this *No* the creature is able to know himself as the work and as the possession of the creator. It is exactly in this *No* that God is known as God. In this *No*, God is known also as the origin and the goal of the thoughts about himself that humankind in the darkness of their culture and decadence habitually form.

Then, showing himself at this time to be closer to the roots of the idealistic dialectical thought of Schelling and Hegel (wherein every thesis has the roots of its antithesis within itself and vice versa) than he would want to admit, Barth stated that this *No said in all finality and said by means of revelation is not without that deep secret Yes. The Yes is under and above the No,* as Luther has said. It is this *Yes* that we should grasp with a firm faith.[71] At the end of the letter Barth stated that he did not intend to entrench himself in the positions in which Harnack had placed him, not only because he did not recognize himself in them but also because he knew how "frightfully relative everything is" that one can say about theology. He knew also, therefore, that in the future, it would be necessary to speak in a totally new way from his present insight.[72]

The correspondence ended with a postscript from Harnack in which he thanked Barth for his contributions to the correspondence, stated again that theology and witness must be kept separate if they were to remain healthy, and that science had but one method, one task, "the pure cognition of its object." He questioned Barth's exclusivistic interpretation of the Christian faith and, with the kind of graciousness for which he was famous, Harnack ended the letter by saying that the purpose of the correspondence was to reach clarity in the matter vis-a-vis a theological friend.[73]

III. The Debate with Heinrich Scholz

Barth's lecture, "Theology and Modern Man," was to become the first link in the chain of friendly conversations between Barth and his friend, Heinrich Scholz about theology as a science. The lecture (which Barth first delivered at a student conference at Burg Lauenstein in Thuringia, in 1927 and then repeated at Frankfurt and Heidelberg in 1930) gave Barth an opportunity to explain his understanding of theology as "a particular science." Theology is not a neutral but a personal affair, a matter that engages the theologian at the very core of his being.[74] It calls for decision. Nevertheless, as Barth had insisted ever since the first edition of the *Römerbrief,* theology as a science can never rest on anthropological grounds. It can "never rest on the meaning of *our being* simply because the sense of our being has been lost." Theology is, in fact, a theology of the church for "in the church understanding rests on the basis of the Word." This Word is a word that one cannot say to oneself. The Word that promises existence, forgiveness and hope is "the Word of God." Theology, the "critical understanding" of the church, is done only on the basis of the same Word on which the church itself is founded and is brought forth, as the church continually reflects upon and considers the Word.[75]

Thus, "Theology is that science in which the church gives an account of its activities without any thought of final expectation or of final demands, in order, perhaps, to know how to understand better and do better what she does."[76] The purpose of theology, the critical self-reflection of the church, is to measure the proclamation of the church according to the Word of God. Much like any other science, it has its assumptions or axioms. Such statements, however, are not eternal principles. Their validity is not necessarily assured. Rather, as theological axioms, they have validity from time to time by virtue of what they are able to achieve. Their authenticity rests on the same grace that is operative in prayer *(orent ut intelligant)*.[77] Theology, therefore, has validity only in its own freedom. It is fundamentally *not open* to the grasp of logical consequences nor subject to enthusiastic intuition.[78] By the same token, however, theology can never decree its own authenticity. It can only witness to it. It maintains its own freedom and lives from the living Word of God.

Every theological statement, therefore, can be thought of and pronounced only in obedience to the revelation that stands behind it and before it. It is just because of the distance between the revelation and theological thought that theology makes its statements without assurance, without foundation, without justification. Like the gospel itself, which is *promise* rather than *fulfillment,* so, too, theology never signifies the fulfilled present but always points to future promise.[79]

In a move away from the second edition to the *Römerbrief* wherein negative statements *over against* the world could be and were identified with proper theological statements, now some five years later Barth's mind had changed or at least had shifted.[80] Rather than having primarily negative significance, theology is now to be understood neither as the tearing-down nor as the building-up, neither as negation of what is nor the establishment of what is to be.[81] By the same token, it is, therefore, not up to humankind, not up to the theologian to determine whether or not theology is true or false. Rather, the truth or falsity of any theology depends upon the object of theology, upon God, upon divine election and predestination, i.e., upon God himself choosing theology to reveal himself.

Because theology is completely dependent upon its object, Barth thinks theology is an embarrassment for the other sciences with which it is associated. Theology does not have the inner power to pronounce the veracity or falsity of its own assertions. In that truth is to be understood only as *an event* that rests in the freedom of God in election, it's *event character,* its *actuality,* is always a matter of the *here and now* in the dynamic of God's own freedom. This *actuality of truth* (its *being in act*) means that theological statements can neither be identified with being nor be employed as the point of reference upon which or around which a "world view" can be constructed.[82]

Theology, in other words, knows itself to rest on sheer contingency. It is entirely dependent upon God's decision rather than upon any independent decision of its own. Instead of being bound to principle, it knows only the actuality of being bound (*Bindung*) to its object, the object of its faith.[83] The fact that theology speaks of the Word of God which itself is not timeless but is nothing less than *revelation* (revelation that has become and becomes revelation on specific occasions) means that theology is done in utter trust in the God who has revealed himself. It *wagers* without assurance that God will speak his Word on the basis of the fact that he has already spoken it. This past relatedness of its assurance indicates that theology necessarily is always and primarily memory. "Without remembrance there is no faith, no obedience, no hope."[84]

In the present, then, "theology remains empty. It receives only promise and awaits fulfillment." It is because of this emptiness, the emptiness that in the present can only be filled by obedience to the Word that *decision* is an essential component of *this science*. The theologian always stands in the *decision* between obedience and disobedience. This "decision component" within theology, along with the fact that theology cannot prove its own validity makes it an uncomfortable partner to the other sciences among which it finds itself.

Theology, therefore, "as a critical self-reflection of the church" is necessarily "the science of faith" (*Glaubenswissenschaft*). Only through faith can "human thought count on the Word of God." It is as a *present spoken word* that this Word is present to us. Bound as it is to the Word and to the Word alone, theology has no special insight into history. It has no special psychology that enables it to check out the life of the soul just as humankind has no special organ for the apprehension of the divine. Because theology, as Barth understands it, is utterly different from the other sciences and as different from philosophy as any two areas of human knowledge can possibly be, it has "in the arena of the sciences no eternal resting place (*keine bleibende Stätte*)". By the same token because there is no exact and permanently defined area (*Gebiet*) to which it is confined, in the final analysis theology cannot be separated off from any of the sciences.[85]

Theology, then, is utterly vulnerable. "There is available to the theologian no events by which he can assure himself or others that he does not have a bee in his bonnet (*nicht Grillen fängt*) but rather that he hears and contemplates God's Word (*Gottes Wort vernimmt und bedenkt*)". The only thing the theologian can do, the only thing he can really be certain of is that he cannot assure himself or others that he is acting according to the command [of God]. He can only act so as to witness to the availability of the command. The very vulnerability of his actions witnesses to the fact that as a theologian he "did not come to the command but the command has come to him, that he has not seized the revelation, but that the revelation has seized him."[86] Theology, then, is empowered to witness only when it is penetrated by that to which it refers, when "that which is really theologically said and when that which is theologically meant is actually theologically heard."[87] Nevertheless, because theology is an attempt to speak of the *other* in terms of *this world*, the *diastasis between that* other and this world continues to exist. This in turn implies that theology always stands under judgment *(krisis)*.

On the other hand, if indeed theology is a *science of faith (Glaubens-wissenschaft)*, Barth asks whether or not it may be the case that the other sciences too may not be subject to the same kind of judgment to which theology is subject. The question is whether or not all sciences do not suffer under pseudonymity, whether or not all sciences are not in need of the same kind of "penetration" to which theology is subject in order to accomplish its goal, a penetration that cannot be set out beforehand but can only be believed. In this way, two decades before Michael Polanyi, Barth set out what Polanyi refers to as *the fiduciary factor* in all sciences. Sciences cannot prove their objects. They can only believe them to be. In investigating their objects, they attempt to assemble data to support their basic belief. It is reality itself, or that part of reality that is the *object* of any science, that in the end must become the *subject* of the scientific procedure. In so doing, that to which the science refers, its *object-subject*, testifies to its own existence.[88]

Thus, just as Barth states that one may well reject theology as an impossibility, so too it is quite possible (although Barth himself does not follow this line to the end) to reject any other science as an impossibility as well. All science remains possibility only on the basis of faith. It rests on the faith that the world is such that the human mind can understand it. It is true, of course, that the *truth* with which theology deals or, to put it correctly, the truth that deals with theology, is of a different dimension (it is really beyond dimension) than the objects other sciences attempt to explain. Theology deals with God the Father, the creator, while the other sciences attempt to understand the different aspects of creation of which every scientist and his or her science is a part.

Nevertheless (as Barth hints but does not develop), the operating "principle" of all sciences, including the science, theology, is the same. Science only reveals reality if and when the reality, on which it attempts to focus, shows itself through the procedures of understanding of the science in question. At the same time, these procedures are modified according to the object they attempt to reveal. In this way they become appropriate to their object and are enabled to expose the nature of the specific "reality" toward which they point. This contingency of science generally is especially pertinent for theology. When it does witness to the truth, it is *enabled* to do so only because the sovereign power that theology calls truth, by virtue of its sovereign will (predestination), makes the Word of God audible from time to time as human word. At that point the Word can only be affirmed or rejected. Since this affirmation or rejection is a matter of personal decision, theology is a discipline that operates in a highly personal way demanding a "Yes," or a "No," acceptance or rejection.[89] As Polanyi, who champions the personal relatedness of knowledge, was later to insist, it is only the "act of commitment" that saves this kind of personal knowledge from being merely subjective.[90]

The voice of the living God is *sui generis*. There is neither agreement nor disagreement (*übereinkunft*) with it simply because such agreement or disagreement would presuppose a standard by which the Word itself could be judged. If and when a person who is addressed hears the Word, he or she can only accept it or reject it and live accordingly.[91]

By contrast, Barth states that the history of theology in the last two hundred years showed that rather then accepting its proper dependence on the Word and being obedient to it, theology attempted to become independent and operate on its own. It was most preoccupied with the question of whether or not it was possible to interpret its dependence upon Christ, the Bible, and dogma in such a way that the theologians themselves would be the *subjects* of theology. Theology, so understood, would be in a position to define its own relationships according to its own best judgment.[92] From Schleiermacher to Harnack, therefore, the whole of theology was an effort to understand theology as an historical vehicle, a medium, or symbol by way of which divine truth is recognized. In this way theology became a study of the way in which that "truth" has enlightened us and is grasped by us. This kind of remembering of Christ, the Bible and dogma, however, treats them only as "accidental truths of history" (*zufällige Geschichtswahrheiten*). They are truths that are to be welcomed to be sure, but truths so understood are also to be mastered. The nineteenth-century theologian and the philosopher of religion "set up his own throne of judgment." Rather than being judged by theology he himself became the judge of theology and the domestication of theology (*die Verharmlosung der Theologie*) was the result.[93]

Dogma and dogmatics thus became nothing more than the "expressions of the momentary valid religious convictions." The exegesis of Scripture was understood to be an interpretation of the honorable religious teachings of the prophets and the apostles which had no basic binding character. Even though this theology is invalid, to say the least, proper theology must be well aware of it simply because it is only in rejecting this theology that theology can (in the right sense of the word) become and can remain theology. Barth nevertheless comforted himself with the fact that, as he had learned from Dostoevski, God continues to undergird creation even in its errors and anomalies. Even this anthropocentric theology, therefore, seldom wholly sank to the level of complete non-validity. The continuance of the theological concept of truth did not allow itself to be discredited so easily. Rather, it continued to make itself felt even in the background of the modern religious philosophical teachings and doctrines of faith that follow them.[94]

We are fortunate in having the scientific understanding of theology advocated by Barth set out with succinct adroitness by Eduard Spranger, in a lecture, *"Der Sinn der Voraussetzungslosigkeit in Geisteswissenschaften,"*("The Meaning of the Absence of Presuppositions in the Human Sciences").[95] Spranger's lecture was delivered in January 1929 and was referred to by Scholz in a lecture in the next year when he attacked Barth's position directly. At the time the *classical* understanding of scientific epistemology was being called into question. In 1926 and 1927 respectively, the usual understanding of even physics, that "hardest of the sciences," had been shattered by Werner Heisenberg's discovery of the Principle of Indeterminacy (*Unbestimmtheitsrelation*) and Niels Bohr's Theory of Complementarity. According to the Principle of Indeterminacy, it was impossible to designate both the momentum and the position of a particle simultaneously – the more exact one measurement was, the more inexact was the other. This, in turn, demanded the consideration of the "observer relationship" within science, on the one hand, and called into question the classical understanding of *causality*, on the other. In choosing which of the two phenomena to measure the observer became a part of the equation. Further, in that all particulars of the trajectories of particles could neither be predicted of an experiment nor accounted for afterwards, the classical cause and effect nexus became highly suspect. Bohr's Principle of Complementarity pointed out that both the momentum factor and the position factor, although logically contradictory, were equally necessary for a proper understanding of the physics involved. This, in turn, called into question the legitimacy of a logic of strict coherence that up to the time had been considered the *sine qua non* of science.

Spranger himself made essentially three points that are pertinent to our discussion, all of which one way or another, had been made previously by Barth. The first concerns the fact that it is no longer possible to speak of science as being without *presuppositions*. It no longer adheres to the *independence postulate* of which we will speak later. Since the seventeenth and eighteenth centuries science had been built on the understanding that nature was entirely rational and therefore entirely open to the rational mind. This *ratio sive natura* notion was the unmistakable reminder of the idea that the divine in nature remained the hidden confession of science and gave to the whole of science a religious attribute. Hence, if, as Barth claimed, theology was a *Glaubenswissenschaft* (a science of faith), so too the whole of science rested on the faith that the world was rational. Science was possible, to follow Rene' Descartes, because the rationality of the *res cogitans* (the mind) was paralleled by the rationality of the *res extensa* (the world outside the mind). So also Einstein could say not only, "The eternal mystery of the world is its comprehensibility,"[96] but that "God does not play dice."[97]

Today, however, neither the idea of a totally independent science nor the idea that all prepositions of science are logically consistent with one another are any longer acceptable. We know that all science, including mathematics, rests on presuppositions, so that, as Kurt Gödel has shown, it cannot prove its own consistency. Spranger's statement that the presuppositions of science are not necessarily independent but may well be conditioned by a *world-view* that is quite extraneous to science itself is open to question.[98] There would seem little doubt that every science is dependent upon a *metascience*.

The second point that Spranger stresses is that there is an important subjective element in all sciences and especially in the human sciences. This inevitable subject-relatedness, does not mean that the sciences are no longer subordinate to their objects. It means, however, as both Heisenberg's *Principle of Indeterminacy* and Bohr's *Theory of Complementarity* demand, that experiments be "observer-related". This means that it is no longer possible to disregard the place of the scientist in the understanding of science. The idea of the pure *cognizing self* with an eternal supply of categories of perception is thus no longer admissible. By the same token, neither Husserl's pure perception of essence (*reine Wesenschau*) nor Nietzsche's cold demon of knowledge *(kalter Dämon der Erkenntnis)* are any longer feasible.[99] Rather the natural sciences (*Naturwissenschaften*) and the human sciences (*Geisteswissenschaften*) are dependent upon presuppositions and perspectives. They are, as we would say *theory-laden.* This may mean also that the final objectivity of a science always escapes the subject-influenced formulations of science *per se.* The subjective aspect of science, to refer again to Polanyi, is the personal-relatedness of science that demands personal commitment to escape arbitrariness.[100] Spranger's statement that "only those who personally participate in the Christian *Heilsgeschichte* and Christian community can make fully valid statements", is thus in agreement with Barth (and Polanyi). The third point emphasized by Spranger which is in line with Barth's concept of theology as a science is that "the one law which moves all the sciences diverse as they may be, is that all are directed to 'the idea of truth'. It is the spark which comes out of truth itself that drives every researcher as a living historical individual forward."[101] Taken as a whole, then, Spranger's discussion, which makes no reference to Barth, illustrates to a considerable extent that the kind of "scientific conceptions" with which Barth was operating at the time in his theology were at the very frontier of scientific epistemological considerations.

By contrast, the challenge to Barth's position issued by Scholz, although he was aware of Spranger's statement, was made from the point of view of "classical science" rather than under the impress of the modifications to scientific thinking that had taken place, especially in the physics of the time. In opposition to the position set out by Spranger, Scholz's lecture, *"Wie ist eine evangelische Theologie als Wissenschaft möglich?"* ("How is it Possible for an Evangelical Theology to be a Science?") was intended to be a direct challenge to the scientific nature (*Wissenschaftlichkeit*) of the kind of theology Barth understood to be a science?

Scholz posits three sets of requirements as being "necessary and adequate" for any science whatsoever. In an ascending scale, these are: the minimal requirements, the moderate requirements, and the maximal requirements.[102] Two conditions necessary for all the requirements are the "proposition postulate" (*Satzpostulat*) and the "formalisation postulate" *(Aufspaltbarkeit aller Sätze)*. The first condition refers to the conviction that the only statements admissible are those that are considered true, i.e., those not contradicted by "known facts." The second demands that the components of any science be expressible in statements.[103] Added to the basic conditions at *the minimal requirement level* are the "coherence postulate" *(Kohärenzpostulat)*, which indicates that all statements must refer to a defined sphere of "reality," and the verifiability postulate" (*Kontrollierbarkeitspostulat*), which demands that all propositions of a science be subject to testing.[104]

The moderate requirement level includes the four conditions of the minimal level plus two others that Scholz admits are controversial. The first is the "independence postulate" *(Unabhängigkeitspostulat)* which states that science be free of prejudice and be independent of all inadmissible assumptions. The second is the "concordance postulate" *(Konkordanzpostulat)* which requires that the only statements admissible are those in accord with, i.e., which do not contradict the understanding of reality as recognized by physics and biology.

Scholz would personally prefer the moderate requirement. He realizes, however, even as Spranger had pointed out, and indeed as Aristotle had long since stated in the first chapter of the *Analytica Posteriora*, that there is no such thing as a science without presuppositions. Even the formulae of physics, those of thermo-dynamics, for instance, are in the end "conventions" without absolute proof. More seriously, as said, the then newest developments in physics, namely Heisenberg's "Principle of Indeterminacy" and Bohr's "Theory of Complementarity" had seriously compromised the classical understanding of causality. Nevertheless, Scholz thinks that theology must continue to respect the limitations of nature set by physics and biology and not ascribe to anything that appears to be physically impossible. He thus commends Schleiermacher for respecting the development of science that had taken place in the 300 years prior to his time so that he did not have to disprove physics in order for Christianity to exist.[105]

The maximum requirement level of a science, according to Scholz, is patterned according to the paradigm of mathematics and worked out according to Aristotelian logic. This model includes "basic axioms" or "first order statements", "theorems" or "second order statements" (the truth of which depends upon the truth of the axioms), and the strict application of Aristotelian logic as the means for moving from one order to another. Scholz knew that even in mathematics, Aristotelian logic has been compromised by the work of the Dutchman, L. E. J. Brouwer, for instance, whose revolutionary interpretation of Aristotelian logic called into question Aristotle's "excluded middle". Brouwer's formula, which indicates that the axiom is not false but meaningless, results in the same kind of compromise to logic as do the implications of Heisenberg's Principle of Indeterminacy and Bohr's Theory of Complementarity. Scholz was well aware of the fact that the maximal requirements are beyond the necessities for any evangelical theology. Indeed, in a strict sense, they are beyond the necessities of any science. Nevertheless, he is probably quite right in admonishing theologians to give some attention to the axiomatic system if for no other reason than that the practice of setting theology out in precise statements and order and, under the pressure of Aristotelian logic, could well serve to prevent inadmissible assumptions from entering into the system surreptitiously.[106]

Scholz's conclusions are interesting even if they seem to lack consistency. As stated, he would prefer the moderate level of requirements for an evangelical theology to qualify as a science. He would settle, however, for the minimal level. Nevertheless, in the end and quite unexpectedly, he refuses to judge whether or not any theology fulfills the conditions of being a science simply because any decision in this regard (and here he comes close to Barth, Spranger, and Polanyi) depends upon one's personal perspective, style, and sense of timing. Thus he knows that any decision as to whether or not a body of knowledge constitutes a science cannot be forced. Although Scholz does not explicitly admit it, this means that the decision as to whether or not a discipline is a *science*, like the components of the science itself, is always a matter of personal decision. As Thomas Kuhn has explained, such components and/or such definitions become "scientifically acceptable" when the specific scientific community responsible for the science in question accepts the formulations of one of its members as being a valid representation of the "object" with which the particular group of scientists is concerned.[107]

Despite his concessions Scholz was certain that Barth's statement in *Die Theologie und der heutige Mensch* that theology was an act of blind faith, "a wager", "a dangerous possibility in a dangerous moment", meant that Barth had pulled theology out of the realm of the sciences. Perhaps with more kindness than honesty, Scholz went on to state that he simply does not understand Barth when Barth, after saying that "theology has no final resting place among the sciences," went on to say that there is no evidence available to the theologian by which he is able to convince himself or others that he "does not have a bee in his bonnet *(das er nicht Grillen fängt)* but, in reality, appropriates and is concerned with the Word of God."[108]

In the end and despite his earlier reticence to pronounce upon theology's status as a science, Scholz decided that, in actuality, there is no *evangelical theology* as such nor is there an evangelical theology that could qualify as a science. There are rather a plethora of competing concepts each one claiming to be "evangelical". In addition, the theological statements about God and Christ, as well as those about man and the world (that are supposed to be true even independent of the evangelical character) cannot be proven. Evangelical theology, therefore, Scholz is convinced, is not a science. It is but a confession of faith. And as for Barth's theology, it is "convincing only to those who are already convinced."[109]

In the "Postscript" *(Nachwort)* to his lecture, Scholz notes that the main criticism of his presentation was that he had omitted mention of the main requirement of any science, the *postulate of objectivity (Sachhaltigkeit* or *Gegenstandsmässigkeit)*, i.e., the demand that a science be understood in relationship to its object both in method and in content.[110] He then explained that he had omitted the postulate of objectivity or "whatever one wants to call it," because, "I have yet to meet a criterion, even in a single case of serious disagreement, that was any help at all in deciding whether a given thought was objective or not." For support he refers to Spranger's conclusion that every definition, be it a definition of a state or of a religion, is based on a *confession* of what a genuine state or a genuine religion is supposed to be.[111]

Barth, of course, was not at all convinced by Scholz's *tour de force* with regard to the niceties of the logical tenets of a science in Scholz's sense and he said as much in the Preface to the first volume of his

Kirchliche Dogmatik (1932) where he restates and rejects Scholz's position with some vehemence. Before that, however, he was to write his *Christliche Dogmatik* (1927) and his *Anselm: Fides Quaerens Intellectum* (1931). In the *Christliche Dogmatik* there is somewhat of a shift in Barth's theological conceptuality in relationship to the emphasis he places on the difference between God and man. Although he was not to move into a positive assessment of this relationship until after his book on Anselm, even in the *Christliche Dogmatik*, in contrast to his book on the Pauline Epistle, he found that he had to move away from Kierkegaard. "I could no longer continue to use the theoretical-practical *diastasis* between God and man in the same way that I had used it at the time of the *Römerbrief*." [112] As in the prefaces to his *Römerbrief* and in the Harnack correspondence, however, he continued to protest against neo-Protestantism. [113] And, as before, and in spite of Harnack's admonitions, Barth stated again, "Dogmatics is dogmatic science when its methodological practice is characterized by pondering the relationship of the human word of preaching to the proclamation of the Word of God. [115] It has to do, as it had to do until the eighteenth century, not with *doxa* (opinion) but with the truth given from God with concrete authority.

In his chapter on "Dogmatik als Besinnung auf das Wort Gottes" ("Dogmatics as Reflection on the Word of God") Barth states, "When necessary reflection [on the Word of God] is carried out in a methodological way, then dogmatics is dogmatic science." "Instruction is not possible without seeking a way to put the whole into a definite order." Hence, he agrees with H.H. Wendt with regard to the requirement that science must use every means to insure objective truth, if and only if the means of insuring the objective truth, the selection of the epistemological method, the critical norm and the possibility of proof "is determined by the particularity of the object in question and with the assurance that the object be not in any way violated *(Gewalt angetan werden)* by the demands of the scientific method that is set over it".[116] Barth insists therefore that "construction of a theological *presentation* [I deliberately avoid the term "system" here] is "not an *a priori* construction but is emphatically an *a posteriori* construction." It is reflection on revelation that has happened and that has been understood. The focus is on Jesus Christ in whom the two conditions of the "objective possibilities of revelation" have been fulfilled in relationship to their inner impulses *(Momenten)*. In him both God and man meet us. [117]

IV The Theology of the Word

A radical shift in Barth's theology came about through consideration of the thought of Anselm of Canterbury. Barth first began an
exposition of Anselm in his seminar in Münster in 1926. Barth had
referred to Anselm in the "Introduction" to his *Christliche Dogmatik*
where he mentions Anselm's emphasis that the challenge to the
legitimacy of the content of the Christian discourse must always and
in every situation be tackled anew and from the ground up. It is not as
if nothing has happened before, but because everything has already
happened, "it must happen again through us so that it happens for us."
Anselm takes up the questions of theology in *Cur Deus Homo?*, for
instance, "without any presuppositions whatsoever" and that means
that he attempts to understand Christian dogmas as truth "not
because of their authority" but "according to the *rationabiliter* (reason-
ableness)" of any particular subject as understood within all the
relationships of its particular context *(Sachzusammenhang).*[118]

Interestingly enough, it was after Scholz addressed Barth's Anselm
seminar in Bonn in 1930 on "The Proof of the Existence of God in
Anselm's *Proslogion,* "that Barth felt compelled to deal with Anselm in
a different way than heretofore. The result was his *Anselm: Fides
Quaerens Intellectum,* the book he wrote *with more love* than any of his
other books. The work marks the beginning of Barth's *Anselmian*
Reformation because Anselm's argument was eventually to become
fundamental to Barth's whole theological epistemology and thus to
his understanding of theology as a science.[119] Anselm enabled
Barth to narrow the *diastasis* (the distance) between God and humankind. The abyss was bridged, however, not from the side of humankind as was the constant attempt of nineteenth-century neo-Protestantism, but from the side of God. It was, in fact, the narrowing, or
better said, the understanding of that abyss that forced Barth not only
to delay the revision of the first volume of his *Christliche Dogmatik,* but
in the end to abandon the book entirely. From his Anselm book forward, Barth enters his third period, *The Theology of the Word* as contained in his *Kirchliche Dogmatik.*

For Anselm, as Barth explained him, *credo,* "I believe," does not
mean simply "a striving of the human will towards God", but a
creaturely "participation in God's mode of Being." As Barth had

advocated since the *Römerbrief, credo ut intelligam* must be understood in the sense that it is my very faith itself that summons me to knowledge."[120] Therefore "theological science, as science of the *credo* (of what I believe), can have only a positive character." Further, "*intelligere* (understanding) comes about by reflection on the credo that has already been spoken and affirmed." Nevertheless, it is still true that because God is absolutely unique, "every theological statement is an inadequate expression of its object." In that he alone is true and real, and in a category of his own, "God shatters every syllogism."[121]

That being said, however (and here we see a real change in Barth since both the *Römerbrief* and the *Christliche Dogmatik*), "it is possible for expressions which are really appropriate only to objects that are *not identical* with God, *to be true expressions* . . . even when these expressions *are applied to God* who can never be expressed.[122] Theological statements can be made, therefore, with a "scientific certainty" even though, because of their relative nature, they themselves must be distinguished from faith. The only exception that Anselm makes to this rule is when the statement coincides with the biblical text. Thus, although Barth continues to insist that a theological statement is "an interim-statement, the best that knowledge and conscience can for the present construe; it awaits better instruction from God or man," it may nonetheless be true.[123] The verdict of whether a particular scientific contribution represents a proper understanding rests with the author, his readers, and those who are in conversation with him. Untimately, however, the verdict of truth or falsehood is hidden in God.

The criterion for theology or really for the theologian who is integral to his theology, is the nourishment of Scripture, the necessity of a pure heart, and obedience in the life of the Spirit. The mode of understanding is that of prayer for it is God alone who "enlightens the eyes."[124] Thus, the decisive demand of *scientific objectivity* is that the theologian realize that "everything depends on the fact that God both grants him the grace to think correctly about himself," and that, "God himself comes within his system as the object of this thinking." God (the *object* who is really *subject*) then shows himself to the theologian who thinks about God in such a way that the theologian's thought is modified and corrected until it becomes a proper understanding of the essentiality of God himself.[125]

As with the second edition of the *Römerbrief* in relationship to the first edition, so after his work on Anselm, Barth so altered his *Christliche Dogmatik* in writing his *Kirchliche Dogmatik* that again "hardly one stone was left on the other." He really had to begin again and as he began, he made a point of answering Scholz's challenge to the scientific nature of his theology by first adumbrating Scholz's demands for any undertaking that would rank itself as a science as follows: (1) freedom from contradiction of all presuppositions ("the proposition postulate"); (2) unity in the sphere of its object ("the coherence proposition postulate"); (3) the possibility that all propositions used may be tested by sufficiently attentive readers or hearers ("the verifiability postulate"); (4) respect for that which is physically and biologically possible ("the congruity postulate"); (5) freedom from all pre-judgment ("the independence postulate"); and (6) the possibility of all propositions being broken up into axioms and theorems and demonstrated on this basis ("the formalisability postulate").[126]

Taken as a whole Barth's answer to Scholz is not altogether satisfactory. Rather than going into Scholz's argument point for point and noting the modifications that Scholz himself had made to the requirements of science and the different levels involved, he attacks Scholz's argument as a whole stressing the point that theology dare not allow itself to be compromised by the demands of any procedures outside of its own. Hence, Barth does not bother to consider Scholz's judgemnt that an evangelical theology adhere only to the "minimum" demands of science, that is, the demand for truth, formalisability, inherent consistency, and openness of control. Although these, like the rest of the requirements that Scholz lists, cannot be strict demands upon theology,[127] all "systems" of thought, including Barth's theology, adhere to them to a certain degree. Without admitting what may be termed a *weak case* of adherence to Scholz's *minimal demands* (granted that these demands will be and must be qualified by a *stronger case* for the *objectivity* of theology, i.e., its appropriateness to its object), Barth could not say, as he does, that in addition to being "a human concern with a definite object" like all sciences theology is "a definite and *self consistent* path of knowledge." Like all sciences too, he goes on, "it must give an account of this path to itself and to all others who are capable of concern for this object and of treading the path". [128] Nevertheless, Barth is quite correct in judging Scholz's formal demands as being far and away too "methodologically rigid" for any theology that is concerned to be more *consistent* with the demands of its *object* than with the requirements of its *formal structure*. Were the latter to obtain, theology would be beholden primarily to human logic rather than the *logia* of God.

Barth is also right in thinking that the requirements of science, as defined by Aristotle, are passé. In fact, Aristotelianism has never proven to be a valid basis for science as we know it. Johannes Philoponos in the sixth century, Robert Grosseteste and Roger Bacon in the thirteenth, and especially John Duns Scotus and William of Ockham in the late thirteenth and early fourteenth centuries, had already begun to set Aristotle aside. Aristotelianism was finally broken by the late Renaissance and the Reformation and only on the basis of a *broken Aristotelianism* was modern science able to arise in the first place - a fact which Scholz ignores.

Barth agrees with Scholz's point that the theologian ought to know what he is about when he transgresses the laws of science. In that Barth understood science, other than theological science, as *classical science* he is also quite right in adding, "As a theologian, he cannot help transgressing them." Scholz might even agree with Barth's continued statement, "Not an iota can be yielded here without betraying theology, for any concession at this point involves surrendering the theme of theology." Scholz would simply say in this regard that "if so, then theology, whatever else it is, is not a science". As already discussed, the crux of the matter as Barth points out, is that Scholz did not put a proper emphasis upon "objectivity" *(Sachgemässheit)*, i.e., the appropriateness of every theological statement to the object of theology. This, Barth quite rightly insists, is the "one distinctive rule to which theology may and must adhere."[129]

The real distinction between Barth and Scholz, as we have already indicated (and this analysis is somewhat in contrast to that of both Wolfhart Pannenberg and Gerhard Sauter), is that while Scholz sets out the ground rules for science in general, Barth is much more up-to-date in realizing that every science is *particular* both in content as well as in form. As T.F. Torrance has pointed out so vividly, every science, including its inner logical structure, must be appropriate to its object, i.e., in Barth's terms, *sachlich.*[130] It is exactly for this reason Barth points to the address by Arthur Titius given July 26, 1932, "*Ist systematische Theologie als Wissenschaft möglich?"* ("Is Systematic Theology Possible as a Science?") as being a somewhat more harmless as well as a more general definition of the understanding of science than that given by Scholz. According to Titius, "science is 'present or in process or realization wherever common work exists or is possible in the realm of knowledge.' " Science, in other words is *any discipline which attempts to investigate a particular object in terms most appropriate to the object itself.*[131]

Thus Barth's statement, "If theology allows itself to be called or calls itself, a science, in doing so it cannot accept the obligation of submission to standards valid for the other sciences," may or may not be true simply because Barth's formal definition of science as such, is much more restrictive than his functional understanding of science with regard to theology. Formally he still seems to have in mind the kind of science Scholz proposed, i.e., science as "classical" science. That understanding of science, however, as Spranger had pointed out, was already passé at the end of the twenties. Barth's definition of theology which "cannot think of itself as a link in an ordered cosmos, but only as a stop-gap in a disordered cosmos," is exactly the kind of definition that much of modern science, especially modern physics, follows. Thus, Barth insists that it is just because theology has its own object of inquiry as do the other sciences that it may indeed regard itself as a science, if not from the point of view of "principle," certainly as a possibility.[132]

In realizing the tentativeness, the transitoriness, the dependence of every science upon an object that is too large for its own comprehension, along with the knowledge that no science is complete in itself but depends upon a meta-science that itself is incomplete, modern science resembles proper theology much more than it resembles the classical seventeenth-century Newtonian science and even less Aristotelian science. What is true for theology is also true for the other sciences. The only way that theology has of proving its scientific character is "to devote itself to the task of knowledge as determined by its actual theme and thus to show what it means by true science," as Barth said. Thus Barth is right in insisting that "no science has any manorial rights to the title, nor does any theory of science have absolute power either to grant or withhold the title." Therefore, "theology has no reason not to call itself a science." In fact, "it [theology] may well prove to be more of a science than many or even all the sciences grouped under the above convention."[133]

Barth's three practical reasons as to "why we should quietly insist in describing theology as a science" are applicable not only to theology but to other sciences as well. The first is that theology, as a human concern for truth, "recognizes its solidarity with other such concerns now grouped under the name of science." This, by the way, was Scholz's first postulate, one that Barth failed to emphasize in his discussion. Likewise Barth is right in saying that theology [as all science] must be humble. There is no "ontological exaltation" of theology above the other sciences as might be suggested by older designations, *doctrina* or even *sapientia.* In line with his statement of 1927, that we do not possess any special organ for the reception of the divine, he insists that theology is only secular even as it carries on its activities in its "relatively special way" and "in the highest spheres."[134]

Barth's second reason for not resigning the title of science to others is that in maintaining the designation theology makes a necessary protest against the concept of science that is pagan and is built on the tradition which commences with the name of Aristotle and shows that it is only one among others.[135] Here Barth would seem to be quite correct in refusing to allow only so-called "secular sciences" to dominate or to completely occupy the field of knowledge. At the same time, however, it is well to remember Barth's own admonition that there is no special human organ by which the truth of theology as over against that of other areas of thought, may be grasped.

Barth's third reason follows from his second. Theology should group itself among the sciences because in so doing theology shows that it does not take the sciences' heathen understanding of themselves seriously enough to separate itself from them under another name. Rather, it "reckons them as a part of the Church in spite of their refusal of the theological task and their adoption of the concept of science which is so intolerable to theology." The statement it would seem, is half right and half wrong. It is right in that theology never believes in the "final reality of a heathen pantheon" It is wrong, however, to qualify the sciences other than theology as being heathen just as it would be wrong to claim that theology is somehow "holy." There is a sense, of course, in which all concepts are human and therefore as Christian or heathen as are their authors. All are a part of fallen-redeemed creation. This, as Barth knew full well, must be said about the ideas and statements of the Bible and church doctrine as well as about any other human ideas and statements. That being so, it would seem that to judge a system of thought as being "Christian" or "heathen" would be an ambiguous procedure at best. It may well be that at times, at least, "the sons of this world are wiser in their own generation than the sons of light" (Lk. 16:8).

Thus we see that any judgment of Karl Barth in relation to science must be given an ambivalent answer. The main components of Barth's theological method are: (1) that theology be objective *(Sachlich)*; (2) that the structure and procedures of theology be directed by its own particular object, an object that in the case of theology is always and only *subject* (i.e., that God may be known only as he reveals himself. He is both the object of knowledge and the means by which knowledge of himself may be gained); (3) that the procedures of theology be determined not outside of itself from the other sciences but in accordance with its own precepts as these are focused upon the *object* of theology; and (4) that the assumptions of theology be self-critical; and finally (5) that there be a recognition of the *ad hoc,* always inadequate and tentative nature of theology's formulations and answers.

In his discussion of science other than theology, however, Barth for the most part unfortunately did not move much beyond the so-called "eggshells" of his nineteenth-century predecessors. For them, following in the wake of Schleiermacher, science was classical science. It was a closed system determined not so much by its *object* as by the nature and the conceptual apparatus of its *subject,* i.e., the scientist. It was characterized by the Cartesian mechanistic universe as understood in relationship to the infinite dimensions of the time and space of Newton and formulated according to *a priori* categories of the apperception of Kant. All of these, as Spranger pointed out, were the remains of the *ratio sive natura* (nature as reasonable) which, as stated above, is simply the secularization of the *deus sive natura* of Aristotelian philosophy and Thomistic theology. Hence, rather than Scholz being more right than Barth, (as Wolfhart Pannenberg tends to argue in his discussion of the Barth-Scholz controversy), it would seem that Barth has the edge on Scholz, sometimes in spite of himself, as far as the actual understanding of theology as science is concerned.[136]

As we have seen, however, this does not mean that Barth is a sure guide to all things. A case in point was his refusal to converse with the physicists and philosophers about the relationship of science to theology in the Göttingen Theologian-Physicists conversations that took place between the years 1949-61, in spite of the fact that his friend Günter Howe who had seen parallels between Barth's theology and modern physics plead with Barth to join the group on several occasions. Barth's refusal to join the theologians-physicists conversations was probably a tragic result of his formal *misunderstanding* of "the sciences." Whereas Barth still thought of the natural sciences in their pre-modern mode, the ideas of science, specifically those of Günter Howe, C.F. von Weizsäcker, and Werner Heisenberg, for instance, (all of whom were members of the Göttingen group) were much more congruous with Barth's own theological method than was his own understanding of what "the sciences" were about.[137]

Again, the fact that Barth's actual way of doing theology is much more congruous with modern scientific method than is his realization of the essence of modern science does not mean, nor would he himself want it to mean, that he has said the final word on the matter. Like Neil Armstrong, as he stepped off the lunar module on the surface of the moon, Barth may have made one small step for himself, but he certainly made a giant step for humankind. In breaking with the nineteenth-century idealistically-influenced Enlightenment concepts, he did, in an incomparable way, what no one else in our time has been given to do. As Professor Daniel Lamont of the University of Edinburgh, a disciple of Lord Kelvin but not of Barth, has said, "He has done the biggest thing that a theologian has done since Luther and Calvin ... he has brought back into the light what should never have been allowed to slip into the shade, that God is neither an object among objects nor a subject among subjects but *the Subject* of subjects."[138] In this way Barth quite literally rescued theology in our time as a proper science.

Nevertheless Barth was not able to distance himself entirely from the ninetenth-century neo-Protestantism from which he has done so much to save the rest of us. His idea of the independence of theology that in itself is not only inaccessible to the other sciences but has nothing to learn from them, comes from his once revered but later rejected teacher, Wilhelm Herrmann. Even as late as October 1945 when he wrote the preface to his "Doctrine of Creation" (*Church Dogmatics*, III/1). Barth excuses his not having dealt with the scientific question posed by the doctrine of creation by saying, "There can be no scientific problems, objections or aids in relation to what Holy Scripture and the

Christian Church understand by the divine work of creation."[139] He is quite right when he states, "There is free scope for natural science beyond what theology describes as the work of the Creator," and "Theology can and must move freely where science which really is science, and not secretly a pagan Gnosis or religion, has its appointed limit."[140] However, in explaining creation simply on the basis of a naive Hebrew saga, he not only fails to address many of the questions about creation that in our day cry out for theological discussion, but perhaps even worse, he fails to remember that the old Hebrew "saga" is based upon what was once thought to be a possible valid account of cosmogony just as surely as our modern scientific theories are considered to be possible and valid assumptions about how the world came to be.

The point is, theology and science have been so intermingled from the beginning and certainly from the beginning of the Hellenistic world whose thought-forms influence the doctrines of the Trinity and Incarnation, for instance, which, as Barth recognizes are central to the expression of the Christian faith, that to ignore the discussion with today's science is simply to discuss theology in terms that are related to the science of the by-gone era. Hence Barth has done a tremendous amount for us, much more than any other single theologian of our time. But as he himself would admit, he has not done everything. We are not to follow him, as he himself has said, "If there are Barthians, I am not one of them,"[141] but we are to learn from him and attempt to move forward. Even as he advised that we must hear beyond the Apostle Paul [142] so we must hear beyond Barth.

There can, it would seem, be little or no argument about whether or not Barth thought of theology as a science. As a matter of fact, he thought of theology as a science from the very beginning of his writings. It is one of the most consistent features of his thought. To be sure his theology changed, his understanding of *theology as a science* underwent a metamorphosis as well. Toward the very end of his writing career there are hints of a final alteration in his thoughts regarding the relationship of theology to the *other sciences* that are nothing less than profound. He was not able to work this out in all particulars, but one of the last of his writings, *Evangelical Theology, An Introduction* points the direction to the future.

Barth reiterates that like the other sciences theology too seeks to apprehend a specific *object*. like the other sciences also, its effort of apprehending is *directed* by the object that the science in question is attempting to understand. All sciences, including theology, attempt to understand their objects on their own terms and to speak of these objects along with the full implications of their existence. Barth then identifies theology as a science in quite unmistakable language. The word " 'theology', seems to signify a special science, a very special science, whose task is to apprehend, understand, and speak of God."[143]

Showing deep insight, and in direct contradiction to most discussions about the relationship of theology to philosophy whereby it is usually said that, "theology always speaks in philosophical terms," Barth turns the tables as he points out that there is, "no philosophy that is not to some extent also theology." Whether the philosophers are ready to admit that divinity is the essence of truth or not, even those who deny such a divinity transfer "an identical dignity and function to another object" be it nature, creativity, an unconscious and amorphous will to life, reason, progress or even a "redeeming nothingness". Thus even such apparently "godless" ideologies are theologies. [144] Every system of thought *ipso facto* represents itself as the best. The best can prove itself the best (and here Barth re-iterates the deep insight which he had already stated in 1927) "by the demonstration of the spirit and of its power."[145]

Thus, Barth's way of doing theology that took a decisive turn with his little book on Anselm, reaches its final form in the "late Barth" with regard to method, but also with regard to content. The God of the Gospel no longer only judges humankind, as he was said to do with stringency and severity throughout the dialectical period. Now God does not primarily negate that which is of this world, as Barth so loudly proclaimed in the second edition of the *Römerbrief* and even in the prefaces through the fifth edition. Rather "The God of the Gospel is the God who mercifully dedicates and delivers himself to the life of all men – including their theologies." [146] God no longer says, "No," to the world. On the contrary, he engages himself with it. He continues to transcend the world to be sure but here in contradistinction to the dialectical Barth, God's *Yes* is louder than his *No*. He must still be discovered again and again. He discloses himself ever anew and must be discovered anew. He remains the God over whom theology neither has nor receives sovereignty but he is the God who is *for* the world rather than against it.

In contradistinction to the claims of his friend, Heinrich Scholz, whose ideas about science Barth remembered until the end of his life, the Barth of the *Evangelical Theology* continued to maintain that evangelical theology is "a particular theology," even "a particular science." It is a theology, as Barth had insisted in his Harnack correspondence, that has its legacy in the New Testament and the sixteenth-century Reformation. It is the theology that consciously has God for its object in contradistinction to any theology based on subjective feelings or ideas about God, against which Barth protested from the second edition of the *Römerbrief* onward. "Wherever he [God] becomes the object of the human sciences, both its source and its norm, there is *evangelical theology.*"[147] Evangelical theology (like any other particular science, by the way) must set forth and proceed along its own path which is "fundamentally and totally different from that of other theologies."[148] It does so because it is determined to do so by its *object* who is also its *subject*. It continues to assume a dialectic. The dialectic, however, no longer has primary reference to the complete *diastasis* between God and humankind. It now refers to human existence as understood under the term, *justus et peccator* (justified but sinful).

Thus, theology is "primarily and comprehensively interested in God himself." Its dominant presupposition is "God's own proof of his existence and sovereignty." Any reversal of this relationship, by which, for instance, theologians would attempt to prove God or, instead of pointing to the relation of man to *God*, would really try to relate God to *man* would surrender theology "to a Babylonian captivity." For it is the God with whom theology deals, or who in a real sense deals with theology, that is truth, "truth" in the sense of the Greek word, *aletheia*. As "truth" God is both in the event of self-disclosure and is the content of that event. It is precisely because this God is a living God that theology, which must give an account of his history, must not be stuck in history. Rather, theology has the "character of a living procession." It is not static but it is a *theologia viatorum* (theology of the wayfarer). It follows the living God "in those unfolding historical events in which he is God."[149]

Here once again, one sees how far Barth has moved from his dialectic period where God only negated history. One also sees, by the way, how wrong those commentators are who continue to talk of Barth in terms of "dialectical theology," the theology of crisis, much less in terms of *neo-orthodox*, which of course Barth never was. Barth definitely differentiates himself from his early twenties with the statement, "God is not imprisoned by his own majesty, as though he were bound to be no more than the personal (or impersonal) 'wholly other'."[150] Hence, rather than remain with Nietzsche's definition, a definition which was also adopted by Nietzsche's friend, Overbeck, and echoed very loudly indeed by Barth in the second edition of the *Römerbrief,* namely that man is someone that must be overcome, for the Barth of *Evangelical Theology* "man is the creature destined by God to *be conqueror.*"[151]

For this reason we can understand why Barth no longer speaks of theology as having *keine bleibende Stätte* (no final resting place) among the sciences. Rather he suggests that it is now worth considering the place of theology within the university as an impetus to a discussion "about the reason and justification for locating this modest, free, critical and happy science *sui generis* in such an environment." To be sure, theology as a science, is a human science. It is not to be identified with the Word of God. The fact that the term *theology* includes the concept of *logia,* (logic or language) which is bound to God, *theos,* himself and that this *theos* both makes theology possible and determines it, means that theology can never be anything else but "a human *ana-logia* to the Word itself". As logic, thought, and speech it does not claim to say the Word nor does it attempt to contain it or control it. For this reason, too, it is not creative in the sense of creating its object. Rather, it is only a "praise of the creator" and of his act of creation. It is praise that is truly responsive to the creative act of God.[152]

Thus, although theology does not create God, if, indeed, it is theology, the logos or logia of God, God creates it, God himself summons human thought and speech so that it can respond to his Word, "the Word that God spoke, speaks and will speak in the midst of all men." The Word is the very basis of all "the theological logia, logic and language." The Word that goes forth from God is a sovereign Word. It may be ignored *de facto* but not *de jure.* This Word or "speech of God" gives the theological logia their creative basis and life.[153]

> "This Logos is the creator of theology. By it theology is
> shown its place and assigned its task. Evangelical
> theology exists in the service of the Word of God's
> covenant of grace and peace."[154]

So described, set out, and interpreted, theology is indeed a *happy science.* Barth, then, in taking that small step for himself but a giant step for us has made great strides along his own theological *way*. Following the God in whose footsteps theology must always be, *theologia viatorum*, he like the Reformers of the sixteenth century has again pointed the way that theology must always follow.

V. Theology and Science – A Postscript

So much for Barth's own thoughts regarding theology as a science and theology as related to science in general. Like Kierkegaard who inspired Barth, perhaps one who had admittedly been inspired by Barth may be allowed, if not a *Concluding Unscientific Postscript*, then a postscript about science. In light of the *about face* with regard to theology that begins with Barth's work on Anselm and is completed with his *Evangelical Theology*, it is somewhat regrettable that Barth did not have time to come to the realization that theology ought not only to have *eine bleibende Stätte* (an enduring resting place) among the sciences, but that it should be in direct conversation with them. This move would seem to be called for not only, as said above, because when we do theology we speak in relationship either to the science of today or the science of yesterday but also because science and theology have the common concern of uncovering the truth whether it be the truth of God himself or the truth of the creation that exists in contingent relation to him. These *sciences* are, therefore, mutually supporting. They may even mutually inform and modify one another. Not that theology should ever give up its particular identity, its particular method or, above all, its particular object who determines all else. Its object, God, is forever its subject. Nevertheless, the analogies by means of which God inspires humankind to recognize him, are always analogies that have their roots though not their references in this world, the same world with which all the other sciences have to do and in which theology too has its proper place.

This then brings us back to that third possibility which Barth, in his article, "Theology and Modern Man" in 1927, called "the most dangerous possibility open to theology." The most dangerous possibility is one that one finds theology to be good, welcomes it, has no objections to it, considers it necessary and requisite for a satisfying human world-view, and utilizes it as a body of learning for structuring a way of life *(Lebenskunst)*. At the time Barth compared this theology to the Roman Catholic theology of St. Thomas Aquinas and understandably so since Thomas' *analogia entis,* his analogy of being, condemned his theology to be founded upon creation rather than on the Creator. Barth construed such a possibility as the continuation of neo-Protestant liberalism that extended from Schleiermacher through Harnack. These "liberal Protestant theologians," as Barth had learned as a student, saw theology as the *summum bonum* of Christian culture, the result of human efforts and endeavors at self-salvation. Theology so construed was understood from the position of secure anthropology which arrogated to theology the "honor" of being the highest development of humankind.[155]

We would not want to disregard Barth's warning that God is God and that he is always transcendent in relation to the world. Any legitimate theology must, therefore, continue to be aware of the utter and complete difference between God and any creaturely representation of him. However, in the light of the Barth as inspired by Anselm, and as reflected in the last volumes of the *Church Dogmatics* and especially as seen in the *Evangelical Theology: An introduction,* it may be possible to ask about the ramifications of God's being *for* humankind, his *choosing* humankind *to conquer,* one who is to *overcome,* and how science and theology must cooperate in that effort.

With this positive understanding of theology, the statements of which, by the grace of God, may be true statements with regard to God, would it not be possible to consider theology in the construction of a metaphysic? One would not want to advocate that theology must necessarily dominate all other sciences as was the case with the Thomistic medieval synthesis and against which Barth warned in 1927.[156] However, all sciences may perhaps be able to re-learn from theology that they, like it, are utterly dependent upon faith. In that no science, not even mathematics, is in a position to prove its basic presuppositions, all are in the same position that Barth claimed for theology. Assumptions and formulations may be checked for validity only in the working out of the particular science to which they belong. Every statement of every science whether an "assumption," "conclusion," or "fact" is, as said, "theory laden." All depend, as Barth said of theology, upon a *wager.* We bet our minds and indeed our lives upon what we believe. All science, as Barth said early on of theology, is thus *Glaubenswissenschaft.* All are *faith-dependent.* We witness to what we *believe* even in mathematics and physics as well as in theology by our commitment.[157]

With this in mind, it may indeed be possible to recommend what Barth distinctly rejected, namely, that there be an "heuristical theology whose task would be, with fatherly intelligence to make clear to modern man that one who thinks he can get along without the Christian faith, must necessarily entangle himself in self-contradiction," or if not in self-contradiction, certainly in the realization that anyone who denies the Christian faith stands in the same state of epistemological vulnerability as does anyone who accepts it. Contrary to Barth, it may not be wrong, therefore, to have a doctrine of history, the truth of which conforms exactly to that which the Bible depicts as the relationship of God and man. Nor would anthropology necessarily have to be structured so as only to expose the negative aspects of Christology.[158] Indeed, a proper Christology may well find itself enabled to inform anthropology.

This reversal of the meaning of Barth's statements in order to give them a positive connotation would seem to follow from his own latest understanding of theology. If this interpretation is at all correct, it fits hand in glove with science's own understanding of itself as interpreted in the light of modern physics. Such a science depends upon faith. It cannot prove either its assumptions or its conclusions. It has its own special procedures as dictated by its object. Its answers are always *ad hoc* and tentative. Although they may be cumulative, these answers are but the best that can be arrived at according to the evidence available and in relationship to the context in which science is actually done.[159]

Were theology to be in conversation with this kind of science, it would not mean necessarily, as Barth feared, that theology, the science of faith, would also be metaphysics, apologetics, anthropology, the doctrine of history, heuristics, or whatever else one calls it. It would certainly not mean a return to the medieval theology of Thomas Aquinas. It may mean, however, that those relationships defined by theology between God and creation, including humankind, as well as those that exist within creation itself could be regarded as being relevant to the whole of existence. These understandings may then even play a role in "shaping any metaphysic, doctrine of history, heuristic, or whatever science is really science."[160] This would not obviate the fact that faith itself, as indeed science also, continues to be "a wager" without any human guarantee as to its validity whatsoever. As Einstein put it, science is verified only by its "success".[161]

Bonhoeffer pointed out, that "certain manifestations of historical life would at the same time be divine ordinances," a possibility that

Barth rejected in 1927, a rejection that he did not rescind.[162] Certainly, as Barth emphasized, such a theology would indeed be a special science among the sciences. If, as he insisted, the exact dimensions of its realm of enquiry would ever remain somewhat ambiguous, were it to maintain its focus upon its particular *object*, it would have no difficulty differentiating itself from philosophy, the science of history, psychology, or whatever. In that it would undergo constant modification according to the leading of its particular *object* its method of investigation would also be particular. So too, as Barth said as early as in his correspondence with Harnack, were theology genuine theology, the other sciences may well seek relationships with it.

Thus, to repeat, if in 1927, Barth could describe the science of theology as a dangerous possibility in a dangerous moment, certainly in our time, every science stands on that same edge of the abyss. Moreover, if at the end of Barth's dialectical period "modern man" was tired of the atheistic rebellion and pitiful neo-Protestantism and was "about to discover his catholic heart" certainly people of today may well be tired of a theology that either dwells in the categories of the past or deals only with future hope. There is always danger, of course, of people taking refuge in their "catholic heart." We are, after all, everyone of us *naturally* natural theologians. Among most Protestants, however, there may be even a greater danger of continuing a kind of platonically-inspired pietistic inwardness and romantic individualistic sentimentality which encourages us to hide within our own hearts and thus escape the real world.

This does not mean that it is time neatly to seize the scandal of faith to domesticate it and draw it within the confines of our fallible human understanding. Rather it means that, as far as we are given to understand, life without God is scandalous indeed, so scandalous as a matter of fact that, without him, we are unable to recognize the scandal. It means also that the God we know in the light of the gospel, the one whom Barth at the end of his life proclaimed as the God who destined humankind to conquer, the God, who spoke, speaks and will speak in the midst of humankind, is *for* the world and *for* human culture rather than *against* it, [163] is also *for* science. For it is by means of science that the world, people, and culture are both understood and brought to articulation. Although there is certainly the danger of the Grand Inquisitor in every attempt to understand God, as Barth points out, [164] that danger is the danger of misunderstanding, of denying the mystery, of grasping God and putting him into the pockets of our categories rather than of allowing ourselves to realize that, with or without our awareness of him, he is Immanuel, God with us, in the midst of the world. [165] Again, this does not imply that we attempt to evaluate *theology*, our feeble attempts to talk about the God who is in our midst, from outside of theology itself, from some secure place transcendent to it. [166] Rather from within theology itself, as Barth explained, we see God but also from within theology, or at least from a theological perspective we see the totality of the life of the world as contingent upon God.

Understood in this way theology is not a foreigner to the other sciences although it will always be particular. It remains true, as Barth warns, that theologians must always recognize "this last and most dangerous temptation", i.e., the temptation of forcing the world into theological forms. [167] Certainly, an equally dangerous temptation in our time is for theology to continue its ghetto existence, to speak in such a way that only those who are already familiar with the language are enabled to hear, and to be a witness only to those who have been convinced by a theology that not only depends on memory, as all theology must, but one that remains only memory. Such a theology is in danger of continuing to allow the world, and even the church that is in the world, to be dominated either by a sentimental attachment to Christian history or by some anthropologically-centered, psychologically-oriented, bootstrap do-it-yourself self-salvation scheme of the kind that Barth rightly rejected. Theology in conversation with the sciences would at least be aware of the discipines that, whether we like it or not, represent some of the primary shaping forces of the world in which we live. Here we do well to listen carefully to T. F. Torrance:

> "For the first time, then, in the history of thought, Christian theology finds itself in the throes of a new scientific culture which is not antithetical to it, but which operates with a non-dualistic outlook on the universe which is not inconsistent with the Christian faith."[168]

So too we may take Barth's friend, Günter Howe, seriously when he said, "God reveals himself in that he objectifies himself in a piece of the world's reality."[169] That objectification, of course, must be seen through the eyes of faith, eyes that are theologically educated to see the world from God's perspective, eyes that are enabled to see the signs that God erects for us to read. This means, as Howe went on to explain, that theology "has no other choice but to explicate this piece of historical, social [and also physical] reality with the materials of thought that are available at the time and thus make them a part of the church's proclamation and doctrinal system."[170] It is in this way that we may carry out the implications of Bonhoeffer's statement that we must "speak of God not on the boundaries but at the center, not in weakness, but in strength, and therefore not in death and guilt, but in man's life and goodness." Considering the relevance of modern science to our thought structures, it seems no mere matter of coincidence that it was while reading C.F. von Weizsäcker's *World View of Physics* in his prison cell in Berlin-Tegel that Bonhoeffer said this and added, "God is transcendent in the midst of our life,"[171] or to say it again as Barth said it:

> "Evangelical theology is concerned with Immanuel, God with us! [and he added] Having this God for its object, it can be nothing else but the most thankful and [therefore] *happy* science."[172]

Notes

1. Karl Barth, *Evangelical Theology: An Introduction*, 1963, p. 12. For accuracy, this, and a number of subsequent citations from English translations, is altered according to the German text. The term, "Evangelical" in German refers to "Protestant," as over against "Roman Catholic."

2. Karl Barth, *Church Dogmatics*, I.1, 1975, p. 6.

3. Ibid., p. 7.

4. Ibid., pp. 6 f.

5. Barth follows G. Söhngen, "Die kathol. Theo. als Wissenschaft und Weisheit," *Catholica; Vierteljahrschrift für Kontroverstheologie*, April 1932. Cf. Barth, *Ch. Dog.*, I,1, p. 7.

6. Barth, *Church Dogmatics*, I.1, p. 8.

7. Ibid., p. 10.

8. Among the nineteenth century theologians, only A.F.C. Vilmar rejected the term, "science," for theology because "for the time being," at least, it was too heavily loaded. Ibid., p. 7.

9. Karl Barth, *The Epistle to the Romans* [tr. from the sixth edition] (London, Oxford University Press, 1950), pp. 257 ff. Cf. Karl Barth, *Protestant Theology in the Nineteenth Century*, 1972.

10. Barth, *Romans*, pp. 299-301.

11. Ibid., p. 1.
12. Ibid., p. 2.
13. Karl Barth, *How I changed My Mind*, 1966, p. 25.
14. Barth, *Romans*, p. 6.
15. Ibid., p. 6
16. Ibid., p. 8. Italics added.
17. Ibid.
18. Ibid., p. 10.
19. Ibid.
20. Ibid., p. 1.
21. Ibid., p. 10.
22. Ibid.
23. Michael Polanyi, *Personal Knowledge*, 1958, pp. 280 f.
24. Barth, *Romans*, p. 10.
25. Ibid., p. 11.
26. Ibid.
27. Ibid., p. 12.
28. Ibid.
29. Ibid., p. 16.
30. Ibid.
31. Ibid., p. 17.
32. Ibid., p. 18.
33. Ibid.
34. Ibid., p. 19.
35. Ibid.
36. Ibid., pp. 19 f.
37. Ibid., p. 20. Italics added.
38. Ibid.
39. Ibid., pp. 20 f.
40. Ibid., p. 21.
41. Ibid., p. 23.
42. Ibid., p. 25.
43. Eberhard Busch, *Karl Barths Lebenslauf*, 1975, p. 51.
44. Ibid., p. 93.
45. The journal was edited by Barth's friend, Georg Merz. Barth, Gogarten and Thurneysen were contributing editors *(ständige Mitarbeiter)*
46. Barth-Harnack Correspondence, *Die Christliche Welt*, 1923, Nr. 1/2, col. 6-8.
47. Ibid., Nr. 5/6, cols. 88-91.
48. Ibid., Nr. 9/10, cols. 142-144.
49. Ibid., Nr. 16/17, cols. 244-252.
50. Ibid., Nr. 20/21, cols. 305-306.
51. Ibid., Nr. 9/10, col. 142.
52. Ibid., Nr. 5/6, col. 89.
53. Ibid., Nr. 6/7, col. 89.
54. Ibid., Nr. 6/7, col. 89.
55. Ibid., Nr. 1/2, cols. 6-7.
56. Ibid., Nr. 5/6, Col. 89. Cf. Ibid., Nr. 16/17, cols. 245-247.
57. Ibid., Nr. 5/6, col. 89.
58. Ibid., Nr. 5/6, col. 90.

59. Ibid., Nr. 1/2, col. 8

60. Ibid., Nr. 5/6, col. 91.

61. Ibid., Nr. 1/2, col. 8.

62. Ibid., Nr. 5/6, col. 91.

63. Ibid., Nr. 9/10, col. 143.

64. Ibid., col. 144.

65. Ibid., col. 143.

66. Ibid., Nr. 16/17, col. 245.

67. Ibid., col. 246.

68. Ibid., cols. 247-248.

69. Ibid., cols. 248-249.

70. Ibid., col. 249.

71. Ibid., cols. 250-251. It is hardly a coincidence that Hegel, Schelling, and Kant, who were the root of Enlightenment idealism, were all basically Lutheran rather than Calvinist Protestants.

72. Ibid., col. 252.

73. The text of the Barth-Harnack correspondence is reproduced in full in *Theologische Fragen und Antworten.* It has been translated and provided with a book-length commentary by H. Martin Rumscheidt, *Revelation and Theology: An analysis of the Barth-Harnack Correspondence of 1923.* In both publications, Barth's first letter is entitled, "Fifteen [instead of Sixteen] Answers to Professor Adolf von Harnack."

74. Karl Barth, "Die Theologie und der heutige Mensch," *Zwischen den Zeiten,* 1930, pp. 374 f.

75. Ibid., p. 375.

76. Ibid., p. 376.

77. Cf. Augustine, *De doctr. Christ.,* III, 37.

78. Barth, "Die Theologie," p. 378.

79. Ibid., p. 379.

80. For an insightful analysis of Barth's change of mind, cf. *How I Changed My Mind,* ed. John D. Godsey.

81. Barth, "Die Theologie," p. 379.

82. Ibid., p. 380.

83. Ibid., p. 382.

84. Ibid., pp. 380 f.

85. Ibid., p. 383.

86. Ibid., pp. 383 f.

87. Ibid., p. 384.

88. Polanyi, op. cit., pp. 274. f.

89. Barth, "Die Theologie," p. 386.

90. Polanyi, op. cit., p. 61; cf. also pp. 300 ff.

91. Barth, "Die Theologie," p. 387.

92. Ibid., p. 390.

93. Ibid., pp. 390 f.

94. Ibid., pp. 391 f.

95. The lecture was delivered at a meeting of the philosophical section of the Prussian Academy of Science in Berlin on January 10, 1929.

96. Albert Einstein, *Out of My Later Years,* 1974, p. 61.

97. *The Born-Einstein, Letters,* tr. Irene Born (London: Macmillan, 1971), p. 91.

98. Eduard Spranger, *Der Sinn der Voraussetzungslosigkeit in den Geisteswissenschaften,* 1964, p. 9.

99. Ibid., p. 12.

100. Cf. Polanyi, op. cit., pp. 300 ff.

101. Spranger, op. cit., p. 19.

102. Heinrich Scholz, "Wie ist eine evangelische Theologie als Wissenschaft möglich?" *Zwischen den Zeiten*, 1931, pp. 13-15. Scholz gave the lecture first in Barmen-Wuppertal for the Kant Society and then before Barth's seminar on the Reformed Doctrine of Sanctification in Bonn, December 1930. It was printed in *Zwischen den Zeiten* in January, 1931. Cf. Busch, *Barths Lebenslauf,* pp. 191, 220. Barth and Scholz first met in the winter of 1906-7 when both were students in Adolf von Harnack's seminar at the University of Berlin. Scholz, according to Barth, was the brilliant *senior* while he considered himself to be one of the *kleinere Geister* (lesser minds). The two were together again at the University of Münster. Scholz joined the faculty in 1928 as a philosopher of religion and later he was to become professor of mathematical logic and fundamental mathematical research.

103. Ibid., p. 39.

104. Ibid., pp. 19-21.

105. Ibid., pp. 23 f., 37.

106. Ibid., p. 24.

107. Thomas Kuhn, *The Structure of Scientific Revolutions*, 1970, pp. 7 ff.

108. Scholz, "Evangelische Theologie," pp. 28, 45.

109. Ibid., pp. 47 f.

110. Ibid., p. 49.

111. Ibid., p. 52.

112. Busch, op. cit., pp. 186 f.

113. Karl Barth, *Die Christliche Dogmatik*, 1927, p. vii.

114. Ibid., p. 36.

115. Ibid., pp. 112 f.

116. Ibid., pp. 113-115.

117. Ibid., pp. 229 f.

118. Ibid., p. 4. Anselm's thought is, of course, packed with presuppositions, largely those of Platonic philosophy and patristic theology, but he argues *as if* these were not present.

119. Karl Barth, *Anselm; Fides Quaerens Intellectum* [tr. from the second German edition], 1960, pp. 7 f. Cf., Busch, op. cit., p. 219.

120. Barth, *Anselm*, pp. 17 f.

121. Ibid, pp. 26-29.

122. Ibid., pp. 29 f. Italics added.

123. Ibid., pp. 30 f.

124. Ibid., p. 37.

125. Ibid., pp. 34-39.

126. *Church Dogmatics*, I.1, p. 8. The editors of the English translation note that, "These six requirements correspond to: (1) formal consistency, (2) inherent consistency, (3) openness to control through a community of verifiers, (4) antecedent credibility, (5) impartiality or, positively stated, according to the principle of sufficient reason and (6) formalisability." Ibid.

127. Scholz, "Evangelische Theologie," pp. 19-21. Barth does not answer Scholz's third attempt to address the problem of logical consistency in his theology which Scholz put to him in "Was ist unter einer theologischen Aussage zu verstehen?" *Theologische Aufsätze: Karl Barth zum 50. Geburtstag*, 1936, pp. 25-27.

128. Barth, *Church Dogmatics*, I.1, pp. 7 f.

129. Ibid., p. 9.
130. Gerhard Sauter, ed. *Theologie als Wissenschaft*, 1971, pp. 58 ff.; Wolfhart Pannenberg, *Theology and the Philosophy of Science*, 1976, pp. 269-275, 326-330; Thomas F. Torrance, *God and Rationality*, 1971, pp. 1-10.' Thomas F. Torrence, *Theological Science*, 1969, pp. 107-140.
131. Barth, *Church Dogmatics*, I.1, p. 9.
132. Ibid., p. 10.
133. Ibid.
134. Ibid., p. 11.
135. Ibid.
136. Cf. Pannenberg, op. cit., pp. 269-275, 326-330. For a more balanced and very informative discussion of the Barth-Scholz controversy, cf. Sauter, op. cit., pp. 58-64.
137. Harold Nebelsick, *Theology and Science in Mutual Modification*, 1981, pp. 159 ff.
138. Ibid., p. 144.
139. Barth, *Church Dogmatics*, III.1, p. ix.
140. Ibid., p. x.
141. Cf. Otto Weber, *Karl Barth's Church Dogmatics*, 1953.
142. Barth, *Romans*, p. 19.
143. Barth, *Evangelical Theology*, p. 3. Quotations are corrected according to the German edition, *Einführung in die evangelische Theologie*, 1962, p. 9
144. Barth, *Evangelical Theology*, pp. 3 f.
145. Ibid., p. 5.
146. Ibid., p. 6.
147. Ibid.
148. Ibid., p. 7.
149. Ibid., pp. 8 f.
150. Ibid., p. 10.
151. Ibid., p. 12. Italics added.
152. Ibid., pp. 16 f.
153. Ibid., p. 19.
154. Ibid., p. 20.
155. Barth, "Die Theologie," p. 392 f.
156. Ibid., p. 374.
157. Polanyi, op. cit., "The Logic of Affirmation," pp. 259-324.
158. Barth, "Die Theologie," p. 394.
159. Einstein, op. cit., pp. 59 ff.
160. Cf. Barth, "Die Theologie," pp. 394 f.
161. Einstein, op. cit., pp. 61 f.
162. Barth, "Die Theologie," p. 394. Bonhoeffer calls them "mandates." Dietrich Bonhoeffer, *Ethics*, 1965, pp. 207-213, 296, 299, et. al.
163. Cf. Barth, *Evangelical Theology*, pp. 11-18.
164. Barth, "Die Theologie," p. 395.
165. Barth, *Evangelical Theology*, p. 12.
166. Barth, "Die Theologie," p. 396.
167. Ibid.
168. Torrance, *God and Rationality*, p. 270.
169. Günter Howe, *Die Christenheit im Atomzeitalter*, 1970, p. 84.
170. Ibid.
171. Dietrich Bonhoeffer, *Letters and Papers from Prison*, 1971, p. 282.
172. Barth, *Evangelical Theology*, p. 12.

Karl Barth and Patristic Theology
Thomas F. Torrance

Karl Barth was certainly a Reformation theologian steeped in the teaching of Luther and Calvin, but he regarded the Reformation as a decisive stage in the doctrinal development of the One Holy Catholic and Apostolic Church, and not as a new foundation. The struggle of Athanasius over the *homoousion to patri* was a struggle for pure doctrine in the Church, which at the very least was just as important, Barth held, as the struggle of the Reformers over faith and justification, for it had to do with the very foundation presupposed by the Reformation, without which it is not to be understood. Thus far from the new task of the Reformers being in conflict with the inheritance of the ancient Church, it was so filled and burdened with it, as to be unthinkable without it. [1] That is surely how we must think of the new task undertaken by Karl Barth himself in his struggle with Neo-Protestantism for purity in the preaching and teaching of the Church in our times, which he discovered to be basically the same as that of Athanasius and Nicene theology in the fourth century.

For two hundred years there had been developing in Protestant theology, whether rationalist or pietist, ways of thinking which Barth found to be in sharp conflict both with the biblical message and with the real world.[2] These ways of thinking were rooted in the philosophies of dualism and immanence, sharply exemplified in the theology of people like Schleiermacher or Hermann. On the one hand, they operated with a radical dualism between the sensible and the intelligible, or the sensuous and the spiritual, realms, which they confounded with a proper distinction between God and the world, or divine and creaturely being, and, like Kant, they rejected as invalid any knowledge of things in themselves or in their internal relations. On these assumptions God was held to be really unknowable as he is in himself, so that divine revelation was regarded as having no objective truth or informational content. On the other hand, however, they operated paradoxically with a refined doctrine of divine immanence which carried with it the idea of a deep-seated kinship between the divine Spirit and the human spirit, in virtue of which epistemic contact might be made with God in the depths of the religious consciousness or through the kind of self-understanding generated in human beings by the personality of Jesus. What this actually led to, and could not but lead to, was a naturalisation and cultural secularisation of the Gospel with humanistic philosophy and sociology, romantic history and psychology, providing the controlling norms, as was evident, for example, in the relativistic *Religionsphilosophie* of Ernst Troeltsch, not to speak of the strange natural theology of so-called "German Christians" for whom the national folk-consciousness was held to be a revelation of the Spirit of God.[3] Is it any wonder that Barth was angry with Roman theologians who adduced the proposition of St Thomas that "grace does not destroy nature but perfects and completes it", or "supplies its defect"[4], in justification of a concordat between the Vatican and Nazi Germany, or that he was angry with Emil Brunner whose pamphlet *Natur und Gnade* seemed to lend some justification for the "Faith-movement of German Christians" in their appeal to a "point of contact" between the natural reason and the divine?

In his vigorous attempts to liberate the biblical and evangelical Faith from the distorting culture-conditioned framework of modern Protestantism, Barth offered relentless analyses of leading nineteenth century philosophers and theologians, and not least of Harnack, the scion of German liberal theology, who was the greatest patristic scholar of the age.[5] At the same time Barth returned to the teaching of the Reformers themselves and engaged in a critical and constructive reexamination of the Lutheran and Reformed Dogmatics of Protestant scholasticism, notably in the formidable works of Quenstedt and Polanus. But he also set out to master the foundations and indeed the whole corpus of canonical Roman Catholic theology. Particular mention must be made of his use of the works of Heinrich Schmid, *Die Dogmatik der Evangelishen-Lutherischen Kirche,* Heinrich Heppe, *Reformierte Dogmatik,* Heinrich Denzinger, *Enchiridion Symbolorum,* and of the 1916 edition of Peter Lombard, *Libri IV Sententiarum,* all of which were replete with appeals to the writings of the Greek and Latin Fathers.[6] One of the major effects of these studies upon Barth was to throw him back squarely upon the Conciliar Theology hammered out in the ancient Catholic Church in its struggle against heresy to preserve the evangelical substance of the Faith once delivered to the saints and handed down through the Apostolic Scriptures. But he had to think it all out for himself through exegetical and historical examination and find fresh ways of reappropriating and expressing it which would do justice to the Fathers and Reformers alike.

Very soon Karl Barth realised that there was a deep-seated connection between Neo-Protestantism and the Augustinian dualism that underlay all Reformation and especially Lutheran theology. That was very evident in the Augustinian definition of sacraments as *outward and visible signs of inward and invisible grace* found in the catechisms of all the main Reformation Churches. This dualism was built into the fabric of Lutheran theology in a rather stronger form through the doctrine of "the two regiments".[7] Moreover, the dualist epistemological substructure of modern Protestantism could be traced back through Hegelian, Kantian and Cartesian philosophy to Augustinian metaphysics - as Heinrich Barth had also shown in various essays.[8] Barth's rejection of any notion of an inherent kinship or analogy of being between man and God, or any continuity of the uncreated Spirit with man's created spirit, embedded both in Protestant and Roman natural theology and in the Augustinian-Thomist doctrine of grace, brought upon him sharp attacks, not only from Protestant philosophers of religion, but from the Jesuit Erich Przywara in a sophisticated defence of *analogia entis*.[9]

This debate only served to confirm Barth in his analysis of the sweet but insidious effect of Augustinian thought in western theology. By way of reply to Protestant and Roman criticisms, he published in 1929 a set of powerful lectures [10] clarifying basic philosophical problems in relations between nature and spirit, the particular and the universal, being and thought, realism and nominalism, etc., in which he analysed the elusive transition, found in Thomist as well as Kantian and Hegelian thought, from realism to idealism or even nominalism, on the ground of a doctrine of *analogia entis*. In the following year he published another lecture on the doctrine of the Holy Spirit, [11] when he carried further his critique of *analogia entis* especially as advocated by Przywara. In it he not only refuted Liberal Protestant notions of a hidden 'identity' between the Divine Spirit and the human spirit, but exposed with detailed references the Augustinian distortion of the doctrine of grace in the subtle work-righteousness of Tridentine Roman theology. Moreover, Barth replaced the Augustinian-Thomist conception of infused and created grace as the medium bridging the gap between God and man, or God and the world, by a full-orbed rehabilitation of the doctrine of God the Holy

Spirit that clearly bears the imprint of the teaching of John Calvin and the Greek Fathers. In it the proper difference between God and all created being is maintained, while the continuity (the true *analogia entis*) between God and the creature is traced to the activity and presence of the Spirit who as Creator, Reconciler and Redeemer freely sustains the human being in creaturely relation to God, making him open to his Word and giving him likeness to God. In this event the creative relation of God to the creature must be regarded as *irreversible,* for the continuity between the creature and God and his likeness to God do not belong to the creature in virtue of some property he possesses in himself but are freely bestowed upon him in his contingent relation to the Grace of the Creator.

This represents a turning away from the Augustinian idea of *imago Dei* inherent in man even before he becomes partaker of God [12] to the Athanasian conception of it as 'the grace of being in the image' *(he kat'eikona charis).* [13] But it also offers a conception of the analogical relation to God basically the same as that for which Athanasius had argued in his rebuttal of Arian mythological projection of creaturely images, patterns and relationships into God. While divine revelation makes use of analogies *(paradeigmata* is Athanasius' term) to speak of God, they have their force in God's gracious condescension to address us in our familiar human terms, but in such a way that they point beyond themselves altogether. They may not be reversed, therefore, and manipulated by us as comparisons by means of which we may impose upon God in an objectifying way *(kat'epinoian)* ideas we have devised or thought up from a centre in ourselves, for God who is beyond comparison does not take his pattern from man.[14] It is basically the same concept of analogy that was propounded by Hilary, according to whom analogies are essentially signitive rather than descriptive of God. "There can be no comparison between God and earthly things, yet the weakness of our understanding forces us to seek analogies from a lower sphere to explain our meaning about loftier themes... We must therefore regard any comparison as helpful to man rather than descriptive of God, since it suggests, rather than exhausts, the sense we seek."[15]

It should be remarked that Barth's trenchant criticism of Latin theology did not deter him from quarrying effectively, and at times heavily, from the insights of St. Augustine and St. Thomas, for whom, as for Schleiermacher, he retained the highest respect. Nevertheless, it is very clear that the prevailing orientation of Barth's developing theology was toward *Greek* rather than Latin Patristics. This was evident already in his *Christliche Dogmatik,* but that was natural for a *Reformed* theologian determined to renew the Nicene struggle for the purity of the Apostolic and Evangelical Faith. After all John Calvin himself was actually more indebted in the main body of his theology to the Greek than to the Latin Fathers. This must be affirmed in spite of the fact that his citations from Augustine's writings outnumbered all his other citations and references put together, for it was to be expected that in the great debates of the Reformation appeal to and against Rome should be made at every point possible to Augustine as the universally acknowledged *Magister Theologiae.* Calvin's indebtedness to Augustine is most apparent in his doctrine of predestination and in his conception of the sacramental relation, but in his rejection of an essentialist approach to God, in his doctrine of the Holy Trinity, in Christology, Pneumatology, Soteriology, and Eschatology, and in his doctrine of the Church as the Body of Christ, his thinking was decidedly Greek. It is particularly significant that Calvin's doctrine of justification through union with Christ and participation in his obedient Sonship was deeply indebted to Cyril of Alexandria, [16] in contrast to Luther's conception of justification which was heavily influenced by Augustine. That is the inheritance into which Barth himself entered, and which left its distinctive mark on his doctrine of justification.

So far as Calvin's exegesis was concerned, the predominating Patristic influence on him came from the biblical expositions and exhaustive commentaries on the Holy Scriptures by John Chrysostom. Under Greek Patristics, of course, must be included the works of two Fathers who resided in the West, Irenaeus of Lyons who wrote in Greek and had a permanent impact on Athanasius, and Hilary of Poitiers who wrote in Latin but had a thorough knowledge of Greek and shared very fully in the anti-Arian Nicene theology of Athanasius and the Cappadocians. It may be noted that a passage from Hilary twice cited by Peter Lombard, to the effect that in biblical interpretation statements and terms must be understood by reference to the realities they indicate, and not the other way round, for reality is not subjected to word but word to the reality, had a considerable influence on the exegesis of both Luther and Calvin, and through them, as well as directly, upon Karl Barth himself.[17]

It is striking that where Calvin was most dependent on Augustine

Barth himself broke emphatically away, in the doctrine of election. Augustine's statement that Christ is "the mirror of predestination" or "the mirror of election", cited several times by Calvin, [18] was of course fully acceptable to him, but not Augustine's concept of double predestination which influenced Calvin so much. [19] In support of his own doctrine of "Jesus Christ, Electing and Elected," on the other hand, Barth was able to appeal to Athanasius himself. [20]

We may now seek to delineate characteristic features of Karl Barth's theology, especially in the *Church Dogmatics,* from the perspective of his interaction with the teaching of the main Greek Fathers and the Ecumenical Councils of the ancient Church.

(1) It may be helpful to begin with the pervading epistemological problem Barth had to face in the idealist framework of thought with which liberal Protestantism operated in its denigration of *dogma.* It is Adolf von Harnack above all that we must have in mind here, not only because he led the attack upon Barth, but because he was such a typical representative of the moral idealisation of biblical revelation and the Gospel, and of the opposition of Liberal Protestantism to what it called "primitive Christology". According to Barth "It has a horror of *physis,* of externality, of corporeality."[21] That is to say, behind the attack upon Christological and Soteriological dogma as "physical", "naturalistic", "mechanical", lay an axiomatic assumption of a sharp disjunction between a realm of moral ideas and a realm of physical events, or a rationalist antithesis of spirit to nature, which made people regard any idea of the Son of God taking concrete form in physical, spatio-temporal reality or of salvation through the death of the incarnate Son on the Cross, as "mythological" or "magical", and prevented them from making anything of what the New Testament calls *soma, sarx, thanatos, zoe, anastasis* and the like. Thus, as Barth saw, the attack of modernist Protestantism upon dogma was an attack upon the objectivity of divine revelation and of divine redemption upon which the Nicene foundations of the Faith were laid. But he also saw that the rationalistic dualism he found in the liberal framework of thought was essentially the same as the gnostic dualism that had been analysed and exposed so acutely by Irenaeus the acknowledged father of Early Church theology, and the epistemological and moralistic dualism no less acutely analysed and rejected by Athanasius and the Nicene theologians in the Arian controversy. The crux of the whole matter had to do with the *Incarnation,* whether it was to be understood in a

fully realist or in a merely symbolical sense. There cannot be any doubt that it was under the impact of high Patristic theology upon him that Barth set about the task of clarifying the problem of Christology, *Very God and Very Man,* and working out in a realist manner the *dogmatic* structure of the Faith of the One Holy Catholic and Apostolic Church.[22]

(2) We return to the primacy attributed by Karl Barth to the Nicene-Constantinopolitan *homoousion,* which applies both to the Incarnate Son and to the Holy Spirit who are equally of one and the same Being as God the Father. It is upon the fact that it is God himself in his own ultimate Being as God who meets us, reveals himself to us and acts upon us in the Incarnation of his Son and in the coming of his Holy Spirit, that the full reality and objectivity of divine revelation and salvation depend. In Jesus Christ and in the Holy Spirit it is not just with something of God that we have to do, but with God in his very reality as God, for it is none other than his own *Self* that he reveals to us and communicates to us - *Gott allein, Gott ganz, Gott selber,* as Barth once expressed it. [23] This means that neither revelation nor salvation may be thought of as other than God himself with us in his revealing and saving activity, or, expressed the other way round, that in revelation it is God himself that we know and in salvation it is God himself who is our Saviour. It also means that God's self-revealing and self-giving "for us and our salvation" can never cease to be *God in action,* and can never be received or enjoyed apart from the Person and Action of the Giver, but only through personal encounter and communion with him. It was one of Karl Barth's greatest contributions to the development of dogmatic theology that he set himself to think out the profound implications of the *homoousion* for the doctrine of God, Father, Son and Holy Spirit. We shall consider his doctrine of God below, but it may be said right away that no modern theologian has been more indebted to or has contributed more positively to the Nicene-Constantinopolitan theology than he.

At this point it is Barth's handling of the epistemological and soteriological import of the *homoousion* that we must note. In the fourth century the Church was constrained in faithfulness to the Gospel mediated through the Apostolic Scriptures to confess that what God is toward us in Jesus Christ and in the Holy Spirit he is in himself in his own eternal Being as God. Hence, any disjunction between God and his self-revelation through Christ and in the Spirit could only mean that in the last analysis revelation is empty of divine reality, and any disjunction between God and his saving activity through Christ and in the Spirit could only mean that in the last analysis salvation is without divine validity. That is to say, the Gospel of revelation and salvation would not be true, if there were no oneness in Word or Agency between Jesus Christ and the Holy Spirit and God the Father. [24]

Now, as Karl Barth understood it, the same fundamental issue was at stake in the Reformation at its most sensitive points, in the doctrines of the *Word* and of the *Grace* of God. [25] The application of the *homoousion* to the Word made flesh means that the Word of God embodied in Jesus Christ is identical with the Word in the eternal Being of God: God the eternal Word is the actual content of his revealed Word to us in Jesus Christ and his Gospel. The effect of this was to give the Reformation doctrine of the Word of God in Holy Scripture a very different status from that which it was accorded for many centuries in the western Church by establishing its ontological reality and objectivity as Word backed up by God's own ultimate Being as God. [26] What we meet and hear in the Holy Scripture is not only God's Word but God's Word as God himself says it. As Barth used to cite from Calvin, it is none other than "God speaking in Person" [27].

Further, the application of the *homoousion* to the Grace of God means that Grace is to be understood as the undeserved, unconditioned self-giving of God, as the impartation to us not of an impersonal something (an *aliquid*) from God but of God himself. In Jesus Christ and in the Holy Spirit God freely gives himself to us in such a living personal way that the Gift and the Giver are one and the same, and cannot be detached from each other. As such Grace is not a transferable tangible state of the soul that can be possessed by us, or subjected to the control of the Church, any more than God himself, but must be continually given and received in living personal communion with God. [28] The effect of this conception of Grace as both *datum* and *dandum* was not only to call into question Augustinian-Thomist notions of it, but to clarify Reformation conceptions of "the means of grace" which were still entangled in mediaeval instrumentalism and causalism in the sacramental life of the Church and its administration. That is to say, what Karl Barth did was to call in high Patristic theology to redress the theology of the Reformation by bringing to light the essential inner connection between revelation and reconciliation in God's Self-giving to mankind and for mankind in Christ and in the Spirit, thereby making it more fully consistent with the Christological and Trinitarian foundations of the One Holy Catholic and Apostolic Church.

(3) We turn now to Karl Barth's doctrine of the living, acting Triune God, Father, Son and Holy Spirit. If what God the Father is toward us in Jesus Christ and in the Holy Spirit, he is antecedently, inherently and eternally in himself, and what he is antecedently, inherently and eternally in himself he is toward us in Jesus Christ and in the Holy Spirit, then we cannot but affim the essential Deity of Jesus Christ and of the Holy Spirit, and thus the Triunity of God. That is to say, Karl Barth approached the doctrine of the Holy Trinity entirely on the ground of God's self-revelation and self-giving in Christ and in the Spirit interpreted through the *homoousion,* but since the doctrine of the Holy Trinity is rooted in God's revelation of himself in such a way that there is an identity between God and his revelation, it could not but be given primary place in the Church's doctrine of God and a normative role in the whole structure of its dogmatic theology.[29] In spite of the fact that the element of "subordinationism" in Barth's doctrine of the Trinity appears to be a hang-over from western thought, his basic position clearly represents a decided departure from the western theological tradition and a distinct rapprochement to the eastern theological tradition shaped through the great Greek Fathers.[30] Barth's difference from Latin theology is particularly apparent in his rejection of the psychologising approach of St Augustine and the analytical approach of St Thomas with its "split concept of God", as Barth called it. The primacy Barth accorded to the Trinity, however, did have some western forerunners in Peter Lombard and Bonaventura,[31] but it was the Boethian-Thomist teaching that predominated and gave rise to the habit in Roman theology of operating with separate treatises on the One God and the Triune God.[32] Among Reformation theologians it was John Calvin to whom Barth stood closest in trinitarian doctrine. Calvin had been influenced partly by the Franciscan tradition, which went back through Duns Scotus to Richard of St Victor who had rejected the analytical approach of Boethius later adopted by St Thomas, but he was much more indebted to the Greek Fathers, to Gregory Nazianzen in particular.

Bound up with Karl Barth's doctrine of the Trinity is his quite distinctive teaching about God's Being in his Act and his Act in his Being,[33] which he evidently developed with help from St Athanasius' discussion of the one activity *(mia energeia)* of God Father, Son and Holy Spirit intrinsic to his being, and of the one being *(mia ousia)* of God in his saving acts as Father, Son and Holy Spirit. If the Word or Logos addressed to us by God in Jesus Christ inheres in the being of God *(enousios logos)*, then it must also be held that the activity of God for us in Jesus Christ and in his spirit inheres in the Being of God *(enousios energeia)*. [34] This belongs to the general "anaphoral" movement of thought, found in Athanasius and in Barth, in which we "read back" through the *homoousion* what God is in his saving Acts as Father, Son and Holy Spirit into the one eternal Being of God as Father, Son and Holy Spirit, and interpret the saving Acts of God in his gracious condescension toward us as Father, Son and Holy Spirit by reference back to their transcendent ground in the eternal Being of God. In this event we may devoutly claim to be granted in some small measure knowledge of the Triune God in his own *inner relations,* for through the Son and in the Spirit God does not remain ultimately closed to us but has opened up for us knowledge of *God in himself.* On the other hand, as Athanasius saw so clearly, if there were any disjunction or discrepancy between God's Being and his Acts or his Acts and his Being, that would imply that God is not after all *in himself* what he is shown to be in the Gospel through the Incarnate Son and in the Holy Spirit. Thus the very basis of Athanasius' doctrine of the one Triune God in the co-activity and co-essentiality of the Father, the Son and the Holy Spirit, depends on his holding inseparably together the Being and the Activity, the Activity and the Being of God.[35]

What is said of Athanasius in this respect must be said very forcefully about Karl Barth's doctrine of the Trinity, which no less than that of Athanasius is completely integrated with his dynamic conception of the living, acting God, as he who he is in his works. Barth has in fact given unparalleled expression to this in his exposition of *Gottes Sein in der Tat, Gottes Sein als der Liebende,* and *Gottes Sein in der Freiheit.* [36] There he worked out the profound implications of God's reconciling and redeeming activity in the Incarnate Son and in the Holy Spirit for an understanding of the Nature of God in light of the identity between God and his saving revelation, and thus in terms of the inherence of God's Being in his Act and the inherence of his Act in his Being, together with the coinherence of the three Persons, the Father, the Son or the Word, and the Holy Spirit, fully and equally in one another. The fact that God's Word inheres in his Being means that God's Being is speaking Being, not Being that also speaks but Being that speaks precisely as Being, for God's Being and his Word inter-penetrate one another and are inseparably one. Likewise, the fact that God's Act inheres in his Being means that God's Being is acting Being, not Being that also acts but Being that acts precisely as Being, for God's Being and his Act interpenetrate one another and are inseparably one.

Now since God's Being is essentially acting and speaking Being, his Word and his Act must be regarded as interpenetrating one another and as inseparably one in the Being of God. It would seem to be in view of these implications that Barth came to have less hesitation in speaking of God's three "ways of being" as *Persons*, but with the recognition that it is not man but God who is properly *Person*, for it is only God who really is who he is in his Act, and who as such is the one creative Source of all other persons, that is, of "personalised persons."[37] This is very significant, for it helps to remove the suspicion that some people seem to have, that Barth was a "modalist", which is, of course, quite the opposite of the case. That suspicion was evidently due to the fact that in the earlier translation of KD,I.1 the expression "mode of being" was used for *tropos hyparxeos* which Barth had borrowed from the Cappadocian theologians.[38]

The way in which Barth integrated "being" and "act" in his under-standing of the Nature of God has a further significance of particular relevance for us today. While they were integrated, as we have seen, in Athanasian theology, the main stress of Patristic theology was upon the presence of God's Being in his revealing and saving Acts, but before very long the resurgence of dualist modes of thought, in Byzantine as well as Augustinian theology, had the effect of driving a wedge between God's Being and his Act. Western mediaeval theology sought to overcome this with the aid of Aristotelian metaphysics, but in fact only hardened the dualist disjunction between an immutable Deity and a transient world. With the Reformers, on the other hand, the main stress was upon the revealing and saving Acts of God in the presence of his Being as made known in his Word, with prominence characteristically given to atonement. Before long, however, the latent Augustinian dualism of Reformation theology was accentuated by radical dualist modes of thought which invaded it from philosophy and science, with the result that there appeared in Protestant theology, pietist and rationalist alike, a serious detachment of God's saving Acts from his Being. If in late Patristic and Mediaeval theology there was a serious loss of the dynamism, in Protestant theology there was a serious loss of ontology. It was the great contribution of Karl Barth to the history of Christian theology that he brought together the Patristic stress upon the Being of God in his Acts and the Reformation stress upon the Acts of God in his Being within a unifying dogmatic structure comparable only to the theological achievement of the early Ecumenical Councils of the One Holy Catholic and Apostolic Church. Moreover, the way in which he succeeded in integrating the ontological and the dynamic in our knowledge of God and his interaction with the creation, actually anticipated and must be appreciated in the light of the attempts of physical science to overcome the inveterate dualism it has inherited between empirical and theoretical factors in our knowledge of nature, and thus to further the unification of our knowledge of the created universe through integrating the ontological and the dynamic, the corpuscular and the undulatory, theories of light.

(4) Now we must turn the spot-light upon Karl Barth's *Christology* and *Soteriology*. His Christology was thoroughly Patristic, both in its base and in its general orientation, and that may also be said, with some qualification, of his Soteriology into which he incorporated powerful reconstructions of Reformation doctrines of atonement, reconciliation and redemption. It is nevertheless a fact that in *Church Dogmatics*, IV.1-4, explicit references to Patristic theology are astonishingly few, although it may be said of him at this stage what he himself once said of the Reformers, that the teaching of the ancient Church was so implicit in their teaching that they naturally took it for granted. [39]

We have already singled out the centrality of the *homoousion* not only for Barth's Christology but for his doctrine of the Trinity, and thus for the profound interrelation of Christocentric and Theocentric structures in his Dogmatics. To his emphasis upon the *homoousion*, however, we must add the important place he gave to the Chalcedonian doctrine of the *hypostatic union* between the divine nature and the human nature in the one indivisible Person of Christ. It was impossible for Barth to agree with Harnack that the Chalcedonian formulation of the doctrine of Christ was an hellenisation of the Gospel through the irruption of Greek and in particular of Aristotelian philosophical concepts into the understanding of the Church. While important Greek terms *(ousia, hypostasis, physis,* and the like) were taken over, their meaning was so radically altered that their new use actually helped to transform the very foundations of Greek thought and culture. These issues were particularly evident, as Barth realised, in the epistemological role of the *homoousion* and the *hypostatic union* in destroying the underlying dichotomous modes of thought derived from the Greek culture. It was those modes of thought that had given rise, in different ways, to early ebionite, adoptionist and docetic deviations, to gnostic corruptions of the Gospel, and to Arian, Nestorian, and Eutychian heresies, as well as modalist and Sabellian, not to speak of tritheist, notions of the Trinity. As soon as the Gospel began to be preached and to take root in the Graeco-Roman world, the Church found itself caught in a persistent conflict between the unitary, non-dualist outlook of the Biblical revelation and the dualist outlook of classical Greece and Rome. The doctrinal formulations of the Evangelical and Apostolic Faith were all hammered out in the interest of preserving the integrity and unity of the Gospel of Jesus Christ from the inroads of divisive and partitive concepts. Regarded in this way Greek Patristic and Conciliar theology was also an instrument in the evangelising and Christianising of Greek philosophy and culture.

Karl Barth's participation in this struggle for the unity and integrity of the Faith is particularly evident in his understanding and deployment of the theological couplet *anhypostasia* and *enhypostasia,* which was designed to carry understanding of the hypostatic union in Christ further in a positive way. The negative term *an-hypostasis* asserts that *apart from* the Incarnation of the Son of God Jesus would *not* have come into being, but the positive term *en-hypostasis* asserts that with the Incarnation Jesus came into being and exists as a completely human person *in* the full hypostatic reality of the Incarnate Son of God. It asserts that Jesus Christ did not have an independent *hypostasis* which was then adopted into union with the divine *hypostasis* of the Son of God, but that thanks to the pure act of God's grace in coming into being Jesus Christ was given a complete human *hypostasis* in and in perfect oneness with the *hypostasis* of the Son. The couplet expresses in hypostatic terms the essential logic in the irreversible movement of God's grace. It is by grace alone that man comes into being and by grace alone he is saved and made a child of God, which he cannot achieve for himself. However, by grace alone does not in any way mean the diminishing, far less the excluding, of the human but on the contrary its full and complete establishment. The archetypal instance of that was the Virgin Birth of Jesus. The realisation that *anhypostasis* and *enhypostasis* are essentially complementary and must be used together as a double concept derives ultimately from Cyril of Alexandria [40], but Barth himself seems to have taken it from seventeenth century Reformed theologians.[41] As Barth used it, this was a technically precise way of speaking of the reality and integrity of the human nature of Christ in the Incarnation, without lapsing into adoptionism, and of speaking of its perfect oneness with the divine nature of Christ without lapsing into monophysitism.[42] Through maintaining the proper differentiation between God and the creature, the negative term is made to serve the positive term in such a way as to stress the indivisible union of the divine and human natures in their undiminished reality in the one Person of Jesus Christ. It was thus the strongest way devised by Patristic theology after the Council of Chalcedon to reject any form of a schizoid understanding of Jesus Christ such as had been put forward not only in Nestorian heresy, but in the post-Chalcedonian dualism attacked so strongly by Severus of Antioch on the basis of the teaching of Cyril of Alexandria.[43]

The importance of this theologoumenon in Barth's theology can be appreciated in its complete rejection of Nestorian dualism, to which Calvinist theologians have often been prone. That is evident not least in their doctrine of predestination when election was read back into the eternal Being of God apart from what actually took place in the life, death and resurrection of Jesus, which had the effect of driving a wedge between his divine and human natures. Barth's use of this Patristic concept enabled him to reinforce the Athanasian doctrine of the *enousios logos* and *enousios energeia*, namely, that the Word and Act intrinsic to God's Being have once and for all taken concrete form in the Incarnation in such a way that Jesus Christ is identical with the Word and Act of God, and thus identical with the eternal decision or election of God. The application of *anhypostasia* and *enhypostasia* to the Incarnation, therefore, declares in the strongest way that there can be no thought of going behind the back of Jesus Christ, the Incarnate Word and Act of God, for there is no God but this God who has revealed and given *himself* to us in Jesus Christ and who is completely one with Jesus Christ in Word and Act.

Karl Barth's employment of *anhypostasia/enhypostasia* and *hypostatic union* in his Christology, together with his conviction of the inherence in one another of the Being and Act of the Incarnate Son of God, demanded that the doctrines of Incarnation and the Atonement, and thus Christology and Soteriology, must be fully integrated. Since the Incarnation means *God with us and with us as we actually are, God with us as one of us and acting for us in our place,* it must be understood as atoning reconciliation between God and man and man and God at work from the very birth of Jesus, reaching out to its consummation in his death and resurrection as one continuous indivisible saving and sanctifying act of God. Regarded in this way the hypostatic union between the divine and human natures in Jesus Christ is the ontological aspect of atoning reconciliation and atoning reconciliation is the dynamic aspect of hypostatic union, while *anhypostasia/enhypostasia* serve to disclose the inner logic of God's grace running throughout the whole incarnational self-giving of God in Jesus Christ for us and our salvation. Hypostatic union and reconciliation inhere inseparably in one another and are, so to speak, the obverse and reverse of each other. That is the basic position which Barth clearly took up in his Prolegomena to *Church Dogmatics* II.1, and which he developed throughout the whole of Volume IV.

It will be sufficient for our purpose here to focus attention only upon several features of Barth's Soteriology in so far as they reveal something of his affiliation with Greek Patristic understanding of redemption.

With all Patristic theology in the East and West Barth affirmed the *Theotokos* of Mary the mother of Jesus, and fully accepted the clauses of the Apostles' Creed: "conceived by the Holy Ghost", and "born of the Virgin Mary."[44] However, the theological position he adopted regarding "the assumption of the flesh" was decidedly not that of the Latin Fathers but of the Greek Fathers who, at least from the time of Irenaeus, interpreted the teaching of St. Paul to mean that in the Incarnation the Son of God condescended to assume from us our fallen, corrupt, mortal human nature, on the ground that what he did not assume did not come within his healing, saving and sanctifying power. Although the line taken by Irenaeus was followed by the great Fathers such as Athanasius [45], Gregory Nazianzen, Gregory Nyssen, and Cyril of Alexandria, strangely few references were made to their views by Barth. Nevertheless the main burden of their argument, "the unassumed is the unhealed", "what has not been taken up, has not been saved"[46] was appropriated and developed by Barth. They argued against Arians, Eunomians and Apollinarians alike that

in becoming flesh the Son of God was not just externally or acciden-
tally related to us, for without being truly united with us in our actual
condition of sin, corruption and slavery, he could not save us. But they
also argued that in becoming sinful flesh the Son of God did not
become contaminated by our fallen and corrupt condition, but that in
making it his very own for our sakes he changed, healed and sanctified
it, transferring to it his own holiness and virtue. They pointed out also
that while he really became what we are in assuming from us flesh
subjected to sin, he had to be other than we are, pure in order to save
us from impurity, life-giving in order to save us from our corruption,
free in order to emancipate us from our subjection, thereby subduing
the evil inherent in us and remoulding our human nature in himself,
restoring it to the image and likeness of God.[47]

Standing squarely in that Greek Patristic tradition, Karl Barth rejected the idea advanced by Latin theologians, probably to be traced back
to the rather dualist *Tome of Leo,* that the Son of God assumed *neutral*
human nature, that is, human nature unaffected by sin and guilt, and
therefore not under the divine judgement. That meant that in the
atonement Christ could be thought of only as assuming our actual sin
and then only by way of some external moral or forensic transaction,
which for Barth could only imply a serious rift in thought between
Incarnation and Atonement. He had no doubt that in becoming flesh
the Son of God really became what we are, sinners alienated from
God and existing down to the roots of our being in a state of disobedience against him. Otherwise, asks Barth, what concern could we
have with Christ? Thus Barth refused to weaken or obscure "the saving truth" that in his incarnation the Son of God penetrated into the
dark recesses of our human existence and condition where we are
enslaved in original sin, in order to bring the redeeming Love of God
to bear upon us in the distorted ontological depths of our human
being. He took seriously, therefore, the teaching of St. Paul that Christ
was made man in the concrete likeness of the flesh of sin under the law
of sin and death, and in an explicable sense was "made sin" and "made
a curse" for us, in order to redeem and save us from sin and death. Yet
in appropriating our sinful and rebellious nature like that, instead of
sinning himself, Christ did the very opposite, for by bringing the holiness and righteousness of God to bear upon it, he condemned sin in
the flesh, and through his atoning self-offering and self-consecration
in our place he healed, redeemed and sanctified in and through

himself what he had assumed. It is supremely important to realize therefore and this is the thrust of Barth's position that in the very act of taking our fallen nature upon himself Christ was at work healing, redeeming and sanctifying it. Although he was made sin for us, he himself was wholly without sin. Far from his nature being sinful, therefore, it was utterly sinless and holy, for the very nature he had appropriated from us he renewed and purified at the same time. All this means that Incarnation and Atonement are entwined in one another from the very birth of Jesus and operate unceasingly together as they press toward the climactic accomplishment of his vicarious ministry of reconciliation and redemption in his death and resurrection. In the centre of it all is the *person* of Jesus Christ, the *Mediator*, God with us in such a way that in him we are with God. In the deepest sense Jesus Christ is himself the Atonement.

In working this out Karl Barth knitted together primary features of Reformed and Patristic theology. He allowed the *Covenant* to constitute the general framework of his thought, recalling his earlier discussion in CD III.1 in which he showed that the Covenant and the Creation are internally linked together in such a way that, while the Creation is the external presupposition and ground of the Covenant, the Covenant is the internal presupposition and ground of the Creation. In view of the breach resulting from the Fall in that relation between Creation and Covenant, the creature and God, the doctrine of reconciliation has to do with the free act of God's faithfulness in which he took the lost cause of man, who has denied him as Creator and ruined himself as creature, and made it his own in Jesus Christ in order to fulfil the purpose of his Creation, thereby maintaining and manifesting his own glory in the world. At the heart of that doctrine, however, is Jesus Christ, the divinely provided *Mediator* who, as God and Man, fulfils the Covenant in his own Person, both from the side of God toward man and from the side of man toward God, healing the breach between the world and God and restoring man to communion with God. In becoming one with us in our estrangement from God, while remaining the eternal Son of God, Jesus Christ in his own Incarnate Person as Mediator, bridged the chasm between God the Creator and Judge, on the one side, and man the creature and guilty sinner, on the other side, precisely in order to effect reconciliation and bring creation to its goal in the Love of God. The fulfilling of the Covenant in and through Jesus Christ was thus inseparably bound up with the functioning of the hypostatic union in the Incarnate constitution of his

Person as Mediator, so that the hypostatic union and the atonement must be regarded as ontologically and dynamically involved in one another throughout the whole life and ministry of our Lord. Moreover the fact that Creator and creature were hypostatically united in the Person of Christ, the one Mediator between God and man, meant that the integration of creation and atonement characterised the whole life and ministry of our Lord as well.

There is another feature characterising Karl Barth's Soteriology that we must consider, a train of thought which he took over from Nicene Theology in respect of *the inner relation of the Son to the Father*. The crucial significance of this came out during the controversy with the Arians and semi-Arians who held that in the last analysis the Son must be placed on the creaturely side of the boundary between God and the creation, which meant that they could operate only with an external/moral relation between the Son and the Father. However, if the Son in his essential nature is one with the Father within the eternal Being of the Triune God, then the implications of that for Incarnation and Atonement are very far-reaching indeed. It means that the Incarnation must be regarded as falling within the life of God, and that the atoning work carried out by Jesus Christ must be thought out in terms of his internal relation to God, that is, as taking place within the Person of the Mediator and as the reconciling operation of the hypostatic union inserted into our estranged humanity. Taken together with Barth's doctrine of the Being and Act of God, which applies also to the Being and Act of the Incarnate Son, this immensely reinforced the way in which he incorporated his understanding of the Person and of the Work of the Son into one another.

Here he made considerable use of a leading motif found in both Reformed and Greek theology, the Biblical concept of the *Servant-Son* that derives particularly from the Epistle to the Hebrews. The Arians had seized upon this concept in order to demonstrate the servile, creaturely nature of the Son. But Athanasius turned the tables on them by showing that *the form of a Servant* was deliberately assumed by the Son when he partook of our human nature subjected to sin and slavery, precisely in order to redeem us.[48] The Son must be understood as making our forfeited disobedient sonship his own, in order to convert it back to true and faithful sonship through his own obedient self-offering to the Father in our place and on our behalf. Athanasius, and Cyril of Alexandria after him, expounded that by linking closely together the obedience of the Incarnate Son and his *priestly* self-offering to the Father.[49] The same motif was employed by Calvin [50], evidently after his study of the 1528 translation of Cyril's *Opera*. Within his use of the *triple munus* Calvin also laid emphasis on the priestly obedience of Christ, but the *munus sacerdotale* does not figure so prominently in the Dogmatics of Barth as it did in the teaching of the Greek Fathers, or even of Calvin. On the other hand, in his explication of the atoning obedience of the Son, Barth brought into prominence the motif of the Judge judged in our place [51], which was by no means wanting in the teaching of Athanasius and Cyril. Moreover, like Cyril particularly, and like Calvin, Barth related the vicarious obedience of Christ the Servant-Son to the doctrine of justification. [52]

It remains to be added to this characterisation of Barth's Soteriology in its relation to Patristic theology, that he laid quite immense emphasis upon the *bodily resurrection* of Jesus Christ, which led him, in a typically Eastern rather than a Western way, to crown his doctrine of atoning reconciliation and justification with an account of the exaltation of man in, through and with the exaltation of Jesus Christ, the Servant as Lord.[53] It is just in this light that we may appreciate the attention he gave to the Virgin Birth of Jesus.[54] Far from being of peripheral or incidental significance it occupied at the beginning of the Incarnate Life of the Son an essential place intrinsic to the whole reconciling and redeeming work of Christ, complementary to that of the Resurrection at its end. It is indeed in the resurrection that the mystery of the Virgin Birth becomes unveiled, for there we see that while Christ was born of Mary, a sinner like ourselves in desperate need of redemption, what took place at the Virgin Birth was a mighty saving Act of God in the recreation of our humanity in Jesus Christ, the First-born of the new creation. Just as the vicarious death of Christ on the Cross had its beginning with his birth into our mortal existence, so the Resurrection of Jesus had its beginning also in the miracle of his birth. Thus the Virgin Birth belongs with the Resurrection to the essential movement of the saving Grace of God in the indissoluble unity of the Life and Work of Jesus from Birth to Resurrection.

(5) Karl Barth's doctrine of the Holy Spirit, to which we now turn, was clearly influenced by the arguments and expositions of the Greek Fathers that led up to the formulation at the Council of Constantinople of short clauses on the Spirit, which were designed to complement

those on the Son formulated at the Council of Nicaea, and were incorporated with them in the definitive version of the Creed. Barth found that the problems which Nicene theologians encountered, especially among Semi-Arians, were much the same as those which had cropped up again in Roman semi-Pelagian notions of grace and in post-Reformation Protestantism, so that it is not surprising that he took his own cue from the dogma of the Nicene-Constantinopolitan Creed. [55]

Where Barth differed from the original Greek version of the Creed, in giving his support for the Western addition of the *Filioque,* he did so on the ground of the inseparable unity in being and activity of the Spirit with the Son, adducing arguments not only from Augustine, but from Athanasius, Cyril of Alexandria and Epiphanius.[56] Barth was surely right in his insistence on the inseparable relation of the Spirit and the Son, together with his claim that the application of the *homoousion* to the Spirit demanded that the "historial mission" of the Spirit from the Incarnate Son, be regarded as grounded in the inner Trinitarian Communion of the Eternal Spirit with the Son and the Father. However, this could have been maintained with equal force through resort to the Athanasian formula "from the Father, through the Son and in the Spirit". As it was, his support for the Latin text of the Creed left him with an element of "subordinationism" in his doctrine of the Trinity which went beyond that of Gregory Nazianzen who had influenced Calvin so much as well as himself.

In his early writing Barth had set out to demolish the notion of a created medium between God and man which in different but parallel ways had infected Roman and Protestant theology alike, and to replace it by restoring a doctrine of the creative presence and direct activity of the Holy Spirit as God and Lord in the fullness of Deity. *Mutatis mutandis* that was the burden of Athanasius' *Letters to Serapion* in which he demolished the idea advocated by the Semi-Arians that the Spirit was a created intermediary between God and man, and argued that unless the *homoousion* was applied to the Spirit as well as the Son, the doctrine of the Son, and of the Holy Trinity, would be undermined. [57] Like Athanasius Barth showed that knowledge of the Spirit must be taken from our knowledge of the Son, for he is the One Word through whom all revelation of God is given, even though the Spirit himself contributes to that knowledge in a distinctive and ineffable way. Like Athanasius Barth argued from the co-activity of the Spirit and the Son to their co-essentiality as God the Son and God the

Holy Spirit, for they are in themselves, in one another and in the Father, what they are in their saving and sanctifying activity toward us. And like Athanasius Barth showed that, even when with him we speak of the "subjective" operation of the Holy Spirit in us, or of our being "in the Spirit" *(en Pneumati)*, that is to be understood in an objective, ontological sense, as a being *in God.* [58] The co-activity and co-essentiality of the Spirit with the Son meant that the doctrine of the Spirit must be allowed to interpenetrate the doctrine of Christ and his revealing and reconciling work, for it is the Spirit who mediates the Son as it is the Son who mediates the Spirit - hence the structured place given by Barth to the doctrine of the Holy Spirit throughout his exposition of Christology and Soteriology.

Here in the *Church Dogmatics* we also have a further development of Barth's earlier teaching about the Holy Spirit as *Creator* which he put forward as a counter to Platonic and rational-mystical notions in Roman and Neo-Protestant theology of an ontological continuity between the human spirit and the Divine. There certainly is an ontological continuity, Barth argued, but it derives from the *Creator-creature* relation which by its very nature is contingent and which, while stable and continuous, unceasingly sustained in the faithfulness of God, may not be reversed into a *creature-Creator* relation, in virtue of which claims might be made upon God, for the latter is entirely dependent on the former. In the Dogmatics Barth offered a more positive Pneumatological account of that relation, which appears to reflect at crucial points the teaching of St. Basil.[59] The Holy Spirit is God himself who is inconceivably able, without ceasing to be God, to be present to the creature in a very real way, and in virtue of that presence to realise the relation of the creature toward himself which it needs in order to live. Far from overwhelming the creature, therefore, or diminishing its nature, by his divine Presence, the Spirit is continuously active, not just externally or from above, but from below and from within the existence of the creature, upholding and preserving it, and giving it freedom to realise its full creatureliness before God. God establishes this relation between the creature and himself 'by his own presence in the creature, in the form of a relation of himself to himself. The Spirit of God is God in his freedom to be present to the creature, and so to create this relation and thereby be the life of the creature."[60]

Barth adds that this Creator-creature relation constantly and

contingently maintained by the presence of the Holy Spirit to the creature is presupposed in divine revelation. By embracing man within
the circle of his own presence of himself to himself, and thus through
meeting himself from man's end and from within him, God makes
man open to his revelation, capable and ready for it beyond any
possibility that he may be considered to possess on his own merely as
a rational human being. Thus while divine revelation does come to
man from above and beyond him, in making God known to him, it
takes place on the ground of the creative and sustaining presence of
his Spirit, whereby God gives existence and life to his creatures. By
revelation, of course, Barth did not mean that the Holy Spirit brings us
any new knowledge or imparts any content independent of and other
than that which is mediated to us through God's Word, but rather that
in and through the Spirit divine revelation is actualised subjectively
within human experience and understanding in a way without which
its intention as revelation of God would not be fulfilled.

It should be added that it is not in revelation only that Barth regarded this existence-giving and being-sustaining relation in the Spirit to
be presupposed, but in all God's ways and works, and throughout all
his interaction with human beings. This is true above all in his reconciling and redeeming activity where the Holy Spirit is at work bringing the people of God freedom from alien subjection, and actualising
the union of the Church with Christ, thereby constituting it as the
Body of Christ, that is, as "the earthly-historical form of Christ's own
existence in the world", and realising within its existence and mission
in space and time the participation of God's children in the Light, Life
and Love of God himself. As Barth understood it, therefore, the Holy
Spirit as Creator, along with the Father and the Son, brings into existence and faithfully sustains the "created correspondence" between
God and his creation. His distinctive operation, as the freedom of God
to be present to his creation and to realise its relation to himself, is that
of actualising within the contingent structures of space and time the
profound interrelation between the Covenant and the Creation, as
through his redemptive activity he brings it to its true end in the Love
of God. Hence, in spite of the contradiction between man and God
introduced into the created order through disobedience and sin, and
on the ground of atoning reconciliation through the Incarnate Son,
the Holy Spirit effectuates the Covenant as the inner presupposition
and ground of the Creation, and liberates the Creation to be the outer

ground and presupposition of the Covenant. Karl Barth went so far as to insist, in a way that must astonish many of his critics, that the doctrine of the Holy Spirit does not have to do only with the unity of the Father and the Son in the eternal Life of the Godhead, but also with God's activity in the world, where the Spirit is the divine Reality by which the creature is unceasingly sustained in its creaturely being and man is made open in his heart and mind to God, and made free, able and willing to receive him. The Holy Spirit is, then, "the unity between the creature and God, the bond between eternity and time."[61]

Notes

1. *Die christliche Dogmatik im Entwurf,* 1927, p. 197f; cf. p. 300.
2. See CD I.1, p. 34, where Barth characterises the problem as "pietistic and rationalistic Modernism rooted in mediaeval mysticism and the humanistic Renaissance".
3. See Barth's analysis in *Theologische Existenz heute/, Beiheft 2* of *Zwischen den Zeiten,* 1933.
4. St. Thomas Aquinas, *Summa Theologica,* 1 q.1.8 ad 2; q.2.2 ad 1, etc.
5. See *Ein Briefwechsel mit Adolf von Harnack,* in *Die Christliche Welt,* 1923, Heft 1/2, republished in *Theologische Fragen und Antworten,* 1957, pp. 3-31.
6. Peter Lombard's appeal, however, was mainly to the Latin Fathers. See my reviews of the critical edition of *Sententiae,* I and II, 1971, and III and IV, 1981, in *S.J.T.,* vol. 26, no. 4, 1973, pp. 488-90, vol. 36, no. 1, 1983, pp. 129-131.
7. For references see Torrance, *Kingdom and Church,* 1956, pp. 11, 16ff, 23, 30f, 45, 56f, 87f, 155ff.
8. Cf. *Zwischen den Zeiten,* 1928, 1929, and 1932; *Die Geistfrage im deutschen Idealismus* in *Zur Lehre vom Heiligen Geist, Beiheft 1 zu Zwischen den Zeiten,* 1930, a publication which he shared with Karl Barth
9. *Religionsphilosophie Katholischer Theologie,* 1926, Eng. tr., *Polarity,* 1935.
10. *Schicksal und Idee in der Theologie,* 1929, reprinted in *Theologische Fragen und Antworten,* 1957, pp. 54-92. See Torrance, *Karl Barth, An Introduction to his Early Theology, 1910-1931,* 1962, pp. 148-171.
11. *Zur Lehre vom Heiligen Geist,* Eng. tr. *The Holy Ghost and the Christian Life,* 1938.
12. Augustine, *De Trinitate,* XIV.8.11.
13. Athanasius, *De Incarnatione,* 5 & 7, etc.
14. See *Con. Arianos,* 1.11-36, 57, etc.; *Ad Serapionem,* 1.19f; 2.5f; 4.1 ff. See further Torrance, "The Logic and Analogic of Biblical and Theological Statements in the Greek Fathers," *Theology in Reconstruction,* 1965, pp. 30-45.
15. Hilary, *De Trinitate,* I.19. For further references see "Hermeneutics, or the Interpretation of Biblical and Theological statements according to Hilary of Poitiers," in *Abba Salama,* Vol. VI, 1975, pp. 37-69.
16. See the edition of Cyril's *Opera* translated into Latin in three tomes by Trapezontius and Oecolampadius, Basel, 1524, with which Calvin was clearly very familiar.
17. Hilary, *De Trinitate,* IV.14 cited by Peter Lombard, *Sententiae,* I.d.V.c.1 & I.d.XXV.c.2; and by Karl Barth, CD, I.1, p. 354. Cf. also Hilary, *De Trinitate,* I.30.
18. *Institutio,* 2.17.1: 3.22.1; 3.24.5, etc.

19. Cf., for example, *Enchiridion*, 100, the little hand-book on Christian doctrine that was widely used in mediaeval Latin theology.

20. *Con. Arianos*, II.75-77, in CD, II.2, pp. 108-110.

21. CD I.2, p. 130. See the full analysis offered by Barth, pp. 126-131; and also the excursus appended by Emil Brunner to Ch. VIII of *The Mediator*, to which Barth also referred, p. 127f.

22. See especially CD, I.2, section 15, pp. 122-202.

23. *Christliche Dogmatik*, p. 220.

24. Chr.D., pp. 126ff, 214f; CD I.1, pp. 295ff; I.2, pp. 122ff; II.1, pp. 257ff.

25. *Offenbarung, Kirche, Theologie*, in *Theologische Existenz heute*, 9, 1934; Eng. tr., *God in Action*, 1936, p. 13f.

26. This is the argument massively reproduced by Barth especially in CD I.1, *The Doctrine of the Word of God*, Ch II. Cf. also Johannes Reuchlin, *De Verbo Mirifico*, 1552, in which he applied Nicene consubstantiality to the Word in criticism of conceptions prevailing in the middle ages.

27. Calvin, *Inst.* I.7.4: *Dei loquentis persona;* Barth, CD I.1, p. 304. This is evidently a citation from Athanasius, *De Incarnatione*, 3: *Touto de kai he theia graphe prosemainei legousa ek prosopou tou Theou.*

28. Cf. CD I,1, p. 41f.

29. Chr. D., pp. 126-214. Cf. my discussion in *Karl Barth. An Introduction to his Early Theology, 1910-1931*, pp. 113-118; CD I.1, pp. 295-489.

30. See Torrance, 'Toward an Ecumenical Consensus on the Trinity', *Theologische Zeitschrift*, vol. 31, 1975, pp. 337-350.

31. Barth, CD, I.1, p. 300.

32. Cf. Karl Rahner, *The Trinity*, 1970 (tr. from *Mysterium Salutis*, 1967), p. 15ff.

33. CD II.1, pp. 257-321 on 'The Reality of God'.

34. Athanasius, *Con. Arianos*, II.2; cf. II.28, III.65, IV.1f; *Ad Serapionem* I.14-21; cf. *Theology in Reconciliation*, 1975, pp. 226ff, pp. 235f & 253.

35. Athanasius, *Con. Arianos*, 1.17-20, 28, 36; 2.2; cf. 2.28; 3.65; 4.1f; *Ad Serapionem*, 1.20f, 27, 30; 3.2f, 5; 4.3f. Cf. again *Theology in Reconciliation*, pp. 235ff.

36. Barth, KD, II.1, pp. 288-361; CD, II.1, pp. 257-321.

37. KD, II.1, p. 305; CD, II.1, p. 272 - a translation that needs to be adjusted.

38. See the Editors' Preface to the new translation, CD, I.1, 1975, p. viii.

39. Chr. D., p. 197.

40. *Apol. con. Theodoretum*, MPG 75, 397c; *Hom. Pascalis*, MPG 77, 505d; Cf. Hippolytus, *Con. haer. Noeti*, 15. And see *Theol. in Reconciliation*, p. 166.

41. See Heinrich Heppe, *Reformierte Dogmatik*, new edit. 1935 (with Foreword by Barth), p. 340f; Eng. tr. 1950, p. 428; Karl Barth, CD, I.2, p. 163f; III.2, p. 70; IV.2, pp. 49f, 91f.

42. According to Barth monophysite ideas crept into Lutheran orthodoxy with the application of *perichoresis* to the union of divine and human natures in Christ, which had the effect of reversing *enhypostasis!* Cf. CD, I.2, p. 166.

43. See Iain R. Torrance, *A Theological Introduction to the Letters Between Severus of Antioch and Sergius the Grammarian*, published in *Ekklesia kai Theologia*, 1981, pp. 961-993; 1982, pp. 283-321; 1983, pp. 537-571; 1984, pp. 453-481.

44. For the following see especially CD, I.1, pp. 147ff. and 172ff.

45. This is particularly evident in the two treatises *Contra Apollinarem*, 1.17; 2.6ff; cf. *De Incarn. et con. Arian.* 21 & 53, traditionally attributed to Athanasius. Critical arguments against the Athanasian authorship have now been demolished by George D. Dragas.

46. Gregory Nazianzen, *Epist. ad Cledonium*, 101; Cyril of Alexandria, *In Ioannis Evangelium*, MPG 1xxiv, 89cd; cf. Gregory Nyssen, *Antirrheticus adv. Apollinarem*, 26, MPG xlv. 1180.

47. For references, especially to Cyril, and for what follows, see *Theology in Reconciliation,* pp 168ff.
48. *Con. Arianos,* 1.40ff, 53ff; 2.1ff, etc.
49. For Athanasius, see *Con. Arianos,* 1.41, 59f, 64; 2.7-9, 14, 55, 68-70, 75f; 3.31-35, 56f; 4.6f.
50. E.g., Calvin's Commentary and Sermons on Isaiah 53.
51. See especially CD, IV.1, pp. 211-283.
52. CD, IV.1, pp. 514 ff; IV.2, pp. 499ff.
53. CD, IV.2, pp. 3-377; and cf. IV.3.1,, pp. 3-374.
54. CD, I.1, pp. 172-202.
55. CD, I.1, pp. 468ff.
56. CD, I.1, pp. 477ff.
57. See *The Letters of Saint Athanasius concerning the Holy Spirit,* tr. by C.R.B. Shapland with very helpful notes, 1951.
58. See here Chr.D., pp. 284ff; CD, I.2, pp. 203-279; as well as CD I.1, pp. 526ff, 533ff. The Athanasian position was already developed in *Con. Arianos,* 1.47f, 50, 56; 2.18; 3.15, 24, 44.
59. Basil of Caesarea, *De Spiritu Sancto,* 16.37f. It was not Basil, however, but Gregory Nazianzen who explicity figured in Barth's Pneumatology.
60. CD, I.1, p. 450; cf. p. 472.
61. CD, II.1, p. 669f.

Barth and a New Direction for Natural Theology

Ray S. Anderson

"If [Emil Brunner] is still alive and it is possible," wrote Karl Barth to pastor Peter Vogelsanger in Zurich, "tell him I commend him to *our* God. And tell him the time when I thought I should say No to him is long since past, and we all live only by the fact that a great and merciful God speaks his gracious Yes to all of us."[1]

Readers of the letters of Karl Barth, 1961-1968, would probably be mislead to draw from this poignant "last word" to Brunner the conclusion that Karl Barth in the end recanted. His famous *NEIN!*, written in response to Brunner's tract on *Nature and Grace* in 1934, still stands as a monument to Barth's rejection of natural theology.[2]

We would also be mislead, however, to conclude that the object of Barth's *NEIN!* remains the same. Karl Barth aimed his theological cannon always at a moving target. The so-called "point of contact" *(Anknüpfungspunkt)* which Brunner appeared to advocate and which drew Barth's imperious denial, raised its head under the disguise of Brunner's proposed agenda for "The Other Task of Theology." Despite Brunner's protests that his attempt to speak of a "point of contact" outside of special revelation only pointed to the formal and objective possibility of a natural theology, and not its material and subjective reality, Barth thought that he had sniffed out in this attempt the suspicious odor of heresy. And if Brunner is bound to call this attempt "a way back to a true *theologia naturalis,"* then the cannon has found its target.[3]

Certainly one must read Barth's *NEIN!* in the context of the contemporary situation in Germany at the time of its writing. To those fighting the battle of resistance to Hitler's program of National Socialism with its assimilation of Christianity into the romantic depths of the German nature and culture, any move toward a natural theology could be viewed as capitulation to the enemy. Barth reminds Brunner very sharply of the possibility that his talk of a natural theology and point of contact will play directly into the hands of the "German Christians." Not only has Brunner diverged from the purity of a "theology of the Word," Barth protests, but he has

> calmly claimed Calvin for his own; he has turned
> Calvin into a kind of Jean Alphonse Turrettini; he has
> confronted me together with his "Calvin" and has pat-
> ted me on the shoulder and told me to be a good boy;
> he has seen to it that the "German Christians" can, if
> they wish . . . quote now not only Luther but also
> Calvin in their support. It is the fact that he managed
> to do all these things which I am so far unable to
> forgive Brunner.[4]

What Barth feared in 1932 came to pass in the new totalitarian state following the ascendancy of Hitler in 1933 and the deadly program of military aggression and antisemitism under the ideology of Aryan supremacy. Reflecting back upon these events after the Second World War, Barth saw that a combination of Christian and natural theology lead the German Church to support a "race nationalism" which plunged the country into a holocaust. It was in the first article of the Barmen declaration (1934), recalled Barth, that there finally arose an opposition to this "new combination" in the form of the declaration of Jesus Christ as the "one Word of God" which calls us back to the single task of theology.[5]

In retrospect, the issue of "point of contact," which drew Barth's blast against Brunner is much more complex and more subtle than a campaign against natural theology in any form. For Barth, the dreaded *Anknüpfungspunkt* refers to an attempt to revive the pagan notion that the human spirit is a spark of the divine. Barth did not actually wish to deny an ontological relation between God and the human person. What he vehemently denied was the notion that the human mind par-ticipates in the mind and being of God – that human reason is a shar-ing in the eternal reason of God.

Scripture itself, Barth acknowledged, gives us "another strand" of witness to the Word of God as found in nature. The so-called "nature Psalms" (111, 113-116), together with the relevant passages in Romans 1 and Acts 17 are discussed fully by Barth as a possible basis for a Christian natural theology. In the end, however, Barth argues that this "second line" of witness in Scripture does not stand as a parallel witness to that of the gospel. Nor will Barth allow that these passages teach that there is a knowledge of God which stands in-dependently of God's revelation in Christ. At best, these passages can only point to the readiness of creation and the human person to know God; they cannot be used as evidence that there is a knowledge and witness to the truth of God prior to and resting on a source other than the "readiness of God" in Christ.[6]

Barth's view of natural theology should also be considered in light of his earlier work on ethics (Münster, 1928), in which he developed the three-fold basis for ethics as the command of God under the headings of Creation, Reconciliation, and Redemption. Here Barth does acknowledge a command of God as Creator, not as a "natural" command, but as a Christian command which can be understood as an "order of creation." It is inadvisable, Barth suggested, to "construct an antithesis between the command of the Creator and the command of Christ." The command of God, said Barth, always entails the concrete situation and existence of the "whole man." The goodness of God is one.[7]

It becomes clear in Barth's interaction with G. Söhngen in *Church Dogmatics,* I/2, that there is an ontological relation between God and the human person, but that this relation is a contingent one.[8] That is, the relation of "being-to-being" in the case of God and the human person is contingent upon the "act-to-being" relation of grace. God's being is only known through his act of creating and sustaining the human person as being. It is the contingent relation between God as being and the human person which preserves the true ontological relation and also provides for an authentic "point of contact." There is, after all, for Barth, a theology of creation which includes a real correspondence between an ethics of creation and general ethical themes. This correspondence allows an "overlapping" of theological and secular concerns for truth and moral actions, without giving away the command of God as the basis for both *(Church Dogmatics,* III/4, Chapter 12).

What Barth rejects in natural theology, says Thomas F. Torrance, is not its rational structure as such, but its *independent* character, developed on the basis of "nature alone," in abstraction from the active self-disclosure of God in Christ.[9] Barth is ultimately committed, argues Torrance, "to one coherent framework of theological thought that arises within the unitary interaction of God with our world in creation and Incarnation."[10] Therefore, there is at the core of Barth's theology, an analogical correspondence between the inner intelligibility of the Being and truth of God, and the rational structure immanent in our understanding of it.[11]

Recounting an ancedote concerning a visit with Karl Barth only a few months before his death, Torrance says:

> I was anxious to get Karl Barth's reaction to the way in which I explained to a Thomist or a physicist his attitude to natural theology by referring to Einstein's account of the relation of geometry to experience, or to physics. . . . instead of idealizing geometry by detaching it from experience, and making it an independent conceptual system which was then used as a rigid framework within which physical knowledge is to be pursued and organized, geometry must be brought into the midst of physics where it changes and becomes a kind of natural science. . . . Instead of being swallowed up by physics and disappearing, however, geometry becomes the epistemological structure in the heart of physics, although it is incomplete without physics. It is in a similar way, I argued, that Karl Barth treats natural theology when he rejects its status as a *praeambula fidei*, that is, as a preamble of faith, or an independent conceptual system antecedent to actual knowledge of God . . .[12]

After listening to this, Karl Barth expressed full agreement, and said, of the relation of geometry to physics, "I must have been a blind hen not to have seen that analogy before."[13]

A Change of Direction In Barth's Theology

How then can one understand what appears to be a contradiction between Barth's early rejection of natural theology (and point of contact) and his later admission that there is, in fact, a basis for establishing a correspondence between what can be formally and generally known of God and knowledge of God as pure act?

We have already suggested that Barth's theological cannon was directed toward a moving target, rather than at a particular theological construct. In a lecture given on "The Humanity of God," in 1956, Barth took note of what he called a "change of direction" in his own thought on this subject. Forty years ago, said Barth, our concern was for the deity of God – a God absolutely unique in his relation to human persons and the world. "I should indeed have been somewhat embarrassed if one had invited me to speak on the humanity of God –say in the year 1920, the year in which I stood up in this hall against my great teacher, Adolf von Harnack. We should have suspected evil implications in this topic."[14]

There is, however, another perspective on Barth's early struggle against natural theology, provided by T.F. Torrance. The early Barth, says Torrance, was under the influence of an Augustinian and Lutheran dualism. This dualism was critically conditioned by a Kantian dichotomy between the noumenal and phenomenal world and theologically conditioned by the influence of Wilhelm Hermann of Marburg. This, together with the principle of the "infinite qualitative distinction between God and man," drawn from Kierkegaard, led Barth in his commentary on Romans to attack the synthesis between divine and human of a Thomistic kind, on the one hand, and a cultural protestantism, on the other.[15]

It would not be fair to say, however, that Barth rejected the existence of natural knowledge, nor did he commit himself to a metaphysical refutation of it, but saw it as that which stands in opposition to the Word of God. There is an "openness of man to God," suggested Barth, but it is not yet the "readiness of man for God."[16] The condition of all men apart from a saving knowledge of God, argued Barth, is an "unknowing knowledge." It is a relation to the truth in the form of opposition to the truth.[17] If there be some general knowledge of God, it is not yet true knowledge until it becomes "acknowledgment." The acknowledgment of God in the form of gratitude and thanksgiving, is essential for there to be true knowledge of God.[18]

What Barth failed to develop adequately, according to Torrance, was the intrinsic relation between creation and Incarnation. Barth's theological methodology pointed him in the direction of working out the correlation between scientific statements and theological concepts, suggests Torrance. Both scientific knowledge and theological knowledge fall within the spatio-temporal structures of intelligibility which God has conferred upon the universe, and which he took upon himself in his incarnational self-revelation to us. It is in moving toward a new understanding of the relation between creation and Incarnation, Torrance argues, that one may develop new forms of natural theology which are consistent with Karl Barth's theological insights and methodology.[19]

There are indeed hints in the later writings of Barth which invite us to consider the fact that he did indeed wish to preserve a correspondence between knowledge of God in creation and knowledge of God through Christ. In Volume Four of his *Church Dogmatics*, for example, Barth argues that the creaturely world, the cosmos and even the nature of man is given in an authentic speech and word.

> It is given quite irrespective of whether the man whom it addresses in its self-witness knows or does not know, confesses or denies, that it owes this speech no less than its persistence to the faithfulness of the Creator. . . . However corrupt man may be, they illumine him, and even in the depths of his corruption he does not cease to see and understand them. . . . they are not extinguished by this light [of Christ], nor are their force and significance destroyed . . . As the divine work of reconciliation does not negate the divine work of creation, nor deprive it of meaning, so it does not take from its lights and language, nor tear asunder the original connexion between creaturely *esse* and creaturely *nosse*. [20]

Even more emphatic are Barth's final statements on this subject, published posthumously as *The Christian Life, (Church Dogmatics* Volume IV, part 4, Lecture Fragments).

> If man would know himself in this nature and inalienable orientation of his, if he would be true to himself, he would find himself confronted with the one true God who, in creating him, has made himself known to man and therefore to the world, so that to man and to the world in the very nature he has given them, he is objectively a very well known and not an unknown God. [21]

In the end, Barth is not unwilling to allow that all human persons, by virtue of their being created by God and possessing a creaturely human nature, remain in an ontological relation to God, despite the radical disruption of sin. Not only that, this ontological relation to God experienced as human nature, carries with it the objective reality of knowledge of God, for which the human person, even as sinner, is accountable. Barth clearly says that this is not a knowledge of God restricted only to those who have experienced the saving work of Christ, but ". . . every person has the chance to recognize God in return and therefore to know him. Man, not God, is at fault if a subjective knowledge of God on man's side does not correspond to God's objective knowledge." [22]

We must be fair to Barth, however, and also heed his caveat. "These impressions should not be generalized and systematized along the lines of a natural theology, but when they lay hold of us with serious force, they cannot be denied."[23] The danger in natural theology is that it abstracts nature from grace, both in the creation and Christ, and seeks to establish a criterion for determining the truth of divine revelation outside of the divine Word.

This form of natural theology operates with a dualism between the being of God and the being of the world which must be overcome through the creation of a metaphysical structure of proportionality which operates from the side of created being. This resulted in the fateful *analogia entis* toward which Barth directed his strongest criticism, both in Thomistic theology and in the new forms of "cultural Protestantism" which he saw emerging. While there can be found some evidence of this same problem of dualism in Barth's early theology, T.F. Torrance argues that he overcame this tendency through his relentless pursuit of the sheer objectivity of the living God who reveals his being only in his act. Thus, Torrance suggests, Barth may be viewed more as an interactionist than a dualist, with a trinitarian basis for his understanding of the relation of created to uncreated being. [24]

Rather than positing a synthesis between the uncreated being of God and the created being of human persons, Barth preferred to speak of an "analogy of relation" *(analogia relationis)*. The basis for a positive natural theology lies within the interaction of God as Creator and Redeemer with creation. As we have seen, this was set forth in his 1928 Münster lectures on Ethics. In Chapter VIII of his Dogmatics (II/ 2), Barth developed much further the concept of the command of God as the basis for ethics, arguing that questions about the good in human life are already given to us as answers in the doctrine of God as Creator, Reconciler, and Redeemer.

Barth was not unconcerned for the pedagogical significance of a natural theology which could serve the church in its witness to the transforming and sustaining power of the Word of God. At the same time, he saw nothing but failure in two centuries of Protestant theology in Germany which sought to create this synthesis. [25] He called for a radical transformation of natural theology as the "single" theological task of those who are bound to the God who is "Wholly Other", and remains so in his interaction with the world. This was the battle cry of his *Epistle to the Romans (Der Römerbrief)*, not mitigated in the totally re-written second edition, and continued to be an important part of his theological attack on the synthesis created by natural theology. While Barth came to dissociate himself from talk of God as the "Wholly Other", he never dissociated himself from the function which such talk served in the theological discussion. [26] In the end, looking back on those early battles, Barth could ask:

> Were we right or wrong? We were certainly right! . . .
> Beyond doubt what was then in order was not some
> kind of further shifting around within the complex
> inherited questions, as this was finally attempted by
> Wobbermin, Schaeder, and Otto, but rather a change
> of direction. The ship was threatening to run
> aground; the moment was at hand to turn the rudder
> an angle of exactly 180 degrees. [27]

But one does not ordinarily point directions with a cannon. Many of Barth's contemporaries saw his theological tactics as more of a retreat from engagement with the world than a positive direction toward a new theology of natural life. Even in the end, the stress on the humanity of God seemed to some to represent a neglect of the "humanity of man." If we lay aside the metaphor of the cannon and pick up the metaphor of the compass, can we find in Barth's transformation of theology itself a new direction for natural theology?

It is our conviction that we can. But we must now take the rudder and steer the ship ourselves, ever mindful of Barth's sharp eye on the "magnetic pole" which determines our heading.

A New Direction For Natural Theology

The theological legacy of Barth continues to be his foundations for an authentic evangelical theology. This is a theology which (1) responds to God's gracious act of self disclosure in Christ with hearing and obedience; (2) proceeds from an actual knowledge of God given through the faithful witness of Jesus as the Son of the Father; (3) is liberated from the constraints of ideological titanism and cultural pretension to experience the command of God; (4) is directed toward the reconciliation of creation in anticipation of the "all things made new" which has occurred through the death and resurrection of Christ.

It is in this last tenet of evangelical theology as suggested by Barth's new direction that we can look for the transformation of the task of natural theology.

Whereas the direction of the older natural theology was a movement from "being-to-being," with the nature of created being providing a clue to the synthesis, the new direction is from "act-to-being," with God's act of Incarnation and creation seen as a unitary action of grace by which creaturely being is determined and upheld. A key theme in Barth's doctrine of God is the matter of God's freedom, both negatively in terms of his freedom from all else as unconditioned being, but also positively in terms of his freedom to create and to interact freely with his creation. "God's freedom is the freedom proper to and characteristic of Him," says Barth. "It is His freedom not merely to be like the reality different from Himself, but to be as the Creator, Reconciler and Redeemer acting towards it and in it, and therefore as its sovereign Lord."[28] This freedom of God from and toward his creation posits the openness of creation to him in its own divinely given order. This freedom and openness is what Torrance describes more fully as the contingent relation between creation and the Creator. We have chosen to use Torrance's concept of contingence in this essay as a more precise term which includes both the freedom and openness of God as Creator in his relation to creation, as Barth described it. What Barth says of this relation of freedom and openness well states what we mean by contingence:

> God's freedom in relation to all that is not God
> signifies that He is distinct from everything, that He is
> self-sufficient and independent in relation to it, and

that He is so in a peculiar and pre-eminent fashion – as no created being confronts any other . . . If they all have their being and specific nature, God in His freedom has conferred it upon them: not because He was obliged to do so, or because His purpose was influenced by their being and nature, but because their being and nature is conditioned by His being and nature. [29]

What Barth has spoken of as the freedom of God as the unconditioned One who, nonetheless "conditions" the being and nature of all else, is what we now mean by a contingent relation between creaturely nature and the being of God. It is this contingent relation by which God interacts with his creation that provides the ontological, and therefore the epistemological and ethical structures of a natural theology.

This form of contingence, one might call "evangelical contingence." It is a contingence toward God, as T.F. Torrance likes to put it. [30] It is a contingence which issues from the freedom of God to act within the structures of our time/space world without being brought under the control and determinism of that world. A contingent relation between God and the world allows for a unitary structure of reality in which the created realm has its own divinely given order and structure. At the same time, the reality of God as the source of that created order impinges at every point in the created realm through the trinitarian relations which God reveals as the nature of his own being in act.

The problem with the traditional form of natural theology was its attempt to understand the being of God as Creator in abstraction from his revelation as Father, Son and Holy Spirit. The being of creation was then linked in some necessary, even though analogical way with the being of God as Creator. It was Barth's judgement that this way of thinking had to be challenged at its very core, on two counts. It established a criterion for a judgement concerning the being and Word of God outside of the act (revelation) of God himself; and it destroyed the freedom of God to remain God as the "wholly other" in his relation to the world. Both of these had the effect of undermining the grace of God as the basis on which all human knowledge and life with God rests. Thus, this kind of theology could not be evangelical theology.

This is why Karl Barth insisted so relentlessly on the Incarnation as the criterion by which creation itself is understood. Far from being a simplistic reduction of all theology to Christology, as some have charged, Barth's insight at this point opens up creation to the full freedom it is meant to have as a contingent order, having its own created nature, resting on the freedom of God's grace as its source. [31] Because the created order is given ontological status of its own in the contingent relation it has with the creative Word of God, it also is given a structure of intelligibility by which the intrinsic laws and principles which belong to that created order may be discovered and thought out.

Because the ontological status of the created world is contingent upon the sheer objectivity of God as its source, it does not rest upon its own nature as that which ultimately defines or determines it. This liberates the created order from the fatalism and nihilism which would inevitably result if left to its own nature to determine its meaning and destiny. Even when the created order falls away from its contingence toward God, it cannot establish its own autonomy and independence from God. Through sin, the created order experiences contingence away from God as a negative contingence, experienced as disorder. Through the Incarnation of God in Jesus Christ, the ontological status of the created order is returned to its contingence toward God through the humanity of Christ, which is bound up with the essential and eternal relations of Christ as the Son of the Father.

This is given dramatic emphasis by the Apostle Paul's cosmic interpretation of the effects of the fall and the eschatological hope for its ultimate redemption in Christ.

> For the creation waits with eager longing for the revealing of the sons of God; for the creation was subjected to futility, not of its own will but by the will of him who subjected it in hope; because the creation itself will be set free from its bondage to decay and obtain the glorious liberty of the children of God (Ro. 8:19-21)

Paul makes it clear that the creation does not have a "will of its own", but that it stands in a contingent relation to the will of God. Nor does

Paul speak of creation other than its being comprehended also in that gracious predestination of God the Father which takes place through the Son, who is "the first-born among many brethren." (Ro. 8:29) Therefore, it is the trinitarian act of God within which the entire cosmos and creation has its existence by the sheer grace and freedom of God. More than that. It is the love of God "in Christ Jesus our Lord" which holds the creation in its positive contingence toward God and which assures the "many brethren" that they can never be separated from God (8:38-39).

This trinitarian, and incarnational thrust in Barth's theology enabled him to sever the artificial and speculative link which natural theology had attempted to construct between humanity and deity as a "being-to-being" synthesis. At the same time, it freed the human and created life of man to discover the authentic ontological, epistemological, and ethical dimensions which are proper to true knowledge of God and of self. This is a theme which the Apostle Paul develops in Romans, chapters one and two, where he argues that it is not the law which constitutes the sole criterion for the moral conscience. Rather, both Jews and Gentiles, both those under the law as well as those "without the law," are related by virtue of their creation by God the Father to God the Son (Christ). At the same time, by virtue of their being included in the justification accomplished by God the Son (Christ) they are held accountable for their knowledge of God as their Creator. The Gentiles who are "without the law" are not "without Christ." For Christ, as the Incarnation of God in human flesh and human form, has revealed the true humanity of all people to be in a gracious contingence to God as Creator. And it is in this contingent relation that Paul sees the epistemological as well as the moral structures of human life related to God.

The interests of a truly evangelical theology in natural theology must henceforth be developed along the lines of a contingent relation between God and the created world, with a unitary view of the relation of Incarnation to Creation. This we will attempt to do, in a tentative and modest proposal.

Toward A Natural Theology of Human Life

In his original treatise on Nature and Grace, Brunner made an insightful comment when he said: "This much is clear: the theologian's attitude to *theologia naturalis* decides the character of his ethics." [32] In his response, Barth summarily dismissed the discussion on ethics as being but one more attempt to establish a point of contact as "the other task of theology." For Barth, ethics is never a task outside of the single task of theology itself. Even with his shift toward a more positive view of the "neighbor" as the concrete occasion for the ethical dimension of the command of God in his later Dogmatics, Barth did not wish to surrender ethics to a criterion outside of the particular and concrete demand of God upon one's personal existence. [33]

Yet, we are encouraged to see a new direction for natural theology precisely in the realm of theological ethics, particularly as an extension of the thought of Karl Barth with respect to the interaction of Incarnation and creation. T.F. Torrance, in his perceptive essay on "Natural Theology in the Thought of Karl Barth", suggests that a starting point for such a new direction might be "the problem of how, in view of the fact that justification by grace calls in question and sets aside our natural goodness, Barth relates the Christian life to natural goodness, or Christian ethics to general ethics."[34] If such a correlation cannot be established, then the charge that Barth's ethic is incapable of public discussion or general application would be validated. [35] If there is no relation between the Christian's life in Christ and the imperative of goodness located in the very structure of humanity itself, then a fatal chasm has opened up between grace and nature, with the "Wholly Other" theme carried out with a vengeance.

But this is not primarily an ethical question, first of all, Barth would remind us. It is a question of the relation of the "new man" in Christ to "man" as such as the good creation of God. It is finally a question, as we have suggested above, of the contingent relation of the "good" as a created order to God himself. If goodness be an attribute of a created order, it is not that it partakes of some necessary quality which is first of all an abstract or universal principle. This would set the discussion of ethics firmly outside of the theological task, and ultimately give to "nature" a sovereign autonomy or an inalienable right to align itself with an ideological principle which preserves its own existence at the expense of all else. Such a catastrophe had already begun to take place in the program of National Socialism in Germany, thought Barth.

The first task of theological ethics is to displace ethics as an autonomous sphere, with its moorings in "orders of creation," such as

Barth saw Brunner attempting in his "other task of theology." The second task of theological ethics would then be to work out a transformation of natural theology with a new understanding of the ethical imperative which binds grace to nature in a contingent relation. "Does Barth," asks Torrance, "actually work this out so far as the rational structure of our *human* understanding is concerned in its relation to the reconstruction of that understanding which befalls man in grace?" In Torrance's judgement, Barth drew back from this second task of ethics, apparently out of anxiety lest the old corruption with its naturalistic fallacies creep back in. [36]

The meaning of contingence as developed by T. F. Torrance has significant applications for our attempt to seek new directions for a natural theology as a basis for a moral theology of human life. Contingence toward God has often been interpreted totally in theological terms, with contingence away from God in ethical terms. But these two forms of contingence are both included in the unitary relation between God and the world through Incarnation and creation. The "impasse" of a Christocentric ethics versus a general ethics can be overcome when contingence is properly understood, says Torrance. [37] Contingency and moral reason are not mutually exclusive. Moral reason does not have access to an independent principle of the good which stands totally outside of the contingent relation of moral creatures to God, their Creator. When such an independent basis for moral reason is assumed, contingency can be replaced by a form of ethical determinism – for example, casuistic ethics. Or, it can result in indeterminacy – for example, situational ethics.

Because reason itself is a created reality in human persons, who bear the divine image and likeness as a gracious endowment, and because the good is a determination of God alone (Genesis 1; Mark 10:18), moral reason in human persons is contingent upon God as Creator and Lord. Contingency, understood in this positive way, gives freedom to human persons to know the good and to experience the good as a structure of created reality. This is a contingency "away from God" which is experienced in the freedom of God, and gives human persons freedom and responsibility to think and act in accordance with this "natural human life." But this contingency "away from God" which is experienced as the freedom given by God is a positive aspect of the contingence toward God which constitutes human life in its natural form and therefore limits ethical formulations. [38]

With the concept of contingence now before us as a basis for understanding the correlation between the created order and God's grace, and with a deeper appreciation for the way in which Karl Barth pointed the way toward a new understanding of Incarnation and creation, we can now think out a new direction for natural theology. This new direction in natural theology can most profitably be taken as we follow out the implications of Barth's theological anthropology as providing a new ontological structure for the consideration of a moral theology of human life. In taking this direction, we are not suggesting that this is the only direction which one could take in working out a new form of natural theology within the tradition of Barth. There are epistemological and ontological implications in this new direction as well as ethical ones. We have chosen to focus on the ethical implications of natural theology for the purpose of showing how contingence may serve to resolve the impasse between theological and general ethics. Also in consideration in choosing this focus, are the crucial questions about quality of human life being raised as ethical problems in our contemporary society.

On the face of it, it is surprising that Barth's immense contribution to theological anthropology (cf. CD III/2) has not been recognized as offering a common forum for ethical discussion. Read apart from the polemic against a natural theology which seeks a criterion for ethics in the universalizing of created orders, or the idealizing of "nature," Barth's view of humanity as determined by God in the form of co-humanity *(Mitmenschlichkeit)*, concretely existing as freedom for the other, offers great promise for ethical discussion. While Barth consistently works out his anthropology in accordance with his theological method – we go to Christ to learn about Adam – he takes seriously the actuality of "real humanity" as the locus of the command of God and as the imperative for the Christian life. It does not occur to Barth that he needs an ethical criterion outside of God's revelation as gracious act, because the humanity of God includes, and does not diminish, the humanity of human persons.

In a discussion of the nature of human love, which seems to have escaped the notice of many, Barth refuses to support the concept of Christian love as over and against human love. The popular distinction between eros and agape, with eros representing a sub-christian kind of love is rejected by Barth. Humanity in the being of one person for the other "gladly" is neither eros nor agape; both forms of love as a common form of humanity can and ought to be qualified by grace and thus manifestations of the love of God. Barth thus identifies a form of humanity common to Christian and non-Christian alike, despite the fact that agape and eros are quite distinct from each other. [39]

The Incarnation of God does not take place in a privileged sphere nor in something less than real humanity. In the humanity of Jesus Christ, the actual humanity of every human person has been taken up, judged, put to death, and justified. Jesus Christ is not only the Son of the Father. He is at the same time the brother of every brother and sister. Through the Incarnation, it is determined that humanity, in its concrete and particular form as co-humanity, is a more fundamental and authentic humanity than that which exists merely as "nature," including all racial and cultural forms.

Through the concrete and particular form of humanity as co-humanity, the determination of God is experienced in terms of the other as both a "near" and "distant" neighbor. [40] In this form of humanity as co-humanity, the creaturely and natural aspect of human personhood is "humanized" without the need to appeal to "orders of preservation" or "institutions of sanctification."

The difference between the natural theology of Brunner and the theology of human nature as held by Barth can easily be seen in their respective views of sexual ethics. For Brunner, the erotic sexual impulse, while created as good, has fallen from its natural state and must be "contained" within marriage as the optimal ethical solution to the "relation between the sexes." [41] Marriage, for Brunner, is an order of creation which has the capacity to determine a moral relation between persons, which otherwise would not be accessible to them.

For Barth, the question of the sexual nature of human persons or of sexual relations is not identical with the question of marriage. "The command of God," says Barth, "sanctifies man by including his sexuality within his humanity, and challenging him even in his bodily nature and therefore in his sexual life, in his answering of the problem of sex relationship, to be true man: . . ."[42] When the definition of marriage is ultimately culturally relative and, to a certain degree, ambiguous, a natural theology which seeks to set forth an ethical principle under the category of an "order of creation," is viewed as preposterous by Barth.

On the other hand, wherever human persons are found, says Barth, whatever the racial or cultural factors, there will be found the inescapable and unavoidable ethical responsibility of living freely for and with the other. The Incarnation did not "christianize" humanity, it "humanized" humanity. The correlation between the "new humanity" in Christ and the goodness of created humanity is first of all an ontological structure of Created humanity before it is an ethical principle or criterion.

Human Life As Criterion For Moral Theology

The humanity of man is not replaced by the humanity of God in the form of Jesus Christ. Rather, the humanity of man is grasped in its contingent order and related again to the humanity of God as that upon which it is contingent. At the same time, it is related to the "other person" in the form of co-humanity.

The authentic form of humanity is to be found in its contingence toward God and toward the neighbor, both near and distant. In our modern era, the lack of a natural theology which speaks for and from the perspective of the concrete and actual humanity of every human person, has left the evangelical church ethically hesitant, if not ethically impotent.

With modern society no longer under the tutelege of a natural theology which subordinated human life to "orders of creation," the "world come of age" that Bonhoeffer prophetically spoke of from his prison cell has swept like a tidal wave over western civilization. In claiming autonomy as a "natural right," humanity today experiences contingence away from God in its full negative force.

It is humanity in its contingence away from God which seeks to reify nature, race, and culture under the religious rubric of "orders of creation." It is humanity in its contingence away from God which thinks of justice in terms of natural rights and fairness in terms of sharing what one would otherwise have for oneself. It is humanity in its contingence away from God which becomes vulnerable, weak, and exploitable. It is humanity in its contingence away from God which surrenders to the state the prerogatives for determining what is best for the "common good." It is humanity in its contingence away from God which bows before the absolute right of the machine to regulate the human organism.

What Barth correctly saw as a fatal plunge into ethical ambivalence in Brunner's optimism concerning "orders of preservation" has come to pass. But what Brunner saw as a fatal chasm between Barth's sheer Christological event of revelation and the natural goodness of life continues to plague the evangelical church.

What is at stake, is a forum of public ethical discussion which can overcome the ethical ambivalence of humanity bound to its own natural instincts. What is at issue are the criteria for moral actions which can break through the self interests of the powerful and the privileged. What is at the heart of the moral dilemma of the present age is the source of a transforming moral authority which is radical in its judgement of moral disorder and reconciling in its healing and renewal of the natural goodness which humanity carries as divine determination and promise.

The Public Nature of Moral Issues

The Incarnation of God in Jesus Christ destroyed the antithesis between Jew and Gentile, and so "broke down the dividing wall of hostility," wrote Paul to the Ephesians (Eph. 2:14). Paul drew out the ethical implications of this fact in his letter to the Roman Christians, where he argued that all human persons are morally as well as spiritually accountable precisely because they are *human* creatures (Chapters one and two). We said earlier that the Incarnation did not "Christianize" human persons, but that it "humanized" persons by freeing them to know their true humanity as created by God and oriented to God and the other person in a positive contingence of responsible love. Contingence means that apart from this positive orientation to God, humanity can only be a self-determination of individual rights based on natural instincts for survival.

The Incarnation, as Bonhoeffer began to see, meant that there is no longer a sacred and secular sphere, but that "Christ, reality and the good" comprise a single sphere of moral and spiritual unity.[43] To do the will of God, for Bonhoeffer, became the single task of the Christian. But the will of God is not an abstract moral or spiritual principle; it is bound up in the humanity of the other person, with Christ himself the middle term in that relation. Theological ethics and general ethics can now be a matter of public discussion, for the Incarnation has directed the moral concerns of God toward the secular and worldly character of human life with infinite concern and loving passion.

The humanity of God, as Barth came to think of it, was not the result of the assumption of creaturely flesh through the Incarnation, but God can become human because "he is human." Barth carries out the implications of this in a radical way:

> But just because God is human in this sense, it is actually *due* to man and may not be denied him through any pessimistic judgement, whatever its basis. On the basis of the eternal will of God we have to think of *every human being*, even the oddest, most villainous or miserable, as one to whom Jesus Christ is Brother and God is Father; and we have to deal with him on this assumption. [44]

This does not mean that a Christian ethic views ordinary and natural humanity "as if" each person were potentially related to Christ. Barth will have none of that! The Incarnation establishes the actuality of every person's objective relation to the humanity of God through Christ. But this means that whatever there is of human goodness and wherever there is concern for what upholds and sustains this human goodness, this is of common concern to theological and general ethics.

The agenda for ethical discussion as a public discussion is not a privileged theological or spiritual set of issues. The issues are set deeply into the nature of humanity as such. The Incarnation sets the issues precisely in the human situation where they rightly belong because of the act of God in creation itself. The christian theologian ought to see these issues more clearly and accurately than anyone else precisely because of the revelation of God in Christ. But the Christian theologian does not have ethical issues which are other than these issues of natural human life as endowed by God with goodness.

Because natural human goodness is contingent upon this endowment from the creator, this does not surrender to humanity in its contingence away from God an absolute moral right. If the moral issues are defined in terms of an absolute moral principle intrinsic to human dignity by those who do not recognize this contingence toward God, this does not preempt the agenda for public moral discussion between Christians and non-christians. The agenda for moral discussion at the public level is determined by the nature of human personhood itself. As Bonhoeffer came to see, one did not need to be a confessing Christian in order to enter into a coalition, and even a conspiracy, to overcome the evil and inhuman actions of the Third Reich. That he did so himself as a confessing Christian, is a mark of his theological integrity as well as of his ethical sensitivity.

The Criteria For Moral Actions

It follows from what has been said that the will of God as the criterion for moral responsibility and moral actions, cannot be abstracted from the concrete actuality of human life with all of the appropriate criteria which pertain to that life. The "command of God," which Barth saw as the single basis for ethical responsibility, is not spoken in a vacuum, nor heard in a vacuum. The command of God is always heard in the particularities of language, location, history, race, and human social realities, argued Barth. [45] The Incarnation, with the "judge judged in our place," is a direct confrontation of God with humanity, and "reveals the full seriousness of the human situation." [46]

The criteria for moral action are thus set squarely within the structures of humanity itself. The single criterion is the will and command of God which directs us to these criteria. The poor, the hungry, the dispossed, the oppressed, as well as the oppressor, constitute the criteria for responsible moral action. Poverty is not itself the criterion, nor is oppression. For this would leave the rich and the oppressor without a criterion for moral self reflection and self criticism. The criteria are lodged within the *relation* of one to the other. As a result, the impoverishment of one is immediately a matter of moral concern to the other. In the same way, the act of oppression is of moral concern to the oppressed one. It is not enough to be liberated from the oppressor. One must also seek reconciliation with the oppressor for the sake of the humanity of the oppressor. Being oppressed does not free one from the moral demand of co-humanity. Nor does being hungry free one from the moral responsibility to seek the good of those who have plenty.

Access to moral criteria is not a theological or Christian prerogative – it is a human prerogative as well as a human responsibility. One could paraphrase Barth by saying that all persons can be presumed to have moral openness, but not moral readiness. This would seem to allow for a natural theology which takes into account a common ground for moral responsibility which finds its criteria in the natural goodness of humanity. Even when that natural goodness has become sheer contingence away from God. The Christian theologian is, or ought to be, aware of the resources for moral courage and moral action through God's revelation in Christ. And the Christian theologian will know that all moral criteria are contingent upon the endowment of moral good as a quality of human life.

The Cross and the Transformation of Moral Authority

We agree that the agenda for moral discussion is of public nature, and not a privileged sphere of theological ethics. We agree with the insight of Brunner that the theologian's attitude to *theologia naturalis* decides the character of his ethics. We agree with Barth that there is an openness of all human persons to knowledge of God, but not the readiness.

We have attempted to bring the concerns of Brunner for a viable *theologia naturalis* into closer proximity to Barth's concern for the "single task of theology." We have sought to establish a new direction for natural theology within Barth's trajectory of evangelical theology through closer attention to the structure of Barth's theological anthropology. The natural goodness of humanity continues to be a matter of divine determination, despite the effects of the fall. God does not abandon humanity in its sheer contingence away from his grace. Instead, he continually seeks to uphold the humanity of all persons, even in their state of sin and rebellion. Through the Incarnation, the ontological status of all human persons is brought back within the positive contingence toward God through the fact that Jesus Christ is not only the Son of God, but at the same time, the brother to every brother and sister in the human family.

Yet, in agreeing to all of this, we still have not touched the heart of the matter. For as Barth clearly stated, and as Brunner well knew, more is required than openness to the good, there must also be the readiness to seek and do the good.

Here it is that we see that moral persuasion is not enough. Here we discover that moral argument is insufficient to penetrate through to the stubborn core of the human heart which is not *ready* to acknowledge what is already objectively known. It is indeed true, as Barth put it, "man, not God is at fault."[47]

The criterion for moral action cannot be the conscience, as the Apostle Paul clearly saw. The conscience is the center of moral ambivalence, not moral authority. True, conscience does "bear witness," as Paul wrote, but it also is the center of "conflicting thoughts" which both "accuse and excuse." (Ro. 2:15) That which conscience points to are the criteria for moral responsibility sunk deep into the structures of created human goodness experienced as co-humanity. But the single criterion for moral action is the command of God which positively orients us to God himself as the source of all human natural goodness.

When a natural theology is based on creation alone and upon human nature as a bearer of a truth which points to God, this theology masks the inveterate sin which plagues all human moral action and turns it into self preservation at the expense of the other. The formation of moral authority without the transformation of moral power will leave the powerless weak and will strengthen the hand of the powerful. A natural theology which does not have at the center a cross sunk deep into human flesh will not find transforming love at the center of human moral action.

It is through the death and resurrection of Jesus Christ that the transformation of moral authority takes place. Here, as Paul clearly states, all of the old antitheses and the natural hostilities are brought to an end (Eph. 2:16). No longer can sexual status, economic status, or racial distinctives be used as criteria for relationship with God or for seeking advantage over others. The Incarnation is not for the purpose of putting the humanity of God upon the cross, but for the purpose of sinking the cross deeply into the humanity of man. When "God dies" upon the cross, what is put to death is all that is inhuman in humanity.

While there is a continuing structure of historical and temporal life, and while human persons continue to survive even as sinners, all of this has come to an end in Jesus Christ who is the *eschatos* of humanity. Through his death and resurrection, Jesus is not the *terminus* of humanity, but the eschatological savior of humanity. The New Testament social ethic, says Leonhard Goppelt, is a Christian calling to life in existing historical structures, but not on the basis of a natural justice or social idealism. Rather, the Christian is called to exercize a role of responsible witness to the new and true humanity which has been obtained through Jesus Christ. [48]

It is not enough to have an agenda for moral discussion which is public in nature and which gives every person access to the criteria for moral discernment. Moral discussions without moral authority to transform existing social and personal evils are themselves immoral discussions. To speak words of encouragement and peace to those in dire need of the basic subsistence of life without actually giving what is needed is not faith, says James; it is dead (James 2:14-17).

A theology which does not include "social repentance" as an evidence of the transformation of the moral authority by which one lives among others, cannot be a truly evangelical theology, nor can it be an authentic natural theology. The atonement which the cross provides through the death of Christ can never be a legal or forensic construct in abstraction from the common humanity which Christ shares with all human persons. To have experienced the grace of the cross and forgiveness of sins is to have received the grace of repentance as well. This theme of John McLeod Campbell establishes the vicarious humanity of Christ as the basis for the transformation of natural human life. Not only does the gospel say that Christ gives me God as my Father, says Campbell, but it also says that "He gives me men as my brethren."[49]

It would indeed be a new and liberating theology which took seriously the Incarnation as the radical criterion by which human social, economic, and political relations are now to be brought under judgement and restored to God's intended order, as "preparation of the way of the Lord." It would indeed be a new direction in natural theology for the transforming grace of the death and resurrection of Christ to be displayed in the public arena through serious moral commitment to the humanizing of human persons.

It would indeed be an approproate testimony to the theological legacy of Karl Barth for evangelical theology to move in this new direction. And perhaps there might even be some who had felt it necessary to say No to Barth on this count, who would have some Angel give him a message: "Tell him that the time when we should say No to him is now past, and we all live only by the fact that a great and merciful God speaks his gracious Yes to all of us."

Notes

1. *Karl Barth Letters (1961-1968),* edited by Juergen Fangmeir and Hinrich Stoevsandt; translated by Geoffrey W. Bromiley (Grand Rapids: Eerdmans Publishing Co., 1981), pp. 202-3. Vogelsanger received Barth's letter on the morning of 5th April, rushed to the hospital, where Brunner was weak but alive and conscious, and read the letter with Barth's greeting. "A slight but beautiful smile came over Brunner's features and he quietly pressed Vogelsanger's hand. A few minutes later Brunner went into a coma from which he did not awake, dying peacefully near midday on 6th April. Barth's seems to have been his last earthly greeting." Ibid.
2. *Natural Theology: Comprising "Nature and Grace" by Professor Dr. Emil Brunner and the reply "No!" by Dr. Karl Barth.* Translated by Peter Fraenkel (London: Geoffrey Bles, The Centenary Press, 1946).
3. Ibid., p. 59
4. Ibid., p. 105. T.F. Torrance also reminds us of the importance of reading Barth's sharp response to Brunner in the context of the events in Germany at that time. Cf. his essay, "Natural Theology in the Thought of Karl Barth," in *Transformation and Convergence in the Frame of Knowledge,* T.F. Torrance (Grand Rapids: Eerdmans Publishing Co., 1984), pp 287ff.
5. *Church Dogmatics,* II/1, pp. 173-178.
6. Ibid., pp. 97-126.
7. *Ethics,* Edited by Dietrich Braun, translated by Geoffrey W. Bromiley (New York: The Seabury Press, 1981), pp. 118-119. In a pithy response to a letter sent to Barth by a Miss Heitmann, Barth wrote (6 August, 1966): "Since God does in fact address man in his Word, he obviously treats him as addressable in spite of the fact that man as a sinner closes his ears and heart to him. And as God awakens man to faith by his Holy Spirit, he himself posits the necessary point of contact. But he is greater than our heart, making the deaf to hear and the blind to see. That's the way it is." *Letters: 1961-1968,* p. 217.
8. *Church Dogmatics,* I/2, pp. 81ff.
9. Torrance, "Natural Theology in the Thought of Karl Barth", p. 294. The American theologian Carl F.H. Henry also states that a natural theology which attempts to establish a basis in human thought alone is not in accord with evangelical theology: "But Reformed theology insists as well that natural theology supplies no possibility of theological understanding. It rejects both Roman Catholic and modernistic notions that the knowledge of God is a realization of a spiritual potential in man as man. ... Because of the deforming effects of sin, the notion that Christians and unbelievers possess a common system of truths or overlapping principles in view of man's created status in the knowledge of God has therefore no essential basis." *God, Revelation and Authority,* Vol. I (Waco, Texas: Word Books, 1976), pp. 399, 400. Henry compromises his own statement, however, when he also says, "The truth of revelation is intended for sinners, and the unbeliever can indeed examine the content of theology. ... The new birth ... is not prerequisite to a knowledge of the truth of God." Ibid., p. 229.
10. Ibid., p. 295.
11. Ibid., pp. 295-6.
12. *Space, Time and Resurrection* (Grand Rapids: Eerdmans Publishing Co., 1976), preface, pp. xx, ix, x.
13. Ibid.
14. *The Humanity of God* (London: Collins, Fontana Library, 1967), pp. 33-34.
15. Torrance, "Natural Theology in the Thought of Karl Barth," pp. 287f.

16. *Church Dogmatics,* II/1, p. 130.
17. *Church Dogmatics,* I/2, p. 305.
18. *Church Dogmatics,* II/1, p. 218.
19. Torrance, "Natural Theology in the Thought of Karl Barth," pp. 295-6; 299-300
20. *Church Dogmatics,* IV/3, p. 139.
21. *The Christian Life* Translated by Geoffrey W. Bromiley, (Grand Rapids: Eerdmans Publishing Co., 1981) p. 120.
22. Ibid., p. 121.
23. Ibid., p. 122.
24. Torrance, "Natural Theology in the Thought of Karl Barth," pp. 287-8
25. Cf. *Church Dogmatics,* II/1, pp. 90-94.
26. Cf. *The Humanity of God,* pp. 41-42.
27. Ibid., pp. 37-8.
28. *Church Dogmatics,* II/1, p. 304.
29. Ibid., p. 311.
30. *Divine and Contingent Order* (New York: Oxford, 1981), p. 82.
31. In addition to the criticism of James Gustafson concerning Barth's narrow theological ethic, *Christ and the Moral Life* (University of Chicago Press, 1968) p. 97, other criticisms of Barth as having a Christological exclusivism in theology and ethics include: E. Clinton Gardner, *Christocentrism in Christian Social Ethics: A depth Study of Eight Modern Protestants* (Washington D.C.: University Press of America, 1983); and, Eugene B. Borowitz, *Contemporary Christologies: a Jewish Response* (New York: Paulist Press, 1980).
32. *Nature and Grace,* p. 51.
33. For a discussion of Barth's view of ethics with respect to the "other" and the shift in his focus from a negative to a positive view of the "other" person as ethical responsibility, see, Steven G. Smith, *The Argument to Other – Reason Beyond Reason in the Thought of Karl Barth and Emmanuel Levinas* (Chico, CA: Scholars Press, 1983), pp. 44-46; 158ff.
34. Torrance, "Natural Theology in the Thought of Karl Barth," p. 299.
35. Cf. James M. Gustafson, *Church and the Moral Life,* who criticizes Barth for failing to develop a Christian ethic which appeals to public criteria: "Barth evades the task of stating in nontheological language precisely what the efficacy of Christian faith is on moral behavior . . . there is a new direction and attitude. But he is not interested in trying to explain the 'hows' of that transformation." p. 97. Robin Lovin, as well in, *Christian Faith and Public Choices: The Social Ethics of Barth, Brunner, and Bonhoeffer* (Philadelphia: Fortress Press, 1984), criticizes Barth's grounding of ethics on the will of God, and suggests in return that the will of God must be open to public discussion in order for moral arguments to establish a general obligation. pp. 3, 24.
36. Torrance, "Natural Theology in the Thought of Karl Barth,", pp. 299-300.
37. *Divine and Contingent Order,* pp. 71f.
38. Ibid., pp. 44ff; 52. For a discussion of the concept of contingence as it relates to theological anthropology, see, Ray S. Anderson, *On Being Human* (Grand Rapids: Eerdmans Publishing Company, 1982). Chapter Two: "Humanity as Creatureliness."
39. *Church Dogmatics,* III/2, pp. 274-285.
40. Cf. Barth's discussion of the socio-historical context of the command of God with respect to the "near" and "distant" neighbor, in *Church Dogmatics,* III/4, pp. 285ff.
41. *Love and Marriage* (London: Collins, The Fontana Library, 1970), pp. 183, 195.
42. *Church Dogmatics,* III/4, pp. 118, 140, 132.
43. *Ethics* (New York: Macmillan, 1955), pp. 188f.

44. *The Humanity of God,* p. 50.
45. See *Church Dogmatics,* III/4, pp. 285ff.
46. See, *Church Dogmatics,* IV/1, pp. 211, 222f, 273.
47. *The Christian Life,* p. 121.
48. *Theology of the New Testament,* Vol. 2, translation by John Alsup; edited by Jürgen Roloff (Grand Rapids: Eerdmans Publishing Company, 1982), pp. 146, 157.
49. "Here it may occur, that though to say that Christ gives me God as my Father has indeed a gospel sound, this is not felt equally as to the statement that He gives me men as my brethren. Yet are the gifts related, inseparably connected; their bond being the relation of the second commandment to the first." *The Nature of the Atonement and its Relation to Remission of Sins and Eternal Life* (London: MacMillan and Co. 1878), p. 317.

Barth, Schleiermacher
and the Task of Dogmatics
Alasdair I.C. Heron

"Dogmatic Theology is the science which systematizes the doctrine prevalent in a Christian Church at a given time." (Friedrich Schleiermacher) [1]

"As a theological discipline dogmatics is the scientific self-examination of the Christian Church with respect to the content of its distinctive talk about God." (Karl Barth) [2]

The relation between Barth and Schleiermacher has already been the subject of numerous studies, so the topic I have chosen might appear passé. Yet it has its own interest and significance, if for no other reason than the acknowledged stature and continuing influence of both. The two definitions of the task and nature of dogmatics quoted above have both come to hold almost classical status, and there are worse questions for rising theologians to cut their dogmatic teeth on than that of the similarities and differences between them. *Similarities* exist here as well as *differences* - which brings me to a further reason for the choice of subject.

Many of the comparisons of Barth and Schleiermacher, at least in the English-speaking world, tend to fall into one or the other of two categories.[3] Either they set out to show that Barth got all the things right which Schleiermacher had not; or they aim to support the view that Barth neither properly understood nor adequately overcame Schleiermacher's legacy. Both ways of seeing are inevitably colored by the hermeneutical problem involved in translating and applying the work of either to what is in part a different cultural context. Sometimes, at least, it is an uprooted and withered Barth or Schleiermacher who is brought under the microscope of anglo-saxon commentators for dissection and evaluation - uprooted, that is, from their place in the broad stream of modern germanic protestant, specifically reformed theology. In the process both the similarities and the differences between them can become somewhat refracted, as when Schleiermacher is seen as the godfather of theological relativism and religious pluralism, Barth as the representative *par excellence* of a conservative theological reaction against the whole drift of modern culture. The two had much more in common than such one-sided accounts suggest, and it is only in the light of the resemblances that the real nature and significance of the contrasts can adequately be seen.

Barth on Schleiermacher

Barth himself was well aware of sharing common concerns with Schleiermacher - an awareness in no way weakened by his intensive criticism through more than forty years, for he sensed that Schleiermacher was *the* figure whom he had to counter, but whom at the same time he must not only *criticise* but also *appreciate.* Certainly he could say in his commentary on Ro. 6, 20 with characteristic vehemence:

> ... the Gospel of Christ is a shattering disturbance, an assault which brings everything into question. For this reason, nothing is so meaningless as the attempt to construct a religion out of the Gospel, and to set it as one human possibility in the midst of others. Since Schleiermacher, this attempt has been undertaken more consciously than ever before in Protestant theology - and it is the betrayal of Christ. [4]

Certainly too he could insist in his 1922 lecture, "Das Wort Gottes als Aufgabe der Theologie", [5] that the ancestral series to which he appealed ran back through Kierkegaard to Luther and Calvin, to Paul and Jeremiah, but most emphatically *not* to Schleiermacher. [6] Yet precisely for this reason, Barth devoted one of his early lecture-courses in Göttingen in the winter semester of 1923-24 to - Schleiermacher, whom he treated in a highly original and, though thoroughly critical, by no means unsympathetic way. [7] The remarks with which the lecture manuscript ends are revealing:

> The higher one values Schleiermacher's achievement in and for itself, and the better one sees with what historical necessity it had to come and how well - how only too well - it fitted the whole spirit of Christianity in the 19th and 20th centuries, the more clearly one perceives how easy it is to say No in word but how hard it is to say it in deed, namely with a positive

counter-achievement. Schleiermacher undoubtedly did a good job. It is not enough to know that another job has to be done; what is needed is the ability to do it at least as well as he did his. This is the serious and humbling concern with which I take leave of Schleiermacher; and if you agree with my assessment, I hope you will share this concern. There is no occasion for triumphant superiority at this tomb, but there is occasion for fear and trembling at the seriousness of the moment and in the face of our own inadequacy. [8]

Or, as he put it some years later in his history of protestant theology in the nineteenth century:

We have to do with a hero, the like of which is but seldom bestowed upon theology. Anyone who has never noticed anything of the splendour this figure radiated and still does - I am almost tempted to say, who has never succumbed to it - may honourably pass on to other and possibly better ways, but let him never raise so much as a finger against Schleiermacher. Anyone who has never loved here, and is not in a position to love again may not hate here either. [9]

The same tone of admiration, fascination and criticism runs through the numerous references to Schleiermacher in the *Church Dogmatics,* whereby it is worth noting that in the frequency of such references Schleiermacher runs more or less neck-and-neck with Thomas Aquinas and is surpassed only by Augustine, Luther and Calvin.

Certainly, Barth's criticisms of Schleiermacher's achievement were utterly seriously meant. He regarded Schleiermacher as the apostle of anthropocentric neo-protestantism, the counterpart of ecclesiocentric Roman Catholicism; and on both he declared war. Theology could not make it its business to speak of God by speaking of humanity, religion or the Christian community in a raised voice: it must, precisely as a *human* enterprise, speak *of God* and *from God.* Its calling is to hear and witness to the Word of God which evokes and addresses faith; it cannot properly allow its agenda to be dictated from "outside" if that "outside" is taken to be any kind of philosophical, metaphysical, sociological, psychological or otherwise "scientific" account of human existence in the world rather than the "from without" of the inbreaking, perennially new revelation of God himself. Barth therefore viewed Schleiermacher as the genial advocate of an approach which in effect reduced theology to anthropology; and aimed to set against that approach his own "counterachievement". Yet precisely as a *counter*achievement it was necessarily related to that which it was opposed. Barth and Schleiermacher may indeed be poles apart, but the poles are those of an ellipse, in which the second can best be appreciated in its tension-laden relation to the first. In this light, a number of general resemblances between Barth and Schleiermacher deserve more attention than they are generally given. Both were revolutionary thinkers; both were theologians of rare insight and industry; both sought to open up deeper paths of theological reflection in the light of the circumstances and challenges of their own time.

Some Resemblances and Parallels

Both Schleiermacher and Barth first became prominent as theological *enfants terribles* - Schleiermacher with the *Addresses on Religion* (1799) and Barth with the first and, even more, with the second edition of *The Epistle to the Romans* (1919/1922). Both works were widely regarded as subversive, indeed downright dangerous, if for opposite reasons. What made Schleiermacher suspect was the *pantheistic* tendency of his romantically-tinged view of the relation between the individual and the "universe"; what seemed to be hard to take in Barth was his emphasis on the *opposition*, the "absolute qualitative difference" between God and the world, eternity and history. At this level, the two may seem to have nothing whatsoever in common; and what is more, this level is no mere superficial or trivial one, but that on which the fundamental difference in approach between Barth and Schleiermacher becomes visible *in nuce*. Yet it would perhaps be a mistake simply to leave the matter there, as two considerations may help to show. First, both could, on the negative side, utter similar criticisms of prevailing established conceptions of theology and church. There is more than a mere accidental similarity, for instance, between Schleiermacher's remark somewhere in the *Addresses* that the Scriptures had become the mausoleum of the Spirit and Barth's comment in *Romans* that the crater around which the saints expectantly sit is long burnt-out. Both observations reflect a struggling with the question of the *reality* with which theology has to do, a struggling which led both Schleiermacher and Barth to break out of the accepted, given patterns of theological argument, reflection and construction. Schleiermacher sought to place in the centre the reality of what today might be called the existential dimension of human life in and as part of the cosmos, Barth the reality of the transcendent Word of God. Second, this common concern to search after reality would seem to be what Bultmann rightly discerned when he observed in his preview of the 1922 *Romans* that, although Barth himself would dispute this way of putting it, his work could be seen as belonging to the same tradition as Schleiermacher's *Addresses* or Otto's *Idea of the Holy*, that is, with the modern attempts to demonstrate the distinct nature of the religious *a priori*. [10] Barth himself came to treat this assessment of Bultmann's as proof of how deeply Bultmann had failed to understand him because Bultmann himself was so deeply bound to the tradition of Schleiermacher; [11] but while this reaction of Barth's is understandable and in its own way justified, it should not obscure the fact that behind and beyond the formulations Bultmann used to describe it, there *is* a recognisably similar kind of questioning underlying the early approaches of both Schleiermacher and Barth, even if the questions themselves are posed in opposite directions.

Schleiermacher's concern was to reawaken a direct sense of religious reality (even among the "cultured despisers") by breaking away from the identification of the religious sphere with those of metaphysics or ethics and by pointing to its own distinct character. The Enlightenment had gravely weakened the bonds which earlier generations had sought to forge between Christian faith and metaphysical, physico-theological and natural theology; but the alternative which it offered, most notably in the work of Kant, was, to Schleiermacher's mind, inadequate as an alternative. Kant had removed religion and theology from the sphere of "pure reason", of the "knowable", and relocated them in that of "practical reason", of ethics, with its threefold postulate of God, the immortality of the soul and the reality of the freedom of the will, all of them *practically* necessary in view of the character of the "categorical imperative" experienced by every moral being. Kant understood himself to be restricting the realm of knowledge in order to make room for faith; but the "faith" which resulted, lying in the field delimited by the questions, What can I know? What must I do? For what may I hope? was for Schleiermacher as unsatisfying as the former path of speculative metaphysics. Both lacked the *immediacy* which he felt must belong to what is genuinely religious. So he came to insist in the second of the *Addresses* that the authentic interest of religion has to do neither with *knowledge* nor with *action,* neither with *metaphysics* nor with *ethics,* [12] but with the directly accessible fields of *contemplation* or *intuition (Anschauung)* and *feeling (Gefühl),* with a capacity for apprehension and response given in and with the human condition - a capacity which he was later to define as "the pious self-consciousness", "the consciousness of absolute dependence". [13] In this way, Schleiermacher sought in the *Addresses* to point to the fact of our human existence, the gift of self-consciousness, the experience of our being in and of the world as a primary datum for theological reflection. In this regard the *Addresses* were epoch-breaking and epoch-making, and laid the foundation for Schleiermacher's later attempt to reconstruct the entire substance of Christian dogmatics by reference to that base.

Barth's approach in the early 1920's represented an equally radical break with established patterns of thought, particularly those of what he came to call "cultural protestantism", the form of protestant theology which had so identified itself with contemporary culture and civilisation that it was no longer capable of protesting against the reduction of theology to history and the misuse of Christian ideals to subserve political and military ambitions. Of special significance here was what he called the *dies ater* in August 1914 when a group of German intellectuals, among them many of his own former teachers, issued a manifesto of support for the war aims of the Kaiser. In Barth's eyes this destroyed at a stroke the credibility not only of their politics but of their theology too. "God" had become for them a function of what has more recently come to be called "civil religion". A direct line can be drawn from this moment of profound disillusionment to Barth's subsequent criticism of "religion" as "idolatry", the glorification of human cultural self-affirmation over against God, to which God can and does address his shattering "Nein!" So Barth's *Romans* drew on the prophetic tradition of the Old Testament, the apocalyptic warning of judgment upon the "powers of this world" and the Gospel of the cross and resurrection of Jesus Christ; and brought them to bear with a fresh, blazing urgency upon the claims and pretensions of "cultural Christianity".

How far was this criticism directed against Schleiermacher himself? Only in a differentiated way. Barth remained to the end of his days convinced that Schleiermacher would not have been capable of signing the manifesto of 1914, but insisted at the same time that "the entire theology which had unmasked itself in that manifesto . . . was groun - ded ,determined and influenced decisively by him".[14] The essential difference between them is not to be found by identifying Schleiermacher as a "cultural protestant", but rather in their understandings of "religion". The contrast is most forcefully expressed by Barth in his exegesis of Ro. 7, 14-25 under the heading, "The Reality of Religion", particularly in the introduction to that section, [15] in which he can quote against Schleiermacher the final verse of the poem which Schleiermacher's friend Friedrich Schlegel had written as his own commentary on the *Addresses:*

> The romantic psychologist . . . may represent religion as that human capacity by which "all human ocurrences are.thought of as divine actions"; he may define it as "the solemn music which accompanies all human experience" (Schleiermacher). Against such representations, however, religion is always on its guard. Religion, when it attacks vigorously, when it is fraught with disturbance, when it is non-aesthetic, non-rhetorical, non-pious, when it is the religion of the 39th Psalm, of Job and of Luther and of Kierkegaard, when it is the religion of Paul, bitterly protests against every attempt to make of its grim earnestness some trivial and harmless thing. Religion is aware that it is in no wise the crown and fulfilment of true humanity; it knows itself rather to be a questionable, disturbing, dangerous thing. . . . Religion, so far from being the place where the healthy harmony of human life is lauded, is instead the place where it appears diseased, discordant, and disrupted. Religion is not the sure ground upon which human culture safely rests; it is the place where civilisation and its partner, barbarism, are rendered fundamentally questionable. Nor does the frank judgement of honest men of the world disagree with the opinion of religion about itself.

> The curtain is raised; the music must cease.
> The temple is gone, and far in the distance
> Appeareth the terrible form of the - Sphinx.
> [16]

> Religion must beware lest it tone down in any degree
> the unconverted man's judgement. Conflict and dis-
> tress, sin and death, the devil and hell, make up the
> reality of religion. ... Religion possesses no solution
> of the problem of life; rather it makes of that problem a
> wholly insoluble enigma. ... Religion is neither a
> thing to be enjoyed nor a thing to be celebrated: it
> must be borne as a yoke which cannot be removed.

This passage displays vividly how much more sombre than Schleiermacher's is the early Barth's diagnosis of religion, civilisation and Christian (or indeed human) existence. It is in part a response to the challenges he felt to be confronting faith and proclamation in the crisis of the First World War, in part a reaction against and a reckoning with the tradition represented by Schleiermacher, in part a recovery of authentic biblical and reformation insights into the height and depth of sin and grace, insights which Schleiermacher had tended to level-down and flatten-out. But Schleiermacher is not thereby dis-posed of - neither for Barth nor for us. Both can open our eyes to realities with which our theology must have to do - on the one hand the gift and mystery of human existence as having to do with the reality of God, on the other the reality of the Word of God as a Word of judgment and of mercy upon that existence. In this sense, the early impulses of both Schleiermacher and Barth remain valid, even if Barth's must be recognised as cutting deeper and driving further than Schleiermacher's.

Further similarities can also be seen in the way that the later work of Barth and Schleiermacher developed. Some would characterise these by saying that both became more "conservative" following their first, radical beginnings. But "conservative" is a slippery concept, whether it is understood politically or theologically. [17] It would be more pre-cise to say that both worked out from their starting-points to include and gather in, in an essentially consistent development, a wider and deeper appreciation and appropriation of the fruits of earlier

Christian theology. Both went on to become, in the strict sense of the word, *ecclesiastical* theologians, conscious of the responsibility of their work for the life and witness of the wider Christian community. Once called to chairs of theology - Schleiermacher in Berlin, Barth first of all in Göttingen - they found themselves confronted with other tasks and responsibilities than those of relatively independent thinkers. In particular, they were faced with the question of *how* they were to teach them - a question which can have a sobering effect on the most effervescent spirits if they feel its real force. Both Schleiermacher and Barth did feel that force and got down to the hard work of regular teaching and its necessary accompaniment, intensive study and reflection. Neither of them found this easy or regarded it as a task which could be completed in a brief period and then regarded as finished. For example, Schleiermacher laboured over twenty years at his *Brief Outline of the Study of Theology,* and issued his *The Christian Faith* in two editions, the second extensively reworked and modified; Barth embarked on the project of a *Christian Dogmatics* only to abandon it after volume one had already been published and to make a fresh start on the *Church Dogmatics,* the task which largely occupied the last forty years of his life. Above and beyond these more external resemblances in what, after all, are not entirely untypical careers for theological professors, one common factor stands out: the seriousness and consistency with which both worked, alongside numerous other tasks, at producing a comprehensive treatment of the main themes of Christian dogmatics, and the originality of the powers and insights they both brought to the task, along with the distinctive character and inner coherence of the resultant works. Three aspects deserve in particular to be highlighted.

1) As already indicated above, both came to modify and deepen (not to depart from) their earlier, "radical" insights by drawing in and reworking materials from the earlier history of Christian theology. In Schleiermacher's case this took the form, for example, of a typological restatement of the pattern of the "natural heresies in Christianity . . . the Docetic and the Nazarean, the Manichean and the Pelagian" as well as of "the antithesis between the Roman Catholic and the Protestant" forms in the western church, [18] combined with a thoroughgoing analysis of the "feeling of absolute dependence" in terms of sin and grace as determining the larger, second part of *The Christian Faith* and an account of salvation in terms of the "God-consciousness"

realised in Jesus of Nazareth and communicated by him to all who believe. [19] Barth went further still, in what he not only included in the *Church Dogmatics* extensive consideration of patristic and medieval theology and the teaching of the Reformers, but also (unlike Schleiermacher) took detailed account of the era of protestant orthodoxy as well as of Schleiermacher and his nineteenth- and twentieth-century successors.[20]

2) At the same time, neither Schleiermacher nor Barth equated the hard study necessary for theological enquiry, teaching and proclamation with mere historical research. Their concern was rather with the present task and responsibility of theological work: What is to be said and communicated here and now? What is the abiding substance of the faith? How must received patterns of thought be corrected and modified in order to address the challenges of the contemporary age? Neither intended the answers to these questions to issue in a simple accommodation of the faith to the questions and concerns of contemporary culture as such. Both were concerned rather to speak of the things of the faith in a way which would address that culture. Schleiermacher sought to awaken in his hearers an awareness of the immediate presence of God, a presence achieved and fulfilled in Jesus Christ and emanating from him as "the union of the divine essence with human nature in the form of the common Spirit which animates the corporate life of believers".[21] Barth aimed by contrast to speak of the transcendent power of the Word of God in Jesus Christ - which in later years he identified more and more specifically as "the humanity of God" - as the true ground, object and goal of Christian theology. In this sense, both identified the essential substance of the faith *christologically* - and at the same time as *contemporary*. Certainly there remains here a major difference, and one which always led Barth to doubt whether Schleiermacher's christological emphasis was in fact consistent with the broad pattern of his theology; for Schleiermacher's christology was essentially historically located and his understanding of salvation as horizontally-mediated "God-consciousness" fitted into the same perspective. Barth by contrast sought after a more *transcendental* point of reference, albeit one which was also and at the same time *historically anchored*, not indeed in Jesus' "God-consciousness", but in the interaction of eternity and time in his historical person and work, in his incarnation, life, death and resurrection as the centre and scope of that "history of God with humanity" which

lies behind and before the whole run of human history. It is not hard to see that at this decisive point Barth is more the heir of Hegel than of Schleiermacher, [22] that here too his theological reflection goes further and cuts deeper than Schleiermacher's had done. But for all that, it was concerned to answer the same kind of questions, albeit to answer them differently. With Schleiermacher's example before him, Barth could see that awareness of the transcendent reality of God amounts to more than "the feeling of absolute dependence" and cannot adequately be expressed in purely historical or anthropological categories - and therefore, too, that christology cannot be adequately expressed in these categories, that christological reflection must break them open if it is consistently followed through.

3) In different ways, both Schleiermacher's *The Christian Faith* and Barth's *Church Dogmatics* witness to the rare capacity of both to present the main themes of the faith in an integrated way. Not without cause are they widely regarded as the finest statements in the tradition of reformed dogmatics since Calvin's *Institute.* Not only do they *integrate;* they also *illuminate* each element by setting it in the light of the whole, and so by drawing out the *internal connexions* between the different *loci* instead of merely listing them one after another, like so many pearls on a string. The aim of such an integrated presentation is not merely formal elegance or abstract systematisation but, in the properly scientific sense of the word, objective understanding, understanding which follows the dynamics of the reality being explored. The shape such an attempt at understanding will take does of course depend fundamentally on the underlying conviction as to the nature of that reality itself, and here the differences between Barth and Schleiermacher are too apparent to need underlining yet again. Equally, however, it may be doubted whether contemporary protestant theology in search for orientation can really appreciate what is going on in the *Church Dogmatics* if it has not already paused to learn from what is going on in *The Christian Faith.* Proper appreciation of what Schleiermacher takes to be the object of the enquiry and of the appropriate systematic analysis of its components can at any rate make it easier for us to understand the different characterisations alike of the object and the method which we find in Barth. With this let me now turn to the specific example of similarity and difference between Schleiermacher and Barth which I wish to examine in this connexion: here too we shall find cause for concluding that Barth did not simply *reject* but rather

deepened the approach he found in Schleiermacher, and thereby sharply *qualified it.*

The Task of Dogmatics

At the beginning of this paper I quoted Schleiermacher's definition of dogmatic theology as "the science which systematizes the doctrine prevalent in a Christian Church at a given time". This definition constituted the first proposition of the first edition of *The Christian Faith;* the reconstruction of the introductory sections in the second edition led to its appearing there as §19. Its specific force can best be understood in the light of Schleiermacher's overall account of the theological disciplines in his *Brief Outline of the Study of Theology.* [23] There he distinguished three broad fields: First, *philosophical theology,* subdivided into *apologetics* and *polemics;* second, *historical theology,* subdivided into three areas: *exegetical theology; historical theology* in the narrower sense of *church history; historical knowledge of the present situation of Christianity,* this last being further subdivided into *dogmatic theology* and *ecclesiastical statistics;* third, *practical theology,* dealing with *ministry* and *government* in the church. Dogmatic theology thus had as its special task the establishing of the contemporary doctrine of the theologian's particular confessional tradition and formed on the one hand a conclusion to the work of historical theology and on the other the basis for practical application in the life, worship and administration of the church. It was thus both an *historical* discipline and an *ecclesiastical* one, in both senses with a direct contemporary relevance. In Schleiermacher's case and situation, this meant that the task of dogmatics was to gather up and state the contemporary doctrine of the mixed lutheran and reformed tradition of the Prussian Church Union: but the same formal pattern could also be applied to other ecclesiastical and denominational contexts or indeed to the present-day attempts to construct a new ecumenical theology, one which will relativise and overcome existing confessional differences in a fresh synthesis capable of practical application in a more comprehensive church union. There too, dogmatics can easily come to be looked upon as an essentially historical and ecclesiastical discipline, concerned to gather up and integrate traditional elements of doctrine in a fresh synthesis.

The definition as such is by no means a bad one, but it patently contains within itself the seeds of a dangerous one-sidedness, of a kind of historical horizontalism which sees and treats the forms of expression of the faith itself in purely historical terms and is exposed to the risk of a relative absolutisation of this or that tradition or combination of traditions as if the responsibility of dogmatic theology were *merely* to them - and to the practical demands of the present day. Schleiermacher's own presentation of the substance of dogmatics was indeed preserved from surrender to mere traditionalism and pragmatism by his concern to do justice to the reality of "the pious self-consciousness" as the touchstone and test of the validity of dogmatic utterances. But it may with justice be doubted whether that is enough. What is still missing is the vital dimension to which Barth called attention: that dogmatic theology is concerned with the Word of God in its bearing upon both individual faith and the teaching and practice of the church. That is to say, there is a necessary and unavoidable *critical* element in the work of dogmatics: it has to bring the given tradition, teaching and practice of the church ever and again under confrontation with the message of the Gospel, and to seek to re-express that tradition, teaching and practice afresh under the impact of that confrontation. Dogmatics in this sense remains an historical and ecclesiastical discipline in Schleiermacher's sense, but it has a new critical edge in the sense of openness to radical self-criticism in the light of the Word of God. Hence Barth's reworked definition which was also quoted at the start of the paper:

> As a theological discipline dogmatics is the scientific
> self-examination of the Christian Church with respect
> to the content of its distinctive talk about God.

Or, in the version rendered in the original translation by G.T. Thompson: [24]

> As a theological discipline, dogmatics is the scientific
> test to which the Christian Church puts herself re-
> garding the language about God which is peculiar
> to her.

The more recent translation is by and large the more literal and in that sense more correct; but Thompson's version, which speaks of "the scientific test to which the Christian Church puts herself", is arguably a better rendering into English of Barth's *"Selbstprüfung der christlichen Kirche"* than Bromiley's "self-examination of the Christian Church". "Self-examination" in today's English invites comparison with navel-gazing, and nothing could be further from Barth's meaning. What he means is a *critical self-testing*. Nor is either "distinctive talk about God" nor "the language about God which is peculiar to her" entirely satisfactory as a translation of Barth's *"der ihr eigentümlichen Rede von Gott"*. His meaning can perhaps be better drawn out with the help of a paraphrase rather than a literal translation:

> Dogmatics is the theological discipline whose particular task is the continuing, conscientious, objective and self-critical testing by the Christian Church of the content of her witness to God as expressed in the words and actions of the Church and its members.

What Barth means by this is unfolded at length in the first [25] and seventh [26] sections of the *Church Dogmatics*. In a nutshell, his argument is that the task of dogmatics lies in bringing the contemporary speech and action of the church in its intention to witness and respond to the revelation of God before the criterion of the Word of God himself. That Word is real, concrete and actual in Jesus Christ, to whom the Bible witnesses; but precisely as such, it can never be identified simply with the witness or the tradition of the church, for these always fall short and are therefore in need of constant correction and reorientation in the light of the Word himself. Out of this dialectical self-criticism, understood as a continual, ongoing process, the witness and proclamation of the church is constantly renewed and revived; it lives always and everywhere out of the power of the Word whom it can never contain or encapsulate, represent or embody. Under the conditions of this earthly life it is and will always inevitably be fallible and antepenultimate. Neither biblical conservatism nor confessional rectitude can in themselves guarantee evangelical truth, no more than ecclesiastical traditionalism or pious pragmatism, or even the best and highest dogmatic theology or the most subtle and sensitive analysis of the human condition. All these are in the end of value only as they are continually drawn into subjection to Jesus Christ as "the one Word of God whom we have to hear and obey in life and in death". [27]

Thus where Schleiermacher was inclined, in the wake of the Enlightenment and the Romantic movement, to search for an eternally permanent, self-identical "essence" in Jesus Christ himself as the Word of mercy and judgment, judgment and mercy spoken once for all over all humanity and therefore as the Word which is always new, always immediate, always challenging, always calling, always commissioning. The difference can be expressed by saying that Schleiermacher sought to be an advocate of Christianity, Barth of Jesus Christ. But it would be truer to say that Barth aimed to direct us more radically and directly to what Schleiermacher also sensed and sought after, but pointed to only indirectly.

Notes

1. Fr. Schleiermacher, *The Christian Faith*. ET of the 2nd German edition, edited by H.R. Mackintosh and J.S. Stewart. Edinburgh: T. & T. Clark and Philadelphia: Fortress Press, 1928, 88 (§19).

2. K. Barth, *Church Dogmatics* I/1. 2nd edition, translated by G.W. Bromiley. Edinburgh: T. & T. Clark, 1975, 3 (§1).

3. This seems to be the case at any rate at what might be called the popular academic level. Profounder insights and useful references to further literature can be found in a series of articles in *The Scottish Journal of Theology*, vol. 21 (1968): T.F. Torrance, "Hermeneutics according to F.D.E. Schleiermacher" (pp. 257-267); J.B. Torrance, "Interpretation and Understanding in Schleiermacher's Theology" (pp. 268-282); J.K. Graby, "Reflections on the History of the Interpretation of Schleiermacher" (pp. 283-299); T.N. Tice, "Article Review" of Schleiermacher's *Glaubenslehre* and *Hermeneutik* (pp. 305-311). See also J.E. Davison, "Can God Speak a Word to Man? Barth's Critique of Schleiermacher's Theology". *SJTh* 37 (1984), 189-211; Brian A. Gerrish, *Tradition and the modern World: Reformed Theology in the Nineteenth Century*. Chicago: Univ. of Chicago Press, 1978; id., *A Prince of the Church: Schleiermacher and the Beginnings of Modern Theology*. Philadelphia: Fortress Press, 1984.

4. K. Barth, *The Epistle to the Romans*. Translated from the Sixth Edition by Edwyn C. Hoskyns. London: Oxford Univ. Press, 1933, 225.

5. Reprinted in J. Moltmann (Ed) *Anfänge der dialektischen Theologie*, Munich: Kaiser, 1962, 197-218.

6. Op. cit., 205.

7. Barth, *The Theology of Schleiermacher*. Edited by D. Ritschl; translated by G.W. Bromiley. Grand Rapids: Eerdmans and Edinburgh: T. & T. Clark, 1982.

8. Op. cit., 260. The very last sentences may not have belonged to the original lecture, but have been added by Barth later - cf. n. 16 ad loc. - This volume also contains the illuminating "Concluding Unscientific Postscript on Schleiermacher," which Barth wrote to accompany a selection of readings from Schleiermacher, published as H. Bolli (Ed.), *Schleiermacher-Auswahl* in 1968, and in which he reports autobiographically on his engagement with Schleiermacher over many decades.

9. K. Barth, *From Rousseau to Ritschl*. London: S.C.M., 1969, 308. - This is also perhaps the appropriate point to remember that in the "Concluding Unscientific Postscript on Schleiermacher" (op. cit., 277) Barth concluded a series of probing questions about Schleiermacher's theology and his own struggles with it with the remark, "The only certain consolation which remains for me is to rejoice that in the kingdom of heaven I will be able to discuss all these questions with Schleiermacher extensively... for, let us say, a few centuries." (The English translation by Bromiley speaks only of "a couple of centuries", but both Barth's German and his characteristic style of expression suggest that a more generous temporal allocation would be appropriate.)

10. Bultmann's review appeared in instalments in nos. 18-21 of *Christliche Welt* (1922). It is reprinted in Moltmann (Ed.), *Anfänge der dialektischen Theologie* I, 119 f.

11. Barth, "Concluding Unscientific Postscript on Schleiermacher", op. cit., 270. - On Bultmann's attitude to Schleiermacher in this period see M. Evang, "Rudolf Bultmanns Berufung auf Friedrich Schleiermacher vor und um 1920", in B. Jaspert (Ed.), *Rudolf Bultmanns Werk und Wirkung*. Darmstadt: Wissenschaftliche Buchgesellschaft, 1984, 3-24.

12. It would be instructive, if space permitted, to compare and contrast Schleiermacher's position here with that of the 17th century Puritan and widely influential federal theologian William Ames (Amesius) in a passage he inserted in the third edition of his *Medulla Theologica* (1628), I.2.6. After stating that theology consists of two parts, faith and observance, he continued: "Out of the remnants of these two parts have sprouted among certain philosophers two new theologies –Metaphysics and Ethics. Metaphysics, in fact, is the faith of the Peripatetics and ethics is their observance. Hence, to each of these two disciplines they ascribe that which deals with the highest good of man. ...When theology, therefore, is handed down correctly in these two parts of faith and observance, metaphysics and ethics vanish spontaneously, after they have given evidence to this illustrious distribution." (Quoted from K. Sprunger, *The Learned Doctor William Ames*. Urbana: Univ. of Illinois Press, 1972, 126.) – The net could indeed be cast even wider by drawing a comparison between Barth's attempts to liberate dogmatics from philosophical and metaphysical presuppositions and concerns in the years following the appearance of his *Christliche Dogmatik* of 1927 and the aggressive repudiation of scholastic metaphysics in Melanchthon's *Loci Communes* of 1521.

13. In a seminar following the presentation of this paper at Princeton Theological Seminary in October 1985, Prof. Daniel Migliore pointed to the question whether Schleiermacher's reference to *das fromme Selbstbewusstsein* should properly be translated as being to "the pious self-consciousness", given that the standard translation of *The Christian Faith* speaks in these passages of "the *religious* self-awareness". It is in fact no easy matter to decide on the most appropriate translation of the German *fromm* into English. The word is in fact most usually rendered as "pious", not in the sense of "pietistic" but in that of "faithful", as reflected in the well-known German hymn, "O Gott, Du frommer Gott" - "O God, thou faithful God". The "pious" awareness of which Schleiermacher speaks is certainly that of *Christian* faith, faith conditioned by the sense of sin and grace, and as such a distinctively Christian modification of the more general and diffused *religious* awareness of "absolute" or "sheer dependence upon God". Just for this reason, however, the rendering "religious self-awareness" is inadequate, for it does not contain and encapsulate all that Schleiermacher sees as belonging to *Christian* faith. It would therefore be more accurate to speak of "the self-consciousness of Christian faith" in unpacking Schleiermacher's terminology today. "Pious" in this paper should therefore be understood in this sense as referring to a genuinely and distinctively Christian *pietas*.

14. "Concluding Unscientific Postscript on Schleiermacher", op. cit., 264.

15. K Barth *The Epistle to the Romans*, 257-259; the following quotation is from pp. 257-258.

16. Hoskyns' translation certainly suffers here by comparison with the original: "Der Vorhang reisst und die Musik muss schweigen. / Der Tempel auch verschwand und in der Ferne /Zeigt sich die alte Sphinx in Riesengrösse." In particular, his rendering of the final line is misleading: the Sphinx is not, for Schlegel, *terrible* but *enigmatic*, for it reveals itself after the dramatic preliminaries in Schleiermacher's presentation in the *Speeches* as – itself, larger than ever (in Riesengröbe). Schlegel's point is that after all that Schleiermacher has seemed to promise in the *Addresses*, the old, enigmatic questions still remain. As he is also reported to have said to Schleiermacher, "Dein Gott kommt mir etwas mager vor!" (Your God seems to me pretty thin!")

17. Neither Schleiermacher nor Barth can be described as "conservative" in any normal political sense. Unlike Hegel, for example, Schleiermacher had neither shared the enthusiasm for sheer power-in-action which led Hegel in 1806 to adulate Napoleon as "the World-Spirit on a charger" nor been later inclined to support Hegel's glorification of the "restored" Prussian state. Similarly, Barth's decided opposition to the power-obsessed ideology of the Nazis during the thirteen years of the appallingly shabby and brutal "Thousand-Year Empire" did not commit him to unqualified approbation of the geopolitical strategy (if it deserves the name, which may well be doubted) of the Western Allies in the decades following 1945. He was much more disposed to criticise that strategy, to the discomfort of many in the West who expected and would have preferred some more McCarthy-type of blinkered anti-Communism from the acknowledged leading light of protestant theology.

18. *The Christian Faith*, 2nd edn., §§23, 24.

19. *The Christian Faith*, 2nd edn., §100.

20. Cf. Barth's "Foreword" to H. Heppe, *Reformed Dogmatics: Set out and illustrated from the Sources.* Revised and edited by E. Bizer; translated by G.T. Thomson, London: George Allen & Unwin, 1950, v-vii.

21. *The Christian Faith*, 2nd edn., §123.

22. Cf. G.S. Hendry, "The Transcendental Method in the Theology of Karl Barth". *SJTh* 37 (1984), 213-227.

23. Schleiermacher's *Kurze Darstellung des Theologischen Studiums* was first published in 1810; a second, heavily revised edition appeared in 1830. The summary given here follows the critical edition by Heinrich Scholz (Berlin, 1910), reprinted in 1977 by the Wissenschaftliche Buchgesellschaft, Darmstadt. - On the originality and significance of Schleiermacher's programme, see Edward Farley, *Theologia: The Fragmentation and Unity of Theological Education*, Philadelphia: Fortress Press, 1983, esp. 73-98 ("Schleiermacher and the Beginning of the Encyclopedia Movement"). - A modified (and historically speaking particularly influential) application of Schleiermacher's scheme was developed by Philip Schaff in his *What is Church History? A Vindication of the Idea of Historical Development*, published in 1846 and reprinted in C. Yrigoyen, Jr. and G.M. Bricker (Eds.), *Reformed and Catholic: Selected Historical and Theological Writings of Philip Schaff*, Pittsburgh: Pickwick Press, 1979, 17-144. See esp. the beginning of Section II: "Development of the Idea of Church History" (pp. 44ff.). - The earliest protestant presentation of a theological "Encyclopedia" covering and integrating the various theological disciplines seems to have been that sketched in the mid-sixteenth century by the distinguished Zürich scientist Conrad Gesner in his *Partitiones theologicae:* cf. J. Staedtke, *Reformation und Zeugnis der Kirche*, Zürich 1978, 141-150 ("Conrad Gesner als Theologe").

24. *Church Dogmatics* I/1. Translated by G.T. Thomson. Edinburgh: T. & T. Clark, 1936, 1.

25. *Church Dogmatics* I/1. 2nd edn., translated by G.W. Bromiley Edinburgh: T. & T. Clark, 1975, 3-24.

26. Op. cit., 248-292.
27. Article One of the *Theological Declaration of Barmen* (1934). - It was precisely this sense of being bound to the one Word which has been spoken, is spoken and will be spoken that enabled Barth to describe evangelical theology as a *modest, free, critical* and *happy* science, as in his *Evangelical Theology: an Introduction.* London: Weidenfeld & Nicholson, 1963, 6-12.

Karl Barth and the
Western Intellectual Tradition.
Towards A Theology
After Christendom

Colin Gunton

To place a theologian in so broad and complex a tradition as that of the West requires some sweeping generalisations. They are made in fear and trembling, but with some confidence in their overall accuracy. The first can be made with little fear of contradiction: that among the chief watersheds of our tradition are the massive achievements of Augustine of Hippo and the change of direction attempted by the Enlightenment. The complications come when an attempt is made to assess the systematic significance of the two and Barth's relation to them. A beginning can be made by expressing agreement with Bernard Ramm's perceptive assessment of the significance of Barth as a theologian who attempted to face clearly the intellectual challenge of the Enlightenment [1]. An elaboration of that thesis will be the main burden of this paper. First, however, must come a sketch of the chief complicating factor, the relation of the Enlightenment to Europe's Augustinian heritage. From one point of view, the Enlightenment's project was a root and branch rejection of that tradition. But, from another, because it operated within categories of thought belonging to the tradition, it was in large part a dispute within the family. What, then, are the features of Augustinian Christendom and the Enlightenment that are relevant to an understanding of Barth's theological achievement?

I. Three Features of Western Thought

The conversation partner of Christian theology from its very beginnings was the platonizing tendency to distinguish sharply between the world of sense and the world of intellect. Augustine was not the first to introduce the dualism into Christian thought, but there can be little doubt that his attempted synthesis marked the thought of the

Western world deeply and permanently. The primary dualism of sense and intellect in its turn generated a sharp dichotomy between time and eternity, this world and the transcendent realm under- (or over-) lying it. The Enlightenment can, in its turn, be understood as a reaction both to end in the terms of that latter dualism. On the one hand, it denied its theological legacy while, on the other, it continued to operate within its fundamental framework for thought.

The legacy which it rejected was the essential other-worldliness of much Western theology. By this I mean not so much the orientation to another world which forms so pervasive a feature of medieval culture as the intellectual tendency to locate the weight of ontological and epistemological interests in the realm of the timeless eternal. For Plato, the eternal world of forms represented both what was ultimately real and the true end of knowledge. By contrast, the temporal world was only dubiously real, a realm of becoming mid-way between being and non-being. Neoplatonism, which was so important for Augustine's development, tended to stress still more the essentially problematic nature of the temporal, with the result that although Augustine affirmed the goodness of the created order he never really escaped from a deep pessimism about it. For him, as in different ways for Kant and Kierkegaard after him, the world of time remained inherently unreliable and disorderly. Historians have called attention to Augustine's deep historical pessimism, which fed upon his dualism and led him to adopt what we would now call reactionary political policies [2]. This, too, can be understood as the direct outcome of his orientation to a certain 'otherworldly' view of reality. In the Western world the neoplatonic colouring of Christianity, especially as it was mediated by Augustine and his successors, had implications in a number of areas. There are three of them that are particularly relevant for our theme. They can be identified as the ontological, cultural and epistemological dimensions of one general direction of Western thought.

The ontological dimension centres on the matter of the relation of time and eternity. Christianity has always produced theologies which respect, so to speak, the rights of both the temporal and the eternal. Classically, in the theology of Irenaeus there is a consistently positive linking of the two, the eternal becoming temporal for the sake of the created world. In strong opposition to the theology of those who would deny the goodness of the creation in the name of an abstract and other-worldly eternalizing of the gospel. Of course, there has never been a time in the history of Christianity in which the need to be true to both realities has not produced tensions. With Augustine, however, the tensions resolved themselves in such a way that there was a decisive shift of the balance in favour of eternity. In his theology, Christianity tends to be conceived as the movement out of time into eternity: from the restlessness of the temporal to the eternal rest of the timeless deity. And 'timeless' is the word: for the deity of so much Western theology is not the communal dynamism of the Cappadocian Trinity, but a kind of static fixity standing over against the moving temporal. An example, repeatedly found in our theological tradition, is of what happens to eschatology. When eschatology is linked with the theology of the incarnation it becomes of a piece with a dynamic movement of the eternal into time, generating if not necessarily an optimism, then at least a positive view of human and political possibilities. Without the link, and with an orientation to timeless eternity, eschatology becomes the doctrine of the four last things, as the order of what will happen *outside* time, *after* our life on earth. It was the latter conception that came to dominate in the West.

That outcome links us directly to the second feature of Western thought, the cultural. The view that the Christian life is essentially a preparation for another life has a considerable impact on the way in which Christianity takes institutional form. The church, as representing the timeless eternal, becomes the place where the eternal can be found and the threats of disorderly temporality avoided. The only apparently paradoxical consequence is 'Christendom', wherein the church becomes the representative of our 'religious' duties – duties to eternity – in the midst of time, and so the spiritual arm of what Paul Johnson has called the 'totally Christian society' [3]. On such an understanding, one is a Christian by virtue of being born into Western society and, as a result, either outside or a lesser member of society if one opts out (or is born and remains a Jew). Other only apparently paradoxical consequences are a tendency towards individualism - the church is the place where individuals exercise their spiritual, nontemporal functions - and towards a view of the secular world as almost a separate order of being from the religious.

The third dimension, the epistemological, is parallel to the other two, in that corresponding to dualisms between time and eternity, secular and religious, there is one also between reason and faith. Here,

Augustine's legacy to later centuries was mediated by the hardening of the distinction between faith and reason which took place as a result of the work of Boethius. Here, Joseph Pieper's view of the development of medieval philosophy is perceptive and illuminating [4]. The heart of the matter is to be found in the development of what came to be known as the two-source theory of knowledge. This holds that reason and faith are two distinct sources of human knowledge, operating, so to speak, in two parallel channels. 'As far as you are able,' wrote Boethius, 'join faith to reason - fidem, si poteris, rationemque conjunge' (p. 37). Faith and reason operate in parallel, like church and state in Christendom as, to change the metaphor, two sides of the same coin. Occasionally, there was an outbreak of sceptical philosophy, which took the form of a theory of double truth, in which there were those who came close to advocating intellectual dishonesty, or at least the closing off of one part of the mind from the other. But more characteristic was the claim that because truth was one, we could expect the two sources to say the same kind of thing, or at least compatible things. Josef Pieper sees it to be a determining feature of scholasticism that 'its leading minds Thomas and Bonaventura, say, carried out that co-ordination between believing acceptance of revealed and traditional truth on the one hand and rational argumentation on the other hand with unfailing resoluteness . . .' (p. 28). What was rarely if ever questioned was the duality of sources. "Conjunction of faith and knowledge" - at the bottom that comes down to mentally uniting these two *realms of reality:* on the one hand the totality of created things which lie within the purview of natural cognition . . . and on the other hand the reality exposed to us in God's revelations, that is to say, in faith' (pp. 118f).

Such a conception, as is now widely recognized, contained the seeds of its own downfall. The late medieval nominalists were not the wicked destroyers they are sometimes made out to be but thinkers who exploited the dualism already inherent in the axiom. And Pieper sees that it is no accident that in the fourteenth century two processes, the intellectual and the political, were taking place side by side:

> Just as in the political realm the form of Christianity which had been developed since the end of antiquity, and which had been founded on the special accord between the spiritual and secular powers, was

> beginning to break down, so also in the realm of the
> mind . . . a progressive divergence between faith and
> reason was taking place. Inexorably . . . divorce was
> taking place between *fides* and *ratio* - to whose con-
> junction the energies of almost a thousand years had
> been devoted (pp. 150f).

The movement Pieper observes at the end of the era of scholasticism came to a completion in some of the trends of thought of the Enlightenment. In the ontological dimension, there is a shift to a pre-occupation with time, often instead of and against eternity. Culturally, the Enlightenment asserts the rights of secular society against the authoritarian claims of the church. Epistemologically, the Enlighten-ment championed the claims of reason over against faith, which it ten-ded to relegate to the status of an inferior form of knowing. In all three areas Christian institutions and theology have been in deep perplex-ity ever since. If we are, however, to be aware of their significance and of Barth's response we must remember that the culture of the modern, enlightened, world is the outcome of a choice of one side of the dualisms of the era of Christendom and therefore continues to operate within its dualistic assumptions. It is still assumed that time and eternity are in some sense opposed realms, that the secular and the religious are alternatives and, of particular importance, that reason and faith are to be understood primarily as different faculties. The dif-ference is that they are now played off against each other, rather than being co-ordinated as parallel realms of equal authority. Correspond-ingly, the significance of Barth as a Western thinker is that he refused to think in terms of these dualisms, but attempted theologically to con-strue them in ways that transcend both Augustinianism and its rebellious but true child, the Enlightenment

II. *'Protestant Theology in the Nineteenth Century'* - Some Themes

That Barth was consciously adopting a programme of this kind is evi-dent from the attitude he adopted to the thinkers in his past chron-icled in his *Protestant Theology in the Nineteenth Century* [5]. The opening chapters witness an account of the eighteenth century in which it is interpreted with the help of a political metaphor as 'the age of absolutism'. Absolutism is not, however, merely a political phenomenon, but endemic in all aspects of the culture of the time, and in particular in a 'belief in the omnipotence of human powers' (p. 36). That is to say, the Enlightenment's shift from eternity to time has implications for the way the human person is conceived to be related to reality as a whole. There is at once an anthropocentrism of interest and an ethic of domination. In the sphere of epistemology, the movement takes the form of an exaggeration of the powers of reason and a consequent relegation of 'faith' or 'belief' to a lesser form of knowledge. Reason is that by which the mind dominates, reducing everything 'to absolute form' (p. 58); faith, by contrast, is an increasingly questionable faculty, called in only for those supposedly diminishing features of our experience where reason fails. Barth's treatment of some of his predecessors can be understood in this context as a programme not simply to save theology, but to reorder the epistemological direction of the Western tradition.

The major philosophical thinker linking Barth with Europe's Augustinian past is Immanuel Kant, whose impact upon all theology after his time has been incalculable. His view of the part played by the mind in the creation of knowledge not only completed a decisive shift of interest in philosophy and theology from ontology to epistemology, but also sharpened the division between the world of experience and the eternal world underlying it. Thus Kant may be said to have completed the breach opened by the late medieval philosophers between faith and reason, though in other respects he is an Augustinian thinker [6].

It is true, of course, that Kant claimed to limit the claims of reason in order to make room for faith, but by *faith* he meant something rather different from what had been held by the leading medievals. They saw faith as the acceptance of a body of truth handed down from the past; he as the oblique implicate of the powers of moral reason. As *Religion Within the Limits of Reason Alone* shows quite clearly, faith in the sense of the acceptance of traditional and authoritative doctrines was the last thing to be intended [7]. In that book the conquest of faith by reason is virtually complete, for despite the presence of a secularized version of the Augustinian doctrine of original sin, the historical content of the Gospel operates chiefly as a source of illustrations of timeless philosophical truths. *Faith* changes its meaning, becoming in Kant a way of speaking of practical reason's ability to operate in the noumenal world of moral maxims. The practical effect, whatever Kant sometimes said, is to eliminate one of the two traditional sources of truth altogether. But therein lies his value for Barth, for, according to him, Kant's value is that he compels theology to rethink its conception of rationality. Henceforward, theology cannot depend upon some kind of consensus with philosophy, as prevailed during the heyday of the two-source theory. It must rather recognize 'the point of its departure for its method in revelation, just as decidedly as philosophy sees its point of departure in reason' (*P T*, p. 307). In the light of the two source theory, such a claim would appear to be an appeal to the arbitrary, to faith in opposition to reason. If this were so, it would justify the charges against Barth of 'fideism' and 'positivism'. But the significance of Barth in the Western tradition is that, like Polanyi in another field, he rejects the two source theory for one which wishes to integrate at the outset the mind's approach to theological truth [8]. Reason and rationality are of supreme importance to Barth but their place and function in theology are altered.

Kant's significance for Barth is, on the one hand, that he represents the apogee of the Enlightenment's absolutism - 'a pure rationalism' in which 'we do not understand anyone but the one who speaks to us through our own reason' (*P T*, pp. 251f). But, on the other, there is a far more positive significance, in that Kant has taught theology that there can be no evasion of the question of its relation to philosophy. 'From now on theology would no longer be able to formulate its tenets, no matter on what foundation it might base them, without having acquired a clear conception of the method of reason which it also uses in the construction of its tenets' (p. 273). Kant's critique of reason means that any employment of human reason, unless it makes its rational methodology clear, is in danger of being charged with sophistry, with 'an uncritical adventure of the understanding prompted by obscure feelings' (p. 273). The fact that these points were made when the writing of the many volumes of the *Church Dogmatics* was well into its course suggests that Barth believed that he had made clear 'the method of reason' that he was employing, and that his much discussed rejection of natural theology has to do not with a rejection of reason so much as a particular view of the way it should be employed.

Another of his comments on the significance of Kant for theology confirms this judgement. After Kant there were, Barth believed, three possible courses for theology to take. Two of them represent a basic acceptance of Kant's critique of reason, proceeding to operate either within Kantian lines or attempting to 'broaden and enrich the conception of reason . . . by pointing out that there is yet another capacity *a priori* . . . of human reason, apart from the theoretical and practical ones: the capacity of feeling' (p. 306).

The third possibility was to question Kant's conception of the nature of theology's relation to philosophy. 'This third possibility would, in a word, consist in theology resigning itself to stand on its own feet in relation to philosophy . . . and in theology conducting . . . a dialogue with philosophy, and not, wrapping itself up in the mantle of philosophy, a quasi-philosophical monologue' (p. 307). The two latter possibilities are represented for Barth by Schleiermacher and Hegel respectively, though by Hegel only in a qualified sense. We shall return to this very important passage, which proves that Barth was more concerned to alter the prevailing conception of faith and reason than to reject any relation of philosophy and theology. But at this stage a brief glance at Barth's view of Schleiermacher and Hegel will give substance to the interpretation of Barth as one who wished to out think not ignore the Enlightenment.

Barth's relation to Schleiermacher is increasingly being recognized as one of serious dialogue rather than total rejection. In *Protestant Theology* he gives two reasons for his positive assessment of his predecessor's achievement: Schleiermacher's commitment to both Christianity and modernity (pp. 433f), and the possibility that his enterprise be considered a theology of the Third Article [9]. It is, however, the reasons Barth gives for diverging from the path taken by Schleiermacher which reveal more clearly the relation of faith and reason, and consequently of theology and culture. The heart of the matter lies in the fact that, according to Barth, Schleiermacher's desire to mediate between church and culture is closly related to a deficient conception of truth. Not only does Schleiermacher see truth as lying in the middle between two opposites (*P T,* p. 451) (so losing its orientation to the object to which it must always seek to be loyal), but, more, he relegates truth to at best secondary importance. '(H)e was not very interested in the truth of theological tenets as such for he was in the first place interested in the active life of religion, and then in feeling as the true seat of this life, and only thirdly in the tenets by means of which this life . . . expresses itself' (p. 448). Distorted though this view of Schleiermacher may be, it once again reveals something of Barth's concern for rationality and truth, and in particular his concern that the Kantian challenge to theology be not evaded but faced squarely. For him, claims for truth require a conception of the expressibility of the subject matter in language that aims to say what is the case independently of the experience of the believer. Therefore Schleiermacher's deficiency is in giving the game away to philosophy: 'Truth in the strictly intellectual, expressible sense . . . remains the concern of philosophy; truth in the ultimate, decisive, but also ineffable sense is reserved for mute feeling . . .' (p. 455). But that is not the way to outthink the Enlightenment. It is rather to restate its absolutist anthropocentrism (p. 306).

The pattern of Barth's discussion of Schleiermacher is repeated in the chapters on Hegel, except that here Barth sees more that is of positive merit. Although he holds that the nineteenth century never seriously took account of the possibility of an alternative to Kant, he clearly sees in Hegel the basis - though no more than that - of such a development (pp. 306f). There are four features of Hegel's thought which can be seen to recur in Barth's own thinking, though I do not believe that they affect the content of the theology in the way sometimes claimed [10]. First, there is the crucial matter of epistemology. The Enlightenment, and Kant in particular, attempted to set up criteria of rationality, epistemological strainers which were to separate real and specious claims to knowledge. Hegel's merit - although from one point of view he shares the self-confidence and rationalism of the Enlightenment to a unique degree - is that he refuses to adopt a theory of knowledge in abstraction from the content of what is known. If theology is to be truly scientific, its form must be shaped by the object it strives to know, and not decided in advance by an *a priori* epistemology. 'It was in him (Hegel) to ridicule the demand for a theory of knowledge by saying that there was as much sense in it as the demand of the Gascon who did not want to go into the water before he could swim' (*P T*, p. 393). Such considerations bulk large in Barth's attitude to the question of natural theology, because he sees it to be precisely that: an illegitimate attempt to limit theological possibilities in advance.

Hegel's second merit is that he establishes, in some contrast, it might be noted, to Kant, Schleiermacher and Kierkegaard, the necessity of a conception of the rationality and knowability of God. 'Because to Hegel the rational was historical and the historical rational, he completely and finally disposed of the God who had somehow stood in opposition to reason, who was in some way an offence and foolishness to reason, and who could perhaps be denied through reason' (p. 395). Once again, we find adumbrations of themes later to be found, in somewhat modified form, in the *Church Dogmatics*. Third, and in some contrast to what Barth finds in Schleiermacher, is the priority of truth for Hegel. According to him, 'man lives from the truth, and only from the truth. Truth is his God, whom he dares not forsake if he is to remain human' (p. 412). Barth reads in this a demand to theology that it should take even more seriously than philosophy the centrality of truth. 'It should not be concerned with manifestations of life in general . . . but with truth, with a kind of knowledge which does not have its foundation in some kind of given thing, as such, but in the link of this given thing with the final origin of everything given. If theology does not speak the truth in this sense, then in what sense can it assert that it is speaking of God?' (p. 415).

All three of these points concern the attempt to break out of the intellectual straitjacket imposed on theology by Kant. The fourth is perhaps even more important, for it concerns the tendency, which has been so destructive for theology, to divide truths into two, the necessary, timeless truths of reason and the contingent, time-conditioned statements in which all other efforts at the expression of truth are couched. Its adoption by Lessing, in a famous dictum, as the crucial modern question for Christian theology, has led to a whole literature about the problems of history and, in particular, of relativism. But it is a modernized version of the old two source theory, and it is intellectually barren. One of the lessons Barth attempted to learn from Hegel - though certainly Hegel, and in some respects Barth, failed to appreciate its implications - is that of the temporality of truth. Truth has to happen, to be realized in time; but that does not entail that it is any less truth (p. 415). In response to the rather static view of truth of the Western tradition, and its accompanying static conception of God, Barth was to develop the conception of God as event, in response to whose event-ful revelation our theological words must take particular and temporal form. It was this which enabled him to stand out against the main stream of Western thought. The significance of that move can be better appreciated if we now turn to an area in which Barth emphatically did not share the views of Hegel.

III. An Illuminating Absence.

There are, in *Protestant Theology in the Nineteenth Century*, only four brief references to a figure who was supremely important for that century and had been influential in Barth's own development. Whatever the reasons for the omission, a glance at Søren Kierkegaard will be illuminating for our study of Barth, for he brings to the centre all three of the features of Western culture with which we have been concerned: the ontological, the cultural and the epistemological. By a glance at his relations with Hegel we shall be enabled to see something of the significance of Barth for our understanding of the relation of Church and culture in particular.

From one point of view, Hegel represents the Enlightenment's programme of subordinating eternity to time. Hegel's concern is not with an eternal realm other than time - the God of that realm has to *die* [11] - but with God realised through historical process, in time, that is to say. From another point of view, as Barth sees, Hegel's pedigree is somewhat longer. Hegel set out to 'restore what had been lost since the Middle Ages, the unity of the human and the divine'.(P T, pp 410f) In other words, Hegel's programme was a repristination of Christendom, the social system corresponding to the dualism of eternity and time, reason and faith. That is, as Barth sees 'the tragic meaning of the catastrophe of Hegelianism'.(p. 411)

Here two points are of utmost importance. First, as Stephen Crites has pointed out, it is no accident that linked with Christendom in Kierkegaard's demonology was the philosophy of Hegel [12]. Hegel's tendency towards the divinisation of mankind is, from one point of view, the canonisation of certain directions of thought ultimately Hellenistic in origin but given a radical renewal by leading thinkers of the Enlightenment. Inherent in the human mind are to be discerned the traces of divinity which it is culture's function to bring to full consciousness and realisation. Hegel's attempted repristination of Christendom was achieved by the employment of categories taken from Christian doctrine in order to provide the basis for a modern version of the synthesis. Western culture is the place where divinity must realise itself. Kierkegaard rejected the whole programme out of hand. 'The God-Man is not the unity of God and mankind . . . That the human race is or should be akin to God is ancient paganism . . .' [13].

The second point is that, as a recent study by John Elrod has shown, Kierkegaard identified Christendom with the programme to liberalize and modernize Denmark. Christendom connoted not simply a past historical reality but the legitimation by Christian bishops among others of an ultimately dehumanizing conception of society [14]. It was Kierkegaard's genius to see that an uncritical acceptance of the Enlightenment's choice of time instead of eternity led to another form of Christendom, in which Christianity was identified with the fashionable liberalism of the day. There was a direct if dialectical continuity between the different tendencies to identify Christianity with two very different cultures, the one other-worldly, the other in reaction agressively this-worldly. It was a continuity within the Western dialectic of time and eternity, conceiving Christianity in both cases as the cement of the social system of which it was a part.

Barth had a rather ambivalent attitude to Kierkegaard. On the one hand, the early Barth was strongly influenced by a Kierkegaardian transcendentalism, which forms one of the oft-noted marks of his *Commentary on Romans.* Barth's bombshell was, like Kierkegaard's polemic, a throwing of a strongly dialectical view of eternity in the face of modern theology's tendency, as Barth saw it, to reduce Christianity to an aspect or function of culture. On the other hand, there is no figure from his early authorities he appears in later life so anxious to expunge. Yet Barth's relations to Kierkegaard are an important indicator of his place in the European tradition. For if Christendom is to be theologically transcended, it cannot be done through the thought of Kierkegaard. Kierkegaard's crucial weakness is that he fought the new Christendom with the weapons of the old, with a reforging of that Augustinian negative dialectic of time and eternity which had made old Christendom possible. He may thus have divided Christendom against itself, but certainly did not provide the tools for a new understanding of Christianity's relation to culture. 'I consider him to be a teacher whose school every theologian must enter once. Woe to him who misses it - provided he does not remain in or return to it' [15].

The importance of Kierkegaard for an understanding of the background to Barth is that we see through his eyes the link between the question of Christianity and culture and that of faith and reason. Christendom, we might say, was the era in which a more or less settled peace was made at once between church and society and between faith and reason. In Aquinas both reason and faith have their proper role through a division of functions within a unitary approach to reality; in Hegel, the refurbisher of Christendom, faith has a more ambiguous role, either subordinate to reason or possibly even swallowed up within it, but certainly, as Kierkegaard saw, is in the gravest danger. In both cases the accommodation between the two reflects the accommodation between church and society that is so characteristic of Christendom. Accordingly, there corresponds to Kierkegaard's rejection of cultural Christendom a rejection of its characteristic epistemological form too. It is in part a response learned from Kant, whose teaching on the limits of reason in matters theological is harnessed by Kierkegaard to a more robustly christological conception of faith and hurled in the teeth of those who would make theological discoveries by reason alone. According to Kierkegaard faith is irreducibly paradoxical and the sworn foe of all attempts to rationalize. Moreover, to the dialectic of time and eternity there *corresponds* a dialectic of reason and faith, which resurfaces in Barth's *Commentary on Romans.* Much Anglo-Saxon suspicion of Barth derives from this feature, in which a Christianity of paradox meets and noisily rejects all attempts at rationality. Eternity is set *against* time, faith *against* reason, Christianity *against* culture. But it cannot be emphasized too frequently that the final form of Barth's theology is very different from this.

IV. Theology After Christendom.

The significance of Karl Barth in the Western tradition is to be found in part in a programme for theology after the end of Christendom. If the two source theory is dead, there can be no simple division of labour between philosophy and theology. If the accommodation between church and state has broken down, the matter of theology and culture has to be rethought. If the harmonization of time and eternity in terms of neoplatonic dualism is no longer defensible, a new interpretation of their relation has to be sought. In all these areas, Barth made major contributions. It is not necessary to claim that he was correct in every respect to realise that in Karl Barth we have the first major theological attempt to establish a style of theological existence appropriate at once to the historic Christian faith and to the changed conditions of modernity.

In the first place, the death of Christendom and its intellectual consensus will require a rethinking of the relation of faith and reason. To hold them as two parallel sources is no longer possible. To reduce faith to reason along with Hegel is to lose history in a gnostic and monistic synthesis. To throw faith in the face of reason along with Kierkegaard is certainly an improvement, but, as the history of existentialism after Kierkegaard has shown, faith can so easily turn into its opposite or generate a new rationalism. It is in a context such as this that Barth's recourse to Anselm at a crucial time in his theological career is to be understood. Barth himself frequently asserts the importance of Anselm for his theological method - 'the method of reason which it also uses in the construction of its tenets'. In our context, the significance in the recourse to Anselm is that Barth is reaching back beyond Aquinas and the other proponents of the two source theory to one of the few medieval thinkers to transcend the conventional approach [16]. Anselm is a thinker who exercised great freedom in the use of reason, and Barth is the same. He is free, first of all, in being able to use philosophy eclectically, taking from it those concepts and insights which he believes aid the rational task of theology. It is not philosophy he is against, but philosophy which exercises a procrustean force on theology. In the second place, he is free to treat philosophers as conversation partners, ultimately concerned with the same matters as he is - whether or not they would accept such an assessment - and so as free agents in a dialogue ('a dialogue with philosophy, and not, wrapping itself up in the mantle of philosophy, a quasi-philosophical monologue' [17]), It is reasonable to claim that Barth's conception of method makes him able to take philosophy more seriously than the proponents of old-style natural theology who continue to depend on a version of the two source theory.

However, the heart of the matter is to be found in the reversal of the traditional order of reason followed by faith. As we have seen, the historical outcome was that reason finally swallowed up faith, classically in Hegel but also in empiricist styles of epistemology. Kierkegaard's answer was to assert the primacy of faith in all matters of any existential importance, and apparently to deny the importance of reason. Barth went further. For him faith is in no way a flight from reason but the means whereby the possibility of an authentic employment of reason is established. 'Faith' does not, of course, mean what it did in terms of the two-source theory, the acceptance on authority of propositions believed to be revealed. Faith is the means whereby a relationship with God is established on the basis of which rational language about him may be developed. It is, of course, like the knowledge to which it leads, the gift of God the Holy Spirit, although space forbids further exploration of that theme here [18]. What is worth saying is that Barth is doing in theology what Michael Polanyi, again on the basis of a rejection of both the two source theory and the Enlightenment's radicalisation of it, sought to do for the philosophy of science. In all forms of intellectual enterprise, he believes, rational exploration is only possible on the basis of personal commitment - faith - to the object of enquiry [19]. Reason builds upon that, developing such forms of understanding as are appropriate to the subject matter.

The change of method to a conception of theology as faith seeking understanding is the motive force of Barth's development of a theology that is not only post-critical but has wider significance for theology after the death of Christendom. It was suggested in the first part of the essay that in Christendom the epistemological dimensions of the Western tradition meshed with the cultural and ontological. Barth's theological revolution requires changes in these spheres also. Christendom presupposed a consensus between theology and culture. When the consensus is lost, theology must find its basis in the church, because it must take shape in the place where God's reality is acknowledged. But that is not an evasion of theology's responsibility for culture, any more than the change of method is an evasion of the intellectual task. It is, rather, the quest for a place from which culture may be addressed. The same is true of matters social and political. Readers of the Busch biography of Barth will be able to miss the importance of the social and political context in which all Barth's theological work was done [20]. In no respect is the churchly grounding of theology an escape into a religious eternity. Quite the reverse, for the church is for Barth the community organized around the place where the eternal becomes temporal for all mankind.

That brings us, finally, to the matter of ontology. Christendom, it was argued, is built upon a rather negative view of the relation of time and eternity, from which an essential otherworldliness resulted, with a consequent reduction of eschatology to what is to happen *after* this life. In Barth, there is a move, perhaps not adequately completed to a view of eternity and of eschatology being more positively related to time. Barth learned his eschatology at the feet of two nineteenth century Christians who swam against the stream of post-Enlightenment rationalism. From the Blumhardts, father and son, he learned an eschatological view of Christianity, with the eternal breaking into time for the salvation of the created order. In Barth's mature theology there came to be developed a new ontology, deeply christological and trinitarian, in which the relation of eternal God and temporal creation was rethought in a thoroughgoing way. Once again, this cannot be given detailed exposition here. But, suffice to say, the resulting conception is very different from that of Christendom. In particular should be noted its positive view of the necessity of political and social action. Not only that: Barth's God is *for* the world, despite its fallenness and sin, in a way not possible for the main Augustinian tradition. The conception of election from Augustine to Calvin made it appear that some, perhaps the majority, were outside the loving purposes of God, and other similar weaknesses could be detailed. That Barth is sometimes accused of universalism is an indicator of two facts. The first is that he has changed the way in which the eternal is conceived in its relation to time: positively, dynamically and much nearer to the thought of Irenaeus and the Alexandrians [21] than to that of Augustine. The second is that minds immersed in the categories of Western thought have often been unable to understand him, reading his doctrine of election, for example, through eyes equipped with dualistic and static spectacles. But he cannot be understood in such a way.

There has come into being in recent years something like a scholarly consensus that in certain crucial respects Barth failed to push through the developments he began. This paper is not written to dispute that consensus, but to say that the weaknesses are the perhaps inevitable outcome of the greatness of the achievement. In all main areas of theological endeavour Barth has enabled those who will listen to understand the theological task in ways appropriate to the changed intellectual and cultural conditions of the world after the death of Christendom and under the shadow of a bankrupt Enlightenment. Despite the recent relative eclipse of his thought, there can be little doubt that distance will make possible a more detached view of both strengths and weaknesses, so that the resources to be found in his writings for contemporary theological work will come to be more adequately appreciated on all sides.

Notes

1. Bernard Ramm, *After Fundamentalism. The Future of Evangelical Theology*. San Francisco: Harper and Row, 1983, pp. 46f.

2. Paul Johnson, *A History of Christianity*. Harmondsworth: Penguin Books, 1978, pp. 85, 122, and Norman H. Baynes, 'The political Ideas of St. Augustine's *De Civitate Dei*', in *Byzantine Studies and Other Essays*, London: Athlone Press, 1955, pp. 288-306.

3. Johnson, p. 177.

4. Joseph Pieper, *Scholasticism. Personalities and Problems of Medieval Philosophy*. E.T. by R. and C. Winston, London: Faber and Faber, 1960.

5. Karl Barth, *Protestant Theology in the Nineteenth Century. Its Background and History*. E.T. by Brian Cozens and John Bowden, London: SCM Press, 1972. In the rest of this article page references to this work will appear in parentheses, prefixed where necessary by the abbreviation *P T*.

6. What else are Kant's *phenomena* and *noumena* but the realms of sense and intellect conceived in even sharper distinction from each other?

7. Immanuel Kant, *Religion Within the Limits of Reason Alone*. E.T. by T.M. Greene and H.H. Hudson, New York, Harper Torchbooks, 1960.

8. Michael Polanyi, 'Faith and Reason', *Journal of Religion* 41 (1961) pp. 237-247.

9. The possibility exercised Barth to the end of his life. See 'Nachwort' to *Schleiermacher-Auswahl*. Ed. H. Bolli, München and Hamburg: Siebenstern-Taschenbuch-Verlag, 1968, pp. 290-312

10. Wolfhart Pannenberg, 'Die Subjektivität Gottes und die Trinitätslehre', *Grundfragen systematischer Theologie, Gesammelte Aufsätze* 2, Göttingen, 1980, pp. 96-111, and Jürgen Moltmann, *The Trinity and the Kingdom of God*, E.T. by Margaret Kohl, London: SCM Press, 1981, pp. 139-144 both read too much Hegel into Barth's doctrine of the Trinity.

11. G.W.F. Hegel, *The Phenomenology of Mind*. E.T. by J.B. Baillie, London: Allen and Unwin, 1949, pp. 780ff.

12. Stephen Crites, *In the Twilight of Christendom. Hegel vs Kierkegaard on Faith and History*. Chambersburg, Pa., American Academy of Religion, 1972, p. 59.

13. Søren Kierkegaard, *Training in Christianity*. E.T. by Walter Lowrie, Princeton University Press, 1941, p. 84.

14. John W. Elrod, *Kierkegaard and Christendom*, Princeton University Press, 1981.

15. Karl Barth, 'A Thank-You and a Bow - Kierkegaard's Reveille', *Fragments Grave and Gay*. E.T. by Eric Mosbacher, London: Fontana, pp. 100f.

16. Karl Barth, *Anselm: Fides Quaerens Intellectum. Anselm's Proof of the Existence of God in the Context of his Theological Scheme*. E.T. by Ian W. Robertson, Allison Park: Pickwick Publications, 1985.

17. Above, p. 292.

18. Karl Barth, *Church Dogmatics*, Vol. II, Part I, Chapter V, 'The Knowledge of God'.

19. Michael Polanyi, *Personal Knowledge: Towards a Post-Critical Philosophy*. London: Routledge and Kegan Paul, 2^e, 1962.

20. Eberhard Busch. *Karl Barth. His Life from Letters and Autobiographical Texts*. E.T. by John Bowden, London: SCM Press, 1976.

21. Charles T. Waldrop, *Karl Barth's Christology. Its Basic Alexandrian Character*. Berlin, New York, Amsterdam: Mouton, 1984.

Karl Barth And Ecumenical Affairs
J.K.S. Reid

I. Introduction

Barth's relationship with the Ecumenical Movement manifests two chief aspects. On the one hand are his direct contributions to ecumenical affairs; on the other there is the continuous influence and even pressure which his on-going work exerted. As the vastness of the dogmatic enterprise on which he was engaged unfolded, he became increasingly reluctant to turn aside to answer calls on his attention that would divert him from the concern he had deliberately made his life's work. While immersed in the exposition of the *Church Dogmatics,* he never lost his concern for the unity of the Church, to which also the Ecumenical Movement was devoted. But it became understandably a recurrent rather than a constant interest, reaching occasional rather than continuous expression. As the *Church Dogmatics* developed, and the stature of what was appearing became evident, the relationship between Barth and the Ecumenical Movement came to be altered and even reversed: if Barth now contributed little to the Ecumenical Movement, the Ecumenical Movement needed to pay heed to Barth.

Certain short early works are definitive: they outline positions in relation to church unity from which he never moved. In fact, they have as much or even more to say about his understanding of the Church. But his understanding of church unity is quite dominated by his concept of the Church and arises immediately from it. [1]

II. The Message of 'Theological Existence Today.'

Barth was writing (1933) in a Germany compulsively dominated by convulsive political occurrences. The salient event was the installation of Adolf Hitler as Reichsführer. The immediate corollary was the appointment by the National Socialist Party of a Church Commissioner. The Church in Germany was caught with a mind divided and was immediately plunged into divisive tactics. Barth opposed both the German Christian party and the New Reformation Men, though in different degrees and for different reasons. He instantly realised that Hitler's pledge that "the rights of the Churches will not be diminished, nor their position as regards the State altered" [2] was worthless. His response to a situation grave with immeasurable threat is a passionate call to the Church to be itself. This does not mean necessarily to be a better Church: the Church is a "Church under the cross", and as such "it is impossible for it to be other than obviously human, all too human . . . The real Church under the cross is the Church of the Holy Ghost whose activities, despite their human weakness and foolishness have nonetheless in themselves something profoundly joyful and peaceful, something sabbatical, even festive." [3] Nor should the Church aim at being a bigger Church. The Church ought not to think of attracting more people to fill up its ranks: it "has not 'to do everything' so that the German people may 'find again the way into the Church', but only so that within the Church the people may find the commandment and promise of the free and pure Word of God." [4]

"To be itself" means simply "to depend upon the Word of God" and to "serve the Word of God." [5] This is the "first business" of the Church, and alongside this first business we brook no second as rival." [6] However, the situation was propelling the Church into activity. Barth agreed that it was a time for action. "Of course something has to be done - very much so; but most decidedly nothing other than this, that the church congregations be gathered together again . . . to the Word by means of the Word." [7] The Church is commissioned to serve the Word of God. "But it lies in the very nature of this commission that it cannot possibly be subordinated to, or co-ordinated with, any other interest." Evidently it is right priority that is being established: "we sin not only against God but against the people if this order of preference in our pursuits be allowed in the least to be shaken." [8] This is no prescription for passivity. Despite what he has said about "first business", there is also "second and third business": "we regard every second and third thing . . . as included and taken up in this first concern." [9]

"To be itself" is of course quite different from being "an end in itself": "the Evangelical Church still possesses the Bible . . . . Where the Bible is allowed to be Master, theological existence is present . . . it is then possible for church reform to issue from the Church's own life." [10] "A Church that recognises its position will neither desire nor be able ... to be Church for its own sake. There is the 'Christian believing group'; but this group is sent out." [11]

With the Reichsführer firmly in control, and the Führerprinzip embedded in government establishment, it was natural, perhaps inevitable, that the question of church leadership should occupy the mind of the Church. Barth feels obliged to respond - by offering practical counsel to a Church reeling before the awesome unfolding of events and trying to discover a role, even a raison d'etre. It is this casual occasion that impels Barth to formulate an understanding of leadership in the Church; and from it derives his assessment of the Churches engaged in the Ecumenical Movement.

Barth first of all resists the idea that the Church needs a leader - the notion arises from "a copying of a specific 'government pattern'" with the aim either of having a "similar kind of Church under leadership", or to "strengthen the Church as against the State." [12] "But when this leader-principle is translated into theological language, it discloses something that all the waters of the Rhine cannot wash away, the real, genuine and unmistakable episcopalism of the Roman Church." [13]

Further, "genuine leadership distinguished from rule and guidance" [14] "can in all spheres become genuine only as event." [15] "The principle of leadership ... is sheer nonsense. Leadership exists only as accomplished fact." "When the man who is there who in fact leads, precisely he is the leader." This occasionalist understanding of leadership Barth finds exemplified in both church and secular history. The Church of the Reformation admitted leadership because it was "actually there" in Luther and in Calvin [16]: "it was granted to them to lead." And remarkably enough he continues: "Were I a National Socialist I should argue as follows: ... we did not think the office of leader was good or necessary with which to invest Hitler. On the contrary, Adolf Hitler was there: he led, he *was* the leader, without any need of office." [17] Thus in Barth's mind the notion of office comes to be so associated with secular parallels, with "uncalled for enthusiasm or anxiety to 'assimilate' (the Church) to the government of the day" that its repudiation in ecclesiastical affairs is a matter of course. With the abandonment of "office" as a reality either political or ecclesiastical, the way is open for his chief point to be established. "It is time for the Church soberly to recognise that the German Evangelical Church, so far as it is in the one, holy, universal Church, has its leader in Jesus Christ, the Word of God." [18]

In *Credo* the point is elaborated. "He, Jesus Christ, rules the Church, and none beside him;" and scorn is poured on two misunderstandings: "since man has not created and founded the Church, he cannot be its Lord"; "neither can the assembly and community rule itself - the *democratic* misunderstanding of the Church; nor can it be ruled by an official or by a number of officials - the *monarchic aristocratic* misunderstanding." [19] And in a later 1948 lecture he compares the Church with "the edifying spectacle that I cannot admire enough in Hungary - how in a gypsy band every individual player has his ears and eyes glued on the leading fiddler, concentrating absolutely on the leader's improvisations, and hence playing inevitably and happily with all the others." [20]

But characteristically Barth withdraws from the naked consequences of what he is saying. This sole leadership of Jesus Christ the Word of God does not extinguish the need for "human leaders." The point to be made is that he alone is the source from which "human leaders" [21] are supplied. "The German Evangelical Church has to make up its mind (to be) content with *his* leading, with *his* ability to supply us with leaders." "The obscure village pastor, or even . . . a lay elder . . . (can be) the genuine bishop, if only he knows his Bible and catechism - a bishop as foreseen in Holy Writ." [22] To ask for other leaders "is as vain as the howling of the priests of Baal on Carmel, 'Baal, hear us!'." [23] The only valid "office" is the "office of Chief Pastor." But it does have "a human counterpart in the ministry of the ordained officers of the concrete Churches in the Synodal Union, as they mutually advise and admonish, endorsing and questioning one another, but not in a special office of bishop superior to the officers of the concrete Churches." [24] Here the Roman Church falls into error. It was a right discernment that saw that "the establishment and organization of the monarchical episcopate upon the soil of the Ancient Church, corresponding to the Roman Empire, could be construed as a symptom of the secularising of the Church." [25] Barth calls upon the Evangelical Church to abjure the example of "the Church of the Pope", as, distrusting the ability of the Chief Pastor to supply human leaders, and "trusting in an arm of flesh, (it) wilfully commits its destinies into the custody of a self-elected leader." [26]

These early emphases remain permanent features of Barth's theology and clearly influence his attitude to ecumenical affairs. The Church has only one Chief Pastor. The Church has one only purpose, to serve the Word of God. All that the Church does, all other charac-teristics it manifests, are quite determined by and derivative from its head. Alongside of this the Church exhibits no permanent features. Even leadership is eventual. He has utter distaste for "compromise" [27] As he will later say with even greater emphasis, there is no *and* in Christianity. Hence he profoundly distrusts the contemporary "Faith Movement" [28] or "Reform Movement." [29] "The Holy Ghost needs no movements; the devil has probably invented most of them." [30] - Eventually he came to have an at least slightly more favourable view of the Ecumenical Movement.

III. A Contemporary Estimate.

In 1931 appeared Adolf Keller's study which in English bore a title that highlighted the ecumenical element: *Karl Barth and Christian Uni-ty.* Keller had made contact with Barth at an early stage, being chief pastor at the German-speaking congregation of the National Church in Geneva, where Barth was in 1909 appointed *pasteur suffragant.* Barth found Keller "an uncommonly rich and many-sided personality; theologically too I got on with him very well." [31] Twenty-one years later Keller's study disclosed the other side of a relationship that was marked by mutual sympathy and respect. Keller's work was pro-phetic, and remains sagacious, discerning and even definitive. He found Barthianism "a sort of parallel movement to ecumenism"; and his book ensured that Barthianism cannot any more "evade the Ecumenical Movement than the later can evade Barthianism." [32]

Keller records that "Karl Barth and some of his followers have agreed to co-operate with the theological Commission of the Move-ment" [33] and finds this "hopeful" for their relationship. But dis-crepancy between the two remains. [34] Keller traces this to Barth's false assessment of what happened at Stockholm ('Universal Chris-tian Conference on Life and Work', 1925) - "a lack of insight into the essence of Stockholm's act of faith." [35] It was a disciple of Barth who wrote off Stockholm as "the kiss of death with which the Church be-trays the gospel to a programme of culture." [36]

About the same time, Barth was setting out his own position in *Credo* from which a fairly extensive quotation must be made. "Accord-ing to the express declaration of Mt 28.18f, and also to what can be gathered from the New Testament about the actual practice of the apostles, the commissioning of the Church consists in the task of witnessing through the preaching of the Gospel and the administration of the sacraments. No third thing stands beside these two - which are in fact one only - the *ministerium verbi divini*. Particularly is the word about the keys of heaven (Mt 16.19) to be understood not as an enlargement but as a restriction of this one office and commission of the Church. In receiving and discharging this one commission is the Church *communio sanctorum, congregatio fidelium*, and in no other way. Beside this one commission neither Seelsorge (cure of souls), nor social work, nor enlargement in the tasks of culture or politics can claim place or honour. These are necessary and legitimate only in the measure that they are understood as particular forms for discharging the one commission. Christian parties? Christian newspapers? Christian philosophy? Christian universities? - one must seriously ask whether such undertakings are necessary and legitimate in this sense. Withdrawal at this point is required not out of resignation; and not in order that the Church can and should be content with an existence in a 'private corner of piety.' The reason rather is respect for the commission with which the Church stands or falls and which it can on its own neither better nor surpass; and trust in the goodness and fittingness of this command; and confidence that by pure proclamation and true administration of the sacraments much more is done for the solution of the pressing problems of life than by putting in hand measures to clear up or ameliorate or mitigate them, by which we should be abandoning our small but mighty sphere of action. This sphere is most accurately designated by the ascent to heaven and baptism on the one hand, and eucharist and the coming again on the other. This sphere is rich enough in problems and tasks. It is in limiting itself to this its proper sphere that the Church shows itself master and nowhere else." [37]

Does this statement merit Keller's criticism? Is it true to say that Barth's judgement is "not based upon a thorough-going knowledge, but upon a fundamental prejudice?" [38] The allegation of "prejudice" must be set aside in any ordinary use of the term. It is not "preconceived bias" that Barth cannot surrender, but rather a cardinal principle. The key to the position he occupies is given halfway through the quoted passage, when he denies that engagement by the Church in the practical sphere can stand *"beside the one commission."* This again is the language not of denial but of comparative assessment. The intention is not the affirmation-repudiation of different attitudes but rather the establishment of priorities. He does not say: abjure action, but rather: get your priorities right. Again, "no third thing stands beside Word and sacraments" may no doubt be construed to mean: there is *no* third thing. But this is not Barth's meaning. He clearly affirms a "second thing" (and a third); but they stand not beside the commission but on a wholly lower level; and moreover they are wholly determined as to their content and character by the Word.

Reflecting at a later point on the matter, Barth expressly declares his approval of active interest and concern on the part of the Church. "The last few centuries . . . . brought out this aspect of the Christian message with a much greater clarity than it had for the great Christians of the 16th century. This was the time when the world-wide mission of the Church was taken up in earnest, the time of a new vision and expectation of the kingdom of God as coming and already come, the time of a new awakening of Christianity to its responsibility to state and society, the time of a new consciousness of its ecumenical existence and mission. These are actualities of church history which a Church Dogmatics cannot overlook." [39]

To an amended form of criticism that Keller brings forward Barth may be more vulnerable. Barth suspects that the Ecumenical Movement lacks theological seriousness; and Keller may be right in thinking this means that it does not quite share in his priorities. But Barth does not despise the activist. "I have now", he writes much later, "become a marginal figure in ecumenical circles"; and "theology in general is more tolerated than really listened to in them." But he continues: "in my view people like Niemöller or Hrodmádka or Ernst Wolf, who are close to things, have much more important things to say than I do." [40] - In the moment of complaining about theological shallowness, Barth commends and admires the contribution of men of action. Church unity for Barth is a paramount obligation. But his approach differs from that of many likewise devoted to its achievement. Barth's incessant demand is that the diplomatic approach usual in the Ecumenical Movement be supplemented, if not replaced, by a theological approach.

In a well-known passage in *Dogmatics in Outline*, he makes a further attempt to specify the active and public role proper to the Church. "Services, sacraments, liturgy, theology" - all these are important; but all of them too are no more than aspects of what is more fundamental, the commission by which the Church exists, "proclaim the Gospel to every creature." "The Church runs like a herald to deliver the message. It is not a snail that carries its little house on its back and is so well off in it that only now and then does it stick out its feelers, and then thinks that the 'claim of publicity' has been satisfied. No, the Church lives by its commission as herald; it is la compagnie de Dieu." [41] "Christianity is not 'sacred' . . . it is an out-and-out 'worldly' thing open to all humanity." The commission is all and absolutely first; engagement in other "tasks" is to be undertaken only in the measure that "they are understood as particular forms for discharging the one commission." He has reverted again to the discernment and realisation of priorities which he has put so cryptically: "in the first place, baptism and eucharist and ascended Christ and the coming again - any other activity is on the side." [42]

IV. The Church and the Churches -
A Closer View of Unity

"The unity of the Church is a thing which cannot be manufactured, but must be found and confessed in subordination to that already accomplished oneness of the Church which is Jesus Christ." [43] This key sentence reveals the essence of what Barth is saying in the four lectures given under the above title at the invitation of Adolf Keller in Geneva. [44]

The relationship between Jesus Christ and the Church determines that the Church has a task or commission. The Church has "no life of its own, but lives as the body of which the crucified and risen Christ is the head": "its being is to proclaim." [45]

The relationship determines further the content of the proclamation: "The one and only Word of God has once and for all been uttered for all men to heed in the fact of the incarnation . . . . The task from which the Church derives its being is to proclaim that this has really happened, and to summon men to believe in its reality." [46]

This commission prescribes "the quest for the *one* Church." [47] This quest emanates from New Testament example, where there is indeed "a variety of communities . . . within the one Church", but "no multiplicity of churches." It arises equally from the harm the multiplicity of churches occasions. Internally, for this reason "many members have found themselves alienated from the Church"; [48] externally, because "there is not one Church but many", there is "dissipation of the spiritual and material energies of the mission work"; [49] and the fact that "Churches are in manifold conflict with each other" occasions "hindrance to the hearing of (the Church's) message", "bewilderment to its less attentive hearers," and a "burden to the more serious." [50]

The relationship further prescribes the nature of the oneness "meant by the quest for the *one* Church." [51] It has nothing to do with "the magical fascination of numerical unity", nor with "mental harmony and agreement." Further, the quest "must not be a quest for 'church unity in itself'". "The quest for the unity of the Church must in fact be identical with the quest for Jesus Christ as the concrete Head and Lord of the Church". [52] Jesus Christ "*is* the oneness of the Church, is that unity within which there may be multiplicity of communities, of gifts, of persons within one Church, while through it a multiplicity of churches is excluded." [53]

What then is the nature of the multiplicity which the quest for oneness confronts and opposes? Multiplicity may not be written off as unimportant, by arguing that it belongs to the visible Church, leaving the "invisible or essential" Church unimpaired: "there is no way of escape from the visible to the invisible." [54] Multiplicity is not "an unfolding of the wealth of that grace given to mankind in Jesus Christ." [55] Nor does it arise as "the fruits of a logical necessity, past or present."[56] Its true nature is quite different: "we have no right to explain . . . (it) at all. We have to deal with it as we deal with sin, to recognise it as a fact, to understand it as the impossible thing which has intruded itself." [57] Accordingly, the appropriate action is to pray that it be "forgiven and removed"; [58] "our response . . . must be prayer for forgiveness and sanctification." [59]

Pressed more closely about the nature of the required response, Barth advances several negative considerations. "To prescribe doses of love, patience, and tolerance as a cure is futile." [60] Such notions arise from "political and philosophical principles which are not only alien but even opposed to the Gospel."[61] "Much the same has to be said of . . . federations or alliances" - they do very well in promoting joint activities towards selected ends, but do not focus on "the essential point." In the end, like other human undertakings, they are no more than a "better sort of humanitarianism." [62]

Barth elsewhere confesses that "all in all ... this ecumenical business has not made much of an impression on me." [63] This is hardly surprising; for what he says strikes an unusual, even alien, note. "The task of church unity is essentially ... the task of listening to Christ." [64] At first sight this looks a spare and meagre judgment. But what is said about "listening" uncovers a rich vein of thought, illuminating an aspect of the nature of the Church. It appears that this listening has to be done "within the Churches in their present multiplicity and separation." [65] We are not to abjure the individual Churches, nor the particular church that is our own. "We cannot hear Christ otherwise than ... giving ear to the Church to which we owe allegiance as members, within which we were baptised and brought to belief." [66] "Only in our own Church can we listen to Christ, not in any other, and still less in any neutral ground above or outside the severed Churches." [67] The Churches "in their multiplicity and separation" are yet the Church: in them the Church, really the Church, continues to be fragmented, divided, "severed", even "in manifold conflict" [68] among themselves, they are still the Church - not a second rate Church beside which there is a better: *they are the only Church.*

Listening to Christ is thus not content but context: it is not the prohibition of activity but the perimeter within which church activity is to be prosecuted. Here it is not passivity that Barth advocates. What is commended is not an embargo on activity, but a critical selectivity of activity. The criterion is variously stated: sometimes, as here, "listening to Christ"; or "the truth of Christ"; or simply recognising and realising that Christ is Head of the Church.

The real or true Church does not exist outside and beyond the divided, separated, contention-ridden Church which here and now we know. It is the real and true Church that exists in this deformed shape and condition. From this arises Barth's view of the way to overcome multiplicity and to promote unity. The Ecumenical Movement tends to operate on the following principle: many differences separate denominations; let us minimise or diminish the differences and maximise the similarities, in order that the Churches may come together. Barth prescribes a different strategy. Since the Church exists only by Jesus Christ, and only in a divided state, the road to unity requires perpetuation and exploitation of the differences, while listening to the Head and Lord of the Church. Churches have to be *more* themselves, not less. Of course their true selves is meant: not a Church "that passes no judgment on itself, and is zealous (only) for its own ordinances as such." [69] This course could lead only to self-justification and vindication of the multiplicity that union is designed to overcome. It means that "each several Church should . . . work out its (own) doctrine", not of course in a narrow logical sense from premises that are clearly not ultimate, but "as listening to the Christ of the Scriptures." [70] Barth has in mind positions historically occupied and theological propositions polemically phrased - these are not to be abandoned. But it is not they but Scripture that is the starting point for progress in unity.

From this standpoint Barth advances the startling judgement. Marburg 1529 marked the parting of the ways for the Churches of the Reformation, and the Lutheran and Calvinistic Churches thereafter blazed separate trails. Barth judges that at Marburg "true unity was a present and visible reality"; and, he adds darkly, more "than in certain doings of our own day." It appears that these "certain doings" are not activities of the Ecumenical Movement as such. Rather he is warning against "so much profession of charity that no one had courage enough left to enquire with honesty about the truth." [71]

Barth's message is sufficiently clear. Each separate Church is of the only Church there is. It has consequently to pursue, not deflect, its own approach. Each several Church has to be guided by Christ the one Head of the Church; and, as thus oriented to Christ, must be advancing to a common goal and moving also towards oneness. Paradoxically, Barth is suggesting that there is really no ecumenical activity as such, no reaching out for unity over and above just being the Church and listening to the Church's Head. The Churches necessarily have some form - episcopal, presbyterian, congregationalist. But these reflect the social, political, and cultural circumstances in which the Church lives rather than the nature of the Church as such. No form is to be promoted as such: it all reduces to the simple requirement that the Church has to listen to Christ.

This plea received powerful expression in the later Dogmatics ". . . there is good reason why every Christian fellowship . . . should in some way claim Jesus Christ especially for itself . . . it is in this that the unity of the Church is proclaimed in all its perverse plurality. . . . If only we would everywhere allow Jesus Christ genuinely to speak and to rule, genuinely and continuously subjecting ourselves to his guidance and instruction and direction, genuinely allowing him to be the Lord of the Church! Naturally not in the theory, the historical or speculative philosophy, the dogma, the particular Christology, in which he has been imprisoned and, as it were, encysted, but himself, the living Lord, speaking by the Holy Spirit to the Church today in the witness of the prophets and apostles . . . . If his real presence were really allowed to become event instead of simply being cherished, then everywhere there would be a crisis in ecclesiastical self-consciousness, rather like the proving fire described in I Cor. 3.12f, in which every man's work is made manifest, that which has so far been built on the one foundation beside which there is no other: gold, silver, precious stones, or wood, hay, stubble . . . . The unity of the Church - which is not under the power of any man because the living Lord Jesus Christ in his own power is himself this unity - would then begin not only to be a reality but to be realised as such in the many Churches . . . . In and with him, the One, the unity of his body and therefore of the Church cannot for very long remain completely hidden from the faith which will ascribe and actually grant to him the power to do this." [72] And Barth finds in Zinzendorf perhaps the first genuine ecumenist, because he was the only "Christocentric" of the modern age and founded his brother-hoods of loyal members of particular Churches round their "common Elder Brother" where unity was not and could not be lost. [73]

V. Involvement in Ecumenical Movement Study: "the Living Congregation".

A further stage in Barth's contact with the Ecumenical Movement is reached in 1948. In this year was held in Amsterdam an Assembly that formally constituted the World Council of Churches. The preparation for the event culminated in four major studies, each developing one aspect of the main theme of the Assembly, "Man's Disorder and God's Design," and each forming the subject of discussion for a section of the Assembly, The first study is entitled *The Universal Church in God's Design* and consisted of an international symposium; and since it was evident that "the fundamental problem of the Church is the existence of churches", [74] the first part of the symposium dealt with "The Doctrine of the Church". Barth contributed one of the five interpretations, under the title: "The Living Congregation of the Living Lord Jesus

Christ." He sets out resolutely, even uncompromisingly considering the company in which he speaks, what he understands by Church. "The Church is neither the invisible fellowship nor the visible company, of all those who believe in Christ.... The Church is the 'event' in which two or three are gathered together in the name of Jesus Christ." [75] From this central reality other aspects coruscate. The Church is best described as Gemeinde, a term not easy to translate but approximately meaning congregation or community living by the act of its living Lord; or in the words of *The Heidelberg Catechism for Today:* "Christians in their fellowship with Christ and in their fellowship with one another, without the interposition of an 'office'." [76] It is Ereignis, event; and its primary form is accordingly the local congregation, meeting regularly in a given place and always dependent on the constantly new activity of Jesus Christ. The local community is constituted by regular public worship, which itself is constituted by visible concrete action, including prayer and the proclamation and reception of the Gospel; and for this all members of the congregation are responsible. The congregation is the event in which men unite together over against the world, yet only in order that they may identify themselves with the need and the hope of the world: [77] it is the event in which the witness of the apostles and prophets to Jesus Christ, deposited in Scripture, as such, becomes present, effective and fruitful; and again as such it is the decisive element in the final phase in the story of God's relations with man. [78]

The Church's "unity stands and falls with that 'event' which is the 'gathering' of the congregation by the Word and the Spirit of its living Lord, Jesus Christ." When that activity is checked, the congregation disintegrates and the Church falls apart. [79] Government is what "guarantees the unity of the living congregation ... (with) his Word attested by the scriptures;" and formally it is the concern of the living Lord alone. Yet besides him there is office, or better said *diakonia* and *ministerium* in which the different gifts are exercised: there is precedence, but no higher or lower. Similarly church order is concerned with relations between local congregations. It has one purpose only: to make room for the event that constitutes the existence and renewal of the congregation. [80] The only possible organ for effecting this is a "synodical congregation", made up of certain members from other congregations but sharing in the same life and worship; and this body will not so much govern as counsel. [81] Church order is not an end in itself: [82] while no human effort can ensure that the divine encounter occurs, order has the purpose of clearing obstacles out of the way.

The objection to papal, episcopal, consistorial, and presbyteral order is that they are systems that obstruct, and do not facilitate, the free access of God's Word to the actual congregation: they come be-tween the congregation and the Word. They arise out of unnecessary fear of arbitrary action on the part of members of the living congrega-tion, while scandalously disregarding the arbitrary behaviour of those exercising authority in and over the Church. Members of a congrega-tion really living by the "event" of its Lord will not degenerate into arbitrary action; and equally, individuals aware that they are, equally with all others, recipients of charism of the Holy Spirit, will not be guilty of arbitrary action. [83] It is understandable that the Con-gregationalist "system" has in Barth's view, if not more to commend it, then at least less to condemn it, than the others named.

How does this testimony differ from the other contributions? All these others agree with Barth that the unity and koinonia of the Church are based on Christ. Thus G. Aulen (Lutheran) declares: "the Church has its existence in and through Christ"; [84] and C.T. Craig (from the US): "the nature of the Church ... determined by the rela-tion of a community to Christ." [85] G. Florovsky (Orthodox) says: "first of all (Christians) *are one* in Christ, and only this communion *with* Christ makes the communion of men possible - *in* him," [86] and J.A.F. Gregg (Anglican): "the Church of the Ascended Christ whose body it is ... is a society founded and constituted by an invisible Head in whom resides all its vitality and apart from whom it can do nothing." [87]

There is similar at least near unanimity concerning the primary task of the Church. Aulen: the new fellowship is based on "sending out of the apostles as authorised agents"; [88] Craig: "the Church is the indispensible organ through which Christ makes his life effective in the world"; [89] Florovsky: "the primary task of the historical Church is the proclamation of the Gospel," [90] Gregg: among "the most important duties laid upon the visible Church (is) that of the witness-ing to the revealed truth of God in Christ." [91]

Difference arises on the question of what more may or must be said; or more summarily on the question whether more can be said. The simplest form in which augmentation is suggested appears in Craig:

"while the Church is the body of Christ, it has to be recognised 'that he cannot be fully operative in the world as disembodied spirit: His Spirit must act through some bodily expression if its existence is to be manifest" and effective." [92] Here an advance is being made beyond the pure Church-Christ relationship which constitutes the identity of the Church. This element is not unmatched in Barth's understanding: "there are, however, some cross-relations between individual local congregations, and other forms and organs of their unity. These are the *free associations for service* in the cause of charity (&c, and also) for the guidance of Christian thought and policy."[93] But similarity ends abruptly there. For Barth these associations must regard themselves as essentially *(de iure)* "worshipping congregations", i.e. "Churches in the full sense." [94] But for Craig they have the character of "ecclesiastical institutions." [95] Clearly the concept of institution is incompatible with Barth's dynamic or actualist understanding of the Church. The ecumenical task is correspondingly differently conceived. For Craig and others like him, the Ecumenical Movement has to pay attention to "ecclesiastical institutions"; for Barth the objective of the Ecumenical Movement is to be achieved simply by each separate Church being true to itself, or in other words true to its Head and Lord.

The discrepancy widens. Aulen introduces the notion of "constitutive elements of the Church," [96] naming them as Word and Sacraments; and to these he later subjoins "the ministry of the Church." [97] Florovsky similarly avers that "emphatically, the sacraments constitute the Church. Only in the sacraments does the Christian community pass beyond the purely human measure and become the Church." [98] Gregg supplies sharper edges to this understanding when he invokes the notion of "marks" [99]. The identification of these "marks of the Church" with "marks of essential catholicity" means that a Church cannot be regarded as catholic if it does not display these marks. Thus we are brought face to face with the substance of the celebrated Lambeth Quadrilateral: Scripture, ecumenical creeds, two sacraments, and "*the* apostolic ministry of bishops, priests and deacons, transmitted by those having authority to transmit." And the gage of battle is thrown down: "these few but vital institutions" are "the visible pledges of continuity with the undivided Church"; and union is to be resisted with communions "which either deny the sufficiency or threaten the integrity of the Church's inherited faith or order." [100]

Barth sees order differently. Since the essence of the Church resides in Jesus Christ, order cannot have essential character but only instrumental or pragmatic character, and is therefore of secondary importance.

It is not of importance that a Church is episcopal or presbyterian or congregationalist; it is of sole importance that a Church act as a Church, without allowing form or order (which are largely the product of history and adventitious circumstance) to interfere or dictate. Here there reappears Barth's slight preference for congregationalist polity: he commends "the principle of Congregationalism - the free congregation of the free Word of God." [101] Any organ or court of other decision-making agency should have the form of "synodal congregation." [102] Few people will think that Barth says here all that is to be said. Worship is distinguishable from decision-making. But one must commend the spacious freedom in which Churches would move and act if, following his lead, the awesome burden of precedent were removed or even lightened. How often in deliberative assemblies of the Churches is action stayed because a bureaucratic voice tells them either: there is no precedent for this, or: this would set a precedent.

Two characteristics chiefly differentiate Barth's position from that of his fellow contributors: his so-called "eventualism", and his emphasis on "solely". Barth's thesis compactly expressed is: "the living Christ solely the life of the Church." Each of these characteristics deserves some notice.

"The true Church is an event" [103] is one instance of a frequently recurring phrase. Another is to be found in the more occasional work *Against the Stream* (1954): "the real Church is truly not invisible but visible. But it is visible only when rendered visible by the action of God, by the witness of the Holy Spirit . . . . Just as the dark letters of an illuminated advertisement become visible, legible, eloquent, when the (electric) current is switched on." [104] H.R. Mackintosh was an early critic of Barth's "excessive actualism", his stress on the "dynamic aspects of Christian faith and life at the expense of the static." [105] As example of the same thing more recently said, Colm O'Grady complains of Barth's "excessive event-ecclesiology": [106] and expresses the philosophical difficulty: "how can I form a concept of existence without forming a concept of that which exists?" [107] It is not easy to defend Barth against this objection; and if so, what he says has the force of protest and warning rather than the character of definitive affirmation.

The term "solely" is the other differentiating feature. In Barth's theology it has deep roots. He writes: "the fatal little word 'and' . . . sooner or later (what it signifies) will make an open bid for sole domination." [108] No brief phrase is more characteristic of Barth's ecclesiology - indeed of all his theology. "Jesus Christ as attested to us in Holy Scripture is the one Word of God whom we must hear and whom we must trust and obey in life and in death." [109] To that, no 'and' may be added. But Barth's exact meaning is elusive. The repudiation of 'and' in his early writings received robust and uncompromising expression. It shocked Christian theology into angry reaction. Thus A. Keller adopts E. Przywara's distinction between the "sole-effectiveness" and the "all-effectiveness" of grace. [110] He avers that Roman Catholic doctrine makes use of the second, so that "an ethical action is made possible", whereas "the Barthian insistence on the sole-effectiveness of grace . . . paralyses and empties the human will of the divine, which thus again becomes a law unto itself . . . in a new form the old Pelagian conflict is again fought out." [111] Barth at Keller's time of writing gave occasion for criticism of this kind - the reduction of intermediate agencies, whether man or Church, to ciphers in the divine economy. But his real intention is different. If his early forceful expressions drowned his denials and rendered them inaudible, they are reiterated in his later, even his latest, writings and deserve credence. In *Ethics* he writes: "Theology is not the presentation of the reality of the Word of God addressed to man *and also* the presentation of the reality of the man to whom God's Word is addressed. This is also a reality of course . . . . Theology knows the reality of the Word of God only as that of the Word of God addressed to man and it cannot for a moment abstract itself from this determination of its theme. One may thus say that not just dogmatics but theology in general includes from the very first and at every point the problem of ethics. But the man to whom God's Word is directed can never become the theme or subject of theology. He is not in any sense a second subject of theology which must be approached with a shift of focus. When this transition takes place . . . death is in the pot (2 Kings 4.40)." [112]

Similarly in *The Christian Life* Barth writes: "God's glory and man's salvation, while they are so different, are not two things but one. God validates his own glory in his love . . . in being kind to man. It is up to man for his part to acknowledge the being, will and act of God, and therefore, as his beloved and elect child, judged, saved, healed, carried, and led by him, to praise him and to give him and him alone all the glory." [114]

In the light of such clear affirmation, a more careful assessment of his repudiation of 'and' is necessary. The repudiation is not absolute. For him, 'and' in theology means imparity, never parity; not association but dissociation; a relation of super- and sub-ordination; two things "not on the same plane." [114] John Thompson exemplifies this fairer assessment: since Jesus Christ: "alone is the light of God", he "needs no completion by others . . . no synthesis between him and others is possible, whether Mary and the Church (Roman Catholicism), or general revelation (natural theology) or human self-understanding (Bultmann)." [115] In contrast, C. O'Grady is asking Barth to deny himself and surrender his witness at this crucial point, when he blandly demands that, in the economy of salvation, Barth's "theology of 'response' and 'reflection' must be broadened to include a theology of 'participation';, of 'sub-operation' and 'mediation' - in other words the affirmation that man and Church have a specific salvific part to play." [116] Of course, according to Barth, the Church is important: "the Church is the earthly form of Christ's own heavenly body, the manhood reconciled in him and represented above by him." [117] Moreover, it does have a role to play: God "does not act directly without this people. He gives to this people the necessary qualities." [118] But this does not meet O'Grady's requirements, which Barth could only regard as "sinister leaven": "the man reconciled with God by God has often become a man reconciling himself with himself, the religious man, complacent and self-explained," [119] With O'Grady may be contrasted another Roman Catholic writer, Philip J. Rosato, who offers another defence of Barth by construing him as doing something "to save and even justify the whole attempt to start theology with the believing Christian as the focus." The key to this novel interpretation of Barth is found in his pneumatology; "exactly at the point where the pneumatological solution becomes possible, Barth ceases to condemn (the attempt) because he recognises there a deep resonance with his own theological intention." [120]

A brief excursus will illustrate the continuing importance and relevance of the point Barth is making. At the moment this is being written, all Churches are studying the Faith & Order document emanating from Lima 1982 entitled *Baptism, Eucharist & Ministry*. The degree of agreement expounded in the document in all three areas is impressive and gratifying. In the case of Baptism, this consensus has made possible in this country (and others, even Spain), [121] a Common Baptismal Certificate, which signifies that each Church recognises the Baptism carried out in other Churches unconditionally. Baptism "unites the one baptised with Christ." [122] The Vatican II documents of the Roman Church are in agreement: "by the sacrament of baptism... a man becomes truly incorporated into the crucified and glorified Christ and is reborn to a sharing of the divine life;" [123] "all those justified by faith through Baptism are incorporated into Christ." [124] But now over this apparent total consensus falls a shadow. The brothers and the communities designated as "separated" are in a real sense acknowledged as Christian. But even when "properly baptised", they are only said to be "brought into a certain, though imperfect, communion with the Catholic Church." [125] This constitutes a "defect", since thereby they lack "the fulness of the means of salvation" which is obtainable "through Christ's Catholic Church alone." – So near and yet so far! The differentia intruded here is the role ascribed by Roman Catholicism to the Church: one can be incorporated into Christ by Baptism, but fulness of salvation is obtained only through the Catholic Church. Full salvation is by Christ *and* the Church. Putting it otherwise: all would agree that the Church has a part to play in Baptism as the *agent* of what Christ in Baptism wills to bestow. But according to the *Decree on Ecumenism*, the Church plays a substantive role in the matter of salvation. (A similar situation arises in the case of the Eucharist: though not stated in BEM, the Roman view is that the "minister of the blessed Eucharist" should properly be in communion with the Roman see.) [126] Even so, not all is lost. Agreement in general remains on what is done in Baptism, i.e., on the substance of Baptism. Discord arises only when attention shifts to matters circumstantial or peripheral, to the *context* in which Baptism is administered (to the status of the minister of the Eucharist). Barth's prophecy comes all too near the truth: what is designated by 'and' is making open bid for domination.

VI. Further contacts with the Ecumenical Movement: Amsterdam & Evanston.

For the sake of completeness, something should be said about certain other contacts between Barth and the Ecumenical Movement.

At the Amsterdam Assembly 1948 Barth was himself participant and found "this cooperation and co-responsibility both interesting and important." [127] He delivered an opening lecture which "took the line that the theme should be stood on its head: that we should speak first of God's design and only then of man's disorder." [128] "We shall not be the ones who change this wicked world into a good one. God has not abdicated from his leadership over us.... All that is required of us is that in midst of the political and social disorder of the world, we should simply be his witnesses. We shall have our hands full simply in being that." [129]

Barth participated in the preparation for the World Council of Churches Assembly at Evanston (1954). Of this participation Busch gives some account, together with some of Barth's comments, appreciative and critical. Of the first gathering for preparation in 1951 Barth remarks: "Yes, we sat there and talked for two whole days." He found the second conference 1952 "a much more successful collaboration." Here "we had all . . . read our Bibles and therefore had automatically been brought closer to one another . . . we not only spoke of the Christian hope but also grew together into it." In 1953 he could say: "we have come substantially closer together." While commending the contributions of people like John Baillie, Lesslie Newbigin, and C.H. Dodd, he complained about the "Anglo-Saxons" making "their phylacteries so broad and so long"; and particularly of "an Evening Prayer at which the Lord's Prayer was said twice and the Gloria five or six times. I said to them afterwards: 'If I were the good God, I would reply to you in a voice of thunder: "All right, that will do, I've heard you"'." [130] Barth was unanimously chosen to add a concluding word to the Report for the Assembly. In it he posed some questions to the Churches: "Is it an authentic witness to its Lord and Head? ... Is it the community which can already recognise the coming king in its hungry, thirsty, alien, naked, sick, imprisoned brethren?" [131] - thus imparting a characteristically theological dimension to interests the Ecumenical Movement was not inclined to neglect.

In CD IV/3.1 Barth gives a brief history of the Ecumenical Movement together with some pungent criticisms. Ecumenism he classes with "hopes and efforts" that have continuously opposed the "centrifugal tendency" that has so characterised the life of the Church. He finds common statements to contain "the necessary element of compromise", and the papers preparatory for Amsterdam and Evanston to be enveloped in "the fog of indecision and sterility." On the other hand he insists that "in relation to speech and action undertaken in common with a respect for that which is distinctive yet an avoidance of that which separates, we have no grounds whatever to say that the Church lags far behind advances long since made by the world. In this field it is obvious that it has seized the initiative, that it is quite a few steps ahead of the world and can be an example to it. The outlook today would be quite different if in some negotiations and conferences there were at least as honest and open and practical a concern for the unity of nations as there has been for the unity of the Churches at Edinburgh, Stockholm, Amsterdam, Evanston, &c, and as there is continually in Geneva, not in the Palace of Nations, but in *Route de Malagnou* 17." [132]

VII. Daniel in the Lions' Den - Ad Limina Apostolorum.

Two events made the year 1966 a notable one for Barth. On May 8th he celebrated his 80th birthday - 1000 letters, 50 telegrams, and enough tobacco to keep him for the rest of his life. [133] One slanderous message addressed him as "a worthless old fellow"; [134] but the rest brought unmistakably home to him that his "little bits of thinking, speaking and doing have had ... in the world a significance which I myself ... would never really have ascribed to them;" [135] and he thinks the praise so generously lavished upon him would be better diverted to the unmerited grace of God which must have been at work.

The other event was a visit to Rome. At Amsterdam Barth had expressed disappointment that Rome had not joined the Ecumenical Movement. His concern found outlet and new hope when Hans Urs von Balthasar gave lectures in Basel itself on Karl Barth and Catholicism. [136] Barth attended the lectures (anxious "to learn more about myself"), and he and the lecturer became friends. In von Balthasar Barth discovered a Catholic theologian who "envisaged a kind of reformation of the Catholic Church and of Catholic theology from within." [137]

This revived hope was strengthened by what was happening at Vatican Council II. Two earlier invitations to visit Rome he had had to decline. One, conveyed through Hans Küng, to attend as observer Session 2 of the Council "pleases and honours me - not least because it seems that in the Secretariat (for Promoting Christian Unity) the fear of me as a wild man seems to have been overcome." Six months later Oscar Cullmann suggested that he join the corps of observers for Session 3. [139] But this too, for reasons of health, he had to refuse, stating in his reply that he was following the proceedings in Rome through "a wealth of sources" and "with great interest." [140] Then two and a half years later Barth wrote to Cardinal Bea (Director of the Secretariat for Promoting Christian Unity) expressing "lively desire to come to Rome." [141] Of the consequent "post eventum" visit (Vat II finished Dec. 1965) Barth gives his own meagre but fascinating record in *Ad Limina Apostolorum.* [142]

The visit was undertaken "personally, not as a Protestant but simply as an Evangelical Christian and theologian . . . concerned about the unity of faith and Church, which we seek but which is also to a large extent already present." He returns from the visit still "defiantly evangelical - I should rather say, evangelical-catholic." [143]

In the more relaxed form of letters he says that the visit was a "success." [144] Writing to Cardinal Willebrands (then Secretary of the Secretariat for Promoting Christian Unity), he speaks of the numerous personal meetings and discussions as being as instructive, fraternal, free and cheerful "as I could expect as a separated brother." [145] He found Cardinal Bea (Chairman of the Secretariat) "a good man doing a good job;" [146] and Willebrands "a very good man;" [147] nor did he let himself be too distressed by the "rather dark looks" which two cardinals had given him. [148] He notes with evident satisfaction that in Rome he "experienced the Ecumenical Movement for six days there, and contributed a little to it." [149] A newspaper report that the Lateran University refused to allow "the head of heresy" within its walls was treated by Barth with disdain. [150] And he confessed to being envious of two things: the facility with which everyone spoke Latin, and the red hats of the cardinalate. [151]

Barth had "an hour-long conversation" with Pope Paul VI, who welcomed him with outstretched arms. Barth found him a "wise and in his own way a humble and pious personality." [152] In his presence he found no cause to remember the proud title of *Pontifex Maximus,* and he reflected that in the documents of Vatican II the term *Vicarius Christi* is replaced by "bishop, and *servus servorum Dei."* [153] The difficulty of discharging the papal office and its duties deeply impressed Barth. "After a little praise from me, (the Pope) began with the almost touching statement how hard it is to carry and handle the keys of Peter committed to him by our Lord," [154] "under pressure from the older men around him, and also from the younger"; "it is difficult to determine proper freedom and necessary order in the problems both old and new with which he is faced." [155]

The aim of the visit was not to speak, but rather "to listen, to receive, to understand, to learn." [156] In consequence he could later in the same year declare to E. Schlink that "one may look a little more hopefully than you do to the future of what is now going on (in the Roman Church), in a way that seems to me to be irresistible." [157] This judgement he reiterates: "I have come to know at close quarters a Church and theology caught up in an unmistakable movement, slow but genuine and irreversible." [158] If Vatican II described itself as *"Conciliorum Tridentini et Vaticani I inhaerens vestigiis",* [159] it does so with "the left foot, while with the right it strides forward" to make new footprints on the way to outline new genuine doctrine for present and future. [160] Barth expresses the wish that a corresponding forward movement were apparent among other Churches. Should we not dispense with "the words 'Protestant' and 'Protestantism'?" [161]

Like other commentators Barth notes the radical change embodied in the celebrated *Dei Verbum* document, in which the parity of Scripture and tradition (the traditional *et. . . . et)* gives way to "tradition hands on . . . God's word." [162] Yet great disparities and obstacles persist. Two of special ecumenical importance call for mention. During the visit itself, Barth posed an important question concerning the *fratres seiuncti.* The Decree of Ecumenism speaks of "a movement for the restoration of unity among all Christians" [163] as increasing also among the separated brethren. Barth bluntly asks: why does not Rome acknowledge that this movement began outside the Roman Church, among precisely these separated brethren, and that any similar concern in the Roman Church was a later development? [164] Again: The Decree on Ecumenism appears to define "separated brethren" in terms of plenitude. How is this judgement related to the admission that the Roman Church itself finds it difficult "to express in actual life her full catholicity in all its aspects?" [165] The further question was raised during the audience itself, whether in the formula it was right to lay emphasis on the word *fratres*, really brothers? Barth was given the impression that the Pope so understood the phrase.

The other major divisive issue Barth finds to be Mariology. He gives reasons why he finds the "business of Mariology" [166] unacceptable: it understands wrongly, and in a Bultmannian sense, the relation between faith and history; the *theotokos* is Christological in intention, not Mariological; it is improper to think of the *ancilla Dei* having a crown. The promulgation of 1950 was said to be no more than a recognition of the place which popular devotion accorded to Mary. Barth's wry comment is expressed in English, that theologians must in that case "make the best of it," [167] and at least guard against the worst consequences. In no sense can there be ascribed to Mariology the *anagke* with which Paul invests the Gospel (1 Cor 9:16). Finally Barth applauds the tendency apparent in the thought of Vatican II to accord to Mariology a "decorative" rather than a substantial role. In a letter Barth recalled "the Pope's desire that he (Barth) might get profounder insights regarding the Virgin in his old age." [168] It may be thought that Barth, privately if not expressly, reciprocated the desire!

Notes

1. Since this essay is in English, quotations from and references to these works are made from the English versions and given this pagination. Some alterations to the English translations have been made in the interests of accuracy.
2. *Theological Existence Today*, London: Hodder & Stoughton, 1933, p. 24.
3. Ibid., p. 20f.
4. Ibid., p. 51.
5. Ibid., pp. 12-13.
6. Ibid., p. 13.
7. Ibid., p. 77.
8. Ibid., p. 82.
9. Ibid., p. 13.
10. Ibid., p. 30.
11. *Dogmatics in Outline*, London: SCM, 1949, p. 146f.
12. *Theological Existence Today*, p. 35.
13. Ibid.
14. Ibid., p. 37.
15. Ibid.
16. Ibid., p. 39.
17. Ibid., p. 38.
18. Ibid., p. 45.

19. *Credo,* London: Hodder & Stoughton, 1936, p. 140.
20. Eberhard Busch, *Karl Barth: His Life from Letters and autobiographical Texts,* London: SCM, 1976, p. 354.
21. *Theological Existence Today,* p. 45.
22. Ibid., p. 46.
23. Ibid.
24. Ibid., p. 42.
25. Ibid., p. 37.
26. Ibid., p. 45f.
27. Ibid., p. 70.
28. Ibid., p. 50.
29. Ibid., p. 28.
30. Ibid., p. 78.
31. Busch, op.cit., p. 53.
32. Adolf Keller, *Karl Barth and Christian Unity,* London: Lutterworth, 1931, pp. 289-90.
33. Ibid., pp. xix-xx.
34. Ibid., p. 290.
35. Ibid., p. 291.
36. Ibid.
37. *Credo,* pp. 143-44.
38. Keller, op.cit., p. 280.
39. *C.D.,* IV/I, p. 527.
40. *Karl Barth Letters 1961-1968,* ed. Jürgen Fangmeier and Hinrich Stoevesandt, Edinburgh: T & T Clark, 1981, pp. 38-39.
41. *Dogmatics in Outline,* p. 147.
42. Ibid., cf also *Credo,* p. 143.
43. Karl Barth, *The Church and the Churches,* London: James Clarke & Co., 1937, p. 48.
44. Busch, op.cit., p. 263f.
45. *The Church and the Churches,* op.cit., p. 15.
46. Ibid., pp. 14-15.
47. Ibid., p. 17.
48. Ibid., pp. 13-15.
49. Ibid., pp. 9-10.
50. Ibid., p. 10.
51. Ibid., P. 17.
52. Ibid., pp. 17-19.
53. Ibid., p. 19.
54. Ibid., p. 26.
55. Ibid., pp. 26-27.
56. Ibid., p. 37.
57. Ibid., p. 29.
58. Ibid.
59. Ibid., p. 37.
60. Ibid., p. 32.
61. Ibid., p. 43.
62. Ibid., pp. 44-45.
63. Busch, op.cit., p. 264.
64. Barth, *The Church and the Churches,* p. 57.
65. Ibid.

66. Ibid.
67. Ibid., p. 58.
68. Ibid., p. 10.
69. Ibid., p. 64.
70. Ibid., p. 65.
71. Ibid., p. 67.
72. *C.D.,* IV/I, pp. 681-83.
73. Ibid., p. 683.
74. *The Universal Church in God's Design,* London: SCM, 1948, p. 17.
75. Ibid., p. 73.
76. Karl Barth, *The Heidelberg Catechism for Today,* John Knox Press, 1964, p. 27.
77. 'Living Community', op.cit., p. 68.
78. Ibid., p. 69.
79. Ibid., p. 72.
80. Ibid., p. 73.
81. Ibid., p. 74.
82. Ibid., p. 75.
83. Ibid.
84. Ibid., p. 19.
85. Ibid., p. 39.
86. Ibid., p. 46.
87. Ibid., p. 59.
88. Ibid., p. 19.
89. Ibid., p. 41.
90. Ibid., p. 55.
91. Ibid., p. 63.
92. Ibid., p. 41.
93. Ibid., p. 74.
94. Ibid., p. 94.
95. Ibid., p. 41.
96. Ibid., p. 22.
97. Ibid., p. 27.
98. Ibid., p. 47.
99. Ibid., p. 65.
100. Ibid., p. 66.
101. Ibid., p. 75.
102. Ibid., p. 74.
103. *C.D.,* IV/2, p. 623.
104. Karl Barth, *Against the Stream, Shorter Post-War Writings,* London: SCM, 1954, pp. 63-64.
105. H.R. Mackintosh, *Types of Modern Theology,* London: Nisbet, 1937, p. 314.
106. Colm O'Grady, *The Church in Catholic Theology: Dialogue with Karl Barth,* London: Geoffrey Chapman, 1969, p. 307.
107. Ibid., p. 16.
108. *C.D.,* IV/3, 1, p. 102.
109. Ibid., p. 3.
110. Keller, op.cit., p. 217.
111. Ibid.
112. Karl Barth, *Ethics,* Edinburgh: T & T Clark, 1981, p. 13.
113. Karl Barth, *The Christian Life, C.D.,* IV/4, *Fragments,* Edinburgh: T & T Clark, 1981, p. 30.

114. *Ethics*, op.cit., p. 13.
115. John Thompson, *Christ in Perspective in the Theology of Karl Barth*, The Saint Andrew Press, 1978, p. 184, n. 32.
116. O'Grady, op.cit., p. 339.
117. *C.D.*, II/1, p. 160.
118. Ibid.
119. *C.D.*, IV/2, p. 9.
120. P.J. Rosato, *The Spirit as Lord, The Pneumatology of Karl Barth*, The Saint Andrew Press, 1978, p. 184, n. 32.
121. *Ecumenical Press Service*, 1984, Vol. 12. p. 47.
122. *Baptism, Eucharist and Ministry (BEM) Faith and Order Paper No. 111*, World Council of Churches, Geneva, 1982, p. 12.
123. *The Documents of Vatican II* ed. Walter M. Abbott, S.J., London: Geoffrey Chapman, 1967, p. 363.
124. Ibid., p. 345.
125. Ibid.
126. C.F. Canons 900-11, and for Baptism, Canons 861-63. *The Case of Canon Law*, Collins, 1983.
127. Busch, op.cit., p. 357.
128. Ibid., p. 358.
129. Ibid.
130. Ibid., pp. 395ff.
131. Ibid., p. 400.
132. *C.D.*, IV/3, 1, pp. 36ff.
133. *Letters*, p. 207.
134. Ibid., p. 206.
135. Ibid., p. 213.
136. Hans Urs Von Balthasar, *Karl Barth: Darstellung und Deutung seiner Theologie*, Jacob Hegner, 1962; *The Theology of Karl Barth*, New York: Rinehart and Winston, 1967.
137. Busch, op.cit., p. 362.
138. *Letters*, p. 127
139. Ibid., p. 152.
140. Ibid.
141. Ibid., p. 208.
142. Karl Barth, *Ad Limina Apostolorum. An Appraisal of Vatican II*, Edinburgh: The Saint Andrew Press, 1969.
143. *Letters*, p. 208. Also *Ad Limina Apostolorum*, p. 18.
144. *Letters*, p. 222.
145. Ibid., pp. 222-23.
146. *Ad Limina Apostolorum*, p. 13.
147. *Letters*, p. 222.
148. Ibid., p. 221.
149. Ibid., p. 226.
150. Ibid., p. 228.
151. Ibid., p. 226. See also *Ad Limina Apostolorum*, p. 14.
152. *Ad Limina Apostolorum*, p. 16.
153. Ibid., p. 16.
154. *Letters*, p. 226.
155. Ibid., *Ad Limina*, p. 16.

156. *Letters*, p. 208.
157. Ibid., p. 226.
158. *Ad Limina*, p. 17.
159. Ibid., p. 45.
160. Ibid., pp. 47f.
161. Ibid., p. 17.
162. Abbott, op.cit., p. 117.
163. Ibid., p. 341.
164. *Ad Limina*, p. 30.
165. Ibid.
166. Ibid., p. 59.
167. Ibid., p. 61.
168. *Letters*, p. 243.

The Abiding Significance of Karl Barth
Goeffrey W. Bromiley

A definitive evaluation of Karl Barth is hardly possible in his own century. The preceding studies have obviously revealed the breadth of his work, the originality of his presentation, and the greatness of his contribution and stimulation in many different and important areas. How lasting his influence will prove, what directions it will ultimately take, and whether Barth will finally rank with the select group that includes an Augustine, Aquinas, or Calvin, future generations will have to decide.

The task of general assessment, then, cannot be the more ambitious one of hazardous prediction but only the more modest one of trying to fix Barth's relation to the past, to his own present, and to the immediate post-Barth period. Even this less pretentious task suffers from the complication that after making a striking impact during the earlier part of the century, Barth entered the time of eclipse that tends to overtake even the greatest figures either in their later years or in the decades immediately following their death. The undertaking of the *Gesamtausgabe* with its exciting new materials, the stimulus given by the Karl Barth Societies, and the memories kindled by the centennial have no doubt helped, and will help, to keep alive an interest in Barth and his theology, but the time of drawing breath as it were, when the rush of living thought, word, and work has been stilled, adds to the difficulty of defining Barth's essential contribution.

This much, however, seems to be plain, that Barth gave to the twentieth century church and its theology a new direction which he himself had begun to find, or to receive, in the troubled days at Safenwil. Perhaps, indeed, one might provisionally sum up his work as that of radical reorientation. He discovered not only new insights but new perspectives or dimensions that he then passed on to his contemporaries, first wth the volcanic fire of the early addresses and *Romans*, then in the penetrating biblical and historical studies of the middle period, with a specific practical application to the Hitler crisis, and finally in the more judicious deliberations and more measured cadences of the *Church Dogmatics*.

The reorientation took place first in Barth's own life and ministry. Brought up in conservative circles, he had fallen under the spell of the brilliant Harnack and even more so of the persuasive Herrmann. Geneva had inspired him only with the tenuous dream of a grandiose synthesis of Calvin and Schleiermacher. In the Aargau he had run head on into social and economic issues and espoused the workers' cause with an enthusiasm that earned for him the title of the red parson of Safenwil and that might have opened up for him a political career. Various factors, however, combined to force on him a drastic re-direction: World War I, the support of German theologians and Social Democrats for the Kaiser's war policy, the problems of the pulpit, the human inadequacy so vividly displayed in both religious and secular matters, the experiences of the Blumhardts, the works of writers like Kierkegaard and Dostoievsky, the teachings of the reformers, and not least of all holy scripture, to which Barth now returned in a new search and with eye and mind and heart newly opened to their inherent message.

Perhaps a first thing one might say about this reorientation is that it carried with it the recognition that bad practice bears eloquent testimony to bad theology. For Barth, however, this perception took on the force of an incentive. If bad theology produces bad practice, then the most urgent task is not to correct the practice but to replace the theology. A simple but profound conclusion, which would be with Barth throughout his life, and which has wide and lasting repercussions, is that every practical problem is at root a theological problem, so that a proper ethics must have its foundation in dogmatics. Theology matters, not as a mere means to the answering of intellectual or academic questions, but as the true basis of all activity, including Christian life and ministry. Barth's quest in Romans had from the very outset, if not an immediate practical goal, at least the most direct of practical implications.

One might also say that the quest itself – the quest for a good theology – entailed an immediate shift of direction in biblical studies as such. Barth had grown up academically with the concerns of late nineteenth century scholarship and its historico-critical emphasis. He would never wish to eliminate this aspect of biblical inquiry. Yet with his new theological insight into the contemporary situation, he saw that an unbalanced focus on the human side of scripture was giving a distorted view of its message, blinding people to its real meaning, and reducing its function to irrelevancy. His crucial function in the first addresses and the *Romans* was to redirect people – parsons and parishioners as well as professors – to the strange new world within the Bible, to teach them to read *with* the authors of scripture as well as *about* them, to point the way to an authentically biblical theology in place of substitutes which had only remoter links with scripture, to cast off, so far as possible, the blinkers of culture, and to let the Bible itself say what it has to say on its own terms and according to its own purpose. To some extent other scholars and movements were already helping to push the church in the same general direction. We hardly exaggerate, however, if we claim that more than any single theologian Barth initiated the new era in biblical investigation which would be an era of intensive linguistic study, renewed theological exegesis, and the attempted reconstruction of Old and New Testament theology.

One might say, moreover, that historical re-direction went hand in hand with the reorientation of biblical studies. Surveying the modern predicament, Barth achieved a fresh perspective on the immediate theological past. This came to fruition in the Schleiermacher lectures, the many essays on Schleiermacher, the monumental series on nineteenth (and eighteenth) century theology, and the small-print sections in the *Church Dogmatics* on such varied thinkers as Descartes, Leibniz, Schopenhauer, and Nietzsche. No longer bedazzled by the concept of theological progress, Barth came to see in the modern period of Protestantism the age of the great anthropocentric aberration. His delving into the seventeenth century resulted in the startling insight that this era of supreme orthodoxy, for all its undeniable merits, had offered the original impetus for rampaging heterodoxy by the introduction of rationalism for reasons of apolegetics and systematization. With all the greater appreciation, then, Barth turned to the vital theology of the reformers and the reformation confessions, in which it seemed that the biblical faith had achieved more appropriate expression. Were Barth remembered for nothing else, he would deserve the church's gratitude for the service that he rendered his own and subsequent generations, not merely by his brilliant observations on the course of modern theology, but even more so by his opening up again of the strange new world within the reformation, by his demonstration that the writings of his formative period are in no sense antiquated and irrelevant documents but living and dynamic testimonies with a message no less true and powerful today than it was in its own century. The rediscovery of reformation theology could hardly fail to lead Barth to a similar rereading of even earlier works, particularly those of the fathers, in which he would find much of the fundamental theology that he would try to restate for his own time. Yet perhaps the most significant shift of perspective, for himself and therefore indirectly for the theology that followed him, came with a fresh look at Anselm of Canterbury and his famous *Proslogion*. Finding his cue in the opening prayer, in which the author refers to faith seeking understanding, Barth challenged the line of thought that finds in the work a philosophically ontological proof of God, and suggested a theological approach whose immediate outcome for Barth himself may be seen in the rewriting of *Christian Dogmatics* I as *Church Dogmatics* I, 1 and 2. What exactly the new approach entailed, and how far it is a legitimate understanding, need not detain us here. The point in the present context is that the study confirms yet again the originality of Barth's survey of theological history and the force with which he could give a new turn and new vitality to historical investigation.

The new worlds of scripture and theological history quickly exerted their influence in the sphere of dogmatics, to which Barth increasingly addressed himself after taking up his first academic post in Goettingen. As in the biblical and historical fields, one might say, perhaps, that his first and by no means his least important achievement was in a sense methodological. With a new clarity he perceived the dynamic reality of dogmatics as a discipline in its own right, which must not be changed into mere apologetics, swallowed up in philosophical thought, or reduced to a static and uninteresting scholasticism. Much of Barth's power at this point lay in the fact that in an age which had largely contrived to treat dogmatics as an irrelevant formal orthodoxy, which could not compare in attractiveness with the new heterodoxies and their wrestling with modern movements of thought, he breathed the breath of life into the dead bones, and succeeded in restoring academic validity and intellectual excitement to this apparently outmoded discipline. As if it had not been enough to set biblical studies on a new course, and to give a wholly new force and emphasis to historical inquiry, Barth brought the ultimate dogmatic issues to the forefront of discussion in a way which would have seemed impossible a generation earlier, but which now did not permit alert and perspicacious scholars and church leaders to close their eyes in ignorance or disdain.

One must also say, however, that in his re-directing of the theological ministry Barth did far more than open up new academic vistas, important though that achievement might be for the future of theological education and Christian ministering and mission. With his recommended entry into the astonishingly different world of scripture, he did not merely advocate a drastic change of approach. He attempted himself a personal exploration of this world, and in the process brought a new awareness of the distinction between this biblical world and ours, and restored some of the emphases which, as he saw it, characterized that world. In the *Romans* – his first significant contribution – he also introduced a strange new world of his own which would probably have been just as startling to the apostle as it was to his surprised but in many cases enthralled contemporaries – a world of fresh style, constant paradox, odd mathematical imagery, and newly minted phrases which in some cases would become part of the theological jargon of the century. The presentation, of course, was not in itself the important thing. If it gained an immediate hearing, it would also contribute to the more rapid dating of the work. The distinctive style had its real significance in its correspondence to the distinctiveness of the matter. It gave force to the emphases that Barth was seeking to convey: the transcendence of God, the problem of divine-human communication, the gulf opened up by the fall, the wonder of the incarnation, the one and twofold declaration of pardon and judgment, the inconceivable grace of justification. In the course of further thought and study, Barth would expand and modify the initial emphases, but coming as they did to a disillusioned generation at the end of World War I, in Europe especially they drew attention to dimensions of the biblical message which the facile optimism and superficial platitudes of the previous age had very largely concealed or transmuted.

For Barth himself, of course, the tumultuous utterances of his first period had the primary purpose of a "marginal correction." Yet the correction, if this modest term may be allowed, served also the positive goal of opening the door to a more sober if no less drastic restatement when the dialectical theology yielded to the theology of the Word of God. In this regard, facing the Liberal systems on the one side and Kierkegaardian existentialism on the other, Barth had first to think through the demands of an authentically scientific theology which would be the victim neither of abstraction nor subjectivity. Here again one might say that he helped to set, or at least to indicate, a new direction, not merely in the formal sense of restoring to dogmatics an honorable place but also in the material sense of vindicating its specific claim to be numbered among the sciences. Previously the main features to which appeal had been made in justifying theology as a science had been such things as its rigorously logical procedure, as in the great orthodoxies, or its application of historico-critical criteria, as in the human study of scripture, or its identification with the humanities, as in the comparative study of religion. In contrast Barth combined the involvement of the subject with commitment to the object and thus found the first principle of genuine scientific endeavour in subjection to the control of the object, i.e., in letting the object tell us about itself. A self-evident implication is the role of the particular nature of the object in governing the nature of the investigation. Thus the humanities differ from the natural sciences inasmuch as human beings differ from rocks, stars, plants, or even animals. Similarly divinity differs from the other sciences inasmuch as God, the primary object of its inquiry, differs even more sharply from all creaturely objects. Yet the underlying scientific principle remains the same. As no object can be scientifically known merely as a construct of human thought, but only as it makes itself known, so God is known only through God in a self-disclosure of the object.

This apparently simple truth had momentous consequences in Barth's reorientation of theology. Barth rejected the whole concept of theology as a human construction or projection. Refusing to find a basis for faith's authenticity in a so-called religious *a priori*, he grounded it in the self-revelation of the object. He could find a place for existential involvement insofar as theology can hardly be pursued without a faith-commitment, yet not at the cost of an all-controlling subjectivity. He still insisted on a restructuring of biblical study in which again the correct hermeneutical procedure is to listen to what scripture itself has to tell us. He caught up this demand, however, into the larger insistence upon a theology of revelation. Like all objects, God must disclose himself if he is to be authentically known. But God is not an empirical object. Furthermore the fall has brought a blindness of human eyes, minds, and hearts to what may be known about God from his creative handiwork. Only by a special self-disclosure, then, does a true knowledge of God arise. Christianity means revelation. Christian theology is a theology of the Word of God as the self-revelation of the Triune God without which there can be no Christian faith, or knowledge, or life, or mission, or consequently theology.

Fundamental to the whole reality of this self-revelation, of course, is the fact that God gives himself what Barth calls his "secondary objectivity." Primarily objective to himself, God also makes himself objective to us in the word-event of his history with us which reaches its climax in the incarnation of the Son, finds its normative attestation in the inspired prophetic and apostolic writings of the Old and New Testaments, and comes to each new generation, by the ministry of the spirit in the controlled proclamation of the church. A striking feature of this whole complex is the way in which Barth, adopting the reformation concept of the three forms of the Word of God, integrated the forms into a comprehensive doctrine which even in detail opened up new and exciting vistas on all three.

As regards revelation, Barth rendered the incontestable service of challenging natural theology and exposing human religion as a final manifestation of the revolt against God. Much of the vehemence of Barth's polemic derived from his rejection of the compromise that the German Christians were attempting with the National Socialist regime. Later he would himself open doors to what some might call a new style of natural theology with his doctrine of creation, his thinking about the humanity of God, his finding of other lights, words, and truths, and his conviction that God's enduring purpose will not permit the frustration of his goal for the creature. Indeed, even at an earlier stage Barth could frankly concede that there is a secondary line of revelation in nature and admit that if religion is *aufgehoben* by revelation, *aufgehoben* has in this context the twofold Hegelian sense of both "taken away" and "taken up". Nevertheless, Barth resolutely directed both his own and all future generations not only to the reality but also to the range and depth of the human apostasy from God which may not obliterate our striving after God, nor negate our inherently religious nature, but which brings ineluctable perversion unless the focus and centre be found in God's own seeking after us. In this context Barth developed quite early a distinction which runs through all his work and which enabled him always to refer to the world's knowledge of God as well as its ignorance of God. This was the distinction between the dimension of knowledge which is mere knowledge (*Kennen*) and the dimension which he calls acknowledgment (*Anerkennen*), and the knowledge of faith which pushes on to the ultimate dimension of confession (*Bekennen*). The religions, too, have some knowledge of God, but apart from revelation this knowledge, accompanied as it is by a vast ignorance, can never be authentic acknowledgement, but can issue only in the various forms of religious achievement and the associated corruption of natural theology. Even Christianity, considered or handled solely as a religion, does not escape this negative assessment.

If on the negative side Barth provoked a more critical attitude to human self-achievement in religion and theology, on the positive side he initiated a closer linking even of the form of revelation to the self-revealing Triune God. As the Word of God has the threefold form of the Word revealed, written, and proclaimed, so revelation itself has the threefold form of the revelation of God the Father, God the Son, and God the Holy Spirit. It thus constitutes for Barth the material root of the doctrine of the Trinity. This line of thinking has important consequences both in Barth's own work and in subsequent discussion. Methodologically it solves the problem of a starting-point by enabling Barth to begin simultaneously with revelation and with the self-revealing God. Architecturally it gives the doctrine of the Trinity a rather singular position in dogmatic prolegomena but a logical position in virtue of the equation of the self-revealing Trinity and the trinitarian revelation. It also suggests that, although dogmatic method is intrinsically arbitrary, a trinitarian arrangement of the material, for which history offers impressive precedents, has the advantage of appropriateness to the divine self-revelation and the climax of the history wherein God gives himself secondary objectivity, and in so doing fulfills his creative and reconciling will for humanity, points us very plainly to the dogmatic centrality of Christ, although not in the sense of a christological locus, and certainly not to the exclusion or disparagement of God the Father or God the Holy Spirit. Implicitly by this whole approach Barth reminded us once again of the importance of dogmatic order. Negatively, he alerted us to the danger of imposing a logical structure by singling out a particular doctrine or doctrines and relating all others to this chosen centre. Positively, while leaving a space for God himself at the centre, he contended for the primacy of the subject-matter and the resultant need to find an arrangement that both materially and formally will best do justice to it. In the later *Church Dogmatics* the placing of election within the doctrine of God and the treatment of sin in the context of reconciliation offer provocative results of Barth's own reflections in this respect. The more abiding reorientation, however, lies in the general thesis rather than its detailed execution.

As regard the threefold Word of God, Barth provided his most magnificent stimulus to a renewal of thinking with his rigorous effort to connect the second and third forms of the Word more closely to Christ himself as the revealed and incarnate Word. The reformers had already used the term "Word of God" with a multiple and often ambivalent reference. They had made the distinction that Barth himself adopted between the Word incarnate, written, and spoken. But often they had left the incarnate Word strangely detached from the other two, and related the spoken and the written Word only by seeing in the former the original form of the latter. Barth's re-direction at this point is highly significant, for with the underlying thought of the perichoresis of the Word it brings the incarnate Word of revelation into more essential relationship with the others as witness to it, safeguards the special position of scripture as the normative prophetic and apostolic witness, and allots to biblically informed proclamation the full rank and status of the final form of the Word.

Barth believed that this attempt at a comprehensive doctrine of the Word opened up a new perspective on scripture that could and should deliver the church from the destructive conflict between critical scholarship and defensive apologetics. The relating of scripture to Christ – of the Word of normative witness to the Word of revelation – provided the key. Instead of seeing in scripture either a fallible story of human religion or an infallible text-book validated by its freedom from error, Barth suggested that according to the Bible's own self-understanding what it offers us is the primary testimony to Christ which God himself has instituted within the process of revelation, and by which he continually speaks in the Spirit. Scripture, then, has a qualitatively incomparable authority that does not depend upon its human characteristics but is confirmed by the internal, or, as Barth would prefer to say, the external witness of the Spirit. Along these lines, Barth found that many of the issues in the modern debate were largely irrelevant to the Bible's own purpose and content. He shifted the focus away from such matters as comparative religion, historical verifiability, and literary composition to the function of scripture within the divine revelation. He could make full allowance for the humanity of the records when viewed from the human perspective, and yet preserve intact the normative authority of scripture as the testimony that the Holy Spirit both inspired and still inspires as the second form of the Word by which all the church's thought, speech,

and action is to be informed, examined, and corrected. Not unnatural-
ly, Barth's suggestions in this embattled area have run into criticism.
Thus far indeed, although they have succeeded in outdating the older
Liberalism and opening up new and promising lines of biblical study,
they have overcome neither the critical nor the apologetic fixation. If
they can finally achieve a full breakthrough, they might at least point
the way to an understanding of the written Word that is more faithful
to scripture itself on the one side and more fruitful in its practical
implications on the other. Incidentally, in the penetrating discussions
of authority and freedom in the church Barth offered one impressive
insight which the churches have been far too slow to appreciate but
which may yet sink in and have a long-range influence for the better.
This is the insight that what the churches that over-emphasize authority need to learn is a true understanding of authority, and what the
churches that contend too much for freedom really need is a true
understanding of freedom, namely, the authority and freedom of the
Word itself and our own authority and freedom under it.

Much of the re-direction that Barth achieved in the doctrine of God
has received attention already: the focus on God as the self-revealing
subject, the secondary objectivity of God and the resultant criticism of
natural theology. Along similar lines Barth's reconstruction of the doctrine of analogy might be mentioned. Opposed though he was to the
positing of anything above both God and us, Barth still perceived a
divinely instituted relationship to God in which God himself is the
original and we the similar but also dissimilar reflection. Analogy on
this basis makes possible the valid use of human terminology with
reference to God, but also ensures that such teminology derives its
true content from God and not from us. Thus in describing God as
Father we do not ascribe to God the attributes of the human father; we
learn the true nature of human fatherliness from God, and always
with a sense of the distinction between the divine fatherhood and the
human. Barth also made what might well prove to be some permanent contributions in his discussion of the so-called attributes of God.
His favoured term – the divine perfections – surely deserves to carry
the day over such alternatives as attributes, qualities, or characteristics.
It expresses already the truth to which Barth gave such heavy emphasis, namely, that God does not merely *have* but *is* his perfections.
Whether or not his grouping of the perfections under love and
(sovereign) freedom will finally commend itself may be doubted, but

his counterbalancing of them along the lines of Anselm forms a basis for profitable discussion even while it might arouse dissent in detail. Particularly stimulating individually is the discussion of the divine omnipotence, in which Barth took care to distinguish omnipotence from omnicausality, to show that what it implies is God's power to do all that he wills to do, to insist that like every other perfection it must be defined by God and not define him, to deduce that it may thus take the form of what we might think of as impotence, and to make the point that far from negating human freedom it genuinely establishes it. Even more striking, perhaps, is Barth's tribute to the beauty of God within his account of the divine glory. In this regard Barth sounded forth again a note which theology can neglect only to its detriment, the more so if it fails to heed the accompanying warning that to do full justice to its theme theology itself must strive to achieve a corresponding beauty.

The focus on God in his self-revelation necessarily carried with it a concentration on Christ as himself in person the theme and centre of the divine self-revelation. Indeed, if one were to try to single out the most comprehensive re-direction that we owe to Barth, a good case could be made out for his extensive reworking of theology from a christological standpoint, which brought him the ugly charge of christomonism in some circles. Barth himself had no brief for the concept of christomonism and disputed its relevance to his own work. After all, at the very outset of *Church Dogmatics* had he not set Christ firmly within the triune relationship, stressed the role of Father and Spirit in the divine self-revelation, enunciated again the patristic principle that all persons of the Trinity participate actively and equally in all God's outward works, and adopted for his work a trinitarian structure? Nevertheless as himself the revealed Word in which God does his reconciling work, Christ does obviously stand at the heart of the divine action with us. With this in view, Barth thought it legitimate to teach us, not to make christology an abstract systematic centre, and certainly not to embody it in a cosmic immanentism, as in some incarnational theologies, but to take a fresh look at some of the familiar dogmatic loci in their relation to Christ as God's incarnate Word.

The revolutionary nature of this proposal emerges rapidly when Barth turns his attention to election in the third chapter dealing with the doctrine of God. Not that the relating of election to Christ is all that unusual: we find it in the reformers and the seventeenth century orthodoxy. The stimulating (or provocative) element lies in the rigor with which Barth does it. The bold placing of election in the doctrine of God attracts notice at once. Only a very strict relationship to Christ can justify it. But this is not all, for by seeing in Christ not merely the executor of election but also its subject and object in one, Barth recasts the whole doctrine in a way that raises its own problems – and these call for further discussion – yet also brings election into closer accord with the gospel. Nor does Barth stop here, for he puts rejection, too, in the light of christology by presenting Christ as the vicarious bearer of rejection in his ministry on our behalf. Corresponding to election is the command of God as the second aspect of the covenant of grace, and by linking this, too, as closely as possible to Christ, Barth sets it in the doctrine of God leaving no place for legalism but giving the command an unmistakable evangelical reference. Whether Barth's massive redevelopment will eventually establish itself may be questioned, but the fact remains that future discussion will have to reckon more seriously with Christ's covenantal role than previous debate has normally allowed.

The implications of christology for creation constitute another area in which Barth gave a decisive turn to the discussion. For generations the relation between religion and science had tended to dominate the treatment of creation. Barth himself feared that when he came to this theme he would have to enter fields in which he had neither the necessary equipment nor interest. Certainly the role of the Logos in creation had always been a constitutive part of the doctrine, and from patristic times the fulfilment of creation in and through Christ had had its place, even to the point of raising the question whether there might not have been a consummation in Christ even apart from the fall. Yet seldom had theologians related creation more consistently to Christ, and more recently a preoccupation with evolutionary science had shifted the focus away from Christ to other concerns. When Barth tackled the doctrine, however, he found to his surprise and delight that what seemed to be needed was a theology of creation in the stricter sense, and within the total context of the divine Word and work this meant again a christological exploration. For Barth, this took the primary form of an interrelating of creation and the covenant: creation as the setting for the covenant, the covenant as the meaning of creation. The covenant, however, pointed directly to Christ, and the perception of Christ in creation enabled Barth to affirm with confidence the goodness of creation, giving cogency to the ventures in theodicy which otherwise would produce only amusing eccentricities. By thus applying theologically the great cosmological statements of the New Testament, Barth accomplished a reorientation of critical importance which can and should result in a richer understanding of creation and one that stands in closer connection to the central thesis of the gospel.

Barth took what was, perhaps, an even more radical step when he attempted an anthropology that is not merely theological but strictly christological as well. For too long, in his view, theology had been content to build its anthropology on borrowings from such other disciplines as physiology, archeology, psychology, and sociology. Barth did not contest the validity of these sciences in their own areas. They can, indeed, tell us true and interesting things about humanity. They fail us, however, in two connected areas. They cannot tell us about God in his relation to humanity; only the theology of the Word can do that. Nor can they tell us about real humanity, for they deal only with fallen humanity; again, only God in his Word can open up to us the secret of created humanity. The divine disclosure takes place in Christ, who as true God is also true man, and hence the model of real humanity as God intended it at creation. Barth recognized, of course, the distinction between Christ and us in virtue of his deity. Yet even when allowance is made for the differences, Christ still serves as the mirror in which alone our true divinely created humanity may be seen. An important implication of this christological reference is that it enabled Barth to reverse the usual procedure whereby Christ's humanity is measured by ours instead of ours by his. No less significant is the introduction of the fourfold relation in which the humanity of Christ displays itself: to God, to others, to self, and to time. Particularly in the discussion of Christ as Lord of time Barth deployed all his resources to make an outstanding contribution to a permanent problem. The finding of humanity in relationships opened up many new lines of inquiry, and the overarching christological reference gave a new direction to anthropological thinking while also offering a broader understanding of the implications of the incarnation itself.

Barth applied christology no less consistently to the field of providence. If creation forms the setting for the covenant, providence serves to uphold and overrule creation in fulfilment of God's covenant purpose. In this sense the providential acts of God find their focus in the salvation history that reaches a climax in Christ's first coming and moves on to its culmination in his second coming. Such things as the Jewish people, holy scripture, and the church – all related to Christ – act as signs of God's providential order whereby world history serves covenant history. This presentation allows a serious place for angelology, since angelic action bears additional testimony to the purpose of the divine overruling. The christological reference offers assurance of providential goodness, and it also guarantees a place for free human response, especially in prayer, within the free divine sovereignty. A striking aspect of Barth's interpretation, which demands fuller discussion, is that it leaves room for both light and shadow in the world of divine ordering. Evil, however, comes within God's rule only on the left hand as the impossible possibility of that which God rejects but the creature seizes. In Christ evil may be known as the contradiction that God has already victoriously contradicted. Although Barth insisted that the human struggle against evil must continue until the manifestation of the divine victory at the eschaton, the apparent triumphalism of his view has aroused vigorous dissent, and the feasibility of his solution obviously calls for further investigation.

Barth did not live to complete more than the first sectionof his projected ethics but even here we catch glimpses of the way in which his re-directing to God's revelation in Christ suggests important lines of ethical inquiry. Thus Barth refused to let the divine command be frozen in legalistic demands or static orders. As God makes himself known in living power through scripture, so he makes his will known in living power through commands that he applies to relevant situations. The ethics of freedom as God's saving act in Christ opens us up for free action in the obedience of faith. Christological anthropology discloses the relations – to God, others, self, and time – within which this action takes place. These relations replace the traditional orders, although even Barth himself found difficulty in working out satisfactorily the social implications. Within the relations regular patterns hold good, but the dynamism of the command and the freedom of faith allow scope for borderline exceptions. In his occasional writings Barth initiated discussion on a more direct christological application to social and political life as he wrestled with the problems caused by the Lutheran doctrine of the two kingdoms and with the meaning of the lordship of Christ for the action of the church and its members in the secular world. Hitlerism and Communism in particular raised difficult questions for a theologian who enjoyed the benefits of a representative system in his native Switzerland. His distinctions between the two totalitarianisms would bring considerable criticism on Barth from different quarters and expose him to pressures to enter what he himself regarded as very dubious courses. The coming of nuclear weapons and the proposal that his own country should develop them would also confront him with new issues that his original treatment of war could neither foresee nor answer. Nevertheless, Barth's rigorous attempt to apply his christologically oriented theology to ethics, even if one has to call it incomplete and in many places unconvincing, did at least show that ethics needs a solid theological foundation of some kind. It also suggested some newer approaches which future workers can hardly afford to ignore.

For the fullest application of christology we naturally move on to the doctrine of reconciliation. Here at the heart of God's dealings with the race the centrality of Christ in his incarnation, crucifixion, and resurrection has commanded almost unanimous assent. To talk of reorientation, then, might seem to be somewhat pretentious. Is not a recall or reemphasis the most that one might reasonably claim? In a general sense, this is no doubt true. Yet when we consider the details, we find that Barth again opened up original lines of consideration and applied his christological emphasis with unparalleled stringency. This appears at once in the total scheme within which he presented the whole doctrine of reconciliation. He wove all his themes into a single intricate pattern under the threefold christological heading of Christ as Son of God, Son of Man, and God-Man (in conformity with the orthodox dogma of the hypostatic union of deity and humanity). Structurally and thematically, then, reconciliation stood from the very outset under christological control, which Barth reinforced at once by bringing the doctrine of the threefold office into the christological framework, appropriating the priestly work more specifically to the Son of God, the kingly work to the Son of Man, and the prophetic work to the God-Man.

Many detailed points might be cited to demonstrate the force and freshness with which Barth expounded the familiar material from this predominantly christological angle. The schema that he adopted enabled him to avoid the traditional dogmatic pressure to separate Christ's person and work. Proceeding by way of the priestly, kingly, and prophetic ministries, he could not only see Christ himself in his

vicarious work but also relate this work smoothly and logically to justification, sanctification, and vocation, and thence to the founding,
upbuilding, and sending of the church, and the faith, love, and hope of
individual believers. The same schema led Barth to an unusual interrelating of the humiliation and exaltation of Christ in which he linked
the former to the Son of God and the latter to the Son of Man, but in
which the two ran parallel to each other instead of being chrono-
logically consecutive as in traditional accounts. The simultaneity of
the so-called states and the distinctive way of relating them suggested
to Barth the patristic theme that as we learn to construe the divine
omnipotence in terms of its manifestation it may take the form of what
to human eyes might seem to be impotence. By way of the humiliation
of the Son of God, which was also the exaltation of the Son of Man,
God fulfilled victoriously his revealing and reconciling purpose.

For Barth the same interpretation shed a new and striking light on
human sin as well. Barth pioneered a new approach to sin by dealing
with it, not as a separate theme, but wholly within the doctrine of
reconciliation. As we learn only from Christ what true humanity is, so
we learn only from him – this time by way of antithesis – what the corruption of humanity entails. At this point Barth could use once more
his main christological headings. Christ's priestly self-humbling as the
son of God unmasks the sin of the race as pride, his kingly exaltation as
the Son of Man unmasks it as sloth, and his prophetic self-witness as
the God-Man unmasks it as falsehood. Yet in this depiction Barth
reached back also to the relational structure of humanity that he had
also learned from Christ, and with graphic illustrations from the Old
Testament he portrayed the implications of pride, sloth, and falsehood in the fourfold relation to God, others, self, and the setting of
human life. A first impression might suggest that Barth was depreciat-
ing the seriousness of sin by not giving it autonomous treatment. If
anything, however, the new angle from which he saw and described it
gave it even more sinister force as the contradiction that God has
already powerfully contradicted in Christ's ministry of revelation
and reconciliation.

The concentration on Christ also brought enhanced vigour and
power to the heavily debated doctrine of Christ's vicarious work.
Already from the doctrine of election, in which Christ elects himself
for both election and rejection, we glimpse the determination of Barth
to set all God's dealings with humanity in strict relationship to Christ.

The christological anthropology moves along similar lines, but it is in the reworking of the doctrine of the atonement that the full bearing of this decision becomes apparent. Barth took the concept of vicariousness so seriously that he could describe all human beings but Christ as "displaced persons" before God. Christ lived *for us* his royal life, bringing to light our mediocrity, but also achieving our exaltation with him. Christ died *for us* his priestly death, disclosing our arrogance, but also bearing and bearing away our sin, securing our pardon, and by his resurrection raising us up with him to new and eternal life. Christ gives his prophetic witness *for us*, condemning our untruth, but effecting our entry into the truth and hence into participation in his ministry and mission. Over every aspect of reconciliation there stood for Barth the great christological "for us." For us Christ lived the perfect life, for us he underwent the divine judgment, and for us he bears faithful testimony. God did not deal with us as we are in ourselves, whether individually or collectively. He dealt with us in Christ in an exclusive and all-sufficient act of deliverance that Christ vicariously effected on our behalf.

Vicariousness meant objectivity. In reply to the demythologizing existentialism of Bultmann, which temporarily won such a following, Barth brought the objective implications of the "for us" into new and sharp relief. Already in earlier volumes of the *Church Dogmatics,* as well as in other writings, Barth had been at pains to prevent theology from rushing off into a false existential subjectivity. He revised the original *Christian Dogmatics* mainly because of its inadequate safeguards against subjective interpretation. He constantly insisted that the inner witness of the Spirit, while relating to a subjective work, signifies objective rather than subjective witness. Even when stressing the present "inspiring" of scripture, he stressed the aspects which rule out mere existentiality. He contended strongly for the objective hymn that has God as the primary theme instead of the subjective hymn that involves a pre-Copernican circling around the self. He continually argued that in the knowledge of God the initiative lies with God, who as supreme subject makes himself object to us, so that when we are enlightened to knowledge, this knowledge relates to a real object and stands under no suspicion of speculation or projection. What applies in revelation applies equally in reconciliation. The real event does not take place *in* believers with their awakening to faith or regeneration to a righteous life. It took place *for* them once and for all in the life, death, and resurrection of Christ as this took place before them and without them. All participation in this event of divine identification rests first upon the event itself. Were there no *for* us, there could be no *in* us. Faith is undoubtedly important – personal faith – but only as the means of entry into Christ's finished work on our behalf. With hope, it derives its significance from its object. It comes into being only by reason of Christ's ongoing prophetic ministry in the Spirit. Distinctions of fact and value, or myth and message, had no meaning for Barth: What finally counted in his view was the reality of God and the reality of his saving work for us even down to such contested details as the signs given with the virgin birth and the empty tomb. Not least of Barth's contributions to theology is his reminder to his own and all succeeding generations that the inner reality of the Christian life has no final substance if it does not rest on the outer reality of Christ's own life for us. On this basis it has its own authentic reality as a work of the Spirit. Without this basis it belongs itself to the realm of mythology.

Barth's orientation to Christ, and the implied objectivity of the divine work, also made possible what might well prove to be a lasting contribution to thinking on the church. Recognizing that strictly the church ought to come under pneumatology, Barth still regarded it as important to set his doctrine of the church in the context of reconciliation. In this way, while maintaining the tie to the Spirit, he could keep the church in the closest of relations to Christ, whether in terms of its being as the body of Christ, its edification and order, or its mission and ministry. Thus far theology has made only the first beginnings of working out the full meaning of this development and its practical implications, e.g., for ecumenical relations, the nature of ecclesiastical structures, and the understanding and conduct of mission. Barth himself opened up many new lines of thinking which, if they are more fully explored, might not only enrich ecclesiology but greatly improve the quality of the church's life, the Christian character of its organization, and the consequent effectiveness of its work and witness in the world.

More debatable, if none the less stimulating, were some of the other results of Barth's christological focus. As regards sacramental theology, his reference of the sacraments to Christ led him quickly to the ancient theme of Christ himself as the true sacrament. Instead of working out the significance of this truth for sacramental theology, however, Barth took the highly controversial step of removing even baptism and the Lord's supper from strict dogmatic discussion and giving them a place in his ethics of reconciliation. One also wonders whether Barth's schematization did not introduce problems into his handling of the threefold office, instructive and stimulating though it undoubtedly is. Thus the very close equation of the priestly office with the passion leaves little place for Christ's high priestly intercession, and it is noticeable that Barth made comparatively little use of the Epistle to the Hebrews. Again, the extension of Christ's prophetic ministry to the present work of the church obviously calls for a clarification of the whole relationship of Christ, church, world, and Spirit, e.g., in view of Barth's prior reference to the Spirit as the subjective possibility of revelation. Indeed, Barth's failure to move on to a comprehensive doctrine of the Spirit in *Church Dogmatics* V left a gap of which he himself was acutely conscious and which he hoped that some future theologian would perceptively fill, particularly as he came to see that the theology of the preceding era might perhaps be regarded in good part as a praiseworthy but mistaken attempt at a theology of the Spirit's operation. Finally, after his magnificent demonstration of the relevance of good christology to the political sphere in the *Barmen Declaration*, Barth found greater difficulty in developing the positive implications of christology for politics. One might question, indeed, whether either theological or political thought can ever work out anything in the way of a strict christological politics. Nevertheless, Barth's thinking in this area has not been wholly for nothing. It testifies against an easy separation of church and world which takes no account of the supreme lordship of Christ. It warns against the assimilation of Christian faith to alien ideologies of cultures. It issues to the church a summons which it might finally hear and obey, namely, the summons to cease basing its own order and policy on secular models and to be instead the exemplary society that it ought to be in virtue of its own christological reference as the body of Christ.

Finally, in assessing Barth's abiding significance, one might say that he re-directed theology to its proper place within Christian ministry. Barth himself, of course, was inevitably caught up in the academic round. Nevertheless, he never forgot the problem of the pulpit which in large part had launched him on his theological quest. He maintained a constant concern that theology should neither be isolated nor isolate itself in an intellectualistic ghetto. If he laboured to establish the validity and integrity of divinity as a scientific discipline, he never allowed himself to regard or pursue theology as anything other than a function of the church, and therefore a function of ministry in which theology must necessarily serve the church's total life and thought and mission. Technically, Barth called for the highest standards of scholarship, not only in the classroom, but also in the task of proclamation and discussion. But for him scholarship could never be an end in itself, only a means to the higher end of Christian witness and practice. Service of God and others, he maintained is the meaning, horizon, and goal of theology. Theology attends upon God's Word. It does so by protecting the purity and apostolicity of the message, whether by showing the church what errors it must avoid or by helping it to a fresh expression of the truth through every change of circumstance and culture. Barth was no innovator in this conception, but at a time when the church has come increasingly under the threat of academic specialization on the one hand and diminished theological understanding on the other his emphasis at this point might well prove to be one of his greatest services to the church once there is the vision fully to appreciate and to practice it. Within the same context, one must also refer to the reverent and prayerful spirit which Barth constantly demanded in theology and in which he tried always to fulfil his own theological ministry, even to the point of continuing to open his lectures with prayer and praise when ordered to use the Hitler salute. With developing maturity, and profiting no doubt by the impressive example of Anselm, Barth's commitment to a devotional as well as a rigorously scholarly approach meant the replacement of the explosive outbursts of his revolutionary years by more meditative and constructive deliberations in which he recognized that in its character, too, theology must come under the control of its holy theme, and that no good result can come, even on the basis of the authoritative biblical witness, except with constant prayer for the Holy Spirit, constant thanksgiving, and a constant desire for the hallowing of God's name, the coming of his kingdom, and the doing of his will. Should the thinking and example of Barth finally prevail in regard to the proper function and spirit of theology, then to have restored this dimension of divine and human service to theological work might well prove to be one of the most determinative of all Barth's many contributions not only to theology itself but to the whole church both in its inner life and thought and in the discharge of its outer ministry.